THE D1278755

THE INVENTION OF CAPITALISM

Classical Political Economy and the

Secret History of Primitive Accumulation

MICHAEL PERELMAN

Duke University Press • Durham & London 2000

© 2000 Duke University Press

Printed in the United States of America on acid-free paper ∞

Typeset in Trump Mediaeval by Keystone Typesetting, Inc.

Library of Congress Cataloging-in-Publication Data appear

on the last printed page of this book.

2nd printing, 2001

Contents

THE INVENTION OF CAPITALISM

Introduction: Dark Designs

In order to develop the laws of bourgeois economy . . . it is not necessary to write the real history of the relations of production. But the correct observation and deduction of these laws . . . always leads to primary equations . . . which point toward a past lying behind the system. These indications . . . then offer the key to understanding the past—a work in its own right.—Karl Marx, *Grundrisse*

In the development of a theory, the invisible of a visible field is not generally anything whatever outside and foreign to the visible defined by that field. The invisible is defined by the visible as its invisible, its forbidden vision: the invisible is not therefore simply what is outside the visible (to return to the spatial metaphor), the outer darkness of exclusion—but the inner darkness of exclusion, inside the visible itself.—Louis Althusser, "From Capital to Marx's Philosophy"

The Laissez-faire Message of Classical Political Economy

Classical political economy, the core works of economic literature from the time of William Petty through that of David Ricardo, presents an imposing facade. The towering figures of early political economy forged a new way of thinking systematically about economic affairs in the late seventeenth and early eighteenth centuries with little more than the writings of business people and moral philosophers to guide them. Every one, from Karl Marx, who created the term "classical political economy," to modern-day conservatives, recognizes the enormous intellectual achievement of these early economists.

For more than two centuries, successive generations of economists have been grinding out texts to demonstrate how these early theorists discovered that markets provide the most efficient method for organizing production. An uncompromising advocacy of laissez-faire is, ostensibly, the intended lesson of classical political economy.

Most contemporary readers of Adam Smith, David Ricardo, and the other classical political economists accept their work at face value, assuming these early writers to be uncompromising advocates of laissez-faire. For the most part, even many Marxists accept this interpretation of classical political economy. Alongside their work on pure economic theory, the classical political economists engaged in a parallel project: to promote the forcible reconstruction of society into a purely market-oriented system. While economic historians may debate the depth of involvement in market activities at the time, the incontestable fact remains that most people in Britain did not enthusiastically engage in wage labor—at least so long as they had an alternative.

To make sure that people accepted wage labor, the classical political economists actively advocated measures to deprive people of their traditional means of support. The brutal acts associated with the process of stripping the majority of the people of the means of producing for themselves might seem far removed from the laissez-faire reputation of classical political economy. In reality, the dispossession of the majority of small-scale producers and the construction of laissez-faire are closely connected, so much so that Marx, or at least his translators, labeled this expropriation of the masses as "primitive accumulation."

The very sound of the expression, primitive accumulation, drips with poignant echoes of human consequences. The word "primitive," first of all, suggests a brutality lacking in the subtleties of more modern forms of exploitation. It also implies that primitive accumulation was prior to the form of accumulation that people generally associate with capitalism. Finally, it hints at something that we might associate with "primitive" parts of the world, where capital accumulation has not advanced as far as elsewhere.

The second term, *accumulation*, reminds us that the primary focus of the process was the accumulation of capital and wealth by a small sector of society, or as Marx (1977, 739–40) described it, "the conquest of the world of social wealth. It is the extension of the area of exploited human material and, at the same time, the extension of the indirect and direct sway of the capitalist." Certainly, at least in the early stages of capitalism, primitive accumulation was a central element in the accumulation process.

Although many modern scholars acknowledge the pervasive nature of primitive accumulation during the time that the classical political economists wrote, nobody to my knowledge has recognized the complicity of the classical political economists. They strongly advocated policies that furthered the process of primitive accumulation, often through subterfuge.

While energetically promoting their laissez-faire ideology, they championed time and time again policies that flew in the face of their laissez-faire principles, especially their analysis of the role of small-scale, rural producers. As we will see, the underlying development strategy of the classical political economists was consistent with a crude proto-Marxian model of primitive accumulation, which concluded that nonmarket forces might be required to speed up the process of capitalist assimilation in the countryside. This model also explains why most of the classical political economists expressed positions diametrically opposed to the theories usually credited to them.

The Secret History of Primitive Accumulation

Perhaps because so much of what the classical economists wrote about traditional systems of agricultural production was divorced from their seemingly more timeless remarks about pure theory, later readers have passed over such portions of their works in haste. Although this aspect of classical political economy might have seemed to fall outside the core of the subject, I argue that these interventionist recommendations were a significant element in the overall thrust of their works. Specifically, classical political economy advocated restricting the viability of traditional occupations in the countryside to coerce people to work for wages.

Chapter 1, which deals with the history of primitive accumulation, demonstrates the classical political economists' keen interest in driving rural workers from the countryside and into factories, compelling workers to do the bidding of those who would like to employ them, and eradicating any sign of sloth.

The vitality of these rural producers generally rested on a careful combination of industrial and agricultural pursuits. Despite the efficiency of this arrangement, classical political economy was intent on throttling small producers. Classical political economists often justified their position in terms of the efficiency of the division of labor. They called for measures that would actively promote the separation of agriculture and industry. As we shall see, Marx's concept of the social division of labor is very important in this respect. In contrast to Smith's exclusive emphasis on the division of labor—the arrangement of work within the firm—Marx suggested that we also examine the deployment of resources between individual firms and households—the social division of labor.

Classical political economists paid virtually no attention to the social division of labor in their theoretical works. For example, although Smith offered a detailed description of the division of labor in his famous pin factory, he did not bother to extend his discussion. What does it mean that society is partitioned in such a way that the pin industry purchases its metals or fuels instead of producing them itself? How does such an arrangement originate? Could such changes in the pattern of industries make a difference in an economy, even if technology were unchanging?

These questions were so distant from the purview of classical political economy that more than two centuries later, Ronald Coase won a Nobel Prize for bringing them to the attention of mainstream economists. Following in the wake of Coase, a group of modern economists developed the new institutionalist school of economics (see Perelman 1991a), which contends that economic forces naturally arrange themselves into some optimal pattern. Like many other economists, the new institutionalist school takes pride in locating anticipations of its work in classical political economy, especially in the thought of Smith. Even though the new institutionalist school concerns itself with the social division of labor, its theories are of no use in analyzing the coercive nature of primitive accumulation, since this school sees the economy arranging itself through voluntary contracts.

Chapter 2 concentrates on the theory of primitive accumulation. Most discussions of primitive accumulation address the subject as a shorthand expression for describing the brutality of the initial burst of capitalism. In contrast, this chapter makes the case for treating primitive accumulation as an essential theoretical concept in analyzing the ongoing process of capitalist accumulation.

I suspected that the continuing silence about the social division of labor might have something important to reveal. Following this line of investigation, I looked at what classical political economy had to say about the peasantry and self-sufficient agriculturalists. Here again, the pattern was consistent.

The classical political economists were unwilling to trust market forces to determine the social division of labor because they found the tenacity of traditional rural producers to be distasteful. Rather than contending that market forces should determine the fate of these small-scale producers, classical political economy called for state interventions of one sort or another to hobble these people's ability to produce for their own needs. These policy recommendations amounted to a blatant manipulation of the social division of labor.

We cannot justify such policies on the basis of efficiency. If efficiency were of great importance to them, the classical political economists would not have ignored the law permitting the gentry to ride across small farmers' fields in pursuit of foxes while forbidding the farmers from ridding their land of game that might eat the crops. As we shall see in Chapter 3, these Game Laws destroyed an enormous share of the total agricultural produce.

Chapter 3 describes the extraordinary history of the Game Laws. Although the origin of the Game Laws was feudal, their application and their ferocity peaked during the Industrial Revolution. They were a useful instrument to separate rural people from a major source of sustenance, adding considerable weight to the pressures to accept wage labor. They also incited many poor people in the countryside to rebel.

Chapter 4 discusses the relationship between primitive accumulation and the social division of labor from the standpoint of self-provisioning.

Chapter 5 analyzes classical political economy's implicit proto-Marxian theory of primitive accumulation. In addition, it discusses the pattern of practical measures that altered the social division of labor to the detriment of independent and small-scale producers. This chapter also discusses how classical political economy applied the calculus of primitive accumulation. It details the relationship between early classical political economy and the rural population with an eye toward efforts to create a capitalistic social division of labor. It demonstrates the continual importance that classical political economy placed on the process of primitive accumulation.

The Secret History of Classical Political Economy

Why has the social division of labor as an aspect of primitive accumulation gone unnoticed for so long by so many students of classical political economy? True, the classical political economists generally maintained their silence regarding primitive accumulation when discussing matters of pure economic theory—although they were not absolutely consistent in this regard.

Because of the novelty of their subject, these writers were not entirely in control of their own ideas. Specifically, I found that classical political economy openly expressed its dissatisfaction with the existing social division of labor quite clearly in diaries, letters, and more practical writings about contemporary affairs. This discovery led me to give a substantially new reading to the history of classical political economy.

In their unguarded moments, the intuition of the classical political economists led them to openly express important insights of which they may have been only vaguely, if at all, aware. As a result, they let the idea of the social division of labor surface from time to time even in their more theoretical works. The subject typically cropped up when they were acknowledging that the market seemed incapable of engaging the rural population fast enough to suit them—or more to the point, that people were resisting wage labor. Much of this discussion touched on what we now call primitive accumulation.

Although these slips flew in the face of the laissez-faire theory of classical political economy, they add much to the value of that literature. Indeed, if classical political economy were nothing more than a conscious attempt to come to grips with and justify the emerging forces of capitalism, it would have far less contemporary interest.

Just as a psychologist might detect a crucial revelation in a seemingly offhand remark of a patient, from time to time classical political economy discloses to us insights into its program that the classical political economists would not consciously welcome. These insights will reinforce the conclusions that we draw from their diaries, letters, and more practical writings.

The Invention of Capitalism is novel in four major respects. First, it addresses the question of what determines the social division of labor, the division of society into independent firms and industries from the perspective of classical political economy. It also develops the theoretical implications of primitive accumulation. Third, this book offers a significantly different interpretation of classical political economy, demonstrating that this school of thought supported the process of primitive accumulation. Finally, it analyzes the role of primitive accumulation in the work of Marx. All of these threads come together in helping us to understand how modern capitalism developed and the role of classical political economy in furthering this process.

On Reading Classical Political Economy

Modern economists sometimes present classical political economy as a polestar by which we can fix our bearings and, in rare cases, guide ourselves toward the future. This approach is disingenuous. Despite the invaluable lessons that we can learn from studying classical political economy, economists rarely read this literature with an eye to the future or even the past.

All too often, seemingly open-minded reviews of the past are merely a means to justify preexisting views of the present. Some readers delight in discovering in classical political economy anticipations of recent technical refinements, such as the theory of utility maximization. Others use the classics to cast their contemporaries in an unfavorable light. John Maynard Keynes, for example, contrasted the common sense of the mercantilists with the irrelevant elegance of Professor Pigou. Still other readers find the emphasis of the classics on dynamics, growth, or capital accumulation attractive.

In using classical political economy as a polestar, many economists represent it as if it were a uniform theory accepted by all. Of course, classical political economy was never a fixed body in space, but a heterogeneous collection of literature written over a period of about 100 years. If fixity does appear, it is only in the eye of the beholder. Even if many readers do acknowledge the diversity of the literature, they single out a select group of classical political economists as its stars. In general, they portray classical political economy as orbiting around a point somewhere between Smith and Ricardo. Some hold it to be closer to one or the other, but whatever its center, there is a general consensus as to what constitutes the canonical literature.

In reality, we lack objective standards for selecting the stars of classical political economy. Writing about the entertainment industry, Moshe Adler (1985, 208) has described a process whereby stars can emerge, even when they do not significantly differ in talent from lesser lights:

> The phenomenon of stars exists where consumption requires knowledge. . . . As an example, consider listening to music. Appreciation increases with knowledge. But how does one know about music? By listening to it, *and by discussing it with other persons who know about it.* [We are] better off patronizing the same artist as others do. . . . Stardom is a market device to economize on learning.

Economists studying the selection of technologies have found a similar phenomenon. In the early stages of the development of a technology, seemingly trivial accidents can determine which of several technological paths is chosen. Once industry becomes locked into a particular technological standard, it may continue to follow that line of development even though hindsight shows that the neglected paths might have been superior (see Arthur 1989).

A similar process is at work in the study of classical political economy, notwithstanding the significant variations that exist in the talents of early political economists. Once the status of a book is initially elevated, students are drawn into giving it a deeper consideration. A tradition gradually builds up around what becomes treated as almost sacred texts.

Readers of these canonical works are brought into a multidimensional dialogue that includes the authors under study, their times, and the collective experience of earlier generations of readers of these texts. In this sense, "the real life of an author emanates from his readers, disciples, commentators, opponents, critics. An author has no other existence" (Prezzolini 1967, 190; see also Latour 1987, 40).

By working and reworking these texts, each successive generation finds new levels of meaning, some of which probably eluded even the political economists who created them. As a result, these works acquire a cumulative force—albeit highly symbolic—that calls new generations to confront them once again. This process reinforces the stature of the "founders" of political economy, thereby confirming their status as "stars." Moreover, the erection of this solid structure of scholarship facilitates analysis by providing a cognitive map of the territory, allowing future researchers to navigate with more confidence.

Smith's *Wealth of Nations*, as we shall see, was not a particularly influential book until a generation after its publication. Once opinion leaders found the book useful in promoting their desired political outcomes, its popularity soared. Only then did Smith become a polestar of classical political economy, and his work a reference point by which all others are judged. Because of this flawed selection process, most histories of the period studiously analyze Smith and Ricardo, along with a handful of supposedly secondary figures. Other equally deserving economists generally escape notice altogether.

This book proposes a new reading—a new cosmology so to speak—that remaps classical political economy. Here, the center is nearer to Sir James Steuart and Edward Gibbon Wakefield than to Smith and Ricardo. From this perspective, Adam Smith appears less like the sun than a moon, a lesser body whose light is largely reflected from other sources.

This alternative cosmology is not an arbitrary rearrangement of the stars. It highlights important lessons from classical political economy. Within this context, Adam Smith becomes less original. His importance appears to emanate from the vigor of his ideological project of advocating laissez-faire and obfuscating all information that might cast doubt on his ideology. Others, such as Edward Gibbon Wakefield and John Rae, took a more realistic view about the nature of accumulation, but later economists set their analyses aside to create the impression of a humanitarian heritage of political economy.

Judging from the literature of the history of economic thought, it is clear this view of history has succeeded mightily. *The Invention of Capitalism* represents a plea to correct this legacy of error and omission. From this perspective we can see that, for all its heterogeneity, classical political economy did manage to compress much of the varied experience of its day into a compact body of literature that reflects the history of relations of production. Hence, the study of classical political economy provides an effective vantage point for the study of the history of relations of production.

Chapter 6 analyzes the role of primitive accumulation in the works of such early economists as Sir William Petty, Richard Cantillon, and the Physiocrats.

Chapter 7 concentrates on the important work of Steuart, by far the most interesting and the most incisive theorist of primitive accumulation and the social division of labor prior to Marx. Besides seeing the implications of primitive accumulation more clearly than the other classical political economists, Steuart stood alone in his willingness to write openly and honestly about the subject. This characteristic explains the comparative obscurity of his reputation.

Next, chapters 8 through 10 are devoted exclusively to Smith, who attempted to develop an alternative to Steuart. According to Smithian theory, the social division of labor would evolve in a satisfactory manner without recourse to outside intervention. This chapter demonstrates that even Smith's celebrated discussion of the invisible hand was developed as a means of avoiding the challenge that primitive accumulation posed for his system. By showing that the social division of labor would evolve without recourse to outside intervention, Smith had hoped to put the question of primitive accumulation to rest. Although Smith's theory was accepted as such, practice continued in a different manner. In fact, Smith himself advocated practices that were not in accordance with his theory. This chapter also indicates that Smith was far more interested in changing human behavior than he was with matters of economic development.

Chapter 9 examines how Smith attempted to distort history, sociology, and psychology to provide confirmation of this theory of the naturally evolving social division of labor.

Chapter 10 continues with the work of Adam Smith, who based much of his theory on the experience of the colonies. Although Smith made great use of the colonial experience, the colonials did not take him nearly as seriously as the English did. The reason is not hard to fathom. In harnessing the story of the colonies to his ideological cart, Smith did not do justice to the actual situation in the colonies. By tracing his analysis of the colonies, this chapter delves deeper into the manner in which Smith purposely obscured the nature of the social division of labor.

Chapter 11 continues the study of Smithian theory and practice by comparing Smith with his friend Benjamin Franklin. This genial American was a man of practice rather than theory, yet his practical analysis greatly influenced the theory of his day. Franklin's role is especially key to Smith's theory of colonial development.

Chapter 12 continues the analysis of the relationship of classical political economy and primitive accumulation into the age of David Ricardo and Thomas Robert Malthus. By reading their works and those of their contemporaries in terms of their relationship to political economy, we provide a new twist to the different interpretation of classical political economy. This chapter reveals that despite the adherence to the doctrine of laissez-faire in theory, classical political economists maintained a strong interest in promoting policies that furthered primitive accumulation.

Chapter 13 investigates the reaction against Smith, beginning with the relatively unknown work of Robert Gourlay and the development of his ideas in the practical school of Wakefield, the systemic colonizer who stressed that the social division of labor should be organized for the purpose of capitalist development. The chapter concludes with an analysis of John Rae.

Chapter 14 discusses the commonality between Smith and such later revolutionary leaders as Vladimir Ilyich Lenin and Mao Tse-Tung.

Dark Designs

Classical political economy is the product of a stormy period, distinguished by the emergence of capitalist social relations. These truly momentous changes of the time do not seem to appear in the great theoretical works of the time. Indeed, the classical political economists displayed little interest in conveying information about the great conflicts between capital and labor, or between capital and early precapitalist relations in the countryside. Nonetheless, these matters were of great importance to classical political economy.

While we catch an occasional glimpse of primitive accumulation in the canonical works of classical political economy, for the most part, we must read of the glaring conflicts indirectly. Our tactic is to approach classical political economy in the way that children learn to view a solar eclipse: by punching a small hole in a piece of paper held above another piece. The dark design that appears on the lower paper is the shadow of an eclipse, albeit with some refraction. The classical political economists made this indirect approach necessary because they were generally successful in obscuring the role of primitive accumulation in their theoretical texts. Yet, as mentioned earlier, when we turn to their letters, diaries, and more policy-oriented works, the importance of primitive accumulation becomes far clearer.

We can push our analogy of classical political economy and solar eclipses a bit further. Both represent rare and fascinating events. Past peoples have superstitiously interpreted solar eclipses as signs of impending epochal change. Similarly, the titans of political economy were thought to have been able to see over the heads of their contemporaries into the future. In this sense, their theories foreshadowed coming changes in the structure of society.

Both phenomena, planetary configurations found millions of miles away and the social changes of a century or more ago, reflect important forces that still shape our lives. Specifically, the struggle against self-provisioning is not confined to the distant past. It continues to this day (see Perelman 1991b). In effect, we can look at the eclipse of precapitalist production relations in much the same fashion, with one major exception: in the case of a solar eclipse, the brilliance of the source can destroy our vision. In the case of classical political economy, the source has attempted to obscure our vision.

Revising Classical Political Economy

Our classical forbearers may have been bright, but they were also fallible human beings. They were certainly not wholly disinterested observers. Their theories were intended to advance their own interests or those of the groups with whom they identified. These interests colored their works, whether or not they realized this influence themselves.

In regard to the struggle over primitive accumulation, these writers seem to have been intentionally obscure insofar as they could, lest they undermine their claim to generality for their theory. The struggle against the self-provisioning of rural people cast only a light shadow across the pages of classical political economy, a glimpse of an all-but-forgotten way of life obliterated by the process of primitive accumulation. Consequently, this process has largely gone unnoticed by modern readers of classical political economy.

Although we find ourselves reduced to studying the shadows of this struggle, the attempt is still worth the effort. Indeed, we will see that classical political economy conforms to a consistent pattern of almost always supporting positions that would work to harness small-scale agricultural producers to the interests of capital.

This book may be controversial in that it contradicts the commonly accepted theory that classical political economy offered its unconditional support for the doctrine of laissez-faire. It questions the relative importance of the almost universally admired Smith and makes the case that Smith and other classical authors sought to promote the process of primitive accumulation. This rereading suggests that classical political economy followed a different project, one that contradicts the standard interpretation of classical political economy.

Before turning to the main body of this work, I wish to append a caveat about my imagery of the eclipse. By studying the shadows cast by the classics, we must keep in mind that such images have fewer dimensions than the object under study. One dimension that disappears from the perspective of classical political economy concerns the social relations between labor and capital. Writing from the comfortable heights of their elevated social position, the classical political economists interpreted working-class organization as mere disorder. Because of this insensitivity, a work such as this one is necessarily imbalanced. Much attention is given to the efforts of capital to control labor, but little is devoted to the reverse. I leave the reader with the responsibility of estimating the actual balance of forces.

I hope that this book succeeds in making three points. First, primitive accumulation was an important force in capitalist development. Second, primitive accumulation cannot be relegated to a precapitalist past or even some imagined moment when feudal society suddenly became capitalist. Primitive accumulation played a continuing role in capitalist development. Third, classical political economy was concerned with promoting primitive accumulation in order to foster capitalist development, even though the logic of primitive accumulation was in direct conflict with the classical political economists' purported adherence to the values of laissez-faire.

I recognize that the seeds of capitalism had been planted long before the age of classical political economy, but never before and nowhere else had the process of capital accumulation become so intense. Hopefully, *The Invention of Capitalism* will throw light on the origins of that intensity.

CHAPTER I

The Enduring Importance
of Primitive Accumulation

Common fields and pastures kept alive a vigorous co-operative spirit in the community; enclosures starved it. In champion [sic] country people had to work together amicably, to agree upon crop rotations, stints of common pasture, the upkeep and improvement of their grazings and meadows, the clearing of the ditches, the fencing of the fields. They toiled side by side in the fields, and they walked together from field to village, from farm to heath, morning, afternoon and evening. They all depended on common resources for their fuel, for bedding, and fodder for their stock, and by pooling so many of the necessities of livelihood they were disciplined from early youth to submit to the rules and customs of the community. After enclosure, when every man could fence his own piece of territory and warn his neighbours off, the discipline of sharing things fairly with one's neighbours was relaxed, and every household became an island unto itself. This was the great revolution in men's lives, greater than all the economic changes following enclosure. Yet few people living in this world bequeathed to us by the enclosing and improving farmer are capable of gauging the full significance of a way of life that is now lost.—Joan Thirsk, "Enclosing and Engrossing"

Compulsion and the Creation of a Working Class

The brutal process of separating people from their means of providing for themselves, known as primitive accumulation, caused enormous hardships for the common people. This same primitive accumulation provided a basis for capitalist development. Joan Thirsk, one of the most knowledgeable historians of early British agriculture, describes above the nature of some of the harshest social and personal transformations associated with the enclosures.

Some people denounced this expropriation. Marx (1977, 928) echoed their sentiment, charging: "The expropriation of the direct producers was accomplished by means of the most merciless barbarism, and under the stimulus of the most infamous, the most sordid, the most petty and the most odious of passions."

Formally, this dispossession was perfectly legal. After all, the peasants did not have property rights in the narrow sense. They only had traditional rights. As markets evolved, first land-hungry gentry and later the bourgeoisie used the state to create a legal structure to abrogate these traditional rights (Tigar and Levy 1977).

Simple dispossession from the commons was a necessary, but not always sufficient condition to harness rural people to the labor market. Even after the enclosures, laborers retained privileges in "the shrubs, woods, undergrowth, stone quarries and gravel pits, thereby obtaining fuel for cooking and wood for animal life, crab apples and cob nuts from the hedgerows, brambles, tansy and other wild herbs from any other little patch of waste.... Almost every living thing in the parish however insignificant could be turned to some good use by the frugal peasant-labourer or his wife" (Everitt 1967, 405).

To the extent that the traditional economy might be able to remain intact despite the loss of the commons, a supply of labor satisfactory to capital might not be forthcoming. As a result, the level of real wages would be higher, thereby impeding the process of accumulation. Not surprisingly, one by one, these traditional rights also disappeared. In the eyes of the bourgeoisie, "property became absolute property: all the tolerated 'rights' that the peasantry had acquired or preserved . . . were now rejected" (Foucault 1979, 85).

Primitive accumulation cut through traditional lifeways like scissors. The first blade served to undermine the ability of people to provide for themselves. The other blade was a system of stern measures required to keep people from finding alternative survival strategies outside the system of wage labor. A host of oftentimes brutal laws designed to undermine whatever resistance people maintained against the demands of wage labor accompanied the dispossession of the peasants' rights, even before capitalism had become a significant economic force.

For example, beginning with the Tudors, England enacted a series of stern measures to prevent peasants from drifting into vagrancy or falling back onto welfare systems. According to a 1572 statute, beggars over the age of fourteen were to be severely flogged and branded with a red-hot iron on the left ear unless someone was willing to take them into service for two years. Repeat offenders over eighteen were to be executed unless someone would take them into service. Third offenses automatically resulted in execution (Marx 1977, 896 ff.; Marx 1974, 736; Mantoux 1961, 432). Similar statutes appeared almost simultaneously during the early sixteenth century in England, the Low Countries, and Zurich (LeRoy Ladurie 1974, 137). Eventually, the majority of workers, lacking any alternative, had little choice but to work for wages at something close to subsistence level.

In the wake of primitive accumulation, the wage relationship became a seemingly voluntary affair. Workers needed employment and employers wanted workers. In reality, of course, the underlying process was far from voluntary. As Foucault (1979, 222) argues:

> Historically, the process by which the bourgeoisie became the politically dominant class in the course of the 18th Century was masked by the establishment of an explicitly coded and formally egalitarian juridical framework, made possible by the organization of a parliamentary, representative regime. But the development and generalization of disciplinary mechanisms constituted the other, dark side of these processes . . . supported by these tiny, everyday, physical mechanisms, by all those systems of micro-power that are essentially non-egalitarian.

Indeed, the history of the recruitment of labor is an uninterrupted story of coercion either through the brute force of poverty or more direct regulation, which made a continuation of the old ways impossible (Moore 1951). Of course, the extractions common to traditional relatively self-sufficient household economy kept many people at or just above the subsistence level, but for many the market was a step backward. The disorienting introduction of the individualistic ways of the market cut people off from their traditional networks and created a sense of dehumanization (see Kuczynski 1967, 70). A purported need for discipline justified the harsh measures that the poor endured. Indeed, writers of every persuasion shared an obsessional concern with the creation of a disciplined labor force (Furniss 1965; Appleby 1978). Supporters of such measures typically defended their position by invoking the need to civilize workers or stamp out sloth and indolence. Yet capital required these measures to conquer the household economy in order to be able to extract a greater mass of surplus value. In fact, almost everyone close to the process of primitive accumulation, whether a friend or foe of labor, agreed with Charles Hall's (1805, 144) verdict that "if they were not poor, they would not submit to employments"—at least so long as their remuneration were held low enough to create substantial profits.

Employers were quick to perceive the relationship between poverty and the chance to earn handsome profits. Ambrose Crowley, for example, set up his factory in the north rather than the midlands, for there "the cuntry is verry poore and populous soe workmen must of necessity increase" (cited in Pollard 1965, 197). This process was cumulative. An increase in poverty begat more population, which in turn created further poverty, and so on. In this regard, Marx (1865, 72) noted that the level of wages in the agricultural districts of England varied according to the particular conditions under which the peasantry had emerged from serfdom. The more impoverished the serfs, the lower their descendants' wages would be.

Classical Political Economy and the War on Sloth

The classical political economists joined in the chorus of those condemning the sloth and indolence of the poor. Although they applauded the leisure activities of the rich, they denounced all behavior on the part of the less fortunate that did not yield a maximum of work effort.

Consider the case of Francis Hutcheson—"the never to be forgotten Dr. Hutcheson," as his student, Adam Smith, later described him in a letter to Dr. Archibald Davidson (reprinted in Mossner and Ross 1977, 309)—the same Francis Hutcheson whose *Short Introduction to Moral Philosophy in Three Books* (1742) seems to have served as a model for the economic sections of Smith's Glasgow lectures (see Scott 1965, 235, 240). A later work, his *System of Moral Philosophy*, exemplifies Dr. Hutcheson's contributions to that noble field of moral philosophy. After a few brief notes on the need to raise prices, Hutcheson (1755, 2:318–19) mused: "If a people have not acquired an habit of industry, the cheapness of all the necessaries of life encourages sloth. The best remedy is to raise the demand for all necessaries. . . . Sloth should be punished by temporary servitude *at least*." The menacing "at least" in this citation suggests that the never-to-be-forgotten professor might have had even sterner medicine in mind than mere temporary servitude. What else might the good doctor recommend to earnest students of moral philosophy in the event that temporary servitude proved inadequate in shunting people off to the workplace?

This attitude, of course, is not unique to classical political economy. We might ask, was there ever a nation in which the rich found the poor to be sufficiently industrious? The universal howl of "sloth and indolence" can be heard as far away as nineteenth-century Japan, to cite one example (see T. Smith 1966, 120). However, no country seems to have gone as far as England in its war on sloth. Indeed, writers of the time charged that a want of discipline was responsible for criminality as well as disease. By the late eighteenth century, even hospitals came to be regarded as a proper medium to instill discipline (see Ignatieff 1978, 61 ff.).

Almost poetically, Thomas Mun (1664, 193) railed against "the general leprosy of our piping, potting, feasting, fashions, and misspending of our time in idleness and pleasure." Josiah Tucker (1776a, 44–45) employed a military metaphor to make a similar point:

In a word, the only possible Means of preventing a Rival Nation from running away with your Trade, is to prevent your own People from being more idle and vicious than they are. . . . So the only War, which can be attended with Success in that Respect, is a War against Vice and Idleness; a War, whose Forces must consist of—not Fleets and Armies—but such judicious Taxes and Wise regulations, as will turn the Passion of private Self-Love into the Channel of Public Good.

Primitive Accumulation and the Eradication of Holidays

Although their standard of living may not have been particularly lavish, the people of precapitalistic northern Europe, like most traditional people, enjoyed a great deal of free time (see Ashton 1972, 204; see also V. Smith 1992; Wisman 1989). The common people maintained innumerable religious holidays that punctuated the tempo of work. Joan Thirsk estimated that in the sixteenth and early seventeenth centuries, about one-third of the working days, including Sundays, were spent in leisure (cited in K. Thomas 1964, 63; see also Wilensky 1961). Karl Kautsky (1899, 107) offered a much more extravagant estimate that 204 annual holidays were celebrated in medieval Lower Bavaria.

Despite these frequent holidays, the peasants still managed to produce a significant surplus. In English feudal society, for example, the peasants survived even though the gentry was powerful enough to extract something on the order of 50 percent of the produce (see Postan 1966, 603). As markets evolved, the claims on the peasants' labors multiplied. For instance, in southern France, rents appear to have grown from about one-fourth of the yield in 1540 to one-half by 1665 (LeRoy Ladurie 1974, 117).

Although people increasingly had to curtail their leisure in order to meet the growing demands of nonproducers, many observers still railed against the excessive celebration of holidays. Protestant clergy were especially vocal in this regard (Hill 1967, 145–218; see also Marx 1977, 387; Freudenberger and Cummins 1976). Even as late as the 1830s, we hear the complaint that the Irish working year contained only 200 days after all holidays had been subtracted (Great Britain 1840, 570; cited in Mokyr 1983, 222).

Time, in a market society, is money. As Sir Henry Pollexfen (1700, 45; cited in Furniss 1965, 44) calculated: "For if but 2 million of working people at 6d. a day comes to 500,000£ which upon due inquiry whence our riches must arise, will appear to be so much lost to the nation by every holiday that is kept."

Zeal in the suppression of religious festivals was not an indication that representatives of capital took working-class devotion lightly. In some rural districts of nineteenth-century England, tending to one's garden on the Sabbath was a punishable offense. Some workers were even imprisoned for this crime (Marx 1977, 375–76n). Piety, however, also had its limits. The same worker might be charged with breach of contract should he prefer to attend church on the Sabbath rather than report for work when called to do so (ibid.).

In France, where capital was slower to take charge, the eradication of holidays was likewise slower. Tobias Smollett (1766, 38) complained of the French: "Very nearly half of their time, which might be profitably employed in the exercise of industry, is lost to themselves and the community, in attendance upon the different exhibitions of religious mummery." Voltaire called for the shifting of holidays to the following Sunday. Since Sunday was a day of rest in any case, employers could enjoy approximately forty additional working days per year. This proposal caused the naive Abbe Baudeau to wonder about the wisdom of intensifying work when the countryside was already burdened with an excess population (cited in Weulersse 1959, 28). How could the dispossessed be employed?

Of course, changes in the religious practices of Europe were not induced by a shortage of people but by people's willingness to conform to the needs of capital. For example, the leaders of the French Revolution, who prided themselves on their rationality, decreed a ten-day week with only a single day off. Classical political economists enthusiastically joined in the condemnation of the celebration of an excessive number of holidays (see Cantillon 1755, 95; Senior 1831, 9). The suppression of religious holidays was but a small part of the larger process of primitive accumulation.

Classical Political Economy and the Ideal Working Day

Once capital began to dislodge the traditional moorings of society, the bourgeoisie sought every possible opportunity to engage people in productive work that would turn a profit for employers. Accordingly, classical political economists advocated actions to shape society around the logic of accumulation in order to strengthen the dependency on wage labor.

In the utopia of early classical political economy, the poor would work every waking hour. One writer suggested that the footmen of the gentry could rise early to employ their idle hours making fishing nets along with "disbanded soldiers, poor prisoners, widows and orphans, all poor tradesmen, artificers, and labourers, their wives, children, and servants" (Puckle 1700, 2:380; cited in Appleby 1976, 501).

Joseph Townsend (1786, 442) proposed that when farm workers returned in the evenings from threshing or ploughing, "they might card, they might spin, or they might knit." Many were concerned that children's time might go to waste. William Temple called for the addition of four-year-old children to the labor force. Anticipating modern Skinnerian psychology, Temple (1770, 266; see also Furniss 1965, 114–15) speculated, "for by these means, we hope that the rising generation will be so habituated to constant employment that it would at length prove agreeable and entertaining to them." Not to be outdone, John Locke, often seen as a philosopher of liberty, called for the commencement of work at the ripe age of three (Cranston 1957, 425).

Others called for new institutional arrangements to ensure a steadily increasing flow of wage labor. Fletcher of Saltoun recommended perpetual slavery as the appropriate fate of all who would fail to respond to less harsh measures to integrate them into the labor force (see Marx 1977, 882). Hutcheson, as we have seen, followed suit. Always the idealist, Bishop George Berkeley (1740, 456) preferred that such slavery be limited to "a certain term of years."

No source of labor was to be overlooked. For example, in a movement that Foucault has termed "the great confinement," institutions were founded to take charge indiscriminately of the sick, criminal, and poor (Foucault 1965, 38–65). The purpose was not to better the conditions of the inmates but rather to force them to contribute more to the national wealth (for a selection of citations that reflect more charitably on the early political economists, see Wiles 1968).

Occasionally, writers of the time found signs of progress. By 1723, Daniel Defoe (1724–26, 86; see also 493) was delighted to discover that so much progress had taken place in Norwich that "the very children after four or five years of age, could every one earn their own bread."

For classical political economy such edifying scenes of hard labor were not common enough. To his credit, Jean-Baptiste Say (1821, 50–51; see also Ricardo 1951–73, 8:184), generally a strong proponent of capitalist development, penned one of the few protests of the state of affairs in Britain in a letter to Robert Malthus:

> I shall not attempt to point out the parts of this picture which apply to your country, Sir. . . . But if social life [a term that Say used almost like the social division of labor] were a galley, in which after rowing with all their strength for sixteen hours out of the twenty-four, they might indeed be excused for disliking social life. . . . I maintain no other doctrine when I say that the utility of productions is no longer worth the productive services, at the rate at which we are compelled to pay for them.

Sadly, no other classical political economist was willing to side with Say in this regard.

Bentham and Laissez-faire Authoritarianism

Classical political economy frequently couched its recommendations in a rhetoric of individual liberty, but its conception of liberty was far from all-encompassing. Liberty, for capital, depended on the hard work of common people.

Lionel Robbins (1981, 8), a strong proponent of market society, also alluded to this authoritarian side of laissez-faire, noting, "the necessity of a framework of law and an apparatus of enforcement is an essential part of the concept of a free society." Earlier, he wrote, "If there be any 'invisible hand' in a non-collectivist order, it operates only in a framework of deliberately contrived law and order" (Robbins 1939, 6; see also Samuels 1966). Within this contrived law and order, workers found their rights to organize unions and even to act politically severely restricted. The entire judicial edifice was erected with an eye toward making ownership of capital more profitable (Tigar and Levy 1977).

Max Weber (1921, 108; see also Perelman 1991a, chap. 3) once observed that rational accounting methods are "associated with the social phenomena of 'shop discipline' and appropriation of the means of production, and that means: with the existence of a 'system of domination' [*Herrschaftsverhältniss*]." Similarly, the rational accounting system of political economy required a "system of domination," albeit on a grander scale. Weber concluded, "No special proof is necessary to show that military discipline is the ideal model for the modern capitalist factory" (1156).

In this sense, we may see Jeremy Bentham, rather than Smith, as the archetypal representative of classical political economy. Indeed, Bentham's dogmatic advocacy of laissez-faire far exceeded that of Smith. For example, after Smith made the case for a government role in controlling interest rates, Bentham (1787b, 133) caustically rebuked him with the words, "To prevent our doing mischief to one another, it is but too necessary to put bridles into our mouths."

Although Bentham theoretically championed laissez-faire in the name of freedom, he was intent on subordinating all aspects of life to the interests of accumulation. Bentham limited his passionate concern with laissez-faire to those who conformed to the norms of a capitalist society; a jarring confrontation with state power was to be the lot of the rest. According to Bentham, "Property—not the institution of property, but the constitution of property—has become an end in itself" (Bentham 1952, 1:117).

Bentham was absolutely clear about the need for this "constitution of property." He realized that even though control over labor is a major source of wealth, labor stubbornly resists the will of the capitalist. In Bentham's (1822, 430) inimitable language:

> Human beings are the most powerful instruments of production, and therefore everyone becomes anxious to employ the services of his fellows in multiplying his own comforts. Hence the intense and universal thirst for power; the equally prevalent hatred of subjection. Each man therefore meets with an obstinate resistance to his own will, and this naturally engenders antipathy toward beings who thus baffle and contravene his wishes.

Bentham never acknowledged any contradiction between his advocacy of laissez-faire and his proposals for managing labor. For him: "Between wealth and power, the connexion is most close and intimate: so intimate, indeed, that the disentanglement of them, even in the imagination, is a matter of no small difficulty. They are each of them respectively an instrument of the production of the other" (Bentham 1962, 48; cited in Macpherson 1987, 88–89).

Bentham understood that the struggles to subdue the poor would spill over into every aspect of life. He hoped to turn these struggles into profit for himself and, to a lesser extent, others of his class. Given labor's natural resistance to creating wealth for those who exploited them, unfree labor held an obvious attraction for Bentham. He designed detailed plans for his fabled Panopticon, a prison engineered for maximum control of inmates in order to profit from their labor.

In a 1798 companion piece to his design for the Panopticon, *Pauper Management Improved*, Bentham proposed a National Charity Company modeled after the East India Company—a privately owned, joint stock company partially subsidized by the government. It was to have absolute authority over the "whole body of the burdensome poor," starting with 250 industry houses accommodating a half million people and expanding to 500 houses for one million people (Bentham n.d., 369; cited in Himmelfarb 1985, 78).

Bentham planned to profit handsomely from these inmates, especially those born in the houses, since they would then have to work as apprentices within the company. He rhapsodized, "So many industry-houses, so many crucibles, in which dross of this kind [the poor] is converted into sterling" (cited in Himmelfarb 1985, 80). A strict regimen, unremitting supervision and discipline, and economies of diet, dress, and lodging would make profits possible. Jeremy Bentham, vigorous advocate of freedom of commerce that he was, dreamed of the profits that would accrue from the use of inmate labor:

> What hold can another manufacturer have upon his workmen, equal to what my manufacturer would have upon his? What other master is there that can reduce his workmen, if idle, to a situation next to starving, without suffering them to go elsewhere? What other master is there whose men can never get drunk unless he chooses that they should do so. And who, so far from being able to raise their wages by combination, are obliged to take whatever pittance he thinks it most his interest to allow? (see also Ignatieff 1978, 110; Foucault 1979)

According to classical political economy, all social conditions and all social institutions were to be judged merely on the basis of their effect on the production of wealth. In this spirit, Bentham recommended that children be put to work at four instead of fourteen, bragging that they would thereby be spared the loss of those "ten precious years in which nothing is done! Nothing for industry! Nothing for improvement, moral or intellectual!" (cited in Himmelfarb 1985, 81).

Bentham went even further, intent on subordinating every facet of human existence to the profit motive. He even wanted to promote the "gentlest of all revolutions," the sexual revolution. In this regard, Bentham was not the least concerned with furthering the bounds of human freedom, but with ensuring that the inmates would have as many offspring as possible (ibid., 83). Bentham was even planning to call himself the "Sub-Regulus of the Poor." Unfortunately, because of lack of government support, his plans came to naught. As he complained in his memoirs, "But for George the Third, all the prisoners in England would, years ago, have been made under my management" (Bentham 1830–31, 96).

Alas, Bentham never succeeded in his personal goals. Perhaps he was too greedy. Perhaps his methods were too crude. Instead, as we shall see, capitalism found more subtle methods for harnessing labor. As a result, today we remember Bentham as a valiant defender of the ideals of laissez-faire rather than as the Sub-Regulus of the Poor.

Victory

Classical political economists were generally more coy about their intentions than Bentham. Despite their antipathy to indolence and sloth, they covered themselves with a flurry of rhetoric about natural liberties. On closer examination, we find that the notion of the system of natural liberties was considerably more flexible than it appeared. Let us turn once again to Francis Hutcheson, who taught Smith about the virtue of natural liberty. He contended that "it is the one great design of civil laws to strengthen by political sanctions the several laws of nature. . . . The populace needs to be taught, and *engaged by laws,* into the best methods of managing their own affairs and exercising mechanic art" (Hutcheson 1749, 273; emphasis added). In effect, Hutcheson realized that once primitive accumulation had taken place, the appeal of formal slavery diminished. Extramarket forces of all sorts would become unnecessary, since the market itself would ensure that the working class remained in a continual state of deprivation. Patrick Colquhoun (1815, 110), a London police magistrate, noted:

> Poverty is that state and condition in society where the individual has no surplus labour in store, or, in other words, no property or means of subsistence but what is derived from the constant exercise of industry in the various occupations of life. Poverty is therefore a most necessary and indispensable ingredient in society, without which nations and communities could not exist in a state of civilization. It is the lot of man. *It is the source of wealth,* since without poverty, there could be no labour; there could be *no riches, no refinement, no comfort,* and no benefit to those who may be possessed of wealth.

Or, as Marx (1865, 55–56) phrased it: "We find on the market a set of buyers, possessed of land, machinery, raw materials, and the means of subsistence, all of them, save land, the products of labour, and on the other hand, a set of sellers who have nothing to sell except their labouring power, their working arms and brains."

Later political economists disregarded the compulsion required to force labor into the market, blithely assuming that the market alone was sufficient to guarantee the advancement of the accumulation process without the aid of extramarket forces. Workers at the time generally understood the strategic importance of measures to foster primitive accumulation. In this spirit, Thomas Spence, a courageous working-class advocate, proclaimed that "it is childish . . . to expect . . . to see anything else than the utmost screwing and grinding of the poor, till you quite overturn the present system of landed property" (cited in E. P. Thompson 1963, 805).

The system, however, was not overturned, but instead grew stronger. Workers were forced to surrender more and more of their traditional periods of leisure (see Hill 1967; Reid 1976, 76–101). The working day was lengthened (Hammond and Hammond 1919, 5–7). The working class, in the person of Spence, cried out: "Instead of working only six days a week we are obliged to work at the rate of eight or nine and yet can hardly subsist . . . and still the cry is work—work—ye are idle. . . . We, God help us, have fallen under the hardest set of masters that have ever existed" (cited in Kemp-Ashraf 1966, 277; see also Tawney 1926, esp. 223). This statement was eloquent enough to earn its author a sentence of three years' imprisonment after its publication in 1803—a result typical of the fate of those who challenged the capitalist order. Whenever the working class and its friends effectively protested against capitalism, the *silent compulsion* of capital (Marx 1977, 899) gave way to compulsory silence.

Spence's silencing was not completely effective. Although some merely wrote him off as a "radical crank" (Knox 1977, 73), more recent studies have demonstrated that Spence deserves a more respectful reception (Kemp-Ashraf 1966). Indeed, Spence's biographer asserts that Owenism and the subsequent heritage of British socialism stands in direct line of descent from Spence's critique of capitalism (Rudkin 1966, 191 ff.). Journalists of the time agreed with this evaluation (see Halevy 1961, 44n). Unfortunately, the Spences of the world were unable to reverse or even impede the process of primitive accumulation.

No society went so far as the British in terms of primitive accumulation. This aspect of capitalist development is all but forgotten today. Instead, separated by two centuries, contemporary economists such as Milton Friedman (1962) gloss over the dark side of capitalism, ignoring the requisite subordination, while celebrating the freedom to dispose of one's property. These modern economists, as we shall see, are very much mistaken in their interpretation of the evolution of the so-called free market.

Analytical Preliminaries

Although primitive accumulation was a central concern to classical political economists, the study of this concept began in confusion and later
settled into an unfortunate obscurity. The seemingly Marxian expression,
"primitive accumulation," originally began with Adam Smith's (Smith
1976, 2.3, 277) assertion that "the accumulation of stock must, in the
nature of things, be previous to the division of labour."

Smith's approach to original accumulation is odd, to say the least. Certainly, the division of labor is to be found throughout history. It even
exists in insect societies (see Morely 1954). Yet Smith would have us
believe that the division of labor had to wait for "the accumulation of
stock," his code word for capital. Such an idea is patently false. How could
we interpret the division of labor in an anthill or a beehive as a consequence of the accumulation of stock?

Marx translated Smith's word, "previous" as *"ursprünglich"* (Marx and
Engels 1973, 33:741), which Marx's English translators, in turn, rendered
as "primitive." In the process, Marx rejected Smith's otherworldly conception of previous accumulation. He chided Smith for attempting to
explain the present existence of class by reference to a mythical past that
lies beyond our ability to challenge it. Marx insisted, "Primitive accumulation plays approximately the same role in political economy as original
sin does in theology" (1977, 873). Marx's analogy is apt. Both original sin
and original accumulation divert our attention away from the present to a
mythical past, which supposedly explains the misfortunes that people
suffer today.

In other words, any theory based on either original sin or original accumulation is both excessively and insufficiently historical. It is excessively historical because it situates the subject in a remote past, discon-
nected from contemporary society. It is insufficiently historical because
it relies on a mythical treatment of the past. Etienne Balibar's (1988, 49)
expression, "ahistorical historicism, or the historicity without history in

Marx's thought," is an appropriate characterization of this part of Marx's work.

To underscore his distance from Smith, Marx prefixed the pejorative "so-called" to the title of the final part of the first volume of *Capital*, which he devoted to the study of primitive accumulation. Marx, in essence, dismissed Smith's mythical "previous" accumulation, in order to call attention to the actual historical experience. In contrast to the "so-called" primitive accumulation, Marx analyzed in detail the brutality of the actual historical experience of separating people from their means of production in an effort to lay bare the origin of the capitalist system.

The Historical Basis of Primitive Accumulation

The contrast between Smith's scanty treatment of previous accumulation and Marx's extensive documentation of the subject is striking. Marx's (1977, 915) survey of primitive accumulation carries us through a several-centuries-long process, in which a small group of people brutally expropriated the means of production from the people of precapitalist society around the globe:

> The discovery of gold and silver in America, the extirpation, enslavement and entombment in mines of the indigenous population of that continent, the beginnings of the conquest and plunder of India, and the conversion of Africa into a preserve for the commercial hunting of blackskins, are all things which characterize the dawn of the era of capitalist production. These idyllic proceedings are the chief moments of primitive accumulation.

Marx did not limit his interpretation of primitive accumulation to isolated pockets of the world. The fruits of primitive accumulation are fungible. For example, he insisted that "a great deal of capital, which appears today in the United States without any birth-certificate, was yesterday, in England, the capitalized blood of children" (ibid., 920).

According to Smith, economic development progressed through the voluntary acts of the participants. Marx (ibid., 926), in contrast, believed that "capital comes dripping from head to toe, from every pore, with blood and dirt." Workers were "tortured by grotesquely terroristic laws into accepting the discipline necessary for the system of wage-labour" (ibid., 899). Where Smith scrupulously avoided any analysis of social relations, Marx produced an elaborate study of the connection between the development of capitalistic social relations and so-called primitive accumulation.

In later years, Marx displayed an impatience with those who failed to ground their treatment of primitive accumulation in concrete historical analysis. For example, he chastised Nikolai Mikhailovsky's suprahistorical presentation of primitive accumulation, in which the latter mechanically extrapolated Russia's future from Marx's analysis of the European experience of primitive accumulation (letter to the editorial board of *Otechestvenniye Zapitski*, November 1877, in Marx and Engels 1975, 291–94).

Granted that primitive accumulation is a historical process rather than a mythical event, a further question arises: Why does this process, or at least most accounts of Marx's treatment of it, seem to stop so abruptly with the establishment of a capitalist society? Marx himself offered few examples of primitive accumulation that occurred in the nineteenth century outside of colonial lands.

In his letter to *Otechestvenniye Zapitski*, Marx seemed to take an almost Smithian position, diminishing the importance of primitive accumulation by relegating it to a distant past. Marx even denigrated his chapter in *Capital* on primitive accumulation as "this historical sketch," insisting that it "does not claim to do more than trace the path by which in Western Europe, the capitalist economy emerged from the womb of the feudal economic system. It therefore describes the historical process which by divorcing workers from their means of production converts them into wage workers" (ibid., 293). We must read this letter in its political context. Marx was upset that Mikhailovsky was attempting to use the chapter on primitive accumulation to convey the impression that Russia's future would be mechanically determined by the "inexorable laws" of capitalism (ibid.). Marx was certain that, although the nature of capital might be unchanged, the specifics of Russian and western European development would be quite different. Consequently, he wanted to point out to Mikhailovsky the mistake of thinking that one could mechanically "predict" the Russian outcome on the basis of western European experiences.

At times, Marx did propose a theoretical stance that would seem to confine the importance of primitive accumulation to the historical past. Lucio Colletti (1979, 130) singles out the following extended passage from the *Grundrisse:*

> The conditions which form its [capital's] point of departure in production—the condition that the capitalist, in order to posit himself as capital, must bring values into circulation which he created with his own labour—or by some other means, excepting only already available, previous wage labour—belongs among the antediluvian conditions of capital, belongs to its historic presuppositions, which, pre-

cisely as such historic presuppositions, are past and gone, and hence belong to the history of its formation, but in no way to its contemporary history, i.e., not to the real system of the mode of production ruled by it. While e.g., the flight of serfs to the cities is one of the historic conditions and presuppositions of urbanism, it is not a condition, not a moment of the reality of developed cities but belongs rather to their past presuppositions, to the presuppositions of their becoming which are suspended in their being. The conditions and presuppositions of the becoming, or the arising, of capital presuppose precisely that it is not yet in being but merely in becoming; they therefore disappear as real capital arises, capital which itself, on the basis of its own reality, posits the conditions for its realization. (Marx 1974, 459–60)

In *Capital*, the same idea appears with a similar wording, except for the elimination of some of the more baroque Hegelesque terminology (Marx 1977, 775). Taken very simply, Marx seems to have been suggesting that the initial separation of workers from the means of production was a necessary historical event for the establishment of capitalism. In short, primitive accumulation was an essential component of what Engels (1894, 217) called the "great division of labor between the masses discharging simple manual labour and the few privileged persons directing labour," but it was irrelevant to the ongoing process of capitalism. In *Capital*, Marx also generally appears to restrict the action of primitive accumulation to a short period in which traditional economies converted to capitalism. As he wrote in *Capital*: "The different moments of primitive accumulation can be assigned in particular to Spain, Portugal, Holland, France and England, in more or less chronological order. These different moments are systematically combined together at the end of the seventeenth century in England" (Marx 1977, 915).

Was Smith then correct after all in relegating primitive accumulation to the past—at least in the societies of advanced capitalism? We will see that the answer is an emphatic no.

The Coexistence of Primitive and Capitalist Accumulation

Despite Marx's words to the contrary, the overall presentation of the first volume of *Capital* suggests that he rejected Smith's approach of assigning primitive accumulation to a distant past. Indeed, the material in his part 8, "The So-Called Primitive Accumulation," does not appear to be qualitatively different from what is found in the previous chapter, "The General Theory of Capitalist Accumulation."

When Marx's study of primitive accumulation finally reached the subject of Edward Gibbon Wakefield, Marx did not qualify his appreciation of the father of modern colonial theory by limiting its relevance to an earlier England. Instead, he insisted that Wakefield offered significant insights into the England where Marx lived and worked (Marx 1977, 940; see also Marx 1853, 498).

Read in this light, Marx's letter to Mikhailovsky is also consistent with the idea that the importance of primitive accumulation was not what it taught about backward societies, but about the most advanced ones. In spite of the presumptions of some authors to prove otherwise (see, for example, Foster-Carter 1978, esp. 229), Marx (1976, 400n) himself, referring to the institutions of Mexico, contended that the "nature of capital remains the same in its developed as in its undeveloped forms."

Even so, the presentation in *Capital* still does suggest a temporal cleavage between the initial moment of primitive accumulation, when capitalists accumulated by virtue of direct force, and the era of capitalist accumulation, when capitalists accumulated surplus value in the market. This dichotomy might appeal to our common sense; still, it is itself rather ahistorical.

In conclusion, at some times, Marx's analysis of primitive accumulation sometimes seems to be a process that ceased with the establishment of capitalism. At other times, it seems to be more of an ongoing process. What then is the source of this confusion?

The Primacy of Capitalist Accumulation in Capital

Why was Marx not more explicit about the continuity of primitive accumulation? To answer this question, recall the purpose of Marx's exposition of primitive accumulation. On a theoretical level, Marx was attempting to debunk Smith's theology of previous accumulation, which suggested that capitalists' commanding position was due to their past savings.

In the process, he was attempting to lay bare the historical origins of market relations. He intended this historical analysis to refute the contention of classical political economy that markets supposedly work fairly because invisible hands somehow intelligently guide the world toward inevitable prosperity and even a higher level of culture.

Marx's depiction of primitive accumulation conveyed an overriding sense of the unfairness of that altogether brutal experience. Yet, this portrayal stood in contradiction to the main thrust of *Capital*. After all, Marx's primary message was that the seemingly fair and objective rule of capital necessarily leads to exploitation.

Although Marx accepted that markets were progressive in the long run, insofar as they prepared the ground for socialism, he was convinced that allegedly impartial market forces produced more cruelty than the crude and arbitrary methods of primitive accumulation. To emphasize primitive accumulation would have undermined Marx's critique of capitalism.

Marx would not have wished his readers to believe that measures to eliminate "unjust" instances of primitive accumulation might suffice to bring about a good society. To have stressed the continuing influence of primitive accumulation would have risked throwing readers off track. Certainly, Marx did not want his readers to conclude that the ills of society resulted from unjust actions that were unrelated to the essence of a market society.

On the contrary, Marx insisted that the law of supply and demand, not primitive accumulation, was responsible for the better part of the horrible conditions that the working class experienced. As a result, he subordinated his insights about primitive accumulation to a more telling critique of capitalism; namely, that, *once capitalism had taken hold*, capitalists learned that purely market pressures were more effective in exploiting labor than the brutal act of primitive accumulation. In this sense, Marx's relegation of primitive accumulation to the historical past made sense. By calling attention to the consequences of the market's unique logic, he was reinforcing his basic contention that piecemeal reforms would be inadequate. In this vein, Marx (1977, 899–900) wrote:

> It is not enough that the conditions of labour are concentrated at one pole of society in the shape of capital, while at the other pole are grouped masses of men who have nothing to sell but their labour-power. Nor is it enough that they are compelled to sell themselves voluntarily. The advance of capitalist production develops a working class which by education, tradition and habit looks upon the requirements of that mode of production as self-evident natural laws. The organization of the capitalist process of production, once it is fully developed, breaks down all resistance. The constant generation of a relative surplus population keeps the law of the supply and demand of labour, and therefore wages, within narrow limits which correspond to capital's valorization requirements. The *silent compulsion of economic relations* sets the seal on the *domination of the capitalist over*

the worker. Direct extra-economic force is still of course used, but only in exceptional cases. In the ordinary run of things, the worker can be left to the "natural laws of production," i.e., it is possible to rely on his dependence on capital, which springs from the conditions of production themselves, and is guaranteed in perpetuity by them. It is otherwise during the historical genesis of capitalist production. The rising bourgeoisie needs the power of the state, and uses it to "regulate" wages, i.e., to force them into the limits suitable to make a profit, to lengthen the working day, and to keep the worker himself at his normal level of dependence. This is an essential aspect of so-called primitive accumulation. (emphasis added)

The force of the "silent compulsion" is more effective than the crude methods of primitive accumulation:

> the pretensions of capital in its embryonic state, in its state of becoming, when it cannot yet use the sheer force of economic relations to secure its right to absorb a sufficient quantity of surplus labour, but must be aided by the power of the state. . . . Centuries are required before the "free" worker, owing to the greater development of the capitalist mode of production, makes a voluntary agreement, i.e. is compelled by social conditions to sell the whole of his active life. (ibid., 382)

Again, in describing the centralization of capital, Marx (1981, 3:609) noted how effectively market forces had replaced primitive accumulation: "Profits and losses that result from fluctuations in the price of . . . ownership titles, and also their centralization in the hands of railway magnates . . . now appears in place of labour as the original source of capital ownership, as well as taking the place of brute force."

Marx (ibid., 354) also made the connection between market forces and primitive accumulation when he discussed the tendency of the rate of profit to fall: "This is simply the divorce of the conditions of labour from the producers raised to a higher power. . . . It is in fact this divorce between the conditions of labour on the one hand and the producers on the other that forms the concept of capital, as this arises with primitive accumulation."

Here, Marx (ibid., 348) referred to "expropriating the final residue of direct producers who still have something left to expropriate." This note is important because it indicates that Marx realized the ongoing nature of primitive accumulation, although as I argue he wanted to suppress its importance to highlight the "silent compulsion" of the market.

Judging by his words, Marx was also careful to avoid confusing such "financial primitive accumulation" with primitive accumulation proper. Marx (ibid., 570–71) noted:

> Conceptions that still had a certain meaning at a less developed state of capitalist production now become completely meaningless. Success and failure lead in both cases to the centralization of capitals and hence to expropriation on the most enormous scale. Expropriation now extends here from the immediate producers to the small and medium capitalists themselves. Expropriation is the starting-point of the capitalist mode of production, whose goal it is to carry it through to completion, and even in the last instance to expropriate all individuals.

No matter what his strategic reasons, Marx seems to have downplayed the role of primitive accumulation in order to focus on modern capitalist accumulation. Although he succeeded in that respect, this ahistoricity obscures our understanding of the early process of capitalist development.

Specifically, by relegating primitive accumulation to the precapitalistic past, we lose sight of the twofold time dimension of primitive accumulation. First, as we shall emphasize later, the separation of people from their traditional means of production occurred over time as capital gradually required additional workers to join the labor force. Second, the process of primitive accumulation was a matter of degree. All-out primitive accumulation would not be in the best interests of capital. Instead, capital would manipulate the extent to which workers relied on self-provisioning in order to maximize its advantage.

The Theoretical Context of Primitive Accumulation

Marx's presentation of primitive accumulation had the unfortunate consequence of divorcing the process from political economy. Peter Cressey and John MacInnes (1980, 18) made a similar point, noting:

> Marx argues that primitive accumulation was a process irreducible to the categories of political economy and explicable only in terms of struggle and ultimately force. At first sight it appears that historical analysis of primitive accumulation explains the initial "formal" subordination of labour, in that the workplace capitalist simply appropriates (formally) a production process bequeathed by pre-capitalist society. [Ultimately, the] . . . concept of the formal subordination of labour, like Smith's concept of previous accumulation, is not derived from history but from political economy.

Etienne Balibar's analysis of Marx's use of the term *proletariat* reinforces our case for looking at the concept of primitive accumulation more closely. Balibar noted that Marx's *Capital* rarely mentions the proletariat, but generally refers to the working class. In the first edition of the first volume, the term only appears in the dedication to Wilhelm Wolff and the two final sections on "The General Law of Capitalist Accumulation," which concerned the law of population and the process of primitive accumulation.

On only one occasion do the proletarian and the capitalist confront each other directly in *Capital.* Balibar (1988, 19–20) concluded, "These passages have in common their insistence upon the *insecurity* characteristic of the proletarian condition." On a more general level, Balibar claimed that Marx's use of the term *proletariat* seemed to be intended to infer that the condition of the working class was unstable, that it perpetuated the violence associated with the transition to capitalism, and that the situation is historically untenable (ibid.).

Following Balibar, we might interpret the notion of the proletariat as an abstract concept to describe the situation of people displaced from their traditional livelihoods by primitive accumulation. The concept of the proletariat abstracts from any of the specific conditions that affected these people, with the exception of their lack of control over the means of production, which sets the stage for the introduction of capitalist forces.

Both Balibar's reading of the use of the word *proletariat* and my own understanding of Marx's treatment of primitive accumulation suggest that Marx obscured the phenomena of primitive accumulation in order to focus attention on the working of markets. By relegating the relevance of primitive accumulation to the historical process of proletarianization, we ignore the centrality of the ongoing process of primitive accumulation in shaping the conditions of the working class.

I am convinced that we can benefit from a closer look at primitive accumulation, without losing sight of Marx's invaluable analysis of market forces. In the process of investigating this subject, I will attempt to reintegrate primitive accumulation into the structure of political economy, especially classical political economy.

Acknowledging the Scope of Primitive Accumulation

In reality, primitive accumulation did not suddenly occur just before the transition to European capitalism. Nor was it confined to the countryside of western Europe. Primitive accumulation may be seen as occurring even well before the age of capitalism.

For example, land was already scarce for the majority of people during the Middle Ages. According to M. M. Postan (1966, 622–23):

> about one-half of the peasant population had holdings insufficient to maintain their families at the bare minimum of subsistence. This meant that in order to subsist the average smallholder had to supplement his income in other ways. . . . [I]ndustrial and trading activities might sustain entire villages of smallholders. . . . Most of the opportunities for employment must, however, have lain in agriculture. . . . [I]n almost all the villages some villagers worked for others.

Other factors reinforced the pressure of land scarcity. For example, the twelfth-century Danes levied tribute from the British. This extortion was not primitive accumulation, since it was not intended to coerce workers into the labor market and foster market relations. However, it did impel Britain to monetize its economy in a way that bore some resemblance to primitive accumulation (Sohn-Rethel 1978, 107). Similarly, medieval usury, often simply dismissed as a parasitic intrusion into the economy, prodded the economy to advance (Marx 1967, 3:596–97).

The process of primitive accumulation does not merely extend backward before the epoch of classical political economy. It lasted well into more modern times. In England, as well as in the other countries of advanced capitalism, the conversion of small-scale farmers into proletarians continued throughout the nineteenth century and into the twentieth. This transformation involved more than the "silent compulsion" of market forces. In the case of the destruction of small-scale farming in the United States, the federal government was central in developing the transportation and research systems that tipped the balance in favor of large-scale agriculture (see Perelman 1977; 1991b).

The continuity of primitive accumulation stands in stark contrast to its usual image as the one-time destruction of the peasant economy, the immediate effect of which was to create a society with capitalists on the one side and workers on the other. This perception is understandable, but misleading. Indeed, on the eve of capitalism, the majority of people were peasants or at least had some connection to farming.

Moreover, primitive accumulation was not limited to agriculture. It extended across many, if not all, sectors of the economy (Berg 1986, 70). It took place in the city as well as the countryside. After all, urban people still provide for themselves directly in a multitude of ways other than the growing of food. Depriving people of these means of provision forces a greater dependence on the market just as surely as restricting their access to the means of food production.

Take a relatively modern example. Packing people into crowded urban quarters left little space for doing laundry. As a result, people become dependent on commercial laundries. After World War II, the ability of the typical U.S. family to produce for its own needs continued to diminish, despite the widespread availability of household appliances, such as washing machines, that should have made many types of self-provisioning easier. Likewise, Paul Sweezy (1980, 13) interprets Japan's huge entertainment sector as a partial result of people being forced to live in such cramped quarters that they are unable to socialize in their homes.

The need to purchase such services compels people to sell more labor. We see the impact of this pressure reflected in the recent increase in the number of women in the labor force. Gabriel Kolko (1978, 267) calculates that the share of life years available for wage labor for the average adult has expanded from 39 percent in 1900 to 44.4 percent in 1970, despite rising education levels, better child labor laws, and a shorter workweek. Since that time, work has demanded a rapidly escalating share of the typical family's time. Juliet Schor (1991, 29) estimates that the average person worked 163 more hours in 1987 than in 1969.

This process can feed on itself. Because people have to earn more wages to compensate for the increased difficulty of providing for certain of their own needs, they have less time to do other sorts of work on their own, inducing families to transfer still more labor from the household to the commercial sector. Child care centers are an obvious outcome of this process. In addition, the fast-food industry is predicated on the difficulty of working a job and performing a multitude of other household chores in the same day.

The foregoing discussion suggests that wage labor and nonwage labor are, indeed, inextricably linked. The analysis of one category necessitates consideration of the other. As we shall see later, the concept of the social division of labor enhances our understanding of this mutual interplay of wage and nonwage labor. For now, we need only keep in mind our modern-day examples of goods and services that were once produced within the household, which became commodities sold by commercial firms.

This new arrangement is related, at least in part, to the pattern of ownership of the means of creating these goods and services in the household. Formally, the lack of ownership of a workspace for doing laundry is no different from the lack of ownership of the parcel of land on which a household once grew its own food. In either case, the denial of ownership to a particular means of production creates a change in the mix of wage and nonwage labor.

Ignoring Balibar's warning about the careless use of the word proletariat, we could interpret this restructuring of the life of a modern household as a contemporary variant of the process of primitive accumulation, whereby the mass of people working for wages has increased. In this sense, the concept of primitive accumulation is closely bound up with that of the social division of labor.

Classical Political Economy and Primitive Accumulation

Even though Marx muted his analysis of the continuing nature of primitive accumulation, he was abundantly clear that primitive accumulation resulted in momentous changes in social relations that were central to creation of the capitalist system (see Dobb 1963, 267). Marx's lesson was lost on most later economists. They were content to treat the Industrial Revolution as if it were merely the introduction of superior methods of production. In contrast, the classical political economists saw primitive accumulation as a means of radically reordering the social division of labor, which they recognized as a precondition of the creation of a proletariat. Along this line, Marx (1977, 764), in writing about primitive accumulation, proposed the formula: "Accumulation of capital is . . . multiplication of the proletariat."

We shall see that we can express the classical theory of primitive accumulation as a model that resembles a crude proto-Marxian model stripped of the dialectic. In analyzing this model, keep in mind that Marx began by taking the categories of classical political economy as he found them (see Perelman 1987, chap. 4). By investigating them more fully, he was able to invest the typically static, undialectical categories of classical political economy with a dynamic, dialectical quality.

We will try to follow the same tradition in our study of the classical theory of primitive accumulation. The classical political economists make this task considerably easier. Compared to their analysis of the categories of profits or wages, they adopted a far more dynamic, almost dialectical approach to their analysis of primitive accumulation. Carrying out such an analysis of the classical theory of primitive accumulation has a twofold importance: it reveals a side of classical political economy that previously has gone unnoticed; and it reminds us that primitive accumulation is an ongoing process.

Even modern commentaries on primitive accumulation do not do the topic full justice. Like Marx, most contemporary references relegate the concept to a distant past, except perhaps in the case of the proletarianization that the less-developed countries of Africa, Asia, and Latin America are experiencing. Consequently, the separation of workers from their means of production is implicitly assumed to be a static, once-and-for-all event.

Since the classical political economists grounded their discussions of primitive accumulation in a dynamic framework, scrutiny of the classics has more to offer than more modern commentaries on the subject of primitive accumulation. To some extent, the deficiencies of these commentaries may be understandable. Marx himself often wrote about primitive accumulation with an air of finality and possibly even with a touch of Smithian mythology. For example, the first mention of the concept of primitive accumulation in *Capital* appears in chapter 23, "Simple Reproduction" (Marx 1977, 714). At this point, Marx had to address the question: How does the system come to be structured into capital and labor? He responded: "From our present standpoint it therefore seems likely that the capitalist, once upon a time, became possessed of money by some form of primitive accumulation" (Marx 1977, 714).

Marx's uncharacteristic "once upon a time," which sounded as unreal as Smith's mythical history, was obviously provisional. The words "from our present viewpoint" also suggest that a more thorough analysis would be forthcoming. For reasons already discussed, Marx never provided that thoroughgoing critique. Instead, we find only history.

Yet primitive accumulation remains a key concept for understanding capitalism—and not just the particular phase of capitalism associated with the transition from feudalism, but capitalism proper. Primitive accumulation is a process that continues to this day. Thus, we must carry the history of primitive accumulation through the epoch of classical political economy by connecting this concept with Marx's notion of the social division of labor.

CHAPTER 3

Primitive Accumulation and
the Game Laws

The Feudal Origin of the Game Laws

Earlier we made the assertion that we should not limit our understanding
of primitive accumulation to agriculture alone. As a case in point, let us
begin with the admittedly obscure subject of the Game Laws.

Classical political economy was virtually silent concerning the Game
Laws. Some might contend that this silence is altogether appropriate.
After all, the Game Laws began as an element of feudalism. As we shall
see, however, the Game Laws were one of the most hated institutions of
feudalism, most remembered today for leading the legendary Robin Hood
into a life of crime. More important, they helped to create conditions that
eventually contributed to the undermining of the feudal aristocracy's hegemony in British society.

Laws protecting feudal rights in the forests were common throughout
Europe. Many remained in force as late as the nineteenth century. In
Germany, for example, merely foraging for berries was deemed a crime
(Marx 1842, 234–35). Marx (1970, 19–20; Marx and Engels 1973, 39:466)
himself remarked that the harsh treatment meted out to those who il-
legally gathered wood in the forests was significant enough to have first
drawn his attention to social problems. These prohibitions differed little
from the ancient feudal laws that forbade people from carrying out certain
types of work in their homes in order to preserve the privileged positions
of their masters (see Weber 1923, 120).

Although the English Game Laws also began as a feudal institution,
they lost most of their importance as feudalism waned. By the end of the
sixteenth century, the English state had ceased to enforce these laws,
although they still remained on the books. King Charles I tried to revive
them in 1630 to raise revenue, but both Parliament and the Civil War
conditions prevented him from doing so (Munsche 1980, 189).

The modern English Game Laws began in 1671. The wording of the
preamble sounds far more like the handiwork of avaricious capitalists
intent on maximizing surplus value than an appeal to feudal tradition:

Whereas great mischief do ensure by inferior tradesmen, apprentices, and other dissolute persons neglecting their trades and employments who follow hunting, fishing and other game to the ruin of themselves and their neighbors, therefore, if any such person shall presume to hunt, hawk, fish or fowl (unless in company of the master of such apprentice duly qualified) he shall . . . be subject to the other penalties. (William and Mary 3 and 4, chapter 23, reprinted in Chitty 1812, 1:459–65; also cited in Ignatieff 1978, 26)

In truth, the initial spirit of this Game Law was as feudal as its predecessors. Although it may have sounded capitalistic, this legislation actually reflected a spirit that was inimical to capitalism. The intent of this legislation was to promote a hierarchy of class relationships, not necessarily capitalist in nature. According to one of the few works devoted to the study of this subject, "The Game Laws were born out of a desire to enhance the status of country gentlemen in the bitter aftermath of the Civil War. Their message was that land was superior to money" (Munsche 1980, 164).

While an antibourgeois sentiment may have motivated the Game Laws, these acts represented a direct response to the refusal of the rural poor to accept the landlords' assertion of unprecedented property rights following the Civil War. After all, these new property rights came at the expense of the traditional rights of the poor in the countryside (see Ignatieff 1978, 16).

These traditional rights were far from inconsequential for the rural poor. For them, hunting was an important means of providing for oneself and one's family, rather than simply pleasant recreation. The Game Laws, in this sense, became part of the larger movement to cut off large masses of the rural people from their traditional means of production (E. P. Thompson 1975, 94, 99, 207, 261).

Once English leaders recognized the unexpected benefits of the Game Laws, the people in power went well beyond merely embracing the acts as they found them; they passed increasingly restrictive Game Laws with even more inhumane penalties. In the process, the British Game Laws became the harshest in the world (see Engels 1845, 552–53).

Although the spirit of the Game Laws may have been in tune with modern capitalism, the British system of justice often administered these bourgeois Game Laws in a decidedly feudal style. The case of Richard Dellers became a particularly famous example. On the basis of information from his gamekeeper and a servant, the Duke of Buckingham convicted Dellers. The duke, presiding over the trial in his own drawing room, informed the unfortunate Dellers that if he uttered a single impertinent word, he would be taken to jail or the stocks (Munsche 1980, 76; see also Cobbett 1830, 1:191–93). Henry Brougham, speaking in 1828 when the Dellers affair was still fresh in the minds of the British public, roared: "There is not a worse constituted tribunal on the face of the earth, not even that of the Turkish cadi, than that which summary convictions on the Game Laws constantly take place; I mean a bench or a brace of sporting justices" (cited in Munsche 1980, 76).

Nonetheless, despite the feudal execution and intent of the modern Game Laws, their effect was decidedly capitalistic insofar as they succeeded in accelerating the process of primitive accumulation.

The Scottish Laboratory

Primitive accumulation probably occurred at a faster rate in Scotland than in Britain, in part because it began later in Scotland. As a result, the perception of the role of hunting in that country is of special significance.

In his tour of the Scottish Highlands, Daniel Defoe (1724–26, 666) discovered that "however mountainous and wild the country appeared, the people were extremely well furnished with provisions." Among the major sources of food, he noted "venison exceedingly plentiful, and at all seasons, young or old, which they kill with their guns whenever they find it." Later visitors to Scotland fretted that hunting was a barrier to the expansion of wage labor. Thomas Pennant, a botanist, provided much valuable information about the relationship between hunting and the labor market in his *Tour in Scotland* (1771). While considered to be a sympathetic interpreter of Scottish society—more so than, say, Samuel Johnson—Pennant still regarded those who used hunting rather than wage labor to supplement their livelihood with a jaundiced eye (see Lascelles 1971, xviii).

For example, writing from a spot near Edinburgh, Pennant (1772, 71) noted, "I was informed that labor [sic] is dear here . . . ; the common people not being yet got into a method of working, so do very little for wages." Once he reached the Highlands, he complained: "The manners of the native Highlanders may be expressed in these words: indolent to a high degree, unless roused to war, or any animating amusement" (ibid., 176).

For Pennant (ibid., 115) the energy the Highlanders devoted to hunting contrasted unfavorably with their lack of enthusiasm for wage labor: "The inhabitants live very poorly. . . . The men are thin, but strong; idle and lazy, except when employed in the chace [sic], or anything that looks for amusement; and are content with their hard fare, and will not exert themselves farther than what they deem necessaries [sic]." Pennant's description of the Highlanders closely resembles Adam Smith's (1755–1756, 250) characterization of savages: "The life of a savage, when we take a distant view of it, seems to be a life of either profound indolence, or of great and astonishing adventures" (see also Rae 1834, 131). Here was the problem that the classical model of primitive accumulation highlighted. People preferred their leisure rather than the small value they could obtain from a long stint of wage labor.

Pennant (1772, 126) drew some hope from what he saw in the salmon fisheries on the beaches near Aberdeen, where the women carried their heavy loads of salmon in baskets, which they hoisted onto their shoulders: "And when they have sold their cargo and emptied their basket, [they] will replace part of it with stones: they go sixteen miles to sell or barter their fish; they are very fond of finery, and will load their fingers with trumpery rings, when they want both shoes and stockings." One could only guess how many hours of their drudgery were exchanged for each hour of the jeweler's craft.

In most accounts of the world of the Highlanders, people displayed more reluctance to engage in wage labor. For example, Samuel Johnson observed that a pair of traditional Scottish brogues could be made at home in one hour. Commercially produced shoes sold for one-half crown per pair (Johnson 1774, 50). According to Adam Smith's (1976, I.viii.31) estimates of wage rates for labor in the vicinity of Edinburgh, where workers were undoubtedly paid more than in the countryside, a citizen of that city would have to work for three full days to earn enough money to purchase a pair of shoes. Commercially produced shoes would need to have a great deal of appeal to induce people to work for almost three days to purchase them instead of making their own brogues in an hour, assuming that they could obtain the leather cheaply.

Given the unfavorable exchange between wages and purchased commodities, people in the Highlands generally preferred self-provisioning to wage labor. Seeing this as a problem, Pennant approved of whatever restricted people's opportunity for self-provisioning. For example, he commended the practice of the Earl of Bute, whose "farms were possessed of a set of men, who carried on at the same time the profession of farming and fishing to the manifest injury of both. His lordship drew a line between these incongruent employs, and obliged each to carry on the business he [Bute] preferred, distinct from the other" (Pennant 1774, 2:160).

Pennant did not base his objection to these poor husbandmen on technical grounds. He admitted that "in justice to the old farmers, notice must be taken of their skill in ploughing even in their rudest days, for the ridges were strait [sic], and the ground laid out in a manner that did them credit" (ibid.). Pennant's concerns were not technical. He wanted a new system of dependency. Thus, he praised the management of the Breadalbane estate, where tenants could stay rent free "on the condition that they exercise some trade. [Consequently, Breadalbane] has got some as good workmen, in common trades, as any in his Majesty's kingdom" (Pennant 1772, 90). To establish such dependency, Pennant saw the need to restrict the possibility of hunting for one's own food.

In this vein, James Steuart (1767, 1:37), writing from his native Scotland, wryly praised the suppression of hunting merely as "an augmentation of inland demand for agricultural commodities."

Lord Kames (Henry Home) (1758, 1, 78n), a Scottish aristocrat, explored the nature of the society that the Game Laws were intended to produce, explaining:

> The life of a fisher or hunter is averse to society, except among the members of simple families. The shepherd life promotes larger societies, if that can be called a society, which hath scarce any other than a local connection. But the true spirit of society, which consists in mutual benefits, and in making the industry of individuals profitable to others as well as themselves, was not known till agriculture was invented. Agriculture requires the aid of many other arts. The carpenter, the blacksmith, the mason, and other artificiers, contribute to it. This circumstance connects individuals in an intimate society of mutual support, which again compacts them within a narrow space.

Kames (1758, 1, 78–79n) recognized that this new society would necessarily lead to a hierarchy:

> The intimate union among a multitude of individuals, occasioned by agriculture, discovered a number of social duties, formerly unknown. These behoved to be ascertained by laws, the observation of which must be enforced by punishment. Such operations cannot be carried on, otherwise than by lodging power in one or more persons, to direct the resolutions, and apply the force of the whole society. In short, it may be laid down as an universal maxim, that in every society, the advances of government towards perfection, are strictly proportioned to the advances of the society towards intimacy of union.

For Kames (ibid., 125–26), while this arrangement might lead to a severely unequal distribution of income, the outcome was for the best. After all, he asked, "What place would there be for generosity, benevolence, or charity if the goods of fortune were common to all?"

The Oppressive Nature of the Bourgeois Game Laws

Changing social relations in the countryside influenced the development of the Game Laws. Although the feudal Game Laws were harsh and repressive, the paternalistic obligations that society still expected of the gentry tempered the severity of these restrictions. Generally, those most in need could count on some generosity from the superior orders; however, the social mores were changing.

With the decline of feudal relations, land ownership was becoming more of a business and less a way of life. The economic value of land rose, and the gentry became more bourgeoisified (Wood 1999). Landlords' relations with their tenants became both more distant and more exploitative. Long-term leases became less common. Rental income was on the rise. Cottagers were being eliminated. Casual labor was replacing full-time workers and servants. Any goodwill was fast disappearing from the countryside.

Within this context, the Game Laws became ever more brutal. The Waltham Black Acts of 1722 were among the earliest of the severe measures to punish poachers. This legislation was devised at a time when venison had become a prized delicacy, perhaps because of the great expanse of land required for raising deer (see E. P. Thompson 1975, 30). More and more, poachers began to see the quarry as a commodity rather than an object of direct consumption. A century later, in 1826, a journalist lamented that it was "difficult to make an uneducated man appreciate the sanctity of private property in game [when] . . . the produce of a single night's poach was often more than the wages for several weeks' work" (cited in Shaw 1966, 156).

The penalties for taking small game were initially less severe than for poaching deer until landowners began to take measures to increase their population of deer on their land. In response, the scope of the Game Laws expanded rapidly. During the first six decades of the eighteenth century, for example, only six acts were directed against poachers of small game. The next fifty-six years saw the enactment of thirty-three such laws. As a result, "Meat virtually disappeared from the tables of the rural poor" (Deane and Coale 1965, 41).

Poaching was taken so seriously that it was, on occasion, even equated with treason. The British courts enforced these laws with shocking ferocity. Several poachers were actually executed under the famous Black Acts (E. P. Thompson 1975, 68).

The imposition of draconian penalties for infractions of the supposedly feudal Game Laws at such a late date might seem anomalous for an advancing capitalist economy. Yet the Game Laws were an important part of the intensifying class struggle that was occurring in the countryside during the age of classical political economy. One pamphleteer exclaimed that "the article of game [is] productive of more *disquiet, popular discontent* and *local animosity* than any other law ever established in this kingdom" (Taplin 1792, 168).

The conviction rates indicate the sharpening of this conflict. In 1816, the first year in which national figures were recorded, 868 persons were imprisoned for game offenses; by 1820, the number had risen to 1,467. In Wiltshire, the winter of 1812–1813 saw 8 committals under the Game Laws; by the winter of 1817–1818, the number had risen to 85. In Bedfordshire, 7 people were imprisoned in 1813; 77 in 1819. By the first half of the 1820s, 65 persons annually were imprisoned for infractions of the Game Laws (Munsche 1980, 138). In Wiltshire, the average had risen to 92. Between 1820 and 1827, nearly a quarter of those committed to prison were convicted of poaching (Shaw 1966, 155). In Wiltshire alone, more than 1,300 persons were imprisoned under the Game Laws in the fifteen years after the battle at Waterloo in 1815, more than twice the number for the previous fifty years (Munsche 1980, 138). These numbers undoubtedly understate the conviction rates, since the Justices of the Peace who heard cases frequently neglected to record convictions (Hay 1975, 192).

Despite the reform of the Game Laws in 1831, the number of convictions for poaching still continued their dramatic increase (Munsche 1980, 157). During the 1840s, in some rural counties, 30 to 40 percent of all male convictions were still for infractions of the Game Laws (Horn 1981, 179–80). The Duke of Richmond told the House of Lords on 19 September 1831 that one-seventh of all criminal convictions in England were for violations of the Game Acts (Hammond and Hammond 1927, 167).

The majority of convicts that Britain exiled to Australia supposedly were convicted of poaching. Robert Hughes disputes that view, suggesting that many of the poachers got off lightly. Nonetheless, a substantial number of poachers suffered transportation (Hughes 1987, 170; Munsche 1980, 103).

In addition, the state convicted a good number of poachers of other crimes that grew out of their poaching, such as resisting arrest. Even Hughes (1987, 170), who tried to make the case that the majority of transported convicts were guilty of more serious crimes, shows how the Game Laws were used to rid the labor market of people whom the authorities deemed to be undesirable.

Economic conditions at the time, rather than feudal history, explain the upswing in conviction rates. For example, the Hammonds (1927, 167) asserted that poaching became more intensive when unemployment was high. After the Napoleonic Wars ended in 1812, some 250,000 to 400,000 men were demobilized. During the war, threshing machines had taken many of the traditional jobs in the countryside (see Munsche 1980, 136). Just as people's means of providing for themselves was diminishing, along with the opportunity for jobs, the cost of purchasing food on the market was rising substantially, catching the workers in a cruel trap (Hammond and Hammond 1927, 86 ff.). Hence, many unemployed workers poached because they had no other option for survival.

The Game Laws and Bourgeois Hegemony

Why would the feudal Game Laws become so much harsher under capitalism? The answer lies in the fact that the Game Laws reflected a situation where the interests of capital and the gentry coincided. The gentry could enjoy the prestige of hunting, while the capitalists could enjoy the labor of many of the people who were forbidden to hunt as a means of subsistence.

The Game Laws were bound up with the rise of classical political economy in the sense that both revealed the emerging hegemony of property relations. Political economy offered a justification of a regime dominated by the logic of property relations; the Game Laws defined new forms of property. In this sense, the Game Laws represented an essential bulwark for the social order. Since the taking of game was tantamount to challenging property rights, such acts had to be punished severely. The lesson was not lost on either the gentry or bourgeoisie.

We can see the resentment against the Game Laws in France, where one of the earliest acts of the French Revolution was their repeal. At the time, Arthur Young (1794, 9; see also 441–42) exclaimed, "One would think that every rusty gun in Provence is at work."

Horace Walpole, after noting the speed with which the French Game Laws were eliminated, confided to a Lady Ossory: "I never admired game-acts, but I do not wish to see guns in the hands of all the world, for there are other ferae naturae besides hares and partridges—and when all Europe is admiring and citing our constitution, I am for preserving it where it is" (Walpole 1789, 69; cited in Munsche 1980, 126).

Lord Milton made a similar point to Lord Kenyon in 1791: "The Republican party has made the Game Laws the object of their abuse and detestation; in France, the instant they began to overturn the constitution and level all distinctions, these were the first they pulled down. It therefore seems to me that they should be most respectfully guarded" (ibid., 127).

These modern Game Laws became an effective policy instrument in the process of primitive accumulation because they prohibited the rural poor from keeping weapons (see *Alarm* 1757), thereby diminishing people's ability to resist the onslaught. As William Blackstone (1775, 2:412) noted, "The prevention of popular insurrection and resistance to the government, by disarming the bulk of the people; which last is a reason oftener meant, than avowed, by makers of forest or Game Laws." Later research has confirmed Blackstone's contention, finding that access to weapons was a major factor in determining the level of exploitation (see Pettengill 1981).

The Game Laws were a useful disciplinary device in another respect. Many observers recognized that people would resist drudgery so long as they could hunt instead. As an early writer from the United States warned his readers, "once hunters, farewell to the plough" (de Crèvecoeur 1782, 51). Similarly, John Bellers (1714, 128), the famed Quaker philanthropist of the time, remarked: "Our Forests and great Commons (make the Poor that are upon them too much like the Indians) being a hindrance to Industry, and are Nurseries of Idleness and Insolence" (see also E. P. Thompson 1991, 165).

Blackstone (1775, 4:174-75) agreed that we should view the Game Laws in terms of maintaining discipline within the labor force: "The only rational footing, upon which we can consider it a crime [to violate the Game Laws], is, that in low and indigent persons it promotes idleness and takes them away from their proper employments and callings." William Pitt concurred (cited in Cobbett 1806-20, 32:851).

The Game Laws went beyond directly promoting primitive accumulation; they became an important tool in maintaining labor discipline. We cannot know how well they succeeded in this respect, since we have little opportunity to hear from both sides in the struggle. In at least one instance, however, the Game Laws seem to have stiffened the resolve of one of the participants. William Cobbett wrote in the *Political Register* of 29 March 1823 that a gentleman in Surrey asked a young man how he could live on a half crown per week. "I don't live upon it," said he. "How do you live then?" "Why," he replied, "I *poach*; it is better to be hanged than to be starved to death" (cited in Hammond and Hammond 1927, 167).

The Destructive Nature of the Game Laws

The Game Laws had another dimension. Some animals protected by the laws ravaged the nation's crops. Others, which were zealously hunted, such as the little foxes and martens, were valuable predators that prevented the population of rodents from becoming excessive (Kautsky 1899, 393). Even worse, hunters and their horses trampled much of what the game left growing in the fields. A letter to the editor of the *London Magazine* in 1757 claimed:

> The present scarcity is owing to an evil, felt by the industrious husbandman, who has in many places in this kingdom, seen all his care, labour, and industry sacrificed to the caprice and humors of those who have set their affections so much on game. Numberless are the places and parishes of the kingdom which have had at least one third part of their wheat crop devoured and eat[en] up by hares. (Letter 1757, 87)

A modern student of the Game Laws observed, "Pheasants, if anything, were more destructive" (Munsche 1980, 46).

The destruction of crop by game was a very important phenomenon. In France, for example, on the eve of the revolution, people were given the chance to express their concerns. In almost every case, the people of the countryside demonstrated their exasperation at the devastation caused by game and hunters (see Philipponeau 1956, 29; Young 1794, 9). Given the resentment against the Game Laws in France, we should not be surprised that one of the first acts of the revolutionary government was to repeal the Game Laws.

The grievances of the English peasants were no doubt just as strong as those of the French. A single hunt could cause enormous destruction. One fox hunt, for instance, carried its riders twenty-eight miles through the British countryside (W. Thomas 1936, 43). A recent study points out other costs besides the trampled grain:

> Sportsmen, it was said, continually broke fences, beat down unharvested corn, trampled turnips, disturbed sheep "big with lamb" and generally pursued game with little concern for the damage they caused. The quantity and volume of these complaints suggest that such conduct was common and deeply resented. (Munsche 1980, 45; see also *Alarm* 1757, 14)

The upper classes were generally insensitive to the destruction of crops by hunting. Anthony Trollope's (1929, 56–58) discussion of this matter, first published in the *Pall Mall Gazette* in 1865, is worth citing in detail in this regard:

> In England two or three hundred men claim the right of access to every man's land during the whole period of the winter months! . . . Now and then, in every hunt, some man comes up, who is indeed, more frequently a small proprietor new to the glories of ownership,

48

than a tenant farmer who determines to vindicate his rights and oppose the field. He puts up a wire-fence round his domain . . . and defies
the world around him. It is wonderful how great is the annoyance
which one such man may give, and how thoroughly he may destroy
the comfort of the coverts in his neighborhood.

Trollope (ibid., 59–60) went on to explain:

Farmers as a rule do not think very much of their wheat. When such
riding is practicable, of course they like to see men take the headlands
and furrows; but their hearts are not broken by the tracks of horses
across their wheat fields. I doubt, indeed, whether wheat is ever much
injured by such usage.

Perhaps the owners of some large farms were not aggravated by the loss of
their grain. For a large farm, the swath of destruction caused by a group of
horses would represent a small share of the total crop.

Of course, Trollope wrote long after the controversies about the Game
Laws had subsided, but he reflected a mentality that had been common in
earlier years. One anonymous writer despaired of any communication
with people who were of this persuasion:

It is in vain to argue with a man who will maintain, that the wealth of
his country, and the advancement of cultivation, is of no concern,
when compared to the pleasure of fox-hunting; or, that the farmers
and tenants, instead of following the plough, are much better employed when after the hounds, and while neglecting the culture of
their own grounds, laying waste and ravaging the improvements of
their industrious neighbours. (*Considerations* 1772, 33)

In the 1840s, an estimated quarter of the crops of Buckinghamshire
were destroyed by game (Horn 1981, 179). Parliament indicated an interest in this problem on only one occasion: "For most sportsmen, the season
began with partridge shooting on the first of September . . . , but following
the bad harvest in 1795 . . . , [e]arly in 1796, Parliament voted to post-
pone the start of partridge shooting until the fourteenth of September"
(Munsche 1980, 46). Parliament repeated this provision by the next year.

The most intense application of the Game Laws falls between 1776, the
same year that Smith's *Wealth of Nations* was published, and the 1840s,
an interval often used to mark the age of classical political economy.
Political economists of the time took a lively concern in all matters pertaining to the functioning of the economy. The consequent loss of grain
continued without comment from the ranks of political economists,

whose keen vision rarely left any opportunity for increased productivity pass unnoticed.

For example, political economy devoted an enormous amount of energy to protesting the consequences of the Corn Laws, but it all but completely ignored the Game Laws. Why should classical political economy have taken note of so much of the minutiae of society while remaining oblivious to the monstrous impact of the Game Laws? Here was a set of laws that created substantial hardships for an enormous number of people. They allowed many workers to be incarcerated or transported. They condoned the destruction of valuable crops. Yet, despite the widespread injuries inflicted by the Game Laws, classical political economy generally ignored the implications of this legislation.

How could the classical political economists never have broached the subjects of the trampled grain or the crops lost to the protected wildlife? Surely the damage done to the harvest must have been of the same order of significance as the distortions caused by the Corn Laws. Yet these arbiters of efficiency remained silent.

The classical political economists of the time had to know about the human costs. Even if they were entirely ignorant of the realities of rural life, they had to know transportation was a common punishment inflicted on poachers in the early nineteenth century. Yet, the early economists remained silent about the human costs. Frank Fetter (1980, 192), after noting the attendance and voting patterns of political economists in Parliament, observed, "transportation was not an issue in which many political economists were concerned."

This omission in no way absolves these economists of any responsibility for the repression and destruction associated with the operation of the Game Laws. Silence in the face of such conditions amounted to an effective form of support.

Adam Smith and the Game Laws

A number of observers dismissed the Game Laws as nothing more than an ugly residue of ancient feudalism, irrelevant to modern capitalism. For example, Brian Inglis (1971, 243) claimed that the Game Laws were the only oppressive part of the feudal system that remained on the statute books. The usually astute Jacob Viner (1968, 39–40) was of a similar mind.

Adam Smith, that great master of capitalist apologetics, also attributed the Game Laws to feudalism. In this respect, he was unique among the major classical political economists in even taking note of the Game Laws; however, Smith's purpose was not to call for more equity for the poor. Instead, he merely attempted to denigrate the status of the gentry in order to raise that of the bourgeoisie (Smith 1978, 1.55–57:24).

Smith attributed all the evils of this legislation to feudal oppression: "There can be no reason in equity for this. . . . The reason they give is that the prohibition is made to prevent the lower sort of people from spending their time on such unprofitable employment; but the real reason is that they delight in hunting and the great inclination they have to screw all they can out of their hands."

Smith's interpretation does contain an ounce of truth. The practice of restricting self-provisioning predated capitalism, as we have already mentioned. Smith added that feudal lords also prohibited the use of hand mills to force people to pay to use those that the lords owned (Smith 1978, 2.39:85). Notwithstanding such examples, no class proved itself as effective and as ruthless in separating workers from their means of production as the bourgeoisie.

Smith (1976, V.ii.a.18, 824) also took some notice of the dissipation of resources associated with hunting. He complained that the "large tracts of land which belong to the crown . . . [were] a mere waste and loss of country with respect both of population and produce." His recommendation that such lands be sold seems to have been based on the assumption that private land would be "well-improved and well-cultivated" (ibid.). He did not mention that much of this land would likely go into private hunting preserves.

In *The Wealth of Nations,* without actually mentioning the Game Laws, Smith seemed to treat this legislation as relatively unimportant. He attributed the decline in the economic significance of hunting to the natural evolution of the economy. He speculated:

> Hunting and fishing, the most important employments of mankind in the rude state of society, become in its advanced state their most agreeable amusements, and they pursue for pleasure what they once followed from necessity. In the advanced state of society, therefore, they are all very poor people who follow as a trade, what other people pursue as a pastime. . . .

He continued:

> A poacher is everywhere a very poor man in Great Britain. In countries where the rigour of the law suffers no poachers, the licensed hunter is not in a much better condition. The natural taste for those employments make more people follow them that can live comfortably by them, and the produce of their labour, in proportion to its

quantity, comes always too cheap to market to afford any thing but the most scanty subsistence to the labourers. (ibid., I.x.b.3, 117–18)

Although Smith refused to acknowledge any association between the Game Laws and the interests of capital, he deserves some credit for broaching the subject, since all other political economists failed to make any mention whatsoever.

Although Smith was correct to charge that the gentry want "to screw all they can out of their hands," like the rest of his class, he said nothing and did nothing to lighten the imposition of the Game Laws on the poor, except to mention them in passing with an eye to putting the bourgeoisie in a good light.

The Demise of the Game Laws

Eventually, the existence of the Game Laws became unnecessary. By 1827, the Black Acts had been repealed. In 1831, other measures were eliminated. Over the next two decades, still more of the controversial features were repealed (see Horn 1981, chap. 6).

Long after people ceased to be hung for poaching, however, the law still countenanced the equally harsh, extrajudicial penalties meted out by spring guns and mantraps set to kill or maim the unwary hunter (see S. Smith 1821, 213–34). The outraged journalist William Cobbett (1831, 1:122–23) complained: "I saw divers copies of a hand-bill notifying an approaching public sale of farming stock . . . and [on] one of these bills having been given to me, I saw that, amongst the farming stock were a fire-engine and several steel man-traps. . . . [D]ismal indeed were the times when fire-engines and man-traps formed part of the implements of husbandry!" The courts held that these barbaric devices were legal according to common law. Eventually, in 1827, the devices were prohibited—but only because of the deaths they inflicted on gamekeepers and children, as opposed to the injury of poachers. As Baron Edward Suffield (1825) noted, "poachers are almost the only persons who escape being shot by spring guns" (cited in Munsche 1980, 72).

Other elements of the Game Laws were harder to eradicate. Parliament did not grant farmers the right to kill hares on their land without permission of the landlord until 1880 (Munsche 1980, 157).

Even after the harsh Game Laws ceased to carry much weight in Britain, their influence persisted in other parts of the world. When the western European nations extended their domination to peripheral regions, they were quick to draw on their experience with the Game Laws. For example, in French Equatorial Africa, the Mandja people were banned from hunting (Rodney 1974, 166). Since these people had almost no livestock, hunting provided a major source of meat. This ban was effective in forcing the Mandja to work on the French cotton plantations.

I know of no explanation other than the logic of primitive accumulation to explain why the rise of classical political economy, often identified with a growing commitment to human freedom, coincided with "a crescendo of fierceness" in the enforcement of the Game Laws (Hammond and Hammond 1927, 164).

The Bourgeois Perception of the Game Laws

The barbarism of the existing Game Laws seems to have been somewhat of an embarrassment for some of the bourgeoisie (see Cobbett 1806–20, 32:833 ff.; S. Smith 1819). Now that the old Game Laws seemed to have served their purpose, many bourgeois interests merely preferred less primitive means of accomplishing the same ends. Proponents of the interests of the rising bourgeoisie were especially vocal in calling for reform of the Game Laws in the interests of substantial farmers and their tenants. In general, these "reformers" concurred with the sentiments of Reverend Joseph Townsend (1786, 404), who called for "a peaceable, silent, unremitted pressure" rather than outright force. These reforms were actually supposed to reduce poaching because the pretensions of the gentry symbolized in the Game Laws incited many daring men to poach, despite the obvious risks involved.

The most commonly proposed reform was to make game private property, a bourgeois concept that chipped away at the exalted privileges of the gentry. John Christian Curwin, a leading reformer of the late eighteenth century, asked Parliament in 1796 to follow the lead of Russia by substituting the taxation of game for the Game Laws. Such a tax was viewed as preferable because it "does away with all necessity of restrictions, and puts it out of the power of persons who might injure themselves and the public by misspending their time in pursuit of game" (cited in Cobbett 1806–20, 32:836). His proposal did nothing to reduce the penalties for poaching. In fact, in some ways, it would have made them even stronger.

Even the sympathetic Sydney Smith (1819), who wished "to preserve the lives of . . . the least worthy of God's creatures" with a vigor equal to that which protected "the Christian partridge . . . the immortal pheasant . . . the rational woodcock, or the accountable hare" (cited in Auden 1956), could only see his way toward strengthening the property rights of wealthy landowners in order to treat game as any other commodity.

Making game property also appealed to a Smithian vision of the world. For example, one anonymous pamphlet proposed: "From the system of game becoming property, a durable bond of harmony, and a mutual communication of good offices, are the necessary consequence" (*Considerations* 1772, 31–32). Frequently, the reformers proposed that property qualifications be lowered so that the middle class could enjoy the right to hunt as well, since the highly restrictive English Game Laws prohibited all but about 1 percent of the population from hunting (Broderick 1881, 386–89). These proposed reforms would also allow bourgeois farmers of the middling sort to hunt on their own lands as freely as the gentry could on theirs. Presumably, anybody else with enough money to purchase the right to hunt could do so.

These proposed bourgeoisified Game Laws offered nothing of significance to the lower classes. Although the reforms would give common workers the formal right to hunt, the cost of hunting would preclude them from that activity. Some thought that the reforms could benefit the poor since a few of them could find work as gamekeepers (Munsche 1980, 113).

In a sense, however, the proposed laws were a step backward for the poor. So long as the Game Laws were grounded in traditional rights, the gentry's claim to exclusive hunting rights was subject to some doubt. Under the existing Game Laws, the poor could appeal both to their own traditional rights and certain ambiguities in the law (see Blackstone 1775, 2:410); under the reformed laws, the traditional rights of the poor were irrelevant.

Small farmers could benefit from the right to protect their crops, but hunting would effectively remain the almost exclusive preserve of the wealthy. In contrast, substantial landowners could hire game wardens to augment the game on their land. Indeed, hunting preserves soon became a major source of income for the gentry (see Ross 1973, 249).

Ironies of the Game Laws

On the infrequent occasions when Parliament took notice of the Game Laws during the late eighteenth century, the ruling strata adopted a curious defense of this legislation. Although hunting was deemed to be an improper diversion for the poor, members of Parliament commended hunting for the rich since it was regarded as an encouragement to agricultural production. But how could running horses and hounds through the fields, trampling grain and destroying fences, possibly improve agricultural production?

Keep in mind that the gentry were an idle lot, spending much of their time enjoying the pleasures of the city. The opportunity to hunt seemed to be the only means of bringing the wealthy into contact with their land (see Cobbett 1806-20, 32:833 ff.; Horn 1981, 172). To my knowledge, none of the gentry rose to defend themselves against this characterization of their relationship to the land.

When Parliament debated the Game Laws again in 1830, not one prominent spokesperson for political economy called for their abolition. Instead, Robert Peel, whose family wealth had come from the employment of those who were leaving the land, cautioned Parliament not to act with undue haste: "We are apt to be too sanguine in our anticipations of advantages to be derived from a particular change. He was afraid that we overlooked the love of enterprise and amusement, which rendered the pursuit of game attractive to the common people" (cited in *Hansard's* 1830, 597-98). A leading journalist made a similar point in 1826, commenting that the gentry, "the most useful and valuable class," was "entitled to properly regulated . . . amusement and relaxation after the performance of their public duties." Moreover, the periodic visits to the countryside supposedly contributed to the "virtue and civilization of the English peasant," which saved Britain from the horrors of the French Revolution (cited in Shaw 1966, 156).

The other presumed contribution of the gentry to society was their military service. According to a good many people, hunting was an important means of imbuing the gentry with appropriate martial skills (see Steuart 1767, 1:85). As Karl Kautsky (1899, 25) observed, "the more warfare became a matter for the aristocracy, the more hunting became the sport of nobles." Many members of the ruling classes were reluctant to encourage the spread of such skills among a broader section of the populace.

Policymakers seem to have broadly accepted the military qualifications of the gentry until around 1756, after Britain endured several military defeats during the Seven Years' War. At that time, the middle classes looked to a reinvigorated militia to renew civic virtue (Munsche 1980, 112). Alas, bourgeois society consigned the feudal warrior, like the medieval artisan, to the hazy past. Future battles would be decided by ships and other fixed capital of warfare, together with the mobilization of broader segments of society. Bourgeois captains of the battlefield would manage their operations much the same as bourgeois captains of industry ran their factories (see Smith 1976, V.i.a, 689-708; Marx 1974, 109; and Marx to Engels, 25 September 1857, in Marx and Engels 1975, 91-92). Within this conception of warfare, farmers who were acquainted with firearms would be invaluable. In this context, some inquired of the gentry if they valued their country as much as their partridges (Western 1965, 119). Even Sir

James Steuart, along with his great rival Adam Smith, joined the Poker Club, which was formed to support a Scotch militia, in spite of Steuart's general deference to feudal warriors (see Bell 1960; Rendall 1978; Mossner and Ross 1977, 22n).

Smith, who usually stressed the sloth and lethargy of rural workers, took a different position in discussing the need for free time for training a militia. There, he had to recognize that agricultural progress might have been bought at the expense of the rural workers: "Those improvements in husbandry . . . which the progress of arts and manufactures necessarily introduces, leave the husbandman with as little leisure as the artificer" (Smith 1976, V.i.a.15, 697).

This concern with the decline in the martial spirit, rather than some deep sympathy for workers, led Smith to interject his famous denunciation of the dehumanizing effect of the division of labor:

> In the progress of the division of labour, the employment of the far greater part of those who live by labour . . . comes to be confined by a few very simple operations. . . . But the understandings of the greater part of men are necessarily formed by their ordinary employments. The man whose whole life is spent in performing a few simple operations, of which the effects too are, perhaps, always the same, or very nearly the same, has no occasion to exert his understanding, or to exercise his invention in finding out expedients for removing difficulties which never occur. He naturally . . . becomes as stupid and ignorant as it is possible for a human creature to become. . . . But in every improved and civilized society this is the state into which the labouring poor, that is, the great body of the people, must necessarily fall, unless the government takes some pains to prevent it. (ibid., V.i.f.50, 781–12)

Smith's concerns illustrate a more general point concerning the Game Laws: although this new military vision did move some classical political economists to reconsider the conditions of the rural poor, none of them noticed the connection between these conditions and the Game Laws.

The Game Laws and Bourgeois Vision of Nature

The perception of the role of flora and fauna provides a useful lens through which to view the emerging bourgeois organization of society. For example, while the British elite saw fit to protect game from the lower classes, the organized slaughter by well-bred huntsmen seemed altogether proper. Certainly, the Royal Society for the Preservation of Cruelty to Animals gave no hint of concern about hunted foxes in Victorian England. It concentrated instead on sports enjoyed by the lower classes: bull, bear, and badger baiting; dog fighting; and the mistreatment of working animals in cities, primarily horses (Gould 1988).

With the evolution of capitalism, the role of game changed. Modern hunting practices also emerged. In the words of Sir William Beach Thomas (1936, 9–10):

> Yes: fox-hunting has a long history in England. It flourished in the fourteenth century; and probably there has been no break in its continuity. Nevertheless it is true enough in essentials to argue that hunting as we know it began in the eighteenth century and belongs to modern England, a country of hedges and spinneys and small woods. The Enclosure Acts encouraged it by destroying other sports, especially the hunting of deer.

The Game Laws fit in with changing styles of consumption as well. The new social relations in the countryside led to an evolution in the definition of hospitality. A writer in the 1761 edition of the *Annual Register* explained that the aristocracy could "no longer affect an old-fashioned hospitality, or suffer the locust of the country to eat them up, while they keep open-house and dispense victuals and horns of beer to all comers" (cited in Munsche 1980, 133–34). According to the same source, "genteel entertainment" with "French food and select company" became the style. Indeed, the cuisine was always limited to French foods. A writer of 1815 claimed that game was "an essential ingredient in every entertainment that has the slightest pretension to elegance" (cited in Munsche 1980, 22).

Along with capitalism's increasingly effective control over labor came a new vision of nature. Polite society no longer admired highly artificial landscapes. Nature was to be managed in such a way that it would look natural. Adam Smith is said to have been a major influence in this respect. His *Lectures on Rhetoric and Belles Lettres* appear indirectly to have initiated the craze for deer parks, which were closely managed game reserves (Olwig and Olwig 1979, 19; Whitney 1924; Smith 1762–63, Lecture, 21 January 1763). Later, Smith (1790b, 183; see also Comito 1971) applauded the growing preference for more natural-looking habitats: "It was some years ago the fashion to ornament a garden with yew and holly trees, clipped to the artificial shapes of pyramids, and columns, and vases, and obelisks. It is now the fashion to ridicule this task as unnatural. The figure of a pyramid or obelisk, however, is not more unnatural to a yew-tree than to a block of porphyry or marble."

Indeed, Smith's vision of a "natural" landscape was well suited to the world of the bourgeoisie. Recall Peel's imagery of "enterprise and amusement" to which he alluded in his defense of the Game Laws. John Ruskin (1866, 61) described this bourgeois vision in greater detail:

> Your ideal of human life then is, I think, that it should be passed in a pleasant undulating world, with iron and coal everywhere underneath it. On each pleasant bank of this world is to be a beautiful mansion, with two wings; and stables and coach horses; a moderately sized park; a large garden and hot houses; and pleasant carriage drives through the shrubberies. In this mansion are to live the favoured votaries of the Goddess: the English gentleman, with his gracious wife and his beautiful family; always able to have the boudoir and the jewels for the wife, and the beautiful ball dresses for the daughters, and hunters for the sons, and a shooting in the Highlands for himself. At the bottom of the bank, is to be the mill; not less than a quarter of a mile long, with a steam engine at each end, and two in the middle and a chimney three hundred feet high. In this mill are to be in constant employment from eight hundred to a thousand workers, who never drink, never strike, always go to church on Sunday, and always express themselves in respectful language.

Not all of the bourgeoisie were able to realize this dream, but enough could that the landscape of the nation was transformed.

Thomas Jefferson (1950–, 681–83) took heed of the effect of the enormous land resources devoted to keeping game in France. To his credit, he recognized the economic importance of reserving this land for hunting in a letter dated 28 October 1785 to James Madison (not the future president) from Fontainebleau, where the king hunted each fall: "In Europe the lands are either cultivated or locked up against the cultivator. Manufacture must therefore be resorted to of necessity, not of choice" (Jefferson 1787, 42).

Nowhere, however, had matters proceeded as far as in England. According to Engels (1894, 213; see also Marx 1977, 892–95), for each acre of English common land brought into cultivation by means of enclosures, three acres of Scottish land were eventually transformed into deer parks. Marx (1977, 892) remarked, "Everyone knows that there are no true forests in England. The deer in the parks are demure domestic cattle, as fat as London aldermen. Scotland is therefore the last refuge of the 'noble passion.' "

Marx's discussion of the deer parks is worth noting in one respect. It is the only reference in part 8 of *Capital* that deals with the household economy of England after the era of classical political economy had been completed (ibid., 892–93). The conversion of forest into well-guarded deer parks represented the final extinguishing of the old feudal rights of the peasantry. Hence, this discussion conforms to the narrow interpretation of primitive accumulation as a precapitalistic phenomenon.

In contrast, the substitution of deer for sheep, also explored by Marx in this same section, represents a restriction of the production of food or clothing, which is fully explicable in terms of supply and demand. If the gentry preferred to use their land for hunting, they were not directly attacking people. If wool or mutton became more expensive as a result, we cannot hold an individual culpable. Yet the effect is no less severe for the people who suffer.

I do not intend to push the definition of primitive accumulation far enough to include the substitution of deer for sheep. I only wish to include those cases that directly impact on a household's ability to produce for its own needs. The example of the deer parks does suggest how such primitive accumulation, in the broad sense, can occur without the arbitrary application of force.

CHAPTER 4   The Social Division of Labor
and Household Production

Commodity Production
and the Social Division of Labor

The foundation of every division of labor which has attained a certain level of development, and has been brought about by the exchange of commodities, is the separation of town from country. One might say that the whole history of society is summed up by this antithesis.—Karl Marx, *Capital*

Our examination of the Game Laws has prepared us to look at Marx's concept of the social division of labor. Just as Marx developed the notion of primitive accumulation in opposition to Smith's notion of original accumulation, so too did he forge the category of the social division of labor in opposition of another Smithian concept—that of the division of labor. Certainly, Marx was dissatisfied with Smith's treatment of the division of labor. He once even wrote to Engels, in 1862, that he wished to use *Capital* to show that "in mechanical workshops, the *division of labor*, as forming the basis of manufacturing and described by Adam Smith, does not exist" (Marx and Engels 1985, 351).

Where Smith's division of labor describes the organization of work within an individual pin factory, Marx's social division of labor refers to the partitioning of the economy into independent firms and industries. In other words, the conventional social division of labor concerns the organization within the factory, where the employer divides the work among the employees. Marx's notion of the social division of labor in contrast, describes how work is divided up between different workplaces, which are coordinated by market relations rather than by an authority figure within the workplace.

The resulting compartmentalization of the labor process divides the economy into separate entities that specialize in the production of particular items, such as pins, iron, and food, etc. The social division of labor thus encompasses what contemporary economists call "industrial organization," although it is broader in scope and not limited to commodity production.

In Smith's famous pin factory, the visible hand of management was in control, assigning each worker to a specialized task, while the invisible hand somehow determined how much coal and machinery the pin industry would use. Marx believed that capital consciously manipulated the partitioning of the economy. His concept of the social division of labor calls out to make the forces that determine the industrial organization of an economy as visible as the hand that distributes the labor within the pin factory.

Marx placed considerable weight on his analysis of the social division of labor in his published writings, dating back as far as his *Poverty of Philosophy* (1847, 128, 135). A year earlier, Marx had observed: "The division of labour implies from the outset the division of the *conditions* of labour, of tools and materials, and thus the splitting up of accumulated capital among different owners" (Marx and Engels 1846a, 73).

In *Capital*, Marx went so far as to claim, "The social division of labour . . . forms the foundation for all commodity production" (Marx 1977, 471; see also Lenin 1908, 37–38, where the same idea is repeated twice).

This "foundation for all commodity production," as Lenin (1908, 38) called it in beginning his *Development of Capitalism in Russia*, was discreetly buried within the texts of pre-Marxian classical political economy. In unearthing this history, both petty commodity production and the feudal mode of production must be exhumed, and the roots of capitalism exposed.

The Commodity Form and the Social Division of Labor

Before we explore the reason why Marx believed that the social division of labor formed the basis of commodity production, let us take note of the perspective of conventional economics. In general, conventional economists, dating back even to the days of classical political economy, have been oblivious to the theory of the social division of labor because they take it to be technically determined by the nature of the commodities produced. Consider the following portrait from Joseph Lowe's (1823, 61) *The Present State of England*: "In London the class of shoemakers is divided, says Mr. Gray, into makers of shoes for men, shoes for women, shoes for children; also into boot-cutters, boot makers. Even tailors, though to the public each appears to do the whole of his business, are divided into makers of coats, waistcoats, breeches, gaiters." Lowe's emphasis on differentiation pointed the way toward modern literature on the social division of labor, although in no way could he have foreseen the wide diversity of commodities available in present-day society. Lowe's perspective is true to the vision of Smith and the other classical political economists. A modern text sums up this perspective by asserting that insofar as intermediate goods are concerned, "inputs are produced commodities which are treated as variables, and *not* as parameters" (Walsh and Gram 1980, 5). In other words, the structure of the social division of labor is a predetermined datum rather than the result of individual or collective choice. The set of preexisting commodities, such as Lowe listed, creates a matrix around which the social division of labor forms.

The social division of labor can, in fact, vary considerably, but understanding this phenomenon requires reconsidering the very nature of commodities. A few decades ago, who would have dreamed that contemporary consumers would be faced with a choice between the purchase of ready-baked bread, frozen dough, or even prebuttered bread (see Lancaster 1966)? Faced with this incredible diversity, Robert Triffen (1940, 89) rejected the concept of an industry as a proper category for economics.

Marx (1981, 3:637) himself forcefully made the connection between the changing array of commodities and the social division of labor, noting: "The market for . . . commodities develops by way of the social division of labour; the separation between different productive labours transforms their respective products into commodities, into equivalents for one another, making them serve one another reciprocally as markets."

Marx alluded to the relationship between commodities and the social division of labor by observing that "the bond between independent labours . . . is the fact that their respective products are commodities" (Marx 1977, 475). Money is merely "the objectification of the social bond" (Marx 1974, 160).

To make this relationship clearer, we have to take another step and ask ourselves what it is that commodities have in common. They are the products of labor that are offered for sale in the market. In other words, commodities are products "which are *sold* as commodities . . . since without the sale they cannot be regarded as products" (Marx 1977, 952; see also 166). Then what is a product?

Marx (1977, 475–76n) once examined this question in terms of the umbrella industry of the United States. Prior to the Civil War, umbrella manufacturers were merely assemblers of the umbrella components. Consequently, individual parts, such as umbrella handles, were commodities. If the companies that produced these handles also assembled the umbrellas, then handles would no longer exist as commodities.

The U.S. Congress raised the distinction between components that were and were not commodities during the Civil War, instituting a turnover tax at the time. Producers had to pay a tax when they sold components to an assembler, who in turn had to pay an additional tax on the total value of the finished product. Congress dismissed industry's protest against multiple taxation. Marx concurred with the eventual judgment of Congress: "A thing is produced 'when it is made' and it is made when it is ready for sale" (ibid.). Engels made a similar point in a note inserted into *Capital*: "In order to become a commodity, the product must be transferred to the other person, for whom it serves as a use value, through the medium of exchange" (Marx 1977, 131). We also read in the *Theories of Surplus Value*: "As values, commodities are *social magnitudes*. . . . Value indeed 'implies exchanges,' but exchanges are exchanges between men. In actual fact, the concept 'value' presupposes 'exchanges' of the products" (Marx 1963–71, 129).

Is this a trivial point? Not at all. The above citation concerning congressional legislation reminds us that the form in which commodities appear may be indeterminate. When U.S. umbrella manufacturers were merely assemblers of the components that made up umbrellas, each individual piece was a commodity. Yet if the handle makers, for instance, were to take over the process of assembly, umbrella handles would not circulate in the market.

The Intentional Structuring of the Social Division of Labor

On one occasion, Adam Smith (1976, I.i.4, 15) did allude to the social division of labor with an offhand remark: "The separation of different trades and employments from one another, seems to have taken place, in consequence of this advantage" of specialization arising from the division of labor. But he never took this thought much further. Although he devoted an entire chapter to the proposition that "the division of labour . . . must always be limited by the extent of the market" (Smith 1976, I.iii.1, 31), he did nothing to show exactly how market forces could have created specialization. In fact, the tradition of classical political economy effectively taught later generations of economists to avoid thinking about the social division of labor. Later economists generally did even less than Smith in taking note of the social division of labor. The common neglect of this subject has left a serious gap in modern economic theory (see Marx 1977, 486).

Karl Rodbertus, who other than Marx, was virtually alone in recognizing the theoretical importance of the social division of labor, had argued that a proper analysis of the basic categories of national economy was inconceivable without the prior notion of a social division of labor. Rodbertus (1899, 93–109) was concerned that Smith's division of labor brings one no further than the analysis of individualistic behavior. Thus, he charged that Smith's method is incomplete. The social division of labor must be seen within the context of capital in general. Unfortunately, few if any economists adopted Rodbertus's perspective.

Marx stands out as the exception in this respect. Fortunately, Marx's (1977, 165) reluctance to trust appearances was far stronger than Lowe's. He would not treat an object as a commodity merely because it would be recognizable as a waistcoat or a child's boot.

> Objects of utility become commodities only because they are the products of the labour of private individuals who work independently of each other.... Since the producers do not come into social contact until they exchange the products of their labour, the specific social characteristics of their private labours appear only within this exchange. In other words, *the labour of the private individual manifests itself as an element of the total labour of society only through the relations which the act of exchange establishes between the products, and through their mediation, between the producers.* (emphasis added; see also Marx 1981, 3:1020)

In contrast to Lowe, Marx's (1977, 202, 207) method leads to a definition of industries based on the social relations of the commodity form: "The quantitative articulation of society's productive organism, by which its scattered elements are integrated into the system of the division of labor is as haphazard and spontaneous as its qualitative articulation. ... there develops a whole network of social connections of natural origin, entirely beyond the control of human agents."

Unlike Marx, modern economists have concentrated almost exclusively on the more familiar Smithian division of labor. Where economics, including modern economics, has on rare occasions touched on the social division of labor, it has almost totally excluded considerations of the social relations of production (see Marx 1977, 486; Perelman 1991a). Even when as distinguished an economist as Nicholas Georgescu-Roegan (1971) broached the subject of the social division of labor, this aspect of his work went all but unnoticed.

The Strategic Importance of the Social Division of Labor

According to the typical interpretation of the history of political economy, mercantilists displayed their ignorance of market forces by designing schemes for organizing and controlling economic activity. In contrast, classical political economy, in its wisdom, supposedly deferred to the market. In truth, this dichotomy is misleading. Certainly, classical political economy was concerned about the division of economic activities between different nations.

British political economists, even those that were ostensibly antimercantilist, preferred that the most profitable activities be carried on in Britain, or at least where they would work toward Britain's advantage. Consider, for instance, Nassau Senior's attack on the Corn Laws. He did not merely appeal to the theoretical arguments generally associated with free trade. Instead, he opposed the Corn Laws because of their impact on Britain's global strategy. Senior warned that if the English persisted in protecting their market from food imports, countries such as the United States and Germany would turn to industrial pursuits (see Senior 1841; McCulloch 1841, 10; cited in Fay 1932, 86–87; B. Hilton 1977, 115, 184, 280). According to Senior, opening British markets to the free importation of grain would safeguard English industrial hegemony by inducing potential competitors to specialize in the production of raw materials.

One Whig was quite explicit about this logic, explaining during the parliamentary Corn Law debates in 1846 that free trade was a beneficent "principle" by which "foreign nations would become valuable Colonies to us, without imposing on us the responsibility of governing them" (cited in Semmel 1970, 8). In the words of a modern scholar, abolition of the Corn Laws was supposed to "create a vast English market for foreign grain; in this way, the agricultural nations of the world might be given a stake in England's Empire of Free Trade" (Semmel 1970, 205).

Friedrich List, writing from a German perspective in the same year as Senior, agreed with the Englishman about the impact of free trade, protesting that it would permanently condemn Germany to the subordinate role of England's agricultural supplier. He accused the English of conspiring to maintain Germany as a vassal of England. List was particularly upset about the notorious largesse that the English bestowed on German free traders, including political economists (List 1841, 7–8).

Lucille Brockway (1979) highlighted the lengths to which the British went to structure the international division of labor. In particular, she detailed the role of plant explorers in the construction of the world capitalist system. At first glance, the adventures of Charles Darwin and other British botanists might seem far afield from a study of classical political economy, but they served a vital economic mission. Brockway demonstrates the extent to which even seemingly innocent, scientific activities were actually part of a concerted effort to organize a social division of world labor.

Latin America was blessed with perhaps the most important set of exotic genetic resources then known to the world, but its low population density made tapping this genetic potential an expensive proposition. To exploit Latin America's rubber or Cinchona trees, colonizers would have to harvest the crops in Latin America with scarce domestic or imported labor, or grow such crops elsewhere.

With abundant cheap labor in Asia, the British followed the second option. They brought impoverished Indians to work the plantations of Malaysia, Ceylon, and Mauritius. Although the British imported some Indian workers to plantations in the western hemisphere, moving labor to the depths of South America was expensive. As a result, the British preferred to transfer the genetic resources near to their available pools of cheap labor. One small matter stood in the way: the British did not own the means of propagating such crops. This technicality did not deter them.

The British charged their plant explorers with obtaining the plants by any means possible in order that they could be bred for production in the colonies of British Asia. By and large, they succeeded. The British simply refused to recognize any possible proprietary rights of the people or even of the rulers of these peripheral lands, smuggling many valuable plants out of Latin America, as well as tea cuttings from China, without any thought of compensation—a dramatic example of primitive accumulation of biological resources. Then they bred these plants to make them suitable for production in new locations, allowing the British to restructure the international organization of tropical agriculture.

This reorganization of a key sector of the world economy made an important contribution to England's industrial growth. As List (1841, 70) wrote: "One can establish a rule that the more a nation is richer and more powerful, the more that it exports manufactured products, the more it imports raw materials, and the more it consumes tropical commodities." The British had thought about these choices for some time. Already in 1774, Samuel Johnson (1774, 61) rhetorically asked, "Why does any nation want what it might have? Why are spices not transplanted to [the British colonies] in America? Why does tea continue to be brought from China?"

James Anderson (1777, 188) also discussed the benefits of transplanting valuable spices, alleging that "the French have made an attempt to obtain young plants from the spiceries of the Dutch; and have succeeded, notwithstanding the jealous watchfulness of that suspicious nation." He gave no hint that the indigenous populations in Indonesia or elsewhere had any stake in that matter.

Two years after Samuel Johnson ruminated on the possibility of planting tea elsewhere, Adam Smith brought his readers' attention to the complex social division of labor required to produce a woolen coat: "How much commerce and navigation . . . , how many ship-builders, sailors, sail-makers, rope-makers, must have been employed in order to bring to-gether the different drugs made use of by the dyer, which often come from the remotest corners of the world?" (1976, I.i.11, 23). Significantly, Smith neglected to consider the welfare of those who grew the plants. The con-science of political economy was little troubled by such considerations.

Should we believe that the classical political economists were alto-gether unaware of the importance of shaping the world social division of labor? Were they completely blind to the fact that the social division of labor formed the foundation for commodity production?

Not at all. The classical political economists were not about to ignore labor's will altogether in their great project. They realized that the masses of workers presented a greater challenge than moving and breeding a few seeds and cuttings. Unlike vegetables, people have minds of their own; they can resist the imperative of capital accumulation. In response, classi-cal political economy sought strategies to manipulate the social division of labor in a way that would expand the power of capital vis-à-vis labor.

Social Relations and the Social Division of Labor

Marx developed another distinction that paralleled the dichotomy be-tween the two divisions of labor. He referred to labor employed in the workshop of a particular employer as "variable capital." In contrast, he labeled the labor embodied in the intermediate goods that the employer purchased for use in the workshop "constant capital."

Variable capital is variable because labor power—the worker's capacity to work—leaves a surplus value embodied in the final product when the worker is properly employed. Constant capital, in contrast, merely trans-fers a preexisting value into the final commodity without producing a surplus.

Marx singled out variable capital as the source of surplus value for a perfectly sensible reason. The employer needs to command the worker at the point of production, ensuring that materials are used in an economical way, to earn a profit. Purchasing an intermediate good may help an em-ployer extract surplus value from the labor employed at the job site, but the intermediate good, in itself, does not produce surplus value—at least from Marx's perspective.

Notice that the labor power that produced the constant capital is con-stant capital only from the standpoint of the firm that purchases the commodity. In other words, the materials that the constant capital repre-sents are passive to the capitalists that purchase them. Other employers occupying another niche in the social division of labor, however, earn a profit from the production of these same goods. So, while that labor produces no surplus for the firm that purchases its produce, that same labor power that produced the constant capital is variable capital for the employer who purchases that labor power. As such, this labor power is capable of producing surplus value for that employer.

In this scheme, all employers have to find a market opportunity that offers a potential profit and then choose the appropriate constant capital to employ toward that end. In doing so, employers are responsible for exercising direct authority over the workers in their particular firm. They exercise only indirect authority over other workers by choosing whether or not to buy the intermediate commodities that those other workers produce.

As employers adjust the mix of the constant capitals that they purchase, they alter the social division of labor. With changes in the social division of labor, the same object may appear either as constant capital or not, depending on whether it is marketed or is used within the production process in that form. In Marx's (1981, 2:218), words, in the production process, "the material forms of existence of constant capital" may change.

In terms of the social division of labor, Marx represents a significant advance relative to contemporary economics. While modern economists take for granted that technological change creates new industries and extinguishes others, they have almost never acknowledged that the social division of labor can change with a fixed set of technologies. George Stigler (1941, 76) was perhaps the only modern economist until recently to take note of the indeterminacy of the social division of labor, observing "the portion of the productive process carried out in a particular unit is an accidental consideration." Later he suggested that massive shuffling of the social division of labor reflected the ability of the market to respond to changing conditions. He used the British gun and jewelry industries to demonstrate the fluidity of the social division of labor (Stigler 1951, 147–48; citing Allen 1929, 56–57, 116–17). Elizabeth Bailey and Ann Friedlander (1982, 1028) also credit Edward Robinson (1932) with having seen that price changes can change the social division of labor. Now that business has widely adopted the practice of outsourcing, some economists have begun to recognize that the boundaries of the firm can change, but none of them have come to grips with the full ramifications of an indeterminate social division of labor.

Let us return to the previous case of the umbrella industry to explore the nature of the changing social division of labor. In this example, the constant capital that the handle makers purchased was transformed into a different constant capital, umbrella handles, which were finally incorporated into the finished umbrellas. Umbrella handles would cease to be a commodity if the industry integrated vertically and the umbrella makers produced their own handles. As a result, what is or what is not a commodity defines the partitioning of the social division of labor (for more detail see Perelman 1987, chap. 4).

Over time, the social division of labor becomes increasingly refined. As Alfred Marshall (1920, 241) observed, "This increased subdivision of functions, or 'differentiation,' as it is called, manifests itself with regard to industry . . . as . . . a growing intimacy and firmness of the connections between the separate parts of the industrial organism." Similarly, Wassily Leontief's (1966, 49) analysis of input-output structures caused him to conclude: "The larger and more advanced a economy is, the more complete and articulated is its structure. The U.S. and western Europe respectively produce about a third and a quarter of the world's total output of goods and services. It is not surprising, therefore, that their input-output tables yield the same triangulation [structure of input-output relations]" (see also Kuznets 1965, 195).

Already in his day, Marx (1977, 460) reported that five hundred varieties of hammers were produced in Birmingham alone. Such a proliferation of products reflects the possibility of many alternative patterns of the social division of labor. For example, each time a firm replaced one type of hammer with another in the production process, it modified the social division of labor. Stigler's evidence bears out Marx's supposition that modern industries experience significant vertical disintegration as well as the vertical integration (Stigler 1951; Marx 1981, 2:119).

Concerning the ongoing reorganization of the social division of labor, Marx (1977, 467) observed:

> The larger English glass manufacturers, for instance, make their own earthenware melting-pots, because the success or failure of the process depends to a great extent on their quality. The manufacture of one of the means of production is here united with that of the product. On the other hand, the manufacture of the product may be united with other manufactures, in which the very same product serves in turn as raw material, or with those products the original product is itself subsequently mixed. . . . The various manufactures which have been combined together in this way form more or less separate departments of a complete manufacture, but they are at the same time independent process[es], each with its own division of labour.

Let me emphasize that this outcome is in no way determinate. An infinite number of arrangements are possible. Moreover, the social division of labor evolves dynamically, unlike the Indian villages, where, as Marx (1977, 477) noted, the division of labor was "crystallized, and finally made permanent by law."

Marx did not always follow his own logic. On occasion, he fell into a technological determinism, allowing that the increasing reliance on larger-scale machinery could ultimately determine the social division of labor. He wrote: "In spite of the many advantages offered by this combination of manufactures, it never attains a complete technical unity on its own foundation. This unity only arises when it has been transformed into an industry carried on by machinery" (ibid., 467). Of course, Marx did not have the advantage of seeing the rapid bundling and unbundling of goods and services so common today. At this moment, I am unclear as to whether a telephone will eventually be an extension of a computer or whether a computer will become an extension of a phone, to offer just one example.

In conclusion, the distinction between the Smithian division of labor and Marx's social division of labor is vital to understanding the nature of commodity production. In this respect, Marx (ibid., 474) insisted: "In spite of the numerous analogies and links connecting them, the division of labour in the interior of a society, and that in the interior of a workshop, differ not only in degree, but also in kind." For Marx (ibid., 477), "in a society where the capitalist mode of production prevails, anarchy in the social division of labor and despotism in the manufacturing division of labor mutually condition each other."

Production and the Social Division of Labor

Some economists are exploring a subject that they name "the economics of scope" (Panzer and Willig 1981). This theory describes how a firm might decide to compete by operating within more than one part of the preexisting social division of labor. It does not address the question of how the social division of labor itself might mutate with the creation of an entirely different matrix.

In Marx's example of the umbrella manufacturers, we can easily see how a widespread change in the scope of production could eliminate umbrella handles as a commodity. Running this evolution in the opposite direction, umbrella handles can suddenly appear as a commodity. More generally, the production process can be broken virtually at any point. In other words, rather than completing its production of a finished good, a firm could decide to put unfinished products on the market as commodities. Other firms could create a new industry to carry the process to completion.

Unfortunately, mainstream economists did not take advantage of Marx's discovery of the indeterminacy of the social division of labor. In fact, they did not even seem to be aware of the importance of the social division of labor. Their analysis, therefore, is generally incapable of penetrating what Marx (1977, 279) termed the "hidden abode of production." In fact, at times mainstream economists also seem to have gone out of their way to avoid coming to grips with the visible shell within which production occurred: the firm (see Perelman 1991a).

This practice reflected a deeper problem. For the most part, the economics profession followed Smith's lead in presuming that the firm was nothing more than a passive conduit that merely assists in movement of resources between alternative activities, except where the firm has the opportunity to take advantage of monopolistic powers (Tomlinson 1986, 224).

Although the social division of labor unfolds according to its own particular laws within certain limits, Marx took the position that it is ultimately dependent on the social relations of production. Along these lines, Engels wrote to Conrad Schmidt, in a letter dated 27 October 1890,

> Where there is division of labour on a social scale, the separate labour processes become independent of each other. In the last instance production is the decisive factor. But as soon as trade in products becomes independent of production proper, it has a movement of its own, which, although by and large governed by that of production, nevertheless in particulars and within this general dependence again follows laws of its own inherent in the nature of this new factor; this movement has phases of its own and in turn reacts on the movement of production. (Marx and Engels 1975, 397)

Like Friedrich Hayek (1945), Marx and Engels recognized the spontaneous evolution of the social division of labor, but the spontaneity that they saw was not an aspect of freedom. It reflected instead a disorder that caused great human suffering. Specifically, the spontaneity of market relations was used to highlight the authoritarian conditions that exist within a firm as well as the pressures that force workers to submit to wage labor.

Coercion, Primitive Accumulation, and the Two Divisions of Labor

In commenting on the relationship between coercion and the two divisions of labor, Marx (1847, 136) wrote: "It can even be laid down as a general rule that the less authority presides over the division of labour inside society, the more the division of labour develops inside the work-

shop, and the more it is subjected there to the authority of a single person." We would be true to the spirit of Marx's later work if we were to read
"the less *open* authority." This early citation also downplays the inten-
tional manipulation of the social division of labor in terms of its effect on
specific classes within the development of a capitalist economy.

Despite these qualifications, this passage points out an interesting
break that occurs under capitalism. In precapitalist societies, tradition
(including the personal authority of those who occupied the upper reaches
of the hierarchy) determined both divisions of labor—within society and
within the workplace. Tradition, the most extreme case being India's
caste system, largely determined the social division of labor in the sense
that people generally followed the occupation of their forbearers.

Class-based authoritarianism was absent from the early workshop. Instead, masters were bound by custom. Although they had considerable
control over their apprentices, the apprentices could reasonably expect to
become masters themselves in time.

For Marx, primitive accumulation reflected the acceleration of the rup-
ture of these traditional methods of organizing work. By manipulating the
social division of labor, the owners of the means of production could
coerce people to work for wages under the despotic authority of capitalists. In this sense, the social division of labor was a precondition for the
modern division of labor.

In earlier times when tradition was still strong enough that primitive
accumulation seemed unnatural to many people, workers asserted their
right to control their own labor as a traditional property right. For example, in 1823, cotton weavers protested against the restructuring of their
work, claiming: "The weaver's qualifications may be considered as his
property and support. It is as real property to him as buildings and lands
are to others. Like them his qualifications cost time, application and
money" (cited in Rule 1987, 106; see also Wilentz 1984, 241). In a sense,
the weavers were correct. In effect, their rhetoric implied that primitive
accumulation was a massive transformation of the social division of labor, which extended much further than the formal eviction of the peasants from the land.

The eviction of people from their traditional properties in the countryside set in motion a process that ultimately destroyed the weavers' means
of production—the productivity attributable to their skills—by virtue of a
restructuring of the labor process. Primitive accumulation provided employers a seemingly inexhaustible supply of cheap labor that could undercut the weavers once machinery supplanted the craft of hand work.

The weavers interpreted this restructuring of their cotton industry as still another form of primitive accumulation, represented by the theft of what we might today call their human capital. While the weavers' logic might seem naive, at least they realized that primitive accumulation was intimately bound up with the social relations of the emerging capitalist formation.

In more recent times, Harry Braverman (1974) forcefully reminded his readers about the close relationship between coercion and the division of labor at the work site. He attributed the evolution of the modern division of labor to increasing control of the labor process as a consequence of the separation of mental and manual labor. While the weavers lacked Braverman's sophistication, in associating the social division of labor with the division of labor in the workplace, they went one step beyond Braverman.

The Household as an Agent of Production

Let us be more explicit about the changes that the new social division of labor wrought. Keep in mind that political economy began in an age in which the social division of labor had not yet evolved very far. We would overstate our case if we described the economic environment of the time by citing Marx's (1965, 79) description of precapitalistic society, where "each individual household contains an entire economy, forming as it does an independent center of production" (Marx 1965, 79; 1977, 616n; 1852, 478; Engels 1881, 460); however, such an image would not be terribly inaccurate.

John Rae's (1834, 57–58) depiction of life on the Canadian frontier during the nineteenth century reveals the extent of the self-sufficiency of a typical farmstead, where farmers transformed materials from their own animals into crude woolen clothing and shoes. Obviously, the people whom Rae described were not reliving the exact life of precapitalist England, but his description does convey the flavor of a self-sufficient household.

Similarly, the feudal state was largely self-sufficient. According to Marx, agricultural bookkeeping in the Middle Ages existed only in the monasteries (Marx 1967, 2:134n). Keith Tribe's (1978, chap. 4) history of farm management literature clearly reflects the slow shift to a greater concern for market considerations.

Certainly, the majority of households in early capitalist societies had no conception of modern cost accounting. Before modern capitalist production developed, one could not locate a clear boundary separating those activities directed toward the production of commodities for sale on the market from those performed to reproduce the household.

For example, when seventeenth-century London bakers applied to local authorities for an increase in the price of bread, they sent in an account of the weekly cost of a bakery, including the baker, his wife, four paid journeymen, two apprentices, two maidservants, and three or four of the baker's children. The business, involving the production of thousands of loaves of bread, was carried on in the baker's own house. The care and feeding of the workers, along with members of the baker's own family, was seen as integral to the production process (see Laslett 1971, 1–2; Kautsky 1899, 156; Weber 1923, 172).

Perhaps the most common, modern intermeshing of commercial and domestic economies occurred in the institution of boarding houses. In the United States during the late nineteenth century, nearly one-fifth of the working-class families studied by the Bureau of Labor took in boarders (Smuts 1959, 14; see also Harvey 1976, 282; Stearns 1974, 416). Boarding was especially important for immigrant families. A 1908 study found that among the Slavs of Homestead, Pennsylvania, 43 percent took in boarders. In half of these families, boarders provided more than 25 percent of the total family income (Byington 1910, 142–44; see also Jensen 1980, 20; Greer 1979, 117).

The development of capitalism separated the workplace from the home. This cleavage between household production and commodity production became more and more pronounced as capitalism evolved, although this division of life and work was more apparent than real. The two were closely linked, however, in terms of the overall reproduction process. In Marx's (1977, 718; see also 1033) words: "The maintenance and reproduction of the working class remains a necessary condition for the reproduction of capital. But the capital may safely leave this to the workers' drives for self-preservation and propagation." Consequently, household production must be considered in conjunction with the social labor process in general. As Marx (1977, 717) noted, although the "worker's productive consumption [the use of constant capital in the workplace] and his individual consumption are . . . totally distinct . . . , in the latter [activity] . . . he . . . performs . . . necessary vital productions outside the production process."

The Transformation of the Household

At this point, I want to extend the notion of the social division of labor a bit further. As I mentioned before, Marx's analysis of the social division seemed to refer to the partitioning of the commodity production process into independent units that we might imagine to be firms. Because I am concerned here with the interrelationship between wage and nonwage production, I will interpret the production process to go beyond the direct production of commodities. I will use the concept of the social division of labor to include all labor that is useful from the perspective of the economy, regardless of whether that labor is waged or nonwaged. All labor performed within the household that promotes economic reproduction, as well as production, falls within this definition of the social division of labor. By reproduction, I mean such activities as the replenishment of those who work for wages and the raising of new generations of workers.

Analyzing the role of the household in the production process highlights two crucial points. The first one concerns the importance of the ongoing process of primitive accumulation. Second, such an analysis provides a theoretical matrix that clarifies the policy positions that classical political economists maintained with respect to the social division of labor.

Within this transformed system, capital demanded that the household function as a factory (see Cairncross 1958, 17). In terms of reproduction, households were a special sort of factory that specialized in the production of workers, who "resemble[d] the component parts of the vast machines which they direct" (Senior 1841, 504). All other aspects of life were to be subordinated to this end (see Hammond and Hammond 1919, 6).

Just as a factory combines living labor with other commodities (constant capital) in order to produce goods for sale, a working-class household also mixes living labor with other commodities (variable capital) to produce a salable product, labor power (see Rae 1834, 203; Senior 1928, pt. iv, chap. 2, sec. 3). Consequently, "consumption is not simply a consumption of . . . material [or service], but rather consumption of consumption itself" (Marx 1974, 301).

Ultimately, things consumed in the household were to serve for the production and reproduction of labor power. In this regard, Marx (1977, 719) directed his readers' attention to the integral role of the household as an agent of production, writing, "From a social point of view, therefore, the working class, even when not directly engaged in the labour-process, is just as much an appendage of capital as the ordinary instruments of labour." For Marx (ibid., 323n), "Labor-power itself is, above all else, the material of nature transposed into a human organism" destined to serve as wage labor. Jean-Baptiste Say (1880, 333n) even extended this notion to its logical limits by defining a "full-grown man . . . [as] an accumulated capital" equipped to earn profits.

Although the household is similar to the factory in the sense that both combine labor and other objects in order to produce a final product, the social relations are different. As Marx (1977, 909) explained:

> The spindles and looms, formerly scattered over the face of the countryside, are now crowded together in a few great labour-barracks, together with the workers and the raw material. And spindles, looms and raw material are now transformed from means for independent existence of the spinners and weavers into the means for commanding them and extracting unpaid labour from them.

Some misunderstanding might arise, however, because variable capital is often described as a value that workers receive, whereas constant capital frequently refers to the things that they use in the workplace. In reality, the things brought into factories and households both enter by way of transactions. In the household, however, the people who do the work own the means of production. In this respect, Marx (ibid., 1006; see also 717–18) correctly observed that "although . . . the exchange of money for labour-power . . . does not as such enter into the immediate process of production, it does enter into the production of the relationship as a whole."

Thus we should interpret the household in terms of the contradictory general system of capitalist social relations, although such an effort is no easy matter. We can find within capitalist households the means of both mutual support and mutual oppression (Humphries 1976; Humphries 1977; Lazonick 1978). The French regulation school contributed to our understanding of the complexity of the household in drawing our attention to the new social norms of consumption (see Aglietta 1979, 159 ff.) that were imposed to reinforce the "invisible threads" that bind labor to capital (Marx 1977, 719).

Engels (1891, 191–92; see also Weber 1923, 94) rightly remarked on the relatively declining role of the family as an autonomous unit with the rise of capital. Nevertheless, the productive energies of the household remain absolutely necessary for a capitalist economy, based as it is on wage labor. Hence, we should be careful not to underestimate the continuing importance of the household as a production site in modern capitalism, even though the specifics of its function have changed.

Creating the New Regimen

While capitalism transformed independent household labor processes into a unified "social process" (Marx 1977, 453), it also created a spatial separation of the workplace from the household. At the same time, capitalism joined together independent workplaces into an ever expanding set of market relationships. In the words of Nassau Senior (1836, 76), "Nature seems to have intended that mutual dependence should unite all the inhabitants of the earth into one great commercial family."

The establishment of this "great commercial family" required that the relatively autarkic economic structure of the independent household be broken down in order that it would become doubly dependent. First, it was to become dependent on commodities that were, in general, produced with wage labor. Second, to acquire these commodities, members of the household would have to supply the market with wage labor.

Of course, this mutual dependence of the household and the economy at large was not unique to capitalism. For example, Sir James Steuart (1767, 1:7) reminded his readers that Herodotus had reckoned the cost of the pyramids in terms of carrots and onions; however, the pharaohs were likely to have provided their workers with in-kind payments rather than cash.

Under capitalism, the working class was left with the responsibility of laboring to earn its wages, then exchanging those earnings for its means of subsistence, and finally efficiently combining these commodities with household labor in order to renew its supply of labor power. In this sense, no other form of social organization went so far in "transform[ing] . . . lifetime into labortime" (Marx 1977, 799).

The adaptation of the family economy to the needs of capital was not always a painless process. Marx (1977, 517–18n) wrote of the common use of opiates for want of time for breast-feeding and described the consequences of leisure insufficient for families to teach the young to cook or sew. With biting irony, he added:

> From this we see how capital, for the purposes of its self-valorization, has usurped the family labour necessary for consumption. This crisis [during the cotton famine that the English textile industry experienced during the American Civil War] was also utilized to teach sewing to the daughters of the workers. . . . An American revolution and a universal crisis were needed in order that working girls, who spin for the whole world, might learn to sew! (ibid.)

As E. P. Thompson (1963, 416) noted, "Each stage in industrial differentiation and specialization struck . . . at the family economy, disturbing customary relations between man and wife, parents and children, and differentiating more sharply between 'work' and 'life.'" Such deformations of the traditional family seemed a small price to pay for the promotion of capitalism.

Classical political economists never addressed the transformation of the household. Some formally dismissed activities performed in the household as "unproductive labor" when discussing the aristocratic household, largely because, as we shall see with Smith, they did not want to dignify the spending patterns of the gentry who commonly employed servants to do their household labor. Obviously, the classical political economists could not dismiss the household work of workers so casually. As Marx (1963–1971, 3:166) once noted, "largest part of society, that is to say the working class, must incidentally perform this kind of labor for itself."

This unwillingness to address the nature of the household is most unfortunate. It obscures a vital dimension of the capitalist economy. We shall see that the linkage between the production of commodities in the factory and labor power in the household proved to be a most profitable combination. Even so, many wished that the households could achieve an even higher level of efficiency in order to relieve employers of the need to pay as much in wages.

On the Economy of Domestic Economies

The idea that poor households could get by with a more frugal fare had an obvious appeal. Neil Smelser (1959, 351) notes that beginning in the last decade of the eighteenth century:

> a barrage of pamphlets exhorted the working classes to . . . substitute vegetables, Indian corn, arrow-root, etc., for more expensive items in the budget. Simultaneously several pamphlets explored the means of relieving the burden of the high costs of provisions. Eden devoted almost forty pages of his study of the poor to the frugality of the north, and in 1806 Colquhoun promised that "a greater boon could not be conferred upon the labouring people, than a general circulation of the art of frugal cookery."

Based on his experience in feeding both the Bavarian army and the inmates of the Bavarian poor houses, whose labor he turned to good profit, the American expatriate Count Rumford (1795, 179) supposed that "the number of inhabitants who may be supported in any country upon its internal produce, depends almost as much upon the state of the arts of cooking as upon that of agriculture." This gentleman's main contribution to the culinary arts was in the form of economical soup recipes based on his discovery that water was a perfectly good substitute for food.

Because of the savings associated with the self-maintenance of their human working machines, employers took an active interest in the most personal of acts of their employees. The welfare secretary of the American Iron and Steel Institute urged tutelage of the worker in the

> regulation of his meals, the amount, the character and the mastication of them, the amount and character of drink, the hours of rest and sleep, the ventilation of rooms . . . washing of hands before meals, daily washing of feet, proper fitting of shoes, amount and kind of clothing, care of the eye, ear and nose, brushing of the teeth, and regularity of the bowel. (cited in Montgomery 1979, 40)

This ability to leave labor with the responsibility to fend for itself when wages are insufficient to support a family is an immense boon to capital. Even when no outside income is required, the effort labor expends in organizing and arranging its own affairs relieves capital of much responsibility (Marx 1977, 1033). In fact, in his chapter on "Wages of Labour," Smith suggested that this factor accounted for the superiority of wage labor relative to slavery (1976, I.viii.41, 98; see also Marx 1977, 1033).

However, this distinction should not be carried too far. Slaves also had to use their free time to grow food and perform other tasks (see Fraginals 1978; 1:121; Taussig 1979, 75). In fact, Rodney Hilton (1978, 273) even suggests that European serfdom may have originated in the lands distributed to Roman slaves who were expected to feed themselves. Indeed, many observers made much of the operational similarity between wage labor and slavery. For example, James Mill (1826, 219) remarked, "What is the difference, in the case of a man, who operates by means of a labourer receiving wages (instead of by slaves)? . . . The only difference is, in the mode of purchasing." Others accepted that slaves were different, but considered that this difference worked to the advantage of slaves, who were thought to fare better than free workers (see Cunliffe 1979, 7, 21). This idea finds a modern echo in *Time on the Cross* (Fogel and Engerman 1974).

In one respect, slaves were more fortunate than wage earners. Some slave owners felt an obligation to care for their sick and aged chattel. Employers of wage labor were generally unburdened by such thoughts. In the words of one forthright American manager: "I regard my work-people just as I regard my machinery. . . . They must look out for themselves as I do for myself. When my machines get old and useless, I reject them and get new, and these people are part of my machinery" (cited in Ware 1924, 77).

Eventually, the economic role of household production came to be taken for granted and fell into the background. No longer was the production and consumption of use values emphasized within the household. Instead, an emphasis on exchange values became the order of the day. From the perspective of capital, working-class families merely sold their labor power to purchase commodities marketed by profit-maximizing firms.

The Household as the Locus of Consumption

Perhaps as a legacy of the rejected theory of unproductive labor, modern economics does not generally regard the household as a locus of production, but as an agent of consumption instead. Even so, concern with household economies never completely disappeared. A book titled *The Practical Housekeeper* maintained: "As it is the business of man to provide the means of living comfortably, so it is the province of women to dispose judiciously of those means, and maintain order and harmony in all things" (Matthaei 1982, 115). Peter Stearns (1974, 18; 1974a, 404) provides an extensive catalog of criticisms of British housewives during the Victorian era for their failure to behave economically enough.

Alfred Marshall joined this chorus of complaints. He (1920, 119) objected that British and American housewives were not as accomplished in "making limited means go a less way . . . than the French housewife . . . not because they do not know how to buy, but they cannot produce as good finished commodities out of the raw material of inexpensive joints, vegetables, etc. . . . Domestic economy is often spoken of as belonging to the science of consumption: but that is only half true. The greatest faults in domestic economy, among the sober portion of the Anglo-Saxon working classes . . . are faults of production rather than of consumption." Marshall was unusual in two respects. In the first place, few economists bothered to take note of the importance of the actual consumption process—except those who objected to workers' excessive consumption, especially of alcohol. Even more important, Marshall related household consumption to the total production process.

Philip Wicksteed (1910, 18) was among the few economists who made an allusion to women's productive work, but mostly in regard to the allocation of resources. In *The Common Sense of Political Economy*, he went into great detail concerning the role of the materfamilias in shopping for and doling out food. Later he did mention the example of stuffing a goose and schemes for getting boarders, but all these examples occur within a long list, including family prayers and the cultivation of general aesthetic tastes (ibid., 159). Even here, he was merely setting out to prove his subjectivist thesis that "the principle remains unchallenged that the marginal significance decreases as the volume of total satisfaction swells."

The contrasting presentation of women's work in Marshall and Wicksteed does credit to the former. Although Marshall might have simply been reflecting a Victorian echo of the movement to increase the productive efficiency of the household to further capital accumulation, at least he acknowledged it as an agent of production rather than limiting it to a locus of consumption.

Marshall's distinction between efficiency of consumption and production in the household was at odds with conventional economic theory. Today's reigning neoclassical theory of the household defends the status quo by arguing that capitalism serves the best interests of the household as a consumer, measured in terms of individualistic utility maximization. Accordingly, teachers expect their students to apply the theoretical apparatus of utility maximization to explain such diverse phenomena as the extent of food waste, reading, sleeping, or even family size (Becker 1965, 503, 509, 513–14).

Of course, the personal satisfaction of the working-class family was the farthest thing from the minds of the founders of classical political economy. Marx (1977, 718) correctly dismissed the relevance of any serious consideration of satisfaction as a basic category of analysis in studying the household: "The consumption of food by a beast of burden does not become any less a necessary aspect of the production process because the beast enjoys what it eats." Nassau Senior (1928, 1:172) expressed a similar thought: "And in what does the consumption of food by a labourer differ from that of coals by a steam engine? Simply in that, that the laborer [sic] derives pleasure from what he consumes, and the steam engine does not."

Neoclassical economists should not be singled out for failing to see the relationship between circuits of production and consumption. Many Marxian theorists are not beyond reproach with respect to this subject. Although this failing is less frequent in more recent works that have been conditioned by feminist concerns, all too often marxist works rely on a formal scheme in which precapitalistic formations are identified with the production of use values, in contrast to capitalism, in which production is simply treated as commodity production.

The Evolution of the Theory of Household Production

Notice that we have been making what might seem to be two conflicting claims about the role of household production. Earlier we had emphasized the role of primitive accumulation in promoting the development of capitalism by restricting the efficiency of the household by depriving it of its means of production. This chapter has been emphasizing capital's interest in augmenting the efficiency of household production. How do we resolve this contradiction?

On the grossest level, the attitude toward household production depends on the stage of capitalist development. At a time when self-provisioning was a serious barrier to the extension of the capitalist mode of production, classical political economy expressed an unremitting hostility toward conditions that would support the working-class household's ability to provide for itself. Once political economy became confident that the household economy was sufficiently hobbled that its role as a producer would be subordinated to capitalist commodity production, economists seemed to lose all interest in the evolution of the social division of labor. Instead, they exhorted households to become more efficient producers of labor power. Finally, after problems of effective demand gained more prominence, economists treated the household as a locus of consumption. As a result, the role of the household as a site of production generally fell into oblivion.

Modern political economics, conditioned to look on the household as an agent of consumption, built its justification of capitalism up around its central concept of utility maximization (see Cairncross 1958). Shrouded in this narrow perspective, modern economics has proven itself ill equipped to understand the changing role of household production over time. Even worse, we find a pervasive silence concerning the interest classical political economy took in controlling and regulating the private lives of the working class.

Households and the Changing Social Division of Labor

During the early twentieth century, industry in the United States saw the household appliances that it marketed as being analogous to the industrial equipment that it delivered to factories. In this respect, business attempted to create new markets by discovering appliances that could revolutionize the productive potential of household labor. Its intention was to cause the "owner[s] or operator[s] of appliance[s] . . . to adapt [themselves] . . . to a transformation from a hand and craft technique over into a machine process" (cited in Ewen 1976, 164). For example, during the heyday of Taylorism, appliance producers hired time and motion experts to design kitchens in order to bring capitalist work rhythms into the household (ibid., 166; see also Gideon 1948, 512ff.).

Toady, we regard these household appliances as an aspect of consumption rather than production, even though they are industrial in scope. In fact, "the American worker has at his disposal a larger stock of capital at home than in the factory where he is employed" (Cairncross 1958, 17). A number of factors have drawn our attention away from the productive role of the household. No observer of the modern household could fail to be struck by the enormous number of commodities that reduce the time required for household chores. Food has become processed and clothes ready-made, yet significant opposing tendencies seem to have gone unnoticed.

As capitalism itself became more complex, so too did the demands put on the household. The process of renewing the energies of workers is complicated by the particularly difficult stresses created by work and life in modern capitalist society (Aglietta 1979, 158; Gorz 1968, 88 ff.). In spite of the labor-saving appearance of the modern household, those tasks that do remain within the realm of its economy have frequently become much more demanding. Budgeting and shopping stand out as obvious instances (Walker and Woods 1976). "Women's work" has become, in many respects, more time consuming than ever.

The importance of this unpaid household labor is far from inconsequential. In 1968, when the Gross National Product was $864 billion, one estimate of the market value of the goods and services produced in U.S. households was $212 billion (see Burns 1976, 22; Scitovsky 1976, 86–89, 279–82; Eisner 1979). Of course, such figures of household production are very imprecise. For example, Robert Eisner (1988) estimated that the value of household production ranged from 20 to 50 percent of the measured Gross National Product.

Even the lower estimate represents a significant contribution to our standard of living. Moreover, William Nordhaus and James Tobin (1972, 518) estimate that the ratio of nonmarket to market consumption has been increasing, from 3:5 in 1929 to 3:4 in 1965, although such estimates may well be biased by the exclusion of unreported business transactions (see Bowsher 1980).

Some household consumption can be antithetical to production. Smoking and excessive use of alcohol come to mind. However, consumption can promote production even when it does not seem to be directly related to the replenishing of the physiological capacities of the working class. Take, for example, the ceaseless curiosity of some young people that drew them from playing to creating video games. Developers of video games, in turn, invented techniques that proved invaluable in advancing computer graphics.

Given that the household is a crucial agent of production, we can easily recognize how new commodities affect the social division of labor. As described earlier, U.S. households used to do their own laundry. By the twentieth century, commercial enterprises had taken over much of the laundering for urban households. With the introduction of the washing machine, many families began to do their own laundry either at home or in a laundromat (Hartman 1976). Gary Becker (1965, 508) describes a similar pattern for the history of shaving.

These examples indicate how the home may be gaining as a center of commodity production once again. With the increasing importance of information processing, more businesses are economizing on costly urban office space by furnishing workers with home computer terminals. This system is beneficial to profits in other respects. Wages no longer have to cover the cost of commuting (see Vicker 1981). Moreover, the physical separation of workers reduces the risk that they might organize themselves.

In this sense, modern capital is not unmindful of the position of the household in the economy. Elsewhere I have used this sort of analysis to explain the unseen manner in which the changing social division of labor has furthered the accumulation process within the agricultural sector (Perelman 1991b).

A Simple Schematic of Primitive Accumulation and the Social Labor Process

In this section, I will develop a simple theory to explain the role of household production in the process of capital accumulation. Classical political economists were mindful of the logic of this model, even though nobody ever articulated it in the explicit form presented below. In fact, although the classical political economists generally excluded the role of the subsistence economy from their theoretical works, they were acutely aware of its practical ramifications.

When they did address the process by which the household economy was being harnessed to the needs of capital, they were typically engaged in discussions of practical policy matters, such as Irish politics or the Poor Laws. In these less theoretical works, the classical political economists consistently advocated policies that were intended to affect the subsistence economy so as to promote a new social division of labor that would prove more profitable for capital. This revealing discontinuity between the theoretical expressions and the practical applications of classical political economy becomes obvious once the household is understood to be an integral part of the system of commodity production.

In this model, we observe that the typical working-class household divides its day between working for wages and what we might call "household production." This term includes both self-provisioning and the production of food and some handicrafts for the market. Although the household remains an essential element in the overall process of commodity production, one key feature distinguishes it from capitalist enterprises within the context of a market economy: no value is assigned to household labor devoted to self-provisioning.

Following Marx (1977, 659, 983), we measure the value of labor power by the value of the commodities that are consumed in the course of reproducing that labor power. The value of a commodity depends on the sum of the amount of direct labor used in production together with the indirect labor consumed in the depreciation process. These values ignore the amount of household labor that contributes to the reproduction of labor power because only commodities that are sold on the market have values (see Perelman 1987, chap. 4).

Marx (1981, 3:665) did not make this point explicit in his analysis of the value of labor power, but it does seem to be implied in his assertion that the value of labor power equals the value of variable capital, which "consists materially of the means of subsistence of the workers, a portion of their own product. But it is paid out to them bit by bit in money." In other words, the in-kind consumption of workers seems to be excluded from variable capital.

Just as prices and values for individual commodities may diverge in industrial production, so too, can the value of labor power deviate from the values of the commodities consumed within a working-class household. Some families will have atypical patterns of consumption, but on the whole, such differences will wash out when we deal with averages of a large number of households.

Notice that the changing social division of labor between household labor and wage labor will affect the value of labor power and, thus, the values of the goods produced by that labor power. For example, if the typical household were to begin to bake its own bread rather than purchase it, the labor of commercial bakers would no longer be counted into the value of its labor power. Since the labor used to bake within the household does not enter into the value calculation, the value of labor power would fall by an amount equal to the value of the previously purchased bread, less the value of the ingredients.

In contrast, consider what happens when a firm reduces its consumption of constant capital by incorporating more of the productive process within its boundaries. This reduction in labor power previously embodied in products purchased by the firm as inputs will balance the increase

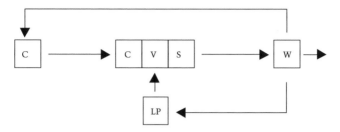

Figure 1. Simplified Production Process

in labor power employed within the firm (see Perelman 1987, chap. 4). Therefore, the value of the commodity produced within the firm remains unchanged.

The Bare Bones Model

We can see the relationship of the household to the total production process more clearly in a simple diagram. Figure 1 shows a representation of the simplified system of commodity production in which the household does not appear as an agent of production. Constant capital (C) is combined with labor power (LP) to produce commodities (W), which go to replace the constant capital and variable capital (V), or are made available for capitalist consumption or accumulation, as shown by the arrow directed from W. Figure 2 recognizes the household as an agent of production. The labor time of the household is divided among household production (H) and commodity production, represented by the dimensions of V and S, where the latter stands for surplus value.

We break the aggregate working day into three segments: (1) the number of hours that households devote to production on their own account; (2) the number of hours in which they work for wages while producing those goods and services they will purchase as commodities; and (3) the number of hours that they work for wages while producing those goods and services that will be bought by other classes. For convenience, assume that the second stretch of time is devoted to the production of necessities and the third to luxuries and goods for capital accumulation. This third segment would measure surplus value.

In addition, assume that all necessities are consumed by the workers and all luxuries by the other classes. Since our model is static, assuming that capital goods last forever and do not require replacement, we can treat capital goods as luxuries. Finally, this model adopts another simplification that is often associated with Marx, but that actually originated in classical political economy (see Senior 1836, 174): the aggregate of all households can be treated as a single entity.

Now let us summarize this bare-bones model. Following the typical approach of classical political economy, our model presumes that workers' standard of living represents a normal subsistence level. To produce these subsistence goods, we assume that the working class labors for a fixed number of hours regardless of whether work is done within the household or firm. This assertion implicitly assumes that the same technology is used in the household or the commodity producing sector.

The Model and Working Day

Today, the assumption of identical technology used in the firm and in the household might seem implausible, but at least during the early stages of economic development, workers performed more or less the same tasks using the same technologies whether they were in the factory or providing for themselves (Marx 1977, 425; Marglin 1974; also the critique of Marglin in Landes 1987). In this sense, Marx (1977, 645, 1019–38) described capital's early control over traditional producers as merely "formal":

> In this simple process it is clear that the capitalist has prepared neither the raw material, nor the instrument, nor the means of subsistence for the weaver and the spinner. All that he has done is to restrict them little by little to one kind of work in which they become dependent on selling, on the *buyer*, the *merchant*, and ultimately produce only *for* and *through* him. He bought their labor originally only by buying their product. (Marx 1974, 510)

Since both the total working day and the amount of time required to produce workers' consumption goods are given, the number of hours used to produce luxuries is also fixed. The more that households produce their necessities on their own account, the less wages they will require to be able to achieve their normal standard of living. Recall that although the time devoted to wage labor is variable, the time devoted to the production of luxuries is not. This feature is central to the model. Consequently, the division of time between the production of necessities in the household and the production of necessities while working for wages is the only variable in the system. Why would the capitalists be concerned about the division of the working day between household labor, or self-provisioning, and wage labor? After all, the amount of luxuries is identical in either case.

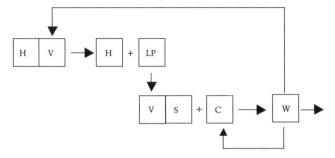

Figure 2. Production Processes with Households Included

The fundamental assumption of this model concerns the length of the working day. The full working day did not represent a universal condition in society, but rather an ideal that capital actively attempted to achieve. This achievement required that capitalists find a way to make the working class engage in wage labor. Still, this goal was no simple matter. So long as workers remained within the household economy, they could enjoy the same standard of living without having to devote time and energy to the production of luxury goods or surplus value.

A simple illustration shows why some outside force would be required to push these workers into wage labor. Suppose that the normal working day is ten hours, of which five are devoted to the production of luxuries. Furthermore, suppose that households work for wages full time. Thus, for each hour worked, the household sector receives wages to purchase commodities that require a half hour of labor to produce. In other words, the rate of exploitation is 100 percent.

Now let us change the conditions so that households work two and a half hours on their own account. Households now need only half as much in wages to maintain their standard of living because of what they produce on their own account. Nonetheless, the amount of time devoted to luxuries does not decline, however. Consequently, for each hour spent working for wages, the household sector receives a payment equivalent to only one-third of an hour of labor. As a result, the rate of exploitation jumps to 300 percent.

I maintain this model captures much of the conflict between classes that occurred during this period, and that much of classical political economy was built around this very struggle. Indeed, when the working class had to exchange a great deal of labor to obtain a relatively small value of commodities in return, it resisted wage labor by producing for itself as much as possible. In this way, labor would be able to shorten the working day in comparison to what it otherwise would be if workers had to produce luxury goods for members of nonworking classes in addition to their own subsistence.

Since capitalism had not developed technologies that were superior to the traditional methods of production, the creation of surplus value depended on capital's success in creating absolute surplus value by lengthening the working day. As a result, the more affluent members of society strenuously condemned all those who chose to remain true to their preindustrial ways.

Factors That Complicate the Model

Although this model is quite simple, it still casts considerable light on the contradictory tendencies of household production. First of all, where households are more engaged in self-provisioning, the money capital required to be a capitalist is lower since the employer has a lower outlay in wages. The greater the reliance on precapitalist economic relations, then, the more successful capitalism is in raising the rate of surplus value.

Let us note some other complications: First, if the process of relying on household production were carried to its limit, the value of variable capital would disappear, and with it wage labor. In addition, even though partial self-provisioning would raise the potential rate of surplus value, each worker must commit more labor to earn enough to purchase a commodity. This situation would be similar to what Samuel Johnson reported regarding the long time that a crafter would have to work to purchase a pair of shoes, although he could make a pair of brogues in an hour.

As a result, while increasing self-provisioning augments the maximum possible rate of exploitation, it can restrict the actual production of surplus value by making people cling even more tenaciously to their traditional employments. Consequently, the mass of surplus value may actually fall as the potential rate rises.

The model does not indicate how much labor will be forthcoming when primitive accumulation comes into play. In reality, primitive accumulationists had to be careful in applying their policies. Excessive pressure could create an exodus from the subsistence sector capable of overwhelming the capacity to employ wage labor. Too little pressure could allow too many people to remain in the traditional sector to satisfy the demands of would-be employers.

I should mention that this model becomes less useful under modern conditions. Although industry and household production initially used the same technology, industrial technology eventually became more productive than the traditional methods used in the household (see Marx 1977, 432). However, even after capitalist technologies progressed to the point that self-provisioning became less technologically efficient than wage labor, workers were often still loathe to engage in wage labor. They frequently opted instead to withhold their labor, preferring to substitute leisure for commodities that they might potentially purchase.

Even though more modern technologies eventually offer substantial economies, traditional household production, especially in the form of the putting-out system, could offer significant savings on capital outlays. One student of the subject observed, "The employer in cottage industry, the merchant manufacturer, has no fixed capital. The cottage workers are his machines. He can leave them unemployed whenever he wants without loosing a penny" (Buecher 1893, 196; cited in Medick 1988, 382).

Finally, living in an era that has until recently been dominated by Keynesian economics, we might consider the demand side of the model. Increasing variable capital increases the demand for commodities. Higher demand offers substantial advantages for capital, although it also implies a lower potential rate of surplus value. As a result, reducing the scope of household production can open up opportunities for capital.

The Basic Value of the Model

Despite the various complications of the model, we can still conclude that, other things being equal, the more activities that could be transferred to the household, the higher the rate of surplus value. This point is crucial. The substitution of household work for work done for wages reduces the value of labor power and raises the rate of surplus value. Ignoring the differences between prices and values, the more that households provide for themselves, the less that employers would have to pay for an hour of work.

All parties seemed to understand what was at stake. For example, early classical political economists realized that the capitalist labor process compelled the working class to labor above and beyond what was needed to support its own needs. In a 26 July 1784 letter, Benjamin Franklin (1905–1907, 9:246) wrote: "It has been computed by some political arithmetician . . . that if every man and woman were to work for four hours each day on some thing useful, that labour would produce sufficient to procure all the necessaries and comforts of life, want and misery would be banished out of the world, and the rest of the twenty-four hours might be leisure and pleasure."

Many of the Ricardian socialists also attempted to make empirical estimates of the ratio of paid to unpaid labor (see King 1981). Although they did not approach the subject theoretically, the workers who were expected to produce the surplus value clearly recognized what was at stake.

The Classics: Primitive Accumulation and Capital Accumulation

To sum up to this point, the classical political economy put forth a theory that held that a greater degree of self-provisioning increases the rate of surplus value, other things being equal. They implicitly applied this model when analyzing the practical problem of resistance to wage labor.

The classical model of primitive accumulation is close to Marx's analysis of capitalist reproduction, in the limited sense that it could be reworked into something similar to what we find in *Capital* without violating any of its particulars. Nonetheless, I must emphasize that it is not Marx's model, however; that is too rigid, too undialectical. It is not Marx; it is classical political economy.

Nonetheless, the classical model of primitive accumulation helps us to understand the reorientation of the household to the production of labor power. This new situation did not come without a struggle on the part of many participants in the traditional economy.

The classical political economists, from Petty in the late seventeenth century to his successors in the mid–nineteenth century, recommended policies that conformed to the model. At least they displayed a keen interest in organizing the social division of labor apparently in order to promote the institution of wage labor.

The idea that political economists would actively concern themselves with the social division of labor might sound odd to many modern students of political economy. The very suggestion of intentionally organizing a social division of labor appears to fly in the face of the general understanding of classical political economy; still, by studying some of their less theoretical works of classical political economy, we shall see how the early economists became active participants in this conflict between capitalist production and household production (including simple commodity production).

At times, classical political economists seemed to take pains to avoid the appearance that they were applying something like this model. For example, Adam Smith, insofar as he addressed the subject, treated the social division of labor as the result of voluntary choices on the part of free people. Even so, on closer inspection, when we review Smith's works as a whole, we find that he also preferred the use of nonmarket forces to manipulate the social division of labor. Specifically, we will see that Smith, like the rest of the early political economists was an ardent advocate of primitive accumulation.

In the process, by demonstrating that this model was an integral part of the program of classical economy, we cast doubt on the current fashion of reading the classics with an eye to showing their preoccupation with the maximizing behavior of individuals. In fact, classical political economy was, first and foremost, meant to be a formula for accelerating the overall accumulation process. The effect of household production in this regard is extremely important from the point of view of capital, which profits from a high rate of surplus value.

We can also read the model from the other side: from the perspective of a hypothetical individual choosing whether or not to engage in wage labor. Of course, the point of the model was to make the case for limiting the choices of such people, rather than to demonstrate the theoretical niceties of individual maximizing behavior.

Nonetheless, the perspective of the individual does cast additional light on the model. While individual choice might be a factor in explaining the evolution of an existing social division once workers come to accept the conditions of wage labor, this model suggests that wage labor would not be likely to arise without some sort of duress. Hence, individual choice is an inadequate explanation for what set the social division of labor in motion in the first place. As the model shows, in an environment where self-sufficient people would be producing all of their own needs, the value of their labor power would be extremely low. Consequently, they would be less than eager to exchange their labor for wages.

Even if the high rate of surplus value would somehow not deter people from accepting wage labor, individuals would still not be likely to choose wage labor because of a first-mover problem. After all, capitalism did not begin in department stores, but in economies where self-sufficiency was quite high. One set of workers could not specialize in the full-time production of shoes, clothing, or even food unless others would make a complementary choice to supply other goods, which the former workers ceased to produce for themselves. We shall return to this problem later in a more detailed discussion of Sir James Steuart.

Even if we accept that this structural impediment could be overcome in time, the classics were still unlikely to leave the fate of capitalism to the free choice of the workers. After all, the working class generally appeared irrational to the superior orders. All too often, the failure of the workers to conform to the approved norms of the bourgeoisie appeared to be striking evidence of their inadequate rationality.

of Primitive Accumulation

The Imperative of Primitive Accumulation

Despite the quasi-dialectical nature of the simple, pre-Marxian model of
primitive accumulation, most writers tended to make their case in terms
of absolutes, emphasizing only one side of the role of household production. The most frequent concern was the potential of workers' resistance
to wage labor. Given the common reluctance to accept the conditions of
wage labor, the creation of artificial scarcities appeared particularly attractive to most early advocates of capitalist development. For example,
almost all representatives of early political economy agreed on the beneficial effects of high food prices in forcing wage labor to work harder (see
Furniss 1965; Wermel 1939, 1–14, 17, 24).

In this vein, Sir William Temple (1758, 30) suggested that the community would be well served if food were taxed when harvests were plentiful lest the working class sink into sloth and debauchery. David Hume
(1752c, 344), for his part, asserted that such policies would even be in the
interests of the poor: " 'Tis always observed, in years of scarcity, if it be not
extreme, that the poor labour more, and really live better."

The advocates of primitive accumulation represented powerful, but not
all-powerful forces. Many people still retained a stubborn attachment to
the land, as well as an abhorrence of wage labor. The early primitive
accumulationists waged a vicious war against the traditional sector, concluding that nothing could coerce people into participating in the social
division of labor so long as they had recourse to what, for want of a better
term, some called the "natural economy." Certainly, modest manipula-
tions of the market would not be effective in coercing self-sufficient peasants to enter into the labor force. How could measures elevating food
prices compel self-sufficient peasants to become wage laborers?

Many observers realized that the natural economy was an abstraction.
People provided for their subsistence by selling their surplus produce
in the local market, as well as by farming and hunting. Even so, many
households, tenaciously holding onto the remnants of their earlier self-

sufficiency, still displayed a general reluctance to accept wage labor. As Rosa Luxemburg (1968, 369) once insisted, self-provisioning "confront[ed] the requirements of capitalism at every turn with rigid barriers" that seemed unlikely to collapse on its own accord.

Even where wage labor paid significantly more than self-provisioning, workers in traditional economies still typically resisted accepting employment as wage laborers (see Pollard 1965, 191). For example, during the Industrial Revolution, Irish women were reported to have been willing to accept half the salary they could earn in a factory if they could do the same work at home (ibid., 173). The case of the handloom weavers is even better known:

> The unwillingness of the hand-loom weavers to enter the mills and manufactories is well known to the whole trade. This arises from them having acquired habits which render the occupation in mills disgusting to them, on account of its uniformity and of the strictness of its discipline. They are unwilling to surrender their imaginary independence, and prefer being enslaved by poverty, to the confinement and unvarying routine of factory employment. (Kay 1835; cited in Pollard 1978, 111)

Edmund Morgan (1975, 64–65) observed that in colonial Virginia, people often preferred a more leisurely subsistence economy despite frequent bouts of hunger and malnutrition. We should acknowledge that the variability of earnings complicates such comparisons.

Alexander Gerschenkron (1962, 9), generalizing from his knowledge of prerevolutionary Russia, concluded that "industrial labor, in the sense of a stable, reliable, and disciplined group that has cut the umbilical cord connecting it with the land and has become suitable for utilization in factories, is not abundant, but extremely scarce in a backward country." Contemporary subsistence farmers still frequently display a remarkable reluctance to work outside the family plot in situations where wage labor would appear to be more remunerative (Bardhan 1973, 1380; 1979).

Capitalists became convinced that they had to take matters into their own hands in order to control the accumulation process. Only a harsher variant of primitive accumulation seemed capable of providing sufficient workers. By crippling the household sector—by depriving it of much of its means of production—the emerging proletariat would be left with no choice but to accept wage labor.

Of course, employers had an alternative to primitive accumulation. Some of the exceptional ones went to great expense to create a relatively appealing environment, such as Robert Owen's villages or the Lowell,

Massachusetts, textile mills. In the case of the Lowell mills, young girls who enjoyed little independence within traditional patriarchal society were often enthusiastic about the opportunity to work in the mills. Besides being free of parental restrictions, they had the prospect of being able to have control of their own earnings. One woman, recalling her youthful labors in an early nineteenth century textile mill in Lowell, explained:

> For hitherto woman had always been a money-saving, rather than a money-earning, member of the community, and her labor could command but a small return. If she worked out as a servant, or help, wages were from fifty cents to one dollar a week; if she went from house to house by the day to spin and weave, or as a tailoress, she could get by seventy-five cents a week and her meals. As a teacher her services were not in demand, and nearly all the arts, the professions and even the trades and industries were closed to her. (H. Robinson 1898, 2)

Unfortunately, few employers were either able or willing to incur the expense of creating attractive opportunities for workers. The majority realized that without the ability to produce enough for themselves, people would have no choice but to engage in wage labor. Thus, employers could acquire surplus value that would otherwise elude them.

Gardening and the Efficiency of the Traditional Sector

Those who prefer the old ways may have solid grounds for their preference; or they might realize the ultimate costs of a dependence on wage labor; or perhaps, these people just prefer to avoid the hectic pace of industrial employment; or finally, maybe they resent the incessant supervision associated with wage labor. This resistance to wage labor perplexes many modern theorists, who habitually presume that wage labor is the "natural" state of humanity (Weber 1923, 260–61; W. Moore 1955, 162; Redford 1926, 19).

Much modern literature portrays anyone who resists wage labor as an enemy of progress. The emotional appeal of the traditional sector seems irrational in such works. For example, the enclosure movement usually forms the backdrop for the traditional story of primitive accumulation. Since many economic historians credit the enclosures with promoting an agricultural revolution, opposition to primitive accumulation (in the form of enclosures) appears as the futile flailing away at the inevitable progress of human society.

In truth, the traditional sector was not nearly as inefficient as many writers would have us believe. Scott Burns (1976), for instance, has pub-

lished a useful, though unscientific catalog of activities in which households can still provide for many of their own needs far more economically
than the commercial sector.

Gardening represents one of the most efficient cases of self-provisioning.
Even the Physiocrats, vigorous advocates of large-scale commercial farming, acknowledged the productivity of traditional methods of producing
food. They estimated that the spade husbandry of the peasants returned
twenty to thirty times as much grain as had been planted. Cultivation with
the plow returned only six times the amount (Weulersse 1959, 154; see also
F. O'Connor 1848a).

Comte de Mirabeau contended that farmers in a suburb of Paris earned
about twenty-eight pounds per year from a single acre of land (Weulersse
1910, 2:317). The physical output of these market gardeners was nothing
short of phenomenal. A Paris gardener, I. Ponce, produced more than
forty-four tons of vegetables per acre, not to mention 250 cubic yards of
topsoil (Ponce 1870, 32–49; Kropotkin 1901, 62ff.; Kropotkin 1906, 220;
Schoenhof 1893, 149; see also the estimates of the produce of an English
market garden in Maitland 1804, 132). By contrast, in the United States,
today's commercial producers manage to harvest only nineteen tons of
onions or thirty-three tons of tomatoes per acre for processing, the highest
yielding vegetables (U.S. Department of Agriculture 1997, 4–22). Other
plants, such as spinach or peppers, only produce four or five tons per acre
in the United States.

Although these gardens were commercial operations, they still suggest
the efficiency of methods of self-provisioning. According to William Pitt,
market gardeners near populated areas in Britain were assessed eleven
pounds, seven shillings per acre (cited in Wordie 1974, 600). Obviously,
they had to be able to earn at least this amount to continue to practice
their trade.

Even in a modern market society, self-provisioning can be efficient.
John Jeavons, a pioneer in the application of the scientific method to
gardening techniques, claims that he can produce a complete diet on
2,800 square feet of marginal land with a daily effort of twenty-eight
minutes, not much more than would be required to shop for the food
(cited in Taper 1979). Although most gardeners cannot match Jeavons's
productivity, Scott Burns (1979) estimates that a typical hour spent in
growing vegetables is worth an average of ten dollars, considerably more
than the typical wage rate at the time of his calculation.

Part of the advantage of self-provisioning is due to the avoidance of the
need to transport and market produce, which generally grows near the
point of consumption. Even if growing vegetables takes less direct labor

on a farm than in a household garden, when we take account of the complexities of the marketing system and the labor embodied in the farm inputs, self-provisioning may well turn out to be superior (see Perelman 1977). Perry Duis (1998, chap. 5) reported that in late-nineteenth-century urban Chicago, lack of refrigeration and an inefficient distribution system made gardening an efficient method of providing for food. These locational advantages can be substantial. For example, despite the enormous rents typical of an urban area, London remained largely self-sufficient with respect to milk until the 1870s (see Atkins 1977).

True enough, not all families had access to garden plots. What is most important to our subject is that the techniques of market gardening have much to offer, even under transformed social relations. In other words, traditional household production can remain a variable alternative even after wage labor has become common. Even in the United States, the poor had no choice to return to gardening when depressions struck. As Duis observed: "Among the poor . . . gardening was sometimes necessary for daily survival, not just a form of ornamentation or a hobby. Even squatters managed to plant a few vegetables to supplement their meager meals, but those efforts were small when compared with what began during the severe depression of 1893–1897, when armies of the unemployed roamed the nation in search of work (Duis 1998, 140). Gardening for food also increased during the Great Depression. We might note that in the early Soviet Union, Nikolai Bukharin and Evgenii Preobrazhensky (Bukharin and Preobrazhensky 1922, 303–4) predicted an important future for the technology of market gardening, based on the experience of the first two years of the Soviet Republic. In addition, during both world wars, the U.S. government devoted considerable energy to promoting victory gardens in an effort to conserve resources.

Classical Political Economy versus the Traditional Sector

Despite the absence of conclusive evidence of the technological superiority of the commercial sector relative to the household sector during the age of classical political economy, the widespread attachment to the traditional sector outraged numerous writers at the time. Many even interpreted the resistance to wage labor as proof of a moral defect. Commentators frequently concluded that potential wage laborers would continue to resist wage labor until some external power separated them from their land. Thomas Hobbes (1651, 387) reflected this concern with overcoming the resistance of the poor, writing:

For such as have strong bodies . . . , they are to be forced to work; and to avoyd the excuse of not finding employment, there ought to be such Lawes, as may encourage all manner of Arts; as Navigation, Agriculture, Fishing, and all manner of Manufacture that requires labour. The multitude of poor, and yet strong people still encreasing, they are to be transplanted into Countries not sufficiently inhabited; where nonetheless, they are not to exterminate those that they find there; but constrain them to inhabit closer together, and not range a great deal of ground together, to snatch what they find; but to court each little Plot with art and labour, to give them their sustenance in due season. And when the world is overcharged with Inhabitants, then the last remedy of all is Warre; which provideth for every man, by Victory, or Death.

As William Robertson (1769a, 84), the Historian Royal of Scotland and a leading figure in Edinburgh literary circles, in a work allegedly based on Smith's then unpublished *Lectures on Jurisprudence* (see Scott 1965, 55–56), wrote with regard to the prospects of naturally developing market relations: "The wants of men, in the original and most simple state of society, are so few, and their desires so limited, that they rest contented with what they can add to these by their own rude industry. They have no superfluities to dispose of, and few necessities that demand a supply." In a similar vein, James Anderson (1777, 61) asserted: "For without commerce or arts, what inducement has the farmer to cultivate the soil? In this case every man will only wish to rear as much as is sufficient for his own sustenance, and no more. . . . For this reason a nation peopled only by farmers must be a region of indolence and misery."

William Temple (1758, 17, 52) was more explicit, calculating: "If mankind employed themselves in nothing but the productions absolutely necessary to life, seven in eight must be idle, or all be idle seven eighths of the time. And yet they might indulge intemperance, and sink into the beastly vices of slovenly gluttony and drunkenness." Finally, let me cite the Reverend Joseph Townsend (1786, 404), in "a Well Wisher to Mankind," argued that "the poor know little of the motives which stimulate the higher ranks to action-pride, honour, and ambition. In general it is only hunger which can spur and goad them on to labour; yet our laws have said, they shall never hunger."

The mind-set of the time might sound fairly crude to some, but it still resonates today. For example, during the Reagan years, George Gilder (1981, 118) bravely revived the spirit of the primitive accumulationists, proclaiming, "In order to succeed, the poor need most of all the spur of poverty," an advantage that was denied to Gilder himself. More recently, the Clinton administration, awash with rhetoric that would have made the primitive accumulationists proud, succeeded in "reforming" the welfare system.

The Creation of Scarcity

The key to avoiding the curse of a comfortable life was to create artificial scarcity for the rural poor. As Arthur Young observed in 1771, "everyone but an idiot knows that the lower classes must be kept poor, or they will never be industrious" (cited in E. P. Thompson 1963, 358). Access to common land touched a particularly sensitive nerve among more affluent property owners. Marx (1977, 881; see also E. P. Thompson 1963, 217) cited a Dr. Hunter, who fretted that "a few acres to the cottage would make the labourers too independent."

Such fears were commonplace during the period of classical political economy. A 1794 report to the Board of Agriculture on Shropshire noted that the use of "the commons now open . . . operates upon the mind as a sort of independence." Others remarked that enclosure would ensure a "subordination of the lower ranks of society which in the present times is so much wanted" (Bishton 1794, 24; cited in McNally 1993, 19). According to one proponent of the eighteenth-century enclosures:

> The possession of a cow or two, with a hog, and a few geese, naturally exalts the peasant. . . . In sauntering after his cattle, he acquires a habit of indolence. Quarter, half, and occasionally whole days, are imperceptibly lost. Day labour becomes disgusting; the aversion increases by indulgence. And at length the sale of a half-fed calf, or hog, furnishes the means of adding intemperance to idleness. (Billingsly 1798, 31; cited in Horn 1981, 52)

John Arbuthnot, a large farmer, expressed a contemptuousness toward pre-enclosure cottagers that was typical for the time. His attack on the supposedly perverse incentives prefigures the modern conservative argument against welfare. In his words:

> The benefit which they are supposed to reap from commons in their present state, I know to be merely nominal; nay, indeed, what is worse, I know that, in many instances, it is an essential injury to them, by being made a plea for their idleness; some few excepted, if you offer them work they will tell you they must look up their sheep,

cut furzes, get their cow out of the pound, or perhaps say they must take their horse to be shod, that he may carry them to the horse race or a cricket-match. (Arbuthnot 1773, 81; see also Wilkinson 1964, 18)

From there, Arbuthnot offered an analysis of chilling clarity. He proposed that if "by converting the little farmers into a body of men who must work for others [by enclosing the commons] more labor is produced, it is an advantage which the nation should wish for" (Arbuthnot 1773, 124; also cited in Marx 1977, 888).

E. P. Thompson (1963, 217) cited the 1796 perspective of a Lord Winchilsea: "Whoever travels through the Midland Counties and will take the trouble of enquiring, will generally receive for answer, that formerly there were a great many cottagers who kept cows, but that land is now thrown to the farmers," not because they want to farm the land, but because "they rather wish to have the labourers more dependent upon them." William Cobbett (1831, 1:88) found much the same attitude among those who hired labor when he proposed to offer each laborer an acre of wasteland on the condition that he enclose, cultivate, and live on it: "Budd said, that to give the labourers a bit of land would make them 'sacy'; Chiddle said, that it would only make them breed 'more children'; and Steel said, it would make them demand 'higher wages.' "

According to Marx (1977, 910–11): "[Capital] transformed the small peasants into wage-labourers, and their means of subsistence and of labour into material elements of capital. . . . Formerly, the peasant family produced means of subsistence and raw materials, which they themselves for the most part consumed. These raw materials and means of subsistence have now become commodities."

In their plan to convert the peasants into wage laborers, the primitive accumulationists were still mindful of the efficiency of self-production. Toward this end, they wanted to allow workers to produce for their own needs, but their access to land was to be at the pleasure of the large farmer who owned it. Here is Arbuthnot's (1773, 83) explanation:

> My plan is to allot to each cottage three or four acres, which should be annexed to it without power of alienation, and without rent, but under the covenant of being kept in grass, except such small part as should be necessary for a garden; this would keep the cottager in more plenty than a very extensive range of common; he and his family must then cultivate the garden, or suffer as they ought to do: and to obviate the plea of their wanting fuel, let it be fenced and planted with ash and other quick growing trees, at the expense of those who are to have the property of the common.

As this struggle to build up the proletariat intensified, workers increasingly lost more of their capacity to provide for themselves. Foreign visitors were struck by the final result of this process, noting that "not one of all the many thousand English factory workers has a square yard of land on which to grow food if he is out of work and draws no wage" (Escher 1814, 35). Indeed, by the nineteenth century, England "presented a unique and amazing spectacle to the enquiring foreigner; it had no peasants" (Hobsbawm and Rude 1968, 3; see also Deane and Coale 1967, 3, 256). Yet primitive accumulation was neither as complete nor as rapid as these visitors might have imagined. For example, as Marx (1977, 911) reminded his readers: "This transformation had already begun in part under the feudal mode of production. For example, hand mills were banned to make people dependent upon the mill belonging to the lord."

The Occasional Acknowledgment of the Economics of Primitive Accumulation

After around 1830, we hear less and less about the urgency of primitive accumulation from the classical political economists. Marx (ibid., 931) interpreted this silence as evidence that they did not understand its importance. He charged that "political economy confuse[d] on principle, two different kinds of private property, one of which rests on the producer himself, and the other on the exploitation of the labour of others." The economists conveniently forgot that the "latter is not only the direct antithesis of the former, but grows on the former's tomb and nowhere else" (ibid., 931; see also Marx 1967, 2:35; for a reflection of this conflict in Japan, see T. Smith 1966, 75).

Marx gave the political economists too little credit. They were not confused at all, but with few exceptions, preferred not to address this matter publicly. Those who did break the code of silence tended to be secondary figures. Take the case of Mountifort Longfield, writing from Ireland, where capitalism still had to contend with a vigorous subsistence farming sector in 1833. Longfield used the unwaged worker to close his system in much the same manner that Ricardo used the concept of no-rent land.

According to Longfield's (1834, 190–91; see also Earle and Hoffman 1980) formulation, the standard of living of the subsistence farmer sets the level of wages, which given the existing technology, determines the rate of profit. Unfortunately, the crucial role of the subsistence sector was not explicitly spelled out.

John Ramsey McCulloch (1854, 34) also stumbled on this relationship between the rate of profit and the subsistence sector. He argued that the degree of poverty among the peasantry determined the wage rate, which within the context of his Ricardian perspective, would have set the rate of profit, given the usual assumptions of his school. As was his practice, McCulloch, however, failed to translate his perceptive observation about the real world into a theoretical analysis.

McCulloch was not alone in this respect. In spite of an intense, practical concern with the subsistence sector, on an abstract level, classical political economy was generally unwilling to openly recognize the antagonism between capital and the traditional economy. Moreover, it generally failed to acknowledge in its theoretical works the role that the subsistence sector played in augmenting profits in the capitalist sector.

Where political economy did come close to confronting this conflict, it appeared to be intentionally obscure. One partial exception was Senior (1836, 74), who chose to treat the matter as a cultural phenomenon, sneering at that "rude state of society [in which] every man possesses, and every man can manage, every sort of instrument." In advocating a market economy based on a more complex social division of labor, he casually noted, "Indirect production is, in a great measure, the result of civilization" (1928, 133).

Even after Senior's concept of indirect labor reappeared in Eugen von Böhm-Bawerk's (see 1959, esp. 1:87) elaborate theory of roundaboutness, the social relations of that category were nowhere to be found. Nonetheless, Senior, for all his other deficiencies, deserves a modicum of credit for raising a concept parallel to the social division of labor to a level faintly approaching abstract theory.

The Silent Compulsion of the Market

The more practical primitive accumulationists wistfully dreamed of a world in which the poor would be forced to "work everyday in the year" (cited in Hill 1967, 278). This vision was attractive enough to win wholehearted support of the majority of the ruling classes for enclosing the common land. Robert Wallace (1809, 17) went beyond the usual crude identity of self-interest and national interest, suggesting that the production of surplus and the creation of a more refined social division of labor could ultimately produce tangible benefits for society in general:

> If the lands be divided into very unequal shares, and in general, may produce much more than will decently support those who cultivate them, the country may notwithstanding be well peopled, if the arts be

encouraged, and the surplus above what would support the labourers of the ground be allotted for such as cultivate the arts and sciences.

At times, the primitive accumulationists seemed to comfort their consciences by imagining themselves as helping to elevate people, while actually thrusting them deeper into poverty. For example, William Temple (1758, 43) calculated:

> If all the lands in the kingdom were to be divided among the people, they would not amount to four acres a-piece. A man is not poor because the refinements of the arts, policy and manners have left him without lands . . . ; but he is poor because he spends what he acquires from the arts of refinement in a foolish manner; or neglects from sloth to make so proper and prudent advantage of those arts as he might.

Given this perspective, Temple concluded, "The best spur to industry is necessity" (ibid., 27). In this spirit, one pamphleteer of the time wrote:

> Nor can I conceive a greater curse upon a body of people, than to be thrown upon a spot of land, where the productions for subsistence and food were, in great measure, spontaneous, and the climate required or admitted little care for raiment or covering. (Forster 1767, 10; see also Steuart 1966, 1:45–46)

In the same vein, Hume (1752d, 266–67) blamed the poverty of France, Italy, and Spain on their benign climates and rich soil.

Temple and his class were too intent on the brutal conquest of the natural economy creating artificial scarcities by limiting the common people's access to natural wealth to bother with the niceties of ideological obfuscation. Some of the forthright accumulationists, however, were sophisticated enough to have realized that once the work of primitive accumulation was complete, what Marx (1977, 899) called the "silent compulsion" of the market could be far more profitable than the brute force of primitive accumulation. Consider again the generous vision of Reverend Joseph Townsend (1786, 404, 407):

> [Direct] legal constraint [to labor] . . . is attended with too much trouble, violence, and noise, . . . whereas hunger is not only a peaceable, silent, unremitted pressure, but as the most natural motive to industry, it calls forth the most powerful exertions. . . . Hunger will tame the fiercest animals, it will teach decency and civility, obedience and subjugation to the most brutish, the most obstinate, and the most perverse.

Similarly, Rodbertus, a German socialist and government minister rather than an outright primitive accumulationist, asserted:

> Originally this compulsion was exercised by the institution of slavery, which came into existence at the same time as tillage of the soil and private ownership of land. . . . When all the land in a country is privately owned, and when the same title to all land has passed into private ownership of land and capital exerts the same compulsion on liberated or free workers. . . . Only now the command of the slave owner has been replaced by the contract between worker and employer, a contract which is free only in form but not really in substance. Hunger makes almost a perfect substitute for the whip, and what was formerly called fodder is now called wages. (cited in Böhm-Bawerk 1959, 253)

As might be expected, Adam Smith put a voluntaristic twist on this silent compulsion. He attributed primitive accumulation to the greed of the feudal aristocracy rather than the rising bourgeoisie, while failing to acknowledge explicitly that this greed arose because the aristocrats began to take on the trappings of the bourgeoisie:

> But what all the violence of the feudal institutions could have never effected, the silent and insensible operation of foreign commerce and manufactures gradually brought about. These gradually furnished the great proprietors with something for which they could exchange the whole surplus produce of their lands . . . without sharing it either with tenants or retainers. All for ourselves, and nothing for the people, seems, in every age of the world, to have been the vile maxim of the masters of mankind. (Smith 1776, 3.4.10, 418)

Presumably, this vile maxim would disappear with the rise of market relationships.

Self-Provisioning as a Subsidy to Capital

Primitive accumulation was largely successful. Once industrial technology became substantially more productive than self-provisioning, the household economy became even less of a threat to the capitalist sector of the economy. At that point, capital could take advantage of the economies of self-provisioning, so long as household labor would not interfere with the commitment to wage labor.

In line with the classical model of primitive accumulation, many agents of capital soon recognized that household labor could serve a useful purpose once workers were engaged in wage labor. Capital could use the household economy to provide for some of the workers' needs. In this way, household production could allow money wages to fall below subsistence level, thus raising the rate of surplus value. In effect, the household economy could help capital profit from relative surplus value (reflecting efficiencies in the production of labor power) rather than absolute surplus value, which depends on the brute extension of the working day—meaning the hours that labor works for wages.

Few poor farmers could aspire to anything like self-sufficiency. Returns from small holdings fell so low that the period between 1788 and 1803 became known as the golden age of handloom weaving, since many small-scale farmers could not survive without augmenting their earnings in this manner (see Smelser 1959, 138).

Despite the worsening circumstances of the petty commodity producers, they could still supply much of their basic subsistence needs themselves, allowing them to survive with a modest level of wages. In light of Mountifort Longfield's observation that petty commodity producers determine the reservation wage, we should not be surprised at Phyllis Deane's (1957, 92) discovery that between 1770 and 1800, real wages in England were falling or at best stagnant.

Even in urban environments, many workers continued to combine agricultural pursuits with industrial employment. For example, in the United States as late as the nineteenth century, urban workers often grew much of their own food (see Smuts 1959, 11–13; Ware 1924, 39, 74). London also had extensive backyard agriculture, including chicken coops, sheepfolds, and pigsties above and below ground (see Dyos and Wolff 1973, 898).

Workers produced much of this food in their spare hours, notwithstanding certain unwelcome environmental consequences of living in close proximity to the animals. These activities may attest either to the strength of the attachment to self-provisioning or to inadequate incomes from wage labor. Either case implies a victory for primitive accumulation.

A number of writers acknowledged that such partial self-provisioning, as opposed to more complete self-provisioning, could be highly profitable for employers. For example, William Thornton observed that the money wages of labor were far lower in medieval times because workers' monetary requirements were minimal then. Workers could squat on neglected land. They had land to grow gardens, to graze a cow, a few sheep, and some geese, poultry, and pigs, as well as access to wood and places to fish (Thornton 1869, 12 ff.). Thus, the decline in household production would raise wages.

Adam Smith noted in passing that workers who farmed or gardened for themselves required less money for their own support (1976, I.x.b.48–49, 133–34). This factor was not irrelevant in England, where gardens adjoining workers' cottages provided important supplements to the commodities purchased with wages (see Chambers and Mingay 1966, 134; E. Thompson 1963, 214, 230, 269, 276; Mantoux 1961, chap. 3; Hammond and Hammond 1919, 3–5; Engels 1845, 9–13).

Others seemed to realize that this combination of industry and agriculture would work best where farmers were poor. For example, Daniel Defoe (1724–1726, 2, 5, 491) noted that manufacturing had already taken hold in "wild, barren, poor country" such as Devonshire on Halifax, where the land was divided into small parcels, presumably because self-provisioning allowed employers to pay less in wages. Similarly, Arthur Young (1794, 412–38; see also Berg 1980b) found a similar pattern during his travels in France.

Sir James Steuart (1767, 1:111), a vehement opponent of the totally self-sufficient household, still allowed that many wage workers "prosecute their manufactures in the country, and avail themselves, at the same time, of small portions of land, proper for gardens, grass for cows, and even for producing certain kinds of fruits necessary for their own maintenance." Here was the same technology that once supported the self-sufficient household economy, yet in an entirely different context, it served to further the process of accumulation. Indeed, Steuart (ibid., 111–12; see also Steuart 1769, 328; Marx 1977, 911) carefully differentiated this form of household production in terms of its social relations:

> This I do not consider as a species of farming. . . . Here the occupation of the inhabitants is principally directed towards the prosecution of their trades: agriculture is but a subaltern consideration, and will be carried on so far only as it occasions no great avocation from the main object. It will however, have the effect to parcel out a small part of the lands into small possessions: a system admirably calculated for the improvement of a barren soil, and advantageous to the population, *when the spirit of industry is not thereby checked.* (emphasis added)

We get an even clearer reflection of the relationship between household labor and the rate of surplus value in an anonymous review of William Cobbett's *Cottage Industry,* a precursor of contemporary self-help books designed to teach families to produce their own food. After first distancing himself from the author's dangerous political views, the reviewer for the prestigious *Edinburgh Review,* probably either Francis Jeffrey or Henry

Brougham (see Fetter 1953, 251), explained the particular advantage of inculcating a spirit of self-sufficiency among the working class:

> Let it be remembered, that after procuring raiment and shelter, almost the whole time and attention of the bulk of the people in every community, is of necessity devoted to the procuring of sustenance, that their comfort depends exactly on the greater or lesser degree of the abundance, and the better or worse quality in which this sustenance is obtained. Whatever therefore, by how little soever an addition, enables them to increase its quantity and mend its composition, brings a solid improvement to their condition and helps the great business of their whole lives. The points to which the book before us directs their attention, are of greater importance, because no cultivation of the economy recommended can be attended without the counteracting check which follows close behind so many other improvements in the labour of the poor, a fall of their wages. Whosoever should teach the reaper to do his work in half the time, would at the same time teach the farmer to give him half the wages, nay, a general practice of working farm work two or three hours extra would not increase his hire, but he will receive as much wages as if he industriously brews and bakes, and tends useful animals at by hours, as if he consumed these and his earnings together at the alehouse. (Review 1823, 119)

We could hardly hope for a more vivid expression of the logic of classical political economy. Although these words did not come from the pen of one of the most important luminaries of classical political economy, they did come from an editor of the *Edinburgh Review*, a position that made the reviewer a highly influential promoter of political economy (see Fetter 1957, 19). Such people knew that the structure of domestic production was no trifling matter. The savings that household labor could offer could be quite substantial. The reviewer of Cobbett's book presumed that the inevitable result would be a fall in the level of wages. An example of this principle is suggested by Steuart (1767, 3:304; see also Smith 1976, I.x.b.48–49, 133–34), who estimated that two days' earnings from spinning were required to nourish a Scottish spinner for a single day during the eighteenth century.

Calibrating the Model of Primitive Accumulation

Classical political economy quickly recognized that once people could no longer grow all their own food, they would become at least partially dependent on the market for their nourishment. As we saw from the proto-Marxian model of primitive accumulation, this dependence was not necessarily absolute.

Writers at the time paid considerable attention to the effect of varying the extent of dependence, or what we might term, "relative primitive accumulation." They wanted to make sure that workers would be able to be self-sufficient enough to raise the rate of surplus value without making them so independent that they would or could resist wage labor. Such calculations about the appropriate extent of household production were exceedingly common in the eighteenth century, as this proposal in an 1800 issue of the *Commercial and Agricultural Magazine* shows:

> A quarter acre of garden-ground will go a great way toward rendering the peasant independent of any assistance. However, in this beneficent intention moderation must be observed, or we may chance to transform the labourer into a petty farmer; from the most beneficial to the most useless of industry. When a labourer becomes possessed of more land than he and his family can cultivate in the evenings . . . the farmer can no longer depend on him for constant work, and the hay-making and harvest . . . must suffer to a degree which . . . would sometimes prove a national inconvenience. (cited in E. Thompson 1963, 219–20)

Robert Gourlay (1822, 145–46), an associate of Arthur Young, made a similar point:

> The half acre of land is condescended upon as being such a quantity as any poor man could make the most of at his spare hours, and from which he could raise sufficient food for a cow, along with his liberty of pasturage on the common; but there are reasons which would make it politic and right to diminish both the extent of the common and the garden plot. A quarter of an acre is the proper size for a garden, and 25 instead of 50 acres of common would be quite sufficient. A rood of land, under good garden culture, will yield a great abundance of every kind of vegetable for a family, besides a little for a cow and pig. . . . It is not the intention to make labourers professional gardeners or farmers! It is intended to confine them to bare convenience. The bad effects of giving too much land to labourers was discovered more than thirty years ago, in the lowlands of Scotland. . . . [T]he bad effects of the little potatoe farms in Ireland are well known; and nothing but dirt and misery is witnessed among the Crofters of the Highlands of Scotland. A tidy garden, with the right of turning out a

cow in a small, well-improved and very well fenced field, would produce efforts of a very different kind indeed.

The earl of Winchilsea, G. Firth (1796, 5–6), offered another example of the calculus of primitive accumulation. In a letter to Sir John Sinclair, president of the British Board of Trade, he wrote:

> Nothing is so beneficial both to them [the laborers] and to the Land Owners, as having Land to be occupied either for the keeping of Cows, or as gardens, according to circumstances. . . . By means of these advantages, the Labourers and their families live better, and are consequently more fit to endure labour; it makes them more contented, and more attached to their situation, and it gives them a sort of independence which makes them set a higher value upon their character. . . . [W]hen a Labourer has obtained a Cow, and Land sufficient to maintain her, the first thing he has thought of, has been, how he could save money enough to buy another.

The earl estimated that four-fifths of the labor put into a garden will come "at extra hours, and when they and their children would otherwise be unemployed" (ibid., 14). As might be expected, he cautioned against allowing a laborer access to even several acres of arable land because that much land "would occupy so much of his time, that the Take would, upon the whole, be injurious to him" (ibid., 13).

Calibration must necessarily adjust with changing technology. For example, progress in spinning, traditionally an agricultural sideline, failed to increase the capacity to weave cloth (see Smelser 1959, 65). Accordingly, the textile industry needed to move more people from part-time farming into full-time spinning.

In this spirit, the British Board of Agriculture attempted to assist those who employed farm labor to benefit from a more self-sufficient labor force. It offered a gold medal "to each of the five persons, who shall, in the most satisfactory manner, prove, by experiment, the practicability of cottagers being enabled to keep one or two milch cows on the produce of the land cultivated with spade and hoe only" (cited in Sinclair 1803, 850).

To be sure, the board did not intend to return to precapitalist subsistence farming. Its president, Sir John Sinclair (ibid., 851), wanted small farming to operate under three principles:

> 1. That a cottager shall raise, by his own labour, some of the most material articles of subsistence for himself and his family;
> 2. That he shall be enabled to supply the adjoining markets with the smaller agricultural productions; and

3. That both he and his family shall have it in their power to assist the neighboring farmers, at all seasons, almost equally as well as if they had no land in their occupation.

Sinclair had two objects in mind, both of which pertained to primitive accumulation. First, he thought that the provision of a small plot of land would make peasants accept enclosures more readily. Second, a glance at Sinclair's three points indicates that he thought that if small-scale farms could be properly proportioned, agricultural employers could profit from a cheap labor force. Sinclair calculated that the cottagers would earn slightly more than half their income from wages. The rest was expected to come from their sales of agricultural produce. Moreover, in excess of one-third of their money wages was expected to return to the landed gentry in the form of rents paid for their tiny plots of land (ibid., 854).

Sinclair's vision, in many respects, had already been put into practice. By the nineteenth century, the bulk of the very small farmers were wage earners who supplemented their earnings with agricultural pursuits (see Wordie 1974; Wells 1979). Even so, Sinclair, like the rest of the primitive accumulationists, agreed that capital had to exert great care lest the worker become "a little gardener instead of a labourer" (cited in Chambers and Mingay 1966, 134).

Josiah Tucker and the Sociology of the Model

Of course, capital was not united with respect to the extent of self-provisioning. Some types of labor are more compatible with a strong household economy than others. Nonetheless, just as we would expect within the context of the classical model of primitive accumulation, more and more people found reasons to support a strengthening of self-provisioning once the initial work of primitive accumulation was completed.

Naturally, these changes in the attitude toward self-provisioning did not follow a smooth and regular path. Cyclical macroeconomic conditions, especially the state of the labor market, affected stances toward self-provisioning. For example, when relatively advanced economies begin to decline, the peasant sector offers a convenient buffer that saves the need for welfare costs. Recall the earlier discussion of the resurgence of gardening during depressions. Once the pace of economic activity picks up, capitalists might look upon self-provisioning as an unwelcome competitor for scarce labor resources.

At one point, Marx seemed about to touch on this matter, almost casually observing, "England is at certain epochs mainly a corn-growing country, at others mainly a cattle-growing country. These periods alternate, and the alternation is accompanied by fluctuations in the extent of peasant cultivation" (Marx 1977, 912). Unfortunately, Marx never followed through with this thought.

Once we recognize some of these more complex considerations, we should not be surprised that we cannot mechanically apply the simple model of primitive accumulation. Indeed, agents of capital rarely spoke with a single tongue with respect to self-provisioning (see Berg 1983b, 64–67 for an excellent discussion of the issues). Those who identified with aspiring lower-middle-class interests differed from those who aligned themselves predominately with agriculture.

Consider Josiah Tucker's (1758, 36) comparison of the economies of Yorkshire, where the household economy retained its importance, and the West Country:

> In many Parts of Yorkshire, the Woolen Manufacture is carried on by small Farmers and Freeholders: These People buy some Wool, and grow some; their Wives, Daughters, and Servants spin it in the long Winter Nights, and at such Times when not employed in the Farms and Dairies; the Master of the Family either sells this produce in the Yarn Market, or hath it wove up himself.

In this competitive environment, no great differences separated the status of workers and employers. Tucker (ibid., 37) reported that:

> [The workers] being so little removed from the Degree and Condition of their masters, and likely to set up for themselves by the Industry and Frugality of a few years. . . . Thus it is, that the working people are generally Moral, Sober and Industrious; that the goods are well made, and exceedingly cheap; and that a riot or a mob is a thing hardly known among them.

By contrast, a more advanced factory system existed in the West Country. There, according to Tucker (ibid., 37–39):

> The Motives to Industry, Frugality and Sobriety are all subverted to this one consideration viz. that they shall always be chained to the same Oar (the Clothier), and never be but Journeymen. . . . Is it little wonder that the trade in Yorkshire should flourish, or the trade in Somersetshire, Wiltshire, and Gloucestershire be found declining every day?
>
> One Person, with a great Stock and large Credit, buys the Wool,

pays for the Spinning, Weaving, Milling, Dying, Shearing, Dressing, etc., etc. That is, he is the Master of the whole Manufacture from first to last, and perhaps employs a Thousand persons under him. This is the Clothier whom all the Rest are to look upon as their Paymaster. But will they not also sometimes look upon him as their Tyrant? And as great Numbers of them work together in the same Shop, will they not have it more in their Power to vitiate and corrupt each other, to cabal and associate against their Masters, and to break out in Mobs and Riots upon every little Occasion? . . . Besides, as the Master is placed so high above the Condition of the Journeymen, both their Conditions approach much nearer that of Planter and Slave in our American Colonies, than might be expected in such a Country as England; and the Vices and Tempers belonging to each Condition are of the same Kind, only in inferior Degree. The Master, for Example, however well-disposed in himself, is naturally tempted by his Situation to be proud and overbearing, to consider his People as the Scum of the earth, whom he has a Right to squeeze whenever he can; because they ought to be kept low, and not to rise up in Compensation with their Superiors. The journeymen on the contrary, are equally tempted by their Situation, to envy the high Station, and superior Fortunes of their Masters; and to envy them the more, in Proportion as they find themselves deprived of the Hopes of advancing themselves to the same Degree by any Stretch of Industry, or superior Skill. Hence their Self-love takes a wrong Turn, destructive to themselves, and others. They think it no Crime to get as much Wages, and to do as little for it as they possibly can, to lie and cheat, and do any other bad Thing; provided it is only against their Master, whom they look upon as their common Enemy, with whom no Faith is kept. . . . their only Happiness is to get Drunk, and to make Life pass away with as little Thought as possible.

Tucker seems to have anticipated the modern literature lauding northern Italy's industrial districts; however, not everybody shared Tucker's enthusiasm for economic development based on small, independent businesses, scattered throughout the countryside.

James Anderson's Alternative Analysis

Unlike Tucker, James Anderson applauded the concentration of workers in urban areas. He argued that urbanization was conducive to superior morality. Anderson, an influential writer on agriculture, probably had his eye on more earthly matters than workers' morality. He worried that the working poor would earn so much spending money from domestic industries that the social relations in the countryside would sour:

> [If] manufacture be of such a nature as to admit of being carried on in separate detached houses in the country, and may be practiced by any single person independent of others, it must invariably happen that the whole of the money that is paid for the working up of these foreign materials flows directly into the hands of the lower ranks of people, often into those of young women and children; who becoming giddy and vain, usually lay out the greatest part of the money thus gained in buying fine cloaths, and other gaudy gewgaws that catch their idle fancies. (Anderson 1777, 26)

Worse yet, these workers might not feel compelled to do low-waged agricultural work.

Another writer was more blunt than Anderson in his dual concern with morality and the labor market, warning that "a daughter, kept home to milk a poor half starv'd cow, who being open to temptations, soon turns harlot, and becomes a distressed ignorant mother, instead of making a good useful servant" (Bishton 1794, 24).

Anderson worried that domestic industry would have other undesirable consequences. Because small farmers resist severing their ties with agriculture, they are willing to pay higher rents than larger farmers. As a result, Anderson (1777, 29) predicted: "The whole order of rich and substantial tenants is totally annihilated, and all the country becomes parceled out into small and trifling possessions, which do not deserve the appellation of farms." Accordingly, he recommended industries that would provide markets for agriculture without seducing away farm labor. Such arrangements would maintain the dependent conditions of the urban workers:

> For if the manufacture necessarily requires to be carried on by people in concert with one another . . . , where those who practice it stand in need of the assistance of each other, so that it must be carried on with a number in one place, it will have attendance to promote rather than retard the progress of agriculture. (ibid., 36)

Both Tucker and Anderson offered a relatively detailed analysis of the manner in which the structure of primitive accumulation affects the sociological characteristics of people in the countryside. Yet both analyses were incomplete. Each advanced an alternative vision of primitive accumulation, without acknowledging the logic behind the perspective of competing visions. Dugald Stewart (1855, chap. 2, pt. 3) was unique, to my knowledge, in attempting to sort out the various approaches to domestic industry, contending:

> a domestic manufacture must *always* be a most unprofitable employ-
> ment for an individual who depends chiefly for his subsistence on the
> produce of a farm.
>
> A man, indeed, who exercises a trade which occupies him from day
> to day, must, of necessity, be disqualified for the management of such
> agricultural concerns as require a constant and undivided attention.
> But it does not appear equally evident, how the improvement of the
> country should be injured by his possessing a few acres as an employ-
> ment for his hours of recreation; nor does it seem likely . . . that his
> professional skill and industry will be more impaired by his occa-
> sional labour in the fields, than by those habits of intemperate dis-
> sipation in which all workmen who have no variety of pursuit are
> prone to indulge. (ibid., 175–76)

Stewart (ibid., 178–79) frowned upon "the extravagance of general declara-
tions in favor of agriculture." He was especially harsh on Arthur Young,
who was brash enough to proclaim, "There is something in manufactures
pestiferous to agriculture" (cited in ibid., 162). Nonetheless, Stewart (ibid.,
177) admitted that "much may be alleged in support of his system," adding, "The fact is, that in all human establishments we may expect to find a
mixture of good and evil; and the only question is, which of the two
predominates."

The Conservative Influence of Petty Commodity Production

Friedrich Engels approached the Anderson-Tucker question from a different angle. He was concerned that in parts of Germany, where workers
heavily relied on self-provisioning as a supplement to their wages, this
arrangement contributed to workers' conservatism in ways that even
Tucker had not realized.

Engels observed that self-provisioning reinforced the power of the German capitalists. First of all, as the reviewer of Cobbett's book had noted,
employers profited from the ability "to deduct from the price of labour
power that which the family earns from its own little garden or field"
(Engels 1887, 301). Petty commodity production offered another dividend,
over and above the boost that it gave to the rate of surplus value. Engels
contended that the ownership of a morsel of property reduced the level of
wages even further by restricting workers' mobility to areas within a short
distance of their land (ibid., 301). In addition, as Engels wrote in a 30 No-

vember 1881 letter to Eduard Bernstein, the very poverty of groups like the Saxony handweavers made them far less resistant to drawn-out struggles (Marx and Engels 1973, 35:237–38).

The domestic industry in which households performed simple piecework tasks for merchants to supplement their pitiful earnings from agriculture, could be held responsible, at least in part, for the abysmal poverty of the German worker (see, in contrast, Sismondi 1827, 230). In response to these German conditions, Engels denounced gardening and domestic industries as "the most powerful lever of capitalist exploitation" (Marx and Engels 1975, 358–59).

Engels was not antagonistic to domestic industries and household work as such. Although he was critical of the cultural deprivation of the traditional economy based on the combination of domestic industries and gardening (see Engels 1845, 9–13), he recognized that this arrangement had earlier formed the basis for a modest prosperity (ibid., 9–13; Engels 1887, 301). The overall impact of this form of work in his day was decidedly negative, however. To begin with, "the kitchen gardening and agriculture of the old rural hand weavers became the cause by virtue of which the struggle of the hand loom against the mechanical loom was everywhere so protracted and has not yet been fought to a conclusion in Germany" (Engels 1887, 301).

Engels's verdict also seems applicable to the case of Flanders. According to the recent testimony of Franklin Mendels (1975, 203; see also Mendels 1972), the influence of domestic industries was "perverse in the sense that it perpetuated the dismal pressures that had first induced its penetration into the countryside."

Of course, Engels did not mean that the elimination of the handloom was an end in itself. His immediate concern was the political situation in Germany, where the unwillingness of many workers to abandon their house garden compelled them to accept employment in domestic industries, long after mechanization had substantially devalued such labor. Not only were these workers reduced to a meager subsistence level, but their competition in the labor markets dragged industrial workers down with them (Engels 1887, 300). Lenin (1894, 317; Engels 1887, 303), too, saw much the same process taking place in his native land.

Even when such peasant workers do find employment in modern industry, they frequently refuse to identify with workers' struggles because they expect to become full-time agriculturalists again in the near future (see Sabel 1982, 102 ff.). German workers, according to Engels, were tolerating the intolerable, but he consoled himself that toleration would soon turn to rebellion as the pressures intensified.

While Engels (1887, 304, 302) opposed the reliance on domestic industries, both German capital and those whom he termed the "bourgeois-social philanthropists" regarded "the introduction of new domestic industries as the sole remedy for all rural distress." He remarked on the irony in this situation. The opponents of capital called for a more rapid introduction of technologies associated with modern capitalism, while the capitalists themselves—perhaps because they reasoned in terms of something like the simple model of primitive accumulation—preferred more primitive methods.

As late as the 1930s in the United States, Henry Ford required that his employees tend gardens; furthermore, a staff of inspectors kept his company informed about those who were remiss in their horticultural responsibilities. Those whose gardens were deemed to be inadequate were dismissed (Sward 1972, 228–29). While Ford might want a full-time effort from his workers on the job, he knew that they would experience irregular employment. Gardens would help tie workers to Ford. They would also blunt the criticism of those who would point to the plight of the workers during their periodic bouts of unemployment.

Engels's condemnation of household production retains much of its relevance in the Third World today. Consider the situation of a twentieth-century wife in an impoverished Bolivian family of miners that depends heavily on household labor:

> The miner is doubly exploited no? Because with such a small wage, the woman has to do much more in the home. And really that's unpaid work we're doing for the boss, isn't it? . . . The wage needed to pay us for what we do in the home, compared to the wages of a cook, a washerwoman, a babysitter, a servant, was much higher than what the men earned in the mine. (Barrios de Chungra 1979, 44–45)

The reasoning expressed by this woman might seem so obvious that it might even appear to be without analytical content. Appearances, in this case, are misleading. For example, compare the insights of this un-schooled Bolivian woman with Thomas C. Smith, a generally insightful student of Japanese agrarian development. Smith (1966, 83, 110) makes repeated reference to the complaints about higher wages paid to Japanese workers during the nineteenth century. Although he notes the loss of access to communal resources (ibid., 99) and the consequent need to purchase more from the market, he gives no indication of being able to recognize the connection between the increase in variable capital and the decline in self-sufficiency (ibid., 144).

The case of domestic industry in Germany or housework in Bolivia illustrates how capital may benefit from a high degree of household self-sufficiency. Obviously, other considerations must be taken into account as well. Engels pointed to the manner in which a resilient household economy impeded technical advances in Germany; however, in Japan, and to a lesser extent in Taiwan, the major force for development had been the manufacturing carried on during the spare time of the peasant household (see T. Smith 1966; Chinn 1979). In this context, domestic production ultimately turned out to be a powerful stimulus in the advancement of modern industrial practices. True, in East Asia, the social relations of production were substantially different from those of the occidental peasant farmer (see Berque 1976).

In conclusion, Engels's analysis suggests that the preferred mix of household labor and wage labor will depend on a complex calculus of class struggle within a given technological matrix. In this sense, the contrast between a Marxian analysis of household production and the classical model of the same phenomenon becomes readily apparent.

The Traditional Sector and Resistance to the
Geographical Extension of Capital

Engels's Germany and Lenin's Russia were at the periphery of capitalist strongholds. In more distant lands, small-scale farming and handicrafts reinforced each other even more effectively. Alone, either form of production might have had difficulty withstanding the competitive pressures from more modern methods of production (see Lenin 1898, 362), but combined, they displayed remarkable resiliency (Marx 1967, 3:333–34; Marx and Engels 1975, 412). As Adam Smith (1976, I.xi.g.28: 224) observed:

> As the money price of food is much lower in India than in Europe, the money price of labour is there lower upon a double account; upon account both of the small quantity of food which it will purchase, and of the low price of that food. But in countries of equal art and industry, the money price of the greater part of manufactures will be in proportion to the money price of labour; and in manufacturing art and industry, China and Indostan, though inferior, seem not to be much inferior to any part of Europe. The money price of the greater part of manufactures, therefore, will naturally be much lower in those great empires than it is anywhere in Europe.

Even counting transport costs, as late as 1780, Indian producers of calico and muslin fabrics had a 60 percent cost advantage over British producers

(Schwartz 1994, 86; citing Kawakasu 1986, 636). In the case of China, Marx quoted a Mr. W. Cooke, who had been a correspondent of the *London Times* at Shanghai and Canton, to demonstrate the efficiency of a combination of small-scale farming and handicrafts. According to Cooke, Chinese costs were so low that British exports often had to be sold in China at prices that barely covered their freight (Marx 1858, 334; Marx to Engels, 8 October 1858, cited in Avineri 1868, 440; see also A. Smith 1978, 491; Myers 1980, 151).

Marx (1967, 3:334) repeated the same idea in the third volume of *Capital*, where he wrote: "The substantial economy and saving in time afforded by the association of agriculture with manufactures put up a stubborn resistance to the products of the big industries, whose prices included the faux frais of the circulation process which pervades them."

Earlier, in 1859, Marx (375) expanded on the nature of the Indian economy, comparing it with that of China:

> It is this same combination of husbandry with manufacturing industry which, for a long time, withstood, and still checks the export of British wares to East India; but there that combination was based upon a peculiar constitution of landed property which the British in their position as the supreme landlords of the country, had it in their power to undermine, and thus forcibly convert part of the Hindoo self-sustaining communities into mere farms, producing opium, cotton, indigo, hemp and other raw materials, in exchange for British stuffs. In China the English have not yet wielded this power nor are they ever likely to do so.

Still earlier, Adam Smith (1976, I.x.b.50, 134) had noted a similar phenomenon: "Stockings in many parts of Scotland are knit much cheaper than they can anywhere be wrought upon the loom. They are the work of servants and labourers, who derive the principal part of their subsistence from some other employment."

The efficiencies associated with primitive self-provisioning did not offer much affluence to its practitioners. In Karl Wittfogel's (1931, 670; cited in Medick 1988, 381) colorful expression, we may see the fate of these traditional economies as "a famishing lilliputian cottage industry choked off large industry."

Around the same time that Marx was writing about the resiliency of the Chinese economy, he associated the resistance of traditional absence of economies with the scale of agriculture (Marx to Engels, 8 October 1858, in Marx and Engels 1985, 347). Rajat Kanta Ray (1988, 271) recently made the same point, observing:

118

Peasants who were part-time artisans and artisans who were part-time peasants were a frustrating combination for the mills, the reason why neither Manchester, nor Bombay, could accomplish their long desired objective, namely monopoly of the immense market for piecegoods in India. Except towards the very end of our period (1929), handloom production kept pace uniformly with mill production.

What was true for China and India had, at one time, also held in England and the other western European nations (see Wieser 1927, 287–88; see also Rodbertus 1851; Marx 1963–1971, pt. 2, chap. 8, pt. 4). In this regard, Marx (1977, 911) observed that "only the destruction of rural domestic industry can give the home market of a country the extension and stability which the capitalist mode of production requires." For example, a nineteenth-century owner of a cotton spinning plant near Portland, Maine, was said to have had to charge nothing for a considerable time until people came to be dependent on his services (Colonial 1816, 62).

Eventually, the technological capacity of the capitalist sector increased by leaps and bounds, especially with the tapping of the power of fossil fuels. Even so, some traditional methods of production can be relatively economical even in modern times. Their relative efficiency must have been considerably greater during the age of classical political economy. This insight reinforces the realization that the purpose of enclosures and other forms of primitive accumulation was not technical. Primitive accumulation appealed to the ruling classes because it was so effective in subordinating the working classes.

The Recapture of Labor Time

Over time, the relative costs and benefits of partial self-provisioning changed. The accumulation of expensive capital goods put a premium on workers' full-time commitment to wage labor.

Because time spent in the household economy limits the number of hours available for wage labor, the tenacious attachment to self-provisioning eventually becomes inconvenient for employers. Business had no interest in adapting itself to the rhythms of the agricultural cycle. In England, for instance, as capitalist farming came to depend more and more on specialized labor in the middle of the eighteenth century, spinning and weaving in the cottages was sometimes prohibited lest it interfere with the supply of agricultural labor (Ashton 1972, 115). As British industrialist Edmund Ashworth told an early-nineteenth-century economist, Nassau

Senior, "When a labourer . . . lays down his spade, he renders useless, for that period, a capital worth eighteen pence. When one of our people leaves the mill, he renders useless a capital that has cost 100 pounds" (Marx 1977, 529–30; citing Senior 1827, 14; see also Baldwin 1983).

Although employers may have preferred the full-time work of their employees, given the cost of eradicating these last vestiges of the traditional economy during the early period of the Industrial Revolution, many employers on both sides of the Atlantic were forced to content themselves with the services of people who worked on their own farms during all but the slack periods of the agricultural cycle (Mantoux 1961, 70; Diamond and Guilfoil 1973, 206).

This arrangement proved troublesome. We hear a report from a Quaker merchant during the Seven Years' War apologizing for a delayed shipment with the excuse: "Our nailors are so much out in harvest time" (cited in George 1953, 44). In addition, the household economy also seemed incapable of adjusting to changing technological requirements. For example, the increasing capacity to weave cloth was unmatched by comparable progress in spinning, traditionally an agricultural sideline (see Smelser 1959, 65).

As capitalism matured, some workers still maintained an attachment to their agricultural endeavors. Until the early 1900s, Belgian coal miners would take time off to tend their potato patches in what were called "potato strikes" (Henneau-Depooter 1959, 117). As late as 1925, J. Russell Smith (1925, 381) told of workers in the southern United States who disdained agricultural wage labor because they could "get an equal amount of food by going hunting, fishing or berrying—facts of profound influence in checking the development of manufacture." Even more recently, Roy Cavender, contractor manager and director of product integrity for the sportswear division of Levi-Strauss, complained, "Many times during the fall in farm areas, there is an increase in absenteeism due to crop harvest" (cited in Sabel 1982, 247).

The report from Levi-Strauss is exceptional in a modern economy. As technology became more capital intensive, firms could no longer afford to let their equipment lie idle for the convenience of its farmer-employees. Consequently, full-time wage labor became imperative.

Extensions of the Calculus

The colonial economies offer clear confirmation of our analysis of capital's need for primitive accumulation. Capitalists were justly appreciative of the work done in the household in these societies, but only after primitive accumulation had progressed far enough to ensure an adequate labor supply. Consider the experience of a Boer farmer in 1852: "I have asked Kaffirs . . . to enter my service, and they have asked whether I was made to suppose that they would go and work for me at 5s. per month, when by the sale of wood, and other articles they could obtain as much as they wanted" (cited in Magubane 1979, 75).

One colonial report recommended that

> native labourers should be encouraged to return to their homes after the completion of the ordinary period of service. The maintenance of the system under which the mines are able to obtain unskilled labour at a rate less than ordinarily paid in industry depends upon this, for otherwise the subsidiary means of subsistence would disappear and the labourer would tend to become a permanent resident . . . with increased requirements. (cited in Meillasoux 1972, 102; see also Deere 1976)

As a result of this sort of arrangement, the modern South African mining industry is free to pay a wage that its own management admits "isn't sufficient to meet the needs of a man and his family unless it's augmented by earnings from a plot of land in the man's homeland. A family man from Johannesburg, for instance, couldn't live on what we pay" (cited in Magubane 1979, 116–17; see also 123).

In late-nineteenth-century Nigeria, Acting Governor Denton applied much the same logic to argue for the continued reliance on slavery: "In much fear that they [the slaves] can find means of subsistence ready to hand without work they will cease to do anything in the way of cultivating the land as soon as the restrictions of domestic slavery are removed" (cited in Hopkins 1966, 96).

Contemporary development studies return to this refrain. The World Bank report for Papua New Guinea reads:

> The prospects for improving traditional agriculture by adding cash crops or by diversifying subsistence production are difficult to assess. Characteristic of New Guinea's subsistence agriculture is its richness; over much of the country, nature's bounty produces enough to eat with relatively little effort. . . . Until enough subsistence farms have their life styles changed by the development of new consumption wants, the relative ease of producing traditional foods may discourage experimentation with new ones. (International Bank 1977, 43; see also Payer 1982, 218–19)

Finally, we might mention that the calculation of the proper degree of self-provisioning is not unique to capitalism. A sixteenth-century Polish writer advised, "The peasant must have as much land as necessary so that in a good year a good worker need not buy bread" (cited in Kula 1976, 49), although the context was quite different in this case, of course.

Concluding Note on Political Economy and Poverty

James Kay-Shuttleworth charged that in England, "the aristocracy is richer and more powerful than in any other country in the world, the poor are more oppressed, more pauperized, more numerous . . . than the poor of any other European nation (cited in E. Smith 1853, 152; see also Sismondi 1827, 195). We should not be surprised that the rich and powerful did painfully little to ameliorate the lot of the poor. After all, the victory of the one group came at the expense of the other.

Neither the Game Laws nor the other aspects of primitive accumulation won a prominent place in the annals of political economy. But then, classical political economy rarely directly addressed the question of poverty. Instead, wealthy members of British society preferred to live in a comfortable state of cognitive dissonance. As Adam Smith (1759, 51) explained:

> The poor man goes out and comes in unheeded, and when in the midst of a crowd is in the same obscurity as if shut up in his own hovel. Those humble cares and painful attentions which occupy those in his situation, afford no amusement to the dissipated and the gay. They turn their eyes from him, or if the extremity of his distress forces them to look at him, it is only to spurn so disagreeable an object from among them. The fortunate and the proud wonder at the insolence of human wretchedness, that it should dare to present itself before them, and with the loathsome aspect of its misery presume to disturb the serenity of their happiness.

The well-to-do, in fact, go to great lengths to avoid confrontations with poverty. For example, Engels (1845, 348) noted how the physical layout of Manchester served to protect the sensitivities of the bourgeoisie:

> And the finest part of the arrangement is this, that the members of this money aristocracy can take the shortest road through the middle of all the labouring districts to their places of business without ever seeing that they are in the midst of the grimy misery that lurks to the right and the left. For the thoroughfares leading from the Exchange in

all directions out of the city are lined, on both sides, with an almost unbroken series of shops, and so are kept in the hands of the middle and lower bourgeoisie, which out of self-interest, cares for a decent and cleanly external appearance.

One could expect the poor in England to keep out of sight. When they dared to impose themselves, they evoked an angry reaction, even when they appeared in small groups. Since the bourgeoisie generally spared itself a direct encounter with poverty in its daily life, it often first witnessed squalor on visits to the Continent or Ireland. There, poverty appeared to be something foreign. The shock of viewing poverty abroad confirmed the belief of the British bourgeoisie in the correctness of the British system.

From time to time, the poverty within the cities drew young people who dared to explore the hinterland of the market economy. The squalid conditions there shocked sensitive people of all stripes who stumbled into the poorer quarters (Engels 1845). Steven Marcus (1974, 28–66), a Dickens scholar, claims the wretchedness of early-nineteenth-century Manchester was so extreme, neither Dickens nor the others could even write articulately about what they had seen.

For some, the study of political economy promised a false hope of finding an answer to the misery of the poor. For example, Alfred Marshall wrote:

> I read Mill's *Political Economy* and got much excited about it. I had doubts as to the propriety of inequalities of opportunity, rather than of material comfort. Then, in my vacations I visited the poorest quarters of several cities and walked through one street after another, looking at the faces of the poorest people. Next, I resolved to make as thorough a study as I could of political economy. (cited in Keynes 1963, 137)

William Stanley Jevons (1972, 67; see also Black and Koenigkamp 1972, 17) also expressed a "curiosity about the dark passages between the strand and the river." However, we have no record of either Jevons or Marshall continuing their firsthand encounters with poverty once they had established themselves as mature economists.

Similarly, we hear virtually nothing in classical political economy about the suffering of those who made possible the success of the market society. This studied pose of ignorance did not mean a lack of awareness. In the discussion of the doctrines of classical political economy that follows, we shall see that political economy applied the classical theory of primitive accumulation with unerring accuracy. In every case, classical political economy called for action with respect to self-provisioning that would maximize the production of surplus value.

The deterioration of the position of the self-sufficient household continued well into the twentieth century. As dispossessed people flocked to the overcrowded, industrial cities, poverty increasingly crept into view.

[A] real state and a real government only arise when class distinctions are already present, when wealth and poverty are far advanced, and when a situation has arisen in which a large number of people can no longer satisfy their needs in the way in which they have been accustomed.—G. W. F. Hegel, *Lectures on the Philosophy of World History*

A Great Beginning

As I have already mentioned, classical political economy was never willing to rely completely on the market to organize production. It called for measures to force those who engaged in self-provisioning to integrate themselves into the cash nexus. This chapter will demonstrate that this assertion holds true for William Petty, Richard Cantillon, the Physiocrats, and other early classical political economists.

For much of classical political economy, self-provisioning was nothing more than a residue of a savage past. True, the classical political economists did not treat self-provisioning as a theoretical category. Instead, they camouflaged their hostility to it under a theoretical apparatus that denied legitimacy to all activity that did not conform to the norm of production by wage labor.

The sociological backdrop to early classical political economy also contained implicit judgments about nonmarket activities. For example, the famous Four Stages theory of Smith and Anne Robert Jacques Turgot proposed that the essence of social development was an inevitable passage from hunting and gathering to animal husbandry, then agriculture, and finally commercial society (see Meek 1977b). This classical anticipation of Marx's base and superstructure theory represented an undeniable advance in the understanding of the past, but it also served an ideological purpose.

Classical political economy often identified the working classes with savages (see Berg 1980a, 136–44). For example, John Rae (1834, chaps. 7, 9) faulted both savages and the working class for an inadequate effective desire for accumulation. Two years later, Nassau Senior (1836, 69) made exactly the same point in terms of his category of abstinence.

In addition, a discipline that associated hunting for one's food with savage life could hardly be expected to display a great deal of sensitivity to the restrictions on hunting that society enforced at the time. After all, Jean-Baptiste Say (see 1821, 165; Platteau 1978, 1:157–70) condemned primitive people as anarchists. On reviewing the major figures in the pantheon of political economy, an unremitting hostility toward self-provisioning of all kinds emerges—at least insofar as it interferes with the recruitment of wage labor.

Sir William Petty: An Introduction

Classical political economy began with a period of adolescent brilliance. Perhaps none of its practitioners was so brilliant or so adolescent as the irrepressible William Petty, whom Marx (1970, 52n; 1977, 384) generously credited with being "the father of English political economy."

Petty was a polymath. Before winning his spurs as a political economist, he had achieved both fame and notoriety as a doctor. He had also served as a professor of music and dabbled in the design of ships.

Petty's scientific activities led him to extreme technological optimism. In his enthusiasm, he predicted that the day would come "when even hogs and more indocile beasts shall be taught to labour; when all vile materials shall be turned to noble use" (cited in Strauss 1954, 137). In general, Petty kept his vivid imagination in check. Instead, his keen powers of perception, together with a vision of a market society, inspired his views. Like others of his day, he caught a glimpse of the power of capital accumulation in the rapid reconstruction of the wealth of London following the Great Fire of 1666 (Petty 1690, 243; see also Appleby 1976, 502).

Petty also recognized that the prospects for the future could be advanced through changes in the system of social organization. Not only did he perceive that a more rational organization of society could increase the quantity of labor, but he also seems to have been the first writer to describe how the division of labor within the workshop results in improved efficiency (Petty 1690, 260; 1683, 473; see also George 1964, 173–75). His example of the manufacture of watches was one of the few areas in which England was a technical innovator rather than a mere imitator (George 1953). Petty's naval experience may have helped him to see the strategic importance of this new method of organizing production. When he traveled to Holland, Petty witnessed firsthand the remarkably refined division of labor in Dutch shipbuilding (Kindleberger 1976). The combination of Petty's parallel interests in the architecture of ships and the social division of labor lends some support as well to Engels's speculation that the division of labor originates in the military (see Marx and Engels 1975, 90–91).

Unlike the other practitioners of classical political economy, for whom the division of labor was primarily a matter of theory, Petty profited from it handsomely in his capacity as the organizer of the great survey of Ireland. After initially winning an appointment as the chief medical officer to Oliver Cromwell's forces in Ireland, he subsequently acquired the contract to survey the newly defeated land.

Private individuals financed a significant part of Cromwell's army, based on the assurance of shares in the 2.5 million acres of Irish land, which the English intended to confiscate. Speed was of the utmost necessity, since Cromwell had to complete the survey before the impatient conquerors could divide the spoils among themselves.

Petty employed a thousand workers who were untrained as surveyors, in this task, first teaching them the rudiments of the separate parts of the profession of surveying (Strauss 1954; Aspromourgos 1988). His work was quick enough, but in the process, Petty picked up 13,000 pounds sterling and 18,000 acres of land for himself in direct violation of the terms of his initial agreement (McNally 1988, 44–45).

Petty's Vision

Petty's analysis is particularly valuable. His broad experiences put him in touch with some of the most dynamic forces of his era. In addition, his survey of Ireland gave him the opportunity to examine the social and economic conditions of an entire people.

Petty's early life as a cabin boy, as well as his military duties in Ireland, suggested England's future as a sea power. This perspective provided him with a different context for analyzing primitive accumulation. Whereas most observers were reluctant to move against the peasant society too quickly because of its ability to produce inexpensive foot soldiers (see Marx 1977, 880–81n; Smith 1976, V.I.a.6, 692–93; Weulersse 1910, 1:246), Petty insisted that England's military future lay with a strong navy rather than an infantry. Certainly, England's geographic position gave naval power considerably more importance than was the case in other nations. England could thus afford to sacrifice some of her peasantry in the course of forming a new society in which defense would rest primarily on a navy (see B. Moore 1966, 30).

Sailors, for Petty (1690, 259), were simultaneously soldiers, artisans, and merchants. He used the following calculation to demonstrate the advantage of his implicitly proposed social division of labor: "The Husbandman of England earns but about 4s. per Week, but the Seamen have as good as 12s. in Wages, Victuals (and as it were housing) with other accommodations, so as a Seaman is in effect three Husbandmen" (ibid.). Indeed, the navy became the eventual foundation for the British imperial system (Frank 1978).

Creating a new social division of labor in England was so integral to Petty's mission that he even attempted to design ships that would best support it (see Strauss 1954). Although his naval designs were not successful, his social program was. The navy that Petty envisioned only made economic sense if the people could be led to produce sufficient commodities for export. Given the diminished need for infantry troops and the importance of increased exports, Petty called for an intensification of primitive accumulation.

Petty found confirmation of his vision of a new social division of labor in the experience of Holland. Indeed, Tony Aspromourgos (1986, 40; see also Petty 1690, 255) believes that a central feature of Petty's work was an attempt to explain the material basis for the contrast between Irish poverty and Dutch success based on his experience living in those two countries. Petty (1690, 266; see also Appleby 1976, chap. 4) claimed that Holland relied on the international economy for much of its food and exported goods, although in reality Holland mostly exported services rather than material products.

Petty's overt concern with revolutionizing the structure of the British economy led him to take notice of the changing social division of labor. He observed: "The Trade of food was branched into Tillage of Corn and grazing of Cattle, that of clothes into Weaver, Tinker, and Taylor, Shewmaker and Tanner and that of Housing in Smith, Mason and Carpenter" (Petty 1927, 1:212). The peasantry, which did not accept wage labor as a matter of course, was unlikely to embrace Petty's vision of a new social division of labor that eliminated the source of their livelihood.

Perhaps because the household economy was so solidly entrenched, Petty did not raise the question of the sort of incentives that might make people forego producing for their own needs in order that they would specialize in narrow occupations. For Petty, however, individual choice was not an issue. Rather, he assigned the government the responsibility for the creation of a new social division of labor.

Petty appropriated the language of bullionism to lend theoretical support to his notion of a new social division of labor. He calculated: "The Wealth of every Nation, consisting chiefly, in the share which they have

128

in the Foreign Trade with the whole Commercial World, rather than in the Domestick Trade, of ordinary Meat, Drink, and Cloaths, &c. which bring in little Gold, Silver, Jewels, and other Universal Wealth" (Petty 1690, 1:295). Petty's universal wealth was merely a sign of power, derived from the development of the economic forces of the nation. Thus he estimated that England was substantially more powerful than her great rival, France (ibid.).

Petty closely associated universal wealth with the rise of a new social division of labor. He expressed this connection even more clearly in a similar passage, which directly follows his estimates about the superior productivity of seamen (259–60)

Petty and the Social Division of Labor

Petty demonstrated a lifelong interest in prodding the government to take actions that would reduce the vitality of household production. Specifically, he recognized the strategic importance of transferring workers out of agriculture (Petty 1690, 256, 267). In his chapter of *Verbum Sapienti* titled "How to Employ the People, and the End Thereof," he explained that an efficiently run society must set people "upon producing Food and Necessaries for the whole People of the Land, by few hands" (Petty 1691, 118–20).

Petty, as was common in his age, wanted to set everybody to work: "Thieves, robbers, beggars, fustian and unworthy Preachers in Divinity in the country schools, . . . Pettifoggers in the Law, . . . Quacksalvers in Physick, and . . . Grammaticasters in the country schools" (cited in Strauss 1954, 137). Petty recommended that the law "should allow the Labourer but just wherewithal to live; for if you allow double, then he works but half so much as he could have done, and otherwise would" (Petty 1662, 87). Toward this end, he insisted that food be kept sufficiently scarce; surplus grain was to be put into granaries rather than allowing it to be "abused by the vile and brutish part of mankind to the prejudice of the commonwealth" (Petty 1690, 275).

Many other writers at the time advocated the value of high food prices (see Furniss 1965; Wermel 1939, 1–14, 17, 24), although not always in language as vigorous as Petty's. With characteristic audacity, Petty (1690, 287) rhapsodized that "that vast Mountainous Island [of Ireland would sink] under Water," thus expropriating its inhabitants from their land and livelihood, and forcing them to migrate to England, where they could be exploited efficiently, "a pleasant and profitable Dream indeed." More practically, Petty (1687, 560; see also 1927, 58–61) called on the government to hasten the development of a proletariat by removing a million Irish to England, leaving the remaining population to manage Ireland as a cattle ranch or in his words as a "Kind of Factory."

Perhaps the only adequate commentary on Petty's social vision came from the acid pen of Jonathan Swift (1729), whose "Modest Proposal" essay suggested consuming the flesh of children. Georgy Wittkowsky (1943) finds numerous stylistic parallels to support his contention that Swift's satire had been chiefly modeled after Petty's work. Gulliver's description of an "odd kind of arithmetick . . . in reckoning the numbers of our people by a computation drawn from the several sects among us in religion and politicks" also seems to be an allusion to Petty (Swift 1726, 131). In addition, Swift (1731, 175) parodied Petty's proposal for the Irish cattle factory, as well as Petty's list of professions that could be put to the productive labor that was cited above.

Given the haphazard data available at the time, Petty's method sometimes invited satire. For example, Guy Routh (1977, 45) provides the flavor of Petty's method:

> In comparing wealth of Holland and Zealand to that of France, he takes guesses by two other people, does not like the results and ends up with a guess of his own. He estimates the population of France from a book that says that it has 27,000 parishes and another book that says that it would be extraordinary if a parish had 600 people. So he supposes the average to be 500 and arrives at a population of 13½ million. And so it goes.

Despite his fanciful predictions and wild guesses, Sir William Petty still managed to set political economy on the course it was to follow for the next three centuries, even though legal intrigues arising from his Irish land grab sapped most of his intellectual energy.

Richard Cantillon

Richard Cantillon, the second major figure of classical political economy, was a shadowy presence. In terms of economic sophistication, Cantillon represented a significant advance over Petty (Brewer 1992). Indeed, Cantillon (1755, 43, 83) was openly contemptuous of Petty's work, which he twice dismissed: once as "fanciful and remote from natural laws"; and once as "purely imaginary and drawn up at hazard."

Unlike most of the writers encountered in the study of primitive accumulation, Cantillon went beyond calling for an intensification of the process. True, he joined in the complaints about the excessive number of holidays enjoyed by people in the countryside (ibid., 95), but so did almost every other political economist at the time. Cantillon (ibid., 43) also wrote, "Individuals are supported not only by the produce of the Land which is cultivated for the benefit of the Owners but also at the Expense of these Same Owners from whose property they derive all that they have."

Much of what we know of Cantillon's life comes from court records. Where Petty was frequently hauled into court for his land speculation, Cantillon was deeply involved in litigations concerning his dealings in credit. Specifically, Cantillon lent people money to buy shares in John Law's scheme. As security, he required that the shares be left in his custody. Anticipating a fall in their value, he sold them. Those to whom he lent the money charged that Cantillon had betrayed their trust. They took the position that merely standing ready to buy new shares was not equivalent to holding the original shares as collateral (see Fage 1952; Hyse 1971).

Indeed, if the price of the shares had risen, Cantillon might have gone bankrupt, leaving him unable to repurchase the stock. His borrowers would have lost any of their own money that they might have invested in those stocks. If the shares fell, Cantillon was guaranteed a double profit, consisting of interest paid on the loan as well as the profit earned from repurchasing the stock at the diminished price. Cantillon's angry clients sued him, setting off a wild sequence of events.

Antoin Murphy (1986) has reconstructed Cantillon's strange story, including the bitter litigation, his scandalous family life, the probable faking of his own death, and his likely ultimate demise incognito in the jungles of South America. Gripping though his personal experiences may be, Cantillon's importance here lies in the realm of theory.

Cantillon, in fact, made several key contributions to economic theory in his famous *Essay,* even though he probably intended it as a contribution to his lawyer's brief (see ibid., 246). To begin with, he clearly pointed out that land generates a surplus, over and above the sustenance of the people who work it. For Cantillon, this surplus represented the material from which all other classes lived. This insight prepared the way for the French Physiocratic school, which we will discuss at length later (see Walsh and Gram 1980, 19).

Even more fundamentally, Cantillon went far beyond Petty's practical call for a reorganization of the economy. Cantillon built this analysis into the structure of his *Essay,* which he divided into three books. The first seems to be about the feudal Irish world in which he was born, and the next two about the monetary world to which he emigrated (Murphy 1986, 17).

According to Cantillon (1755, 63 ff.; Walsh and Gram 1980, 298), the system of prices in the economy that he described in the final sections of the *Essay* could give the same result as a system of direct command over labor typical of a feudal economy. In effect, Cantillon recognized for the first time that market relations could be an effective means of control. His contribution to the political economy of primitive accumulation is thus incalculable.

The French Economy

Almost all observers concurred that the French economy was dysfunctional at the time when classical political economy came to France. Marx (1977, 239) spoke of "the unspeakable misery of the French agricultural population." Alex de Tocqueville (1858, 120) claimed that the peasants on the eve of the French Revolution were worse off than their thirteenth-century forbearers. One mid-eighteenth-century visitor to southern France claimed that he saw no birds because the peasants had consumed them all (Kiernan 1991, 78). The despondent François Fénelon warned that "France was being turned into a desolate and starving poor house" (cited in Salvemini 1954, 53).

As French society veered toward revolution, the educated public began to take a keen interest in economic matters, especially insofar as they pertained to agriculture. Dupont de Nemours noted: "We . . . place at that epoch [1750] the origin of discussions about political economy" (ibid.). In this spirit, Voltaire wrote: "Around 1750, the nation, satiated with verses, tragedies, comedies, operas, novels, romanesque stories, with moral reflections still more romanesque, and with theological disputes over grace and convulsions, set itself to reason about grains" (cited in Weulersse 1910, 1:25). Comte de Mirabeau went so far as to proclaim that "all politics emanates from a grain of wheat" (ibid., 2:2; the source cited by Weulersse appears to be incorrect). We might roughly translate Mirabeau's image to mean that the locus of "principal contradiction" (see Mao 1937, sec. 4) of French society was the agricultural crisis.

Most middle-class observers agreed on the causes of France's plight: An oppressive tax system, which largely exempted both the aristocracy and nobility; a peasantry that was too poor to afford the necessary investment; and a church that contributed to the peasant's laziness by supporting an excessive number of holidays. We have already mentioned Voltaire's proposal for shifting holidays. The cantankerous English novelist, Tobias Smollett (1766, 59, 38) apparently agreed, complaining:

The great number of their holidays not only encourages this lazy behavior, but actually robs them of what their labour would otherwise produce. . . . Very nearly half of their time, which might be profitably employed in the exercise of industry, is lost to themselves and the community, in attendance upon the different exhibitions of religious mummery.

Not everybody conceded that the French economy was as disastrous as these commentators made it out to be, although Say was the only classical political economist who seemed skeptical of the great superiority of the British economy (see above). More recently, some historians and economists have begun to judge the French economy more favorably. Robert Aldrich (1987, 99; see also Kindleberger 1984) sums up this research: "It is possible to consider the long-term development of France as a more humane transition and perhaps a not less effective one in the transition to industrial society."

In other words, France's development may have differed from Britain's, but it was not altogether inferior. Although peasants may have been impoverished, their lot may not have been worse than what the unskilled, urban worker encountered in England. We might even arrive at the conclusion that France's transition to modern capitalism might have been more humane than England's. Unfortunately, a humane transition had less attraction for the primitive accumulationists than the great profits to be had from coercing labor into submission.

The Economic Interests of the Physiocrats

In France, a group of economists, collectively known as the Physiocrats, more or less sought to emulate the British system. As might be expected, they counted themselves among those who would profit from the changes they proposed. In Norman Ware's (1932, 608) words, "The Physiocrats were not professional economists but officials of various sorts emerging from the French bureaucracy and climbing into the land-owning and even the noble classes."

These officials could not easily cease to be bourgeois. They were too poor to ape the aristocracy and treat their estates as playthings. They had to earn revenue. Not surprisingly, their theories justified a new system of production and reform of the archaic financial system that burdened them.

François Quesnay, for example, the leader of the Physiocrats, published his first economic essay in 1756, the year after he bought a large estate and became a nobleman (ibid., 614). According to his economic table, which was a schematic analysis of the new social division of labor, the expected rate of return on agricultural investment was between 250 and 300 percent (Weulersse 1910, 1:354). No wonder that Gabriel Bonnot de Mably was moved to write, "Here then is M. Quesnay entirely occupied with this new object. His first discovery was, that if the price of land increase, the revenue of his new domain would increase equally and he would have made himself an excellent purchase" (cited in Ware 1931, 614).

The Physiocrats built on Cantillon's analytical foundations, centering on rent. The Marquis de Mirabeau, François Quesnay's loyal disciple, claimed to have been in possession of Cantillon's work for sixteen years, planning to publish it as his own. Eventually, he heard that somebody else had a copy and was about to issue the book with the proper attribution. As a result, Mirabeau finally published the book in 1755 as the work of Cantillon (Higgs 1931).

The Physiocratic identification of surplus and rent reflected the prevailing opinion within the French middle classes, as well as Cantillon's theory. At the time, the French bourgeoisie was incapable of imagining any other source of wealth and power than landed property (Nallet and Servolin 1978). For instance, their legal framework gave no indication of an awareness of the potential expansion of capital (ibid.).

Despite their fanatical support for large-scale farming, the Physiocrats understood that small-scale, labor-intensive agriculture could produce substantially higher yields (Weulersse 1910, 2:317). Recall the success of Ponce and the Parisian market gardeners discussed in chapter 5 (see also Kropotkin 1898, 62ff.; 1906, 20; Ponce 1870, 32–49).

True, these market gardeners devoted a prodigious amount of labor to their work. Mirabeau even claimed that the majority of Parisian gardeners slept with a pail of water near their bed to quench the thirst of their plants when they gave off sounds that indicated the need for moisture during the night (Weulersse 1910, 2:317); however, even if their working day had been halved, their output would still have remained substantial.

Attitudes toward Labor

The Physiocrats saw England as the most successful example of what they considered to be a well-functioning society. Still, they distanced themselves from the basic English model of the social division of labor in one respect: they called for the initial concentration of wage labor in agricultural pursuits rather than industry. They looked with suspicion on textile production, the mainstay of the Industrial Revolution in England, since textiles might prove to be an unwelcome competitor for agricultural labor (Weulersse 1959, 28n). In contrast, the British were more troubled by the thought that agricultural activities might compete with industry.

The Physiocratic movement differed from British political economy in one other crucial respect. Although almost everybody in polite society agreed that the French peasants were lazy (Weulersse 1910, 1:321), the Physiocrats did not adopt an ostensibly hostile attitude toward them. Unlike the British, whose typical tone was contentious at best when discussing the common people, the French often expressed concern about the well-being of country folk.

Where the British violently opposed hunting by the lower classes, the French worried that people had to content themselves with coarse food such as chestnuts (ibid., 1:488), now an expensive gourmet item. The Parliament of Toulouse lamented the fate of women who spun at night after spading or even plowing during the day (ibid., 2:687). With a more free form of commerce, such women were promised lighter workloads. Enclosures were even recommended as a method for expanding the demand for labor (Weulersse 1959, 149).

Ultimately, such differences came down to matters of style, since the Physiocrats could be as brutal as anyone in their attitude toward the working classes. Mirabeau (1763, 8) identified the agricultural laborers along with working cattle as tools of cultivation. Certainly Quesnay (1757, 86) did not express much sympathy toward the workers when he wrote:

> It is very harmful to allow people to get used to buying corn at too low a price. As a result they become less hard-working; they spend little on the bread they eat and become lazy and presumptuous; farmers have difficulty in finding workers and servants and are very badly served by them in years of plenty. It is important that the common people should earn more, and they should be spurred on by the need to earn. In the last century, when bread was much dearer, the people were used to it and they earned in proportion, and as a result were more hard working and better off.

Net and Gross Product

What, then, was the advantage of the new technology of large-scale farming? The answer from England, where the French first learned about the new husbandry, seemed clear. One article, published more than a half century after the age of the Physiocrats, reveals the British perspective:

The proprietor of the land, cultivating his farm under the old system, was obliged, we will suppose, to keep ten horses, ten labourers to plough, sow and reap, ten women to card and spin. Under the present system of providing a series of different crops in succession, we may assume that five horses and five labourers are sufficient to carry on the work of the same farm, and that the use of machinery in carding, spinning, and weaving, may enable two women the same quantity of wrought goods, which formerly required the labour of ten. (Edwards 1827, 417)

Boyd Hilton (1977, 121) attributes this citation to Edward Edwards, the same writer whom Joseph Dorfman (1966b) credits with being the author of two books written under the pen name Piercy Ravenstone, generally considered to be two of the most noteworthy works of "Ricardian Socialism." Ravenstone, however, opposed profits, although the author of the above passage does not argue so much against profit as in favor of rent. This divergence lends support to Piero Sraffa's (1951, 11:64) contention that the author of the Ravenstone works was Richard Puller.

Regardless of the authorship, this quote throws light on one important aspect of the new agricultural technologies: although these techniques seemed to save labor, on closer examination, these savings become more ambiguous. To begin with, much of the improved economy of labor was not at all due to the production of more output with a lesser quantity of labor. Instead, it was nothing more than the result of an intensification of labor.

The new system not only speeded up labor (see A. Smith 1976, V.I.a.15, 697); it also redirected it to meet the needs of capital. Under the old system, the demand for agricultural labor was irregular. Specific tasks, such as planting and harvesting, required considerable labor. During other, less demanding periods, agricultural workers had more time available to produce for their own needs. The author of the above cited article considered this activity to be a loss for capital. He recommended that "the occupier of any tenant must have maintained in his own house, or at least within the limits of his own farm, a number of hands, sufficient, not only to perform the work of tillage, but to manufacture all the articles of clothery required by himself, his family, and his working people" (Edwards 1827, 416).

Thus, although in the long run, a far-reaching expansion of the productive powers of labor accompanied the new agricultural technology, the major attraction at the time appeared to be the reduction in the expense of maintaining labor over the extensive periods that rural workers had previously devoted to household production. Workers, who had formerly divided their hours between the production of grain and the production of their other domestic needs, were now required to more or less specialize in grain. As a result, the net product would increase, since fewer workers would be required on the farm to perform those tasks specifically directed to the production of grains (Weulersse 1910, 2:314–15).

Thus, Mirabeau, the self-proclaimed "Friend of the People," justified capitalist farming by virtue of its ability to force people to cease living at the expense of the proprietor (ibid., 2:350; see also Cantillon 1775, 47). Under the Physiocratic program, as L. P. Abeille (1768, 95; cited in Weulersse 1910, 2:686) recommended in his *Principles sur le liberte du commerce des grains*, the worker was to be considered a commodity like all other commodities. To give this program theoretical support, the Physiocrats excluded grain consumed by cultivators (and presumably also all other goods they produced for their own needs) from the national wealth (see Maitland 1804, 125–27).

The Physiocratic contention that the success of agriculture should be judged by the net product did not go uncontested. Others, such as François Forbonnais, countered that the support of people was an end in itself (Weulersse 1910, 2:314–15). In effect, the Physiocrats wanted to convert traditional agricultural production into a commodity-producing enterprise directed toward the creation of surplus value; their critics analyzed agriculture from the point of view of the production of use values. In short, the much vaunted success of the capitalist agriculture recommended by the Physiocrats was not merely a matter of technical improvements.

The Reception of the Physiocrats

The Physiocrats evoked widespread antipathy. For example, David Hume (1769, 216) wrote to a French friend, "I hope that you will thunder them, and crush them, and pound them, and reduce them to dust and ashes. They are, indeed, the set of men the most chimerical and most arrogant that now exist." Baron Grimm, one of their severest critics, ridiculed their pretensions:

> They begin with a good dinner, then they labor; they chop and dig and drain; they do not leave an inch of ground in France. And when they have either labored all day in a charming saloon, cool in summer, and well warmed in winter, they part in the evening well contented, with the happy thought that they have made the Kingdom more flourishing. (cited in Hale and Hale 1887–1888, 1:8)

In a 6 August 1770 letter, Jean-Baptiste-Antoin Suard wrote to Abbé Gal-
liani: "I have been so disgusted by the jargon and the tiresome repetitions
of the economistes, the exportists, the libertyites, etc! But having barely
finished the first four pages [of the Dialogues] I was swept up till the very
end without being able to do anything else" (cited in Kaplan 1976, 593).

What explains this hostility? In part, the Physiocrats appalled conservatives by challenging existing institutions. For example, Tocqueville
(1858, 159, 162) bristled:

> Our Economists had a vast contempt for the past. . . . Starting out
> from this premise, they set to work, and there was no French insti-
> tution, however venerable and well founded, for whose immediate
> suppression they did not clamor if it hampered them even to the
> slightest extent or did not fit in with their neatly ordered scheme of
> government. . . .
>
> According to the Economists the function of the state was not
> merely one of ruling the nation, but also that of recasting it in a given
> mold, of shaping the mentality of the population as a whole in accor-
> dance with a predetermined model and instilling the ideas and senti-
> ments they thought desirable into the minds of all.

Finally, Tocqueville charged that the Physiocrats called for economic but
not political liberty (ibid., 159). Of course, the other classical political
economists also feared universal suffrage. More damaging to the Physiocrats, Tocqueville interpreted their reliance on the state as a form of
socialism (ibid., 164), yet we will see throughout this book that classical political economists generally called for state action to sweep away
traditional barriers to capitalism, although they generally did so more
discreetly.

More recently, both Terrence Hutchison (1988) and Friedrich von Hayek
(1948, 1959, 189) have renewed the charge that the Physiocrats were the
spiritual forbearers of modern communism, although the former grudg-
ingly grants that they were "perhaps rather less dictatorially directed than
the Marxians" (Hutchison 1988, 285). Hutchison's position is especially
curious, since he also condemned what he termed "Colbertist-Stalinist"
tendencies, even though the Physiocrats strenuously opposed Colbert's
system (ibid., 295).

Nonetheless, Adam Smith, the patron saint of laissez-faire, adopted a
great deal of the Physiocratic analysis, except for its specifically French
emphasis on the exclusive productivity of agriculture. He also made his
own version less abstract than the Physiocrats, in the process obscuring

the importance of primitive accumulation. Indeed, Smith's transformation of Physiocratic doctrine led Dugald Stewart, whom we have already met in the context of his clearheaded sorting out of the various theories of domestic industry, to conclude that Physiocrats were more scientific than Smith. However, Stewart (1855, 1:306) judged that the doctrines of Smith were "with very few exceptions, of greater practical utility" to statesmen and businessmen.

Certainly, with respect to primitive accumulation, Stewart's verdict is correct. The Physiocrats put the subject on a much more theoretical basis than any of the classical political economists, but their analytical clarity was unwelcome. In contrast, the English political economists preferred to write as if all hardship were due to the silent compulsion of the market, rather than the intended result of extraeconomic actions.

In conclusion, with the Physiocrats, as with Sir William Petty, we get some idea of the connection between the creation of a new social division of labor and the rise of capitalism—a connection that is generally expressed in terms of hostility toward the self-sufficient household.

CHAPTER 7

Sir James Steuart's Secret History of
Primitive Accumulation

A river may as easily ascend to its source, as a people voluntarily adopt a more operose agriculture than that already established.—Sir James Steuart, *An Inquiry into the Principles of Political Economy*

The Destruction of Feudal Society in Scotland

This chapter concerns Sir James Steuart's contribution to the theory of primitive accumulation. Steuart, forgotten today, was one of the most important of the classical political economists. Steuart's analysis benefited from his upbringing in Scotland. His Scotland was a mysterious world, even for the English visitor in the age of classical political economy. In the early eighteenth century, Defoe (1724–26, 3:663) remarked, "Our geographers seem to be almost as much at a loss in their description of this north part of Scotland as the Romans were to conquer it." Toward the end of the century, Samuel Johnson recalled his tour of the Highlands: "I got an acquisition of more ideas by it than anything that I remember. I saw quite a different system of life" (cited in Boswell 1799, 199).

Tribal values remained strong in the Scottish Highlands. All commentators agreed that the household economy maintained an exceptional degree of self-sufficiency in the countryside (see Marx 1977, 472, 616n; see also Smith 1976, I.iii.2, 31; Anderson 1777, 12–15). Defoe, an enthusiastic prophet of early capitalism, noted that despite the unfavorable environment, the people of the rugged Scottish Highlands could provision themselves with remarkable ease. In his words, "Their employment is chiefly hunting. . . . however mountainous and wild the country appeared, the people were extremely well furnished with provisions" (Defoe 1724–26, 664–67). He specifically mentioned the availability of venison and salmon.

Before the union with England in 1707, clan chiefs ruled the Highlands. The lairds received goods in kind, as well as military service from their people. Custom fixed rents at a nominal sum or a lamb or sheep (Smith 1976, III.iv.6, 414). Here is James Anderson's (1777, 12) portrayal of this society:

Accustomed to an almost independent sovereignty, the chieftains, till of late, lived each in the midst of his own people, and shared with them the produce that his demesnes afforded. Ignorant of the luxuries that commerce had introduced into the other parts of the island, they lived contented with their own homely fare. . . . This naturally produced a kind of warmth of attachment between the vassal and his chief, that is almost entirely unknown in every other stage in the progress of civil society.

Adam Smith (1976, III.iv.11, 419; see also 1978, 202, 248) suggested a more material basis for this pattern of social relations: "In a country where there is no foreign commerce, nor any of the finer manufactures, a man of ten thousand a year cannot well employ his revenue in any other way than in maintaining, perhaps, a thousand families, who are all necessarily at his command."

After the union with Britain, the lairds appreciated that access to the lucrative English market allowed a dramatic rise in the value of cattle, their chief produce (Smith 1976, I.xi.b.8, 165; I.x.1.2, 237–8; Ommer 1986). According to Adam Smith (1976, I.xi.1.3, 239–40), "Of all the commercial advantages, however, which Scotland has derived from the Union with England, this rise in the price of cattle is, perhaps, the greatest. It has not only raised the value of all highland estates, but it has perhaps been the principle cause of the improvement of the low country."

As new opportunities for profit emerged, some lairds started to shift their reference point from the self-sufficient clan economy to the world of the Lowlands and English aristocracy (Ommer 1986). A hunger for money set in (see Smith 1978, 262; see also S. Johnson 1774, 85, 94). Thomas Selkirk (1805, 12) aptly commented on this relationship:

By allowing his tenants to posses their farms at low rents, he secured their services whenever required, and, by the power of removing any one who was refractory, maintained over them the authority of a monarch. The sacrifice of pecuniary interest was of inferior importance. . . . The Highland gentlemen appear to have been so anxious on this subject that they never ventured to raise their rents.

The final defeat of Scottish hopes for independence from Britain at the Battle of Culloden (1745) put an end to the remains of traditional economic structure. James Anderson (1777, 13) explained:

As the government, for wise reasons, found it necessary to deprive the chieftains of that power and authority, . . . many of these, who still remained in the country, finding their authority curtailed, and becoming gradually acquainted with the pleasures of a civilized life, grew less and less fond of that kind of life they had formerly been accustomed to.

Once the union became an accepted fact, the chiefs had little need for the military services of the clan members. This situation offered a pretext for the conversion of the traditional feudal system of land tenure. The lairds ceased to be the head of a traditional feudal society. Instead, they became landlords who saw their land as a source of monetary rent (ibid., 12–14). In the words of Samuel Johnson (1774, 89), "Their chiefs being now deprived of their jurisdiction . . . gradually degenerate from patriarchal rulers to rapacious landlords." As a result, during the third quarter of the nineteenth century, Highland rents quadrupled (see Johnson 1775, 38).

Similarly, Benjamin Franklin (1959, 20:523) noted in 1773, "It seems that some of the Scottish Chiefs, who delight no longer to live upon their Estates . . . chuse rather a Life of Luxury . . . , have lately raised their Rents most grievously to support the Expense."

Despite their increased income, the lairds still fell deeply into debt. J. H. Grey Graham (1937, 29) observed, "It was a tradition that in the days of the Scots Parliament . . . , when the sessions closed, the Cannongate jail was crowded with peers, whom their creditors could seize the moment their period of immunity ceased." Adam Smith's (1976, III.iv.10, 419; see also Carter 1980, 384) contemptuous reference to an effete nobility purchasing a diamond buckle for an amount that could maintain a thousand men was symptomatic of the changes that were occurring.

In some ways, we could compare the Scotland of Steuart's day to ancient Athens while it was transforming itself from a tribal to a civil society. Like Athens, Scotland became a center of intellectual ferment, enjoying what was perhaps the most advanced university system in the world. Likewise, it was to fall victim to the superior military might of a neighbor. Nonetheless, Steuart, as we shall see, identified with Sparta rather than Athens.

Primitive Accumulation in Scotland

To satisfy their newfound lust for luxuries, the lairds cast aside their traditional obligations to the community. Even though originally they only held their land as leader of a clan, they laid claim to clan land as their personal property. Based on questionable property rights, they threw large numbers of people off the land in the name of agricultural improvements. Indeed, the first lairds who turned to raising sheep on this land profited handsomely (Selkirk 1805, 32).

This confiscation of clan property was one of the most dramatic examples of primitive accumulation. Benjamin Franklin (1959–, 20:523; see also S. Johnson 1775, 38) cited an issue of the *Edinburgh Courant* in 1773, which claimed that 1,500 people had emigrated from Sutherlandshire in the space of two years. Many years later, between 1814 and 1820, a descendant of Steuart's wife's cousin, the duchess of Sutherland, took vigorous measures to evict another 15,000 inhabitants. According to Marx's (1977, 891–92; see also Smout 1969, 353–54; Ross 1973, 182–93) description of the event:

> All their villages were destroyed and burnt, all their fields turned to pasturage. British soldiers enforced this mass of evictions, and came to blows with the inhabitants. One old woman was burnt to death in the flames of her hut she refused to leave. It was in this manner that this fine lady appropriated 794,000 acres of land which belonged to the clan since time immemorial. . . . By 1825, the 15,000 Gaels had been replaced by 131,000 sheep.

Although this particular method of eviction might seem overly harsh, we should note that landlords recently applied it to their tenants in India (see Perelman 1977, 149).

Lest our sympathies for the disposed divert our attention too far afield, we should take note that Jean Charles Leonard de Sismondi (1827, 52; see also Ross 1973, 242) reported a few years later that the unfortunate proprietor of the estate had been extremely anxious about the precarious state of her fortunes at the time. Incidentally, Marx (1853a, 491) incorrectly enlisted Steuart in condemning these clearings in his *New York Tribune* article by means of a rare misquotation, where he cited Steuart to the effect that "a plot of land in the highlands of Scotland feeds ten times more people than a farm of the same extent in the richest provinces." Steuart (1767, 1:137) had actually written "value" where Marx cited the word "extent."

Enclosures and clearings, such as the Sutherland affair, might appear to be conducive to progress in the long run, but their immediate effect was devastating to the people who were uprooted in the process of primitive accumulation. Even the purported long-term benefits are somewhat dubious. Recall that the increase in pasturage was followed by an expansion in deer parks (see chapter 3).

The lairds also had political motives for removing people. After all, the peasants were fierce warriors, who expected the lairds to respect traditional rights. In his travel report on Scotland, Samuel Johnson (1774, 97) cynically remarked that "to hinder insurrection, by driving away the people, and to govern peaceably, by having no subjects, is an expedient that argues no profundity of politicks."

Others took a more charitable view of the massive primitive accumulation that was occurring in Scotland. For example, Thomas Pennant (1772, 145; 1774, 145) rhapsodized: "Let a veil be flung over a few excesses consequential to a day of so much benefit to united kingdoms. . . . The Halcyon days are near at hand: oppression will beget depopulation, and depopulation will give us dear-bought tranquility." Years later, the kindly Nassau W. Senior (1868, 282; also cited in Marx 1977, 892) wrote of the work of the duchess of Sutherland as "one of the most beneficent clearings since the memory of man." No wonder the classical political economists could lay claim to the virtue of humanitarianism.

These forced migrations following the first Jacobite rebellion, as well as the Battle of Culloden, resulted in concentrations of propertyless people available for employment. The lairds were anxious to turn this situation to their own advantage. The most important employment for these displaced people was the labor-intensive business of gathering kelp (Gray 1951; Carter 1980, 372; Smith 1976, I.xi.a.2, 160; Matsukawa 1965), an industry employing as many as 50,000 people (see Ross 1973, 230).

The kelp industry was strategically placed during the early years of the industrial revolution (see B. Thomas 1980, 7). This primitive industry provided the alkali needed for the dynamic textile industry. Without kelp, scarce timber would have been burned for potash (Smith 1776, I.xi.a.3, 161).

All of the elements of a capitalist development seemed to be in place. Unfortunately, manufacturing did not take a firm hold in Scotland. English competition swamped the fine Scottish woolen industry, as well as most other manufactures (Campbell 1953, 12). Scottish prosperity did not extend much beyond Glasgow, which benefited from the extension of the Navigation Acts to Scotland rather than from an indigenous economic development (ibid., 12; Devine 1976).

In short, depopulation of the Scottish countryside led to a future of poverty for the kelp gatherers alongside the prosperity of the emerging capitalist potentates. As Thomas Pennant (1771, 180; see also Boswell 1799, 5:221) commented, "The great men begin at the wrong end, with squeezing the bag, before they have helped the poor tenant to fill it, by the introduction of manufactures."

Steuart's Scotland

Sir James Steuart was well suited to serve as the leading theoretician of Scottish development. His family was highly placed. One grandfather was

Lord Provost of Edinburgh. His father led an erratic career, compromised by involvements in Scottish conspiratorial politics; nonetheless, he eventually won appointment as Solicitor-General of Scotland.

He personally embodied the conflict between the traditional economy of the household and capitalist development. Moreover, he displayed a rare "sense of the historical differences in modes of production," a gift perhaps belonging to no other classical political economist except Richard Jones (Marx 1963–71, pt. 3, 399). Elsewhere, Marx (ibid., 43) expanded on this aspect of Steuart's importance:

> His service to the theory of capital is that he shows how the process of separation takes place between the conditions of production, as the property of a definite class, and labour-power. He gives a great deal of attention to this genesis of capital—without as yet seeing it directly as the genesis of capital, although he sees it as a condition for large-scale industry. He examines the process particularly in agriculture: and he rightly considers that manufacturing industry proper only came into being through this process of separation in agriculture. In Adam Smith's writings this process of separation is assumed to be already completed.

Keith Tribe (1978, 88, 94) wrongly ascribed a precommercial understanding of economics to Steuart. True, he stood with one foot firmly planted in the old way of life (see Marx 1974, 83–84). Steuart's native Lanarkshire, although not far from Edinburgh or Glasgow, was surrounded by "the wildest country" that Defoe (1724–1726, 617) saw during his tour of Scotland.

Steuart, however, had his other foot tentatively pawing at the new modes of existence. We have already discussed the evictions that took place in this very region. In fact, Steuart displayed a keen sense of the nature of a market economy. He was not only connected with traditional Scottish society; he also had the opportunity to witness the unfolding of capitalist development from the vantage point of the Scottish Highlands. He also had personal ties with recent capitalistic developments. For example, his own mother, supposedly "for the sake of finding employment to her mind, had taken coal work" (Kippis 1842, 282).

Steuart also had the advantage of extensive travels. In his youth, he had compromised himself by his involvement in Jacobite conspiracies leading up to the battle of Culloden. As a result, he was forced to spend fourteen years in exile on the Continent. Such experience can be invaluable to perceptive economists. Petty's work certainly benefited from his years in Holland and Ireland. Similarly, Cantillon profited from his firsthand knowledge of the difference between Ireland and France.

Steuart himself appreciated that the practical information that he garnered during his years away from Scotland gave him an advantage in comprehending his native economy. In the dedication to his handwritten manuscript of his *Principles* in 1759, he wrote, "The best method I have found to maintain a just balance . . . has been, in discussing general points, to keep my eye off the country I inhabit at the time, and to compare the absent with the absent" (cited in Chamley 1965, 137). By availing himself of this method, even before his return to the British Isles, he was able to anticipate the exceptional nature of what was occurring in his native Scotland.

Intellectual Roots

Andrew Skinner (1966, xxxvii) believes that Steuart drew heavily from Mirabeau's *Friend of the People* (1756), whereas Paul Chamley (1965, 76–81) suggests the flow of ideas may well have gone in the other direction. A third possibility does present itself. The books of both Steuart and Mirabeau bear striking similarity to the work of Richard Cantillon. Steuart's connection with Cantillon was indirect. True, he twice cited the English version of a work published under the name Philip Cantillon (Steuart 1767, 2:22, 67), but in the first book of his, *Principles*, already completed by 1759, the same year that Philip Cantillon's work appeared, the parallels with Cantillon were more pronounced. Yet there, Richard Cantillon was not cited.

Steuart may have had privileged access to Cantillon's work prior to its publication, although I can only speculate. We do know that he dedicated the 1759 handwritten version of his *Principles* to Lady Mary Wortley Montagu (1689–1732), whom Steuart had met in Venice the previous year (Chalmers 1805, 372). This brilliant English woman of letters was often immersed in scandals that were not always literary in nature (see Halsband 1956, 268–79).

This very same Lady Mary Wortley Montagu had become, a quarter century earlier, the close friend of Mary Anne Mahoney, the wife of Richard Cantillon (see Montague 1966–67, 2:25, 29). She wrote to her sister that Cantillon's wife "eclipses most of our London beauties" (ibid., 25). In 1741, she seems to have been referring to Cantillon as "one of the prettiest men I ever saw in any country" in writing of an affair between Cantillon and the wife of the British consul in Naples, where she was staying (ibid.,

213). Almost two decades later, while taking a deep interest in the work of Steuart, she may have called Cantillon's book to the attention of her protégé in case that he himself had not already been familiar with the theories of that most important earlier, peripatetic economist.

Although Steuart depended less on the printed word than did Adam Smith, he did seem to make some use of his predecessors. Steuart wrote extensive notes on Hume's *History*, and sent the *Principles* to Hume for comments before publishing it (Skinner 1966, xlv). Another possible influence on Steuart was Robert Wallace's *A Dissertation on the Numbers of Mankind*, published in 1753, the year after Hume, in his *Political Discourses*, challenged Wallace to publish it (see Hume 1752b, 379; Hume to Montesquieu, June 1753; cited in Rotwein 1955, 184).

Steuart's work also bore some resemblance to that of James Harrington (on Harrington, see Hill 1964; Macpherson 1962). Like Steuart, Harrington opposed smallholders, called for high rents to stimulate labor, and attempted to calculate an appropriate balance among classes in which the nobility was to oversee agriculture and bear arms (see Macpherson 1962, 187, 178–79).

Steuart's Call for an Agrarian Transformation

Steuart clearly recognized the advantages for the gentry in moving with the times, accepting that the future lay in capitalism. He assumed that the nobility would not support themselves by trading. To begin with, they lacked the requisite funds (Steuart 1767, 1:84). More important, to sink to the status of a mere shopkeeper was unthinkable. The proper course for them was to establish themselves as prosperous capitalist farmers.

In a letter of 14 October 1777, he described this outcome in language that could have come from Adam Smith:

> The allurement of gain will soon engage everyone to pursue that branch of industry which succeeds best in his hands. By these means many will follow manufactures and abandon agriculture; others will prosecute their manufactures in the country, and avail themselves at the same time of portions of land, proper for gardens, grass for cows, and even for producing certain kinds of fruit necessary for their own maintenance. (cited in Chamley 1965, 87]

Steuart himself appears to have been adept at the new husbandry (Chalmers 1805, 377; Campbell 1953, 25–26). In the words of one contemporary report on his agricultural practices, "No person who is acquainted with Sir James Stewart [*sic*], but must admire his genius and zeal to promote agriculture" (Wight 1778–1784, 3:544–46). Agricultural successes such as his, however, generally necessitated costly victories over the rights of tenants.

Steuart's proposition that the gentry engage in capitalist farming represented a clarion call to break with tradition by separating large numbers of such people from their means of subsistence. In the process, the farmers would no longer be limited to the customary rents. Steuart (1769, 286) acknowledged that "raising . . . rents was thought [by some] to be robbing the present possessor," but he came out squarely in favor of the new husbandry by virtue of its ability to raise rents (ibid., 287 ff.; Steuart 1767, 1:280 ff.). In this sense, we may judge the new husbandry to have been most successful.

Steuart (1767, 1:204; see also 1:55) justified higher rents because "the surplus of the farmers . . . goes for the subsistence of others," adding, "The surplus I show to be the same thing with the value of rents." Higher rents would also serve to drive those remaining on the land to intensify agricultural production. As a result of such "silent compulsion," market forces would compel them to specialize in the production of commodities for the market, rather than continuing to produce so many goods as pure use values.

Steuart's position about rents is reminiscent of the Physiocratic school, but with a significant difference. In spite of the relatively extensive nature of the new husbandry that the Physiocrats proposed, they could suggest that the commercialization of farming would increase the supply of food on account of the large tracts of unused land in France, even though they ultimately rested their case on the net rather than the gross output.

Steuart made no such claim. Instead, he identified the march of progress with the replacement of cropland by pasture. In fact, he openly admitted that the mass of food produced would fall with the changes he recommended (Steuart 1767, 1:282; see also Malthus 1976, 106–7). The advantage of the extension of pasture was that it could increase the surplus (ibid., 1:55 ff.). When the crops had grown on the land, the people who grew them consumed a significant proportion of the harvest. Pastures require a minimum of labor, thereby leaving almost all the proceeds of the land to its owner.

Steuart versus Traditional Producers

The connection between the creation of a widespread wage-labor relationship and the social division of labor was essential to Steuart. He had no doubts that his plans required the destruction of traditional agriculture. In this respect, Steuart displayed one of his numerous affinities with the

148

Physiocrats (see Weulersse 1910, 2:697). Well before he had begun the formal study of political economy in 1737, he expressed deep concern in a letter about "the laziness of the people," such as the peasants he saw in Spain (cited in Chamley 1965, 127).

Steuart did not even seem to think the self-sufficient peasant worthy of working unimproved land. He asked his readers, "How can extended tracts of bare land be improved, but by subdividing them into small lots of about ten, fifteen or twenty acres, and letting them to those who make their livelihood (by doing) . . . things for hire" (Steuart 1769, 328). He considered it to be "evident" that these lands would be so finely sub-divided that it "is in no way sufficient to enable the possessors to main-tain themselves, and pay their rents out of the product. The land will contribute towards maintaining themselves and their family; their indus-try must support their family and pay the rent" (ibid.).

As far as Steuart (1767, 1:111) was concerned, the mode of existence of the traditional agriculturalist was appropriate only for "rude and un-civilized societies." So long as they had been free to live off the spontane-ous fruits of the earth, they could content themselves with a few wants and much idleness (ibid., 1:48, 62).

Thus Steuart (ibid., 1:65, 77; see also Marx 1977, 649) called for the "separation between parent earth and her laborious children" in order that they no longer be "suckle[d] in idleness." Otherwise, "who will increase his labour, voluntarily, in order to feed people who do not work for him-self?" (Steuart 1767, 2:174). According to him, "Any person who could calculate his labours in agriculture purely for subsistence, would find abundance of idle hours. But the question is, whether in good economy such a person would not be better employed in providing nourishment for others, than in providing for other wants" (ibid., 1:110; see also Weulersse 1910, 1:687). As a result, the lives of rural workers had to be turned to purposes not of their own choosing.

Steuart's program owed not a little to Hume (1752d, 256–57), who had called for the employment of "superfluous hands" as soldiers to extend the power of the state. Taking his cue from his countryman, Hume, and consis-tent with Turgot and the Physiocrats, Steuart joined in the call for the elim-ination of the "free hands" who resided on the land. W. Arthur Lewis recently made this interpretation of rural development fashionable once again (1954).

These superfluous workers represented a substantial "burden on the husbandman" for Steuart (1767, 1:40, 43; see also Hume 1752d, 260–61; Turgot 1766, pars. 4, 8; Weulersse 1910, 1:350; Quesnay 1758, vi). Else-where, he categorized these same people as nothing more than "superfluous mouths" (Steuart 1767, 1:58, 198, 304). Steuart even went so far as to state that insofar as a person exercised the art of agriculture, "as a direct means of subsisting . . . , the state would lose nothing though [he] . . . and his land were both swallowed up by an earthquake" (1767, 1:116; see also 4:314).

In the absence of an earthquake, what would come of the people who would be uprooted from the land? In answering this question, Steuart developed the most sophisticated analysis of primitive accumulation in the entire literature of political economy.

Steuart's Rhetoric of Primitive Accumulation

Steuart (ibid., 2:23) fretted that masses of people detached from the land could pose a serious political threat, given that capitalism threatened to unleash the dread forces of democracy. The danger was all the more troubling because the majority of people considered the property of the lairds to be illegitimate.

Steuart (ibid., 1:98) believed the poor to be incapable of self-government, tracing the "principle cause of decay in modern states [to] . . . liberty" (ibid., 93). He asserted that the Spartan republic of Lycurgus offered "the most perfect plan of political economy" (ibid., 332; see also Hume 1752d, 257–58). At one point, he even seemed to have been comparing himself with Lycurgus, referring to him as "a profound politician, who had travelled over the world with a previous intention to explore the mysteries of the science of government" (ibid., 334).

Steuart's affection for a slave society may shock modern readers, but his sentiments were more common when he was writing. As religion had lost its appeal in some circles, many writers used Sparta as a convenient image for community. For example, Samuel Adams envisioned America's future as a "Christian Sparta" (cited in McCoy 1982, 52).

The frequent admiration of Sparta owed much to Jean-Jacques Rousseau, who emphasized Sparta's collectivism and antipathy to trade (see Therborn 1976, 119–24). Praise of Sparta became a common characteristic of the tradition of civic humanism, which held that property was important because it allowed the possessor the independence to exercise civic virtue (see Pocock 1985a, 115; 1982, 92). In this vein, Goran Therborn (1976, 122) remarked:

> The Enlightenment was strongly attracted by tradition and by collectivist traditions at that. It turned to an antique-pagan heritage, instead of a medieval-christian heritage. . . . The austere public virtues of Sparta, the Roman Republic, and even the Roman Empire at its

zenith, were the social ideals of many of the *philosophes*, not a free-wheeling individualism. Rousseau admired Sparta and in the *Discourse on Inequality*, the Spartan lawgiver Lycurgus is presented as the model of a revolutionary politician.

A number of Scottish writers portrayed Sparta in a positive light, including Adam Smith's "never to be forgotten Dr. Hutcheson" (cited in Mossner and Ross 1977, 309), in his chapter "Of the Nature of Civil Laws and their Execution," commended Lycurgus to modern legislators (Hutcheson 1755, 2:310).

What made Steuart's use of Sparta unique was not his approval of totalitarian methods, but his straightforward recognition that these methods could be used to further capitalist development. He admitted the futility of his hope of re-creating a Spartan republic based on slave labor supporting a commercial society of frugal warriors.

The Slavery of the Market

While Steuart (1767, 1:51) taught that slavery was a "violent method (for) making men laborous in raising food," he understood that the market, properly arranged, could accomplish the same objectives that Spartan slavery promised. In the past, he argued, "men were . . . forced to labour because they were slaves to others; men are now forced to labour because they are slaves to their own wants" (ibid., 1:52).

What did Steuart mean by "wants"? He wrote, "Those who become servants for the sake of food, will soon become slaves" (ibid., 1:28). Thus although wage earners, unlike slaves, are formally free, Steuart understood that workers would be subject to an increasingly strict discipline. In this sense, capitalism seemed to be the next best alternative to a slave society.

Although no other classical political economist would have been so blunt, this idea was not unique to Steuart. For example, Mirabeau, whose work differed from that of Steuart in many respects (see Chamley 1965, 73 ff.), exclaimed, "The whole magic of [a] well-ordered society is that each man works for others, while believing that he is working for himself" (Mirabeau's *Philosophie Rurale*; cited in Meek 1963, 70). Cantillon's analysis of how feudalism and the market could lead to the same outcome offered an even closer parallel.

Not unexpectedly, Steuart's insensitive language did not win much acceptance. For example, one reviewer took Steuart to task on this point:

> In plain English, that by one way or another, men are made slaves by statesmen, in order that the useful may feed the useless. This is,

indeed, the present state of what is called liberty in England. But, in fact, they are not made slaves to their passions and desires, for that is common to all men. It is the hard hand of necessity at present, like that of the taskmasters in preceding times, which compels them to work. The hired husbandman has, indeed, one passion that engages him to become a slave, and to labour; it is the goading dread of starving that enslaves him, and urges him to toil without desire. (Reviewers 1767, 127)

This review should not be read as a refutation of Steuart, but as a clarification. Certainly, the reviewer's semantics, referring to hunger and poverty instead of wants, is more informative than Steuart's. Nonetheless, Steuart's presentation has the merit of reminding us of the power of the silent compulsion of the market.

Steuart (1767, 2:217) realized that the market had many advantages over the crude Spartan system, but he also understood that it could run amok. In his words, "The Lacedemonian form may be compared to the wedge.... Those of the modern states to watches, which are continually going wrong."

As a result, Steuart looked to a statesman to guide the system. This perspective led him to focus his attention on one overriding question: How were wants to be structured so that they would effectively enslave people?

Here we come to the heart of Steuart's work. Steuart found himself in a land where labor had not yet been fully subjugated to the needs of capital. His agricultural experience was well suited to equip him to become the theorist par excellence of primitive accumulation. He knew that the traditional Highlanders had wants, but they were not yet "slaves" to them in the sense that Steuart used the term. In responding to this situation, Steuart went further than any other classical political economist in trying to develop a program to integrate the traditional sector into the economy.

Steuart and The Organizing of Economic Development

Steuart (ibid., 2:80) clearly connected his desire to purge the land of free hands, as well as his antagonism toward subsistence farming, with the rise of commodity production: "Now the frequent sale of articles of the first necessity makes a distribution of inhabitants into labourers, and what we have called 'free hands.' The first are those who produce the necessaries of life; the last are those who buy them." Steuart realized that merely throwing people off the land would not necessarily lay the path for a smooth transition to capitalist social relations. He recognized the complexity of the underlying dynamic of primitive accumulation, along with the need to be specific about the nature of this momentous transformation.

Unlike other classical political economists, Steuart stressed that one cannot overlook the tempo at which changes are introduced. What may be disastrous when suddenly introduced might well be beneficial if it could be accomplished more slowly (ibid., 1:160–61, 284, chap. 19). In Steuart's words, "Sudden revolutions are constantly hurtful, and a good statesman ought to lay down his plan for arriving at perfection by gradual steps" (ibid., 1:111). The recent experience of the countries of the former Soviet Union also suggests how difficult the sudden transition to capitalism can be.

In particular, primitive accumulation required much caution. With this thought in mind, Steuart cautioned (ibid., 1:175), "A young horse is to be caressed when a saddle is put upon his back." For this reason, he called for the gradual conversion of cornfields into pasture (ibid., 1:181). Unfortunately, many modern economists, even with the benefit of hindsight, have failed to take the tempo of their project into account in confidently dismantling traditional agricultural systems around the world. In addition, some of the advisors of post-Soviet Russia could have benefited from looking at the dusty volumes that Steuart wrote.

A second consideration was more substantial. Steuart knew full well that although the Scottish gentry was able to throw masses of people off the land, eviction alone was not sufficient to force people into wage labor. Time and time again, Steuart (ibid., 1:8, 29, 237) repeated that the crux of his investigation was to discover how people came to submit voluntarily to authority. In a capitalist society, submission implied the acceptance of the wage relationship.

A third concern was closely related to the second. How could the first capitalist firm, say a shoe factory, emerge out of a noncapitalist economy? Since the factory would presumably be the first capitalist institution in the economy, the workers there could not exchange their wages to obtain the goods that they customarily consumed, except for shoes. The workers could use some of their earnings to purchase shoes, but in order to be a productive operation, the owners of the factory would have to ensure that the workers would be able to produce more shoes than they could afford to purchase with their wages.

Moreover, the workers have other needs besides shoes, even though no other commodity-producing firms are selling the goods that the workers in the shoe factory might want to purchase. Consequently, the shoe factory presumes the existence of other entities manufacturing consumer goods for sale. This phenomenon was doubly important in eighteenth-century England, where the absence of coin of small denomination led to the common practice of paying workers with a share of their product, which they then had to market on their own.

How, then, would the first factory come into existence? Paul Rosenstein-Rodan (1943; see also Hume 1752d, 260–61), writing in the midst of the devastation of World War II, brought this question to modern economists while wondering about the possibility of the re-creation of a market in war-ravaged southern and eastern Europe. Nurkse (1953) later associated the solution to this problem, which he termed, the "big push," with the Smithian tradition, but it is the very antithesis of Smith's project.

We already alluded to Adam Smith's basic answer, which we shall examine in more detail (see chapter 10). According to Smith, the first institutions were not large factories, but the works of small artisans who gradually increased the scale of their operations. Unfortunately, Smith's approach does not shed any light on the process by which the artisans became wage laborers—a central concern of Steuart and the rest of the classical political economists.

Steuart's Construction of the Social Division of Labor

Steuart (1767, 2:157) explicitly stated that the "object of our enquiry hitherto has been to discover the method of engaging a free people to concur in the advancement of one and the other, as a means of making their society live in ease, by reciprocally contributing to the relief of each others' wants." Politics, for Steuart, rather than the market, was the fundamental determinant of the social division of labor during the initial stages of capitalist development. Specifically, Steuart called upon the state to guarantee an appropriate social division of labor:

> I conclude, that the best way of binding a free society together is by multiplying reciprocal obligations and creating a general dependence between its members. This cannot be better affected, than by appropriating a certain number of the inhabitants, for the production of food required by all, and by distributing the remainder into proper classes for supplying every other want....

Steuart assumed that statesmen, whom he credited with enormous powers, would be capable of manipulating the people to create reciprocity. In his words:

> Nothing is impossible to an able statesman. When a people can be engaged to murder their wives and children, and to burn themselves, rather than submit to a foreign enemy; when they can be brought to

give their most precious effects, their ornaments of gold and silver, for the support of a common cause; . . . I think I may say, that by properly conducting and managing the spirit of a people, nothing is impossible to be accomplished. (ibid., 1:15)

If people could be moved so far to support precapitalist ends, why should the capitalist statesman be less able to direct society? Presumably, the creation of a social division of labor should not raise serious difficulties for capable leaders.

Steuart expected the statesman "to lay down his plan of political economy, and chalk out a distribution of its inhabitants" (ibid., 2:175). Elsewhere he was more specific, calling upon the statesman to "regulate the distribution of . . . classes of his people" (ibid., 2:17). He stressed the importance of this objective (ibid., 1:46).

Steuart frequently returned to the theme of the need to create an appropriate social division of labor in order to ensure a proper structuring of reciprocal wants (see ibid., 1:3, 20, 33, 46, 86, 211, 316; 2:158).

In developing the social division of labor, Steuart called upon his statesman to act "with an impartial hand" (ibid., 2:183), perhaps alluding to the famous impartial spectator of Adam Smith's *Theory of Moral Sentiments* (e.g., Smith 1759, 26).

Steuart even expressed some humanistic concerns. For example, he opposed "excessive misery among the poor" (1767, 1:277). His standards of humanism, however, were not excessively high. For example, he believed that a proper wage could be calculated from the expense accounts of hospitals and workhouses, which were hardly seats of opulence (ibid., 1:415).

But then Steuart also recognized the need to restrain his humanistic impulses: "I am very far from wishing to see any industrious person in distress for want of food. . . . But I think . . . that the more soberly our lowest classes are made to live at all times, the cheaper may our manufactures be sold" (ibid., 2:210). In this spirit, he recommended:

> If the luxurious taste and wealth of the country prevent any one who can do better, from betaking himself to a species of industry lucrative to the nation, but ungrateful to those who exercise it, the statesman must collect the children of the wretched into workhouses, and breed them to this employment, under the best regulations possible for saving every article of unnecessary expence [*sic*]. (ibid., 1:379, 98)

Steuart's proposal may suggest a deeper meaning to the term "infant industries." One can only guess at the expected fate of the poor without the protective measures advocated by Steuart. In short, he supported enslavement without slavery.

For Steuart, the statesman also had an obligation to restrict profits from rising above a certain standard (ibid., 2:185). However, he sounded substantially more emphatic when he turned to this subject, warning that "when a statesman looks coolly on, with his arms across, or takes it into his head, that it is not his business to interpose, the prices of the dexterous workman will rise" (ibid., 1:314).

Steuart and The Dialectics of Household Production

Steuart was the only classical economist to express clearly the dialectical nature of the household economy. Toward this end, he crafted a rich theory of the dialectical role of self-provisioning in the course of economic development. In the process, he provided the outlines of a program to modify the condition of labor. His intention was that more and more people would have no choice but to accept wage labor. In Marx's words, workers would be "powerless as an independent force, that is to say, [they would be unable to exist] outside of this capitalist relationship" (1963–1971, 391).

Steuart (1767, 1:29, 8, 62) ultimately wanted to restrict the masses' access to their traditional means of subsistence in order to ensure their "voluntary subordination," but as we already noted, he understood that this transformation of the populace would have to occur over an extended period of time.

At times, Steuart saw the same problem from the perspective of food prices. He realized that when food is too expensive, wages have to increase to permit subsistence. He also recognized that self-provisioning would lead to a lower price of grain (ibid., 2:89–99). As a result, employers could hold down the wage rate and enjoy a higher rate of surplus value (ibid., 1:197, 304). Recall that many mercantilists, and even David Hume, suggested that when food is too cheap, even those people without access to any substantial degree of self-provisioning, will not feel as much compulsion to labor (see chapter 5).

Steuart saw that low food prices did not represent a serious threat to employers in Scotland, since the economic situation of the people who had been displaced from their land was so dire. For example, Steuart estimated the wage rate of a day laborer according to the cost of grain required for subsistence. He found that spinners required two days' wages to nourish themselves for a single day (ibid., 1:304; see also Smith 1776, I.x.b., 134).

According to Steuart, this enforced poverty was certain to have a wholesome effect on labor. He was confident that leisure would be restricted (Steuart 1767, 1:35; see also Pollard 1978, 144) and labor would become more intense (Steuart 1767, 1:139; 2:176). Specifically, he expected that once workers cease the production of a diverse set of use values, a regime of "good economy" would commence.

Otherwise, how could a family survive? Assuming that the typical worker had a vegetable garden and potato patch in addition to a cow, self-provisioning could help feed the family. Steuart (1769, 291–92) expected that the meager earnings of the wife's spinning would be sufficient to meet all other expenses.

In short, Steuart's hostility to the household economy was conditional, since he recognized its value as a prop to the early capitalist accumulation process. Recall his plan to throw small farmers off the land only after they had improved barren holdings (Steuart 1767, 1:112–13; see also 1769, 328). For Steuart, in the stage of emergent capitalist development, a cottage industry supported by a high degree of self-provisioning was the preferred course, so long as the changes were not overly abrupt. The sort of putting-out system that Steuart recommended, developing in tandem with the strong household economy, could allow business to begin with a minimum of investment in plant and equipment. As Steuart (1767, 1:395) maintained, "People . . . must glean before they can expect to reap."

Steuart anticipated that the market would be especially effective in mobilizing the labor of children as capitalist social relations began to gel. In a market economy, children would no longer dissipate their time on such relatively unproductive chores as the herding of a few geese. Along with women, they would be set to work spinning (ibid., 1:136–38).

Once capitalist relations would take hold, Steuart expected that the economy would prosper because of gains in efficiency, as well as the increased efforts of the workers. He predicted that the typical farm would come to be regulated by a precise economy: "Cattle consume the exact quantity of grain and forage necessary; what remains is money; a superfluous egg is money; a superfluous day of cart, of a horse, a superfluous hour of a farmer is all money to the farmer" (ibid., 1:72).

In an apparent anticipation of the modern economic theory of labor (Schultz 1968), Steuart recognized that with development, "Time becomes more precious" (1767, 1:230; see also 303 ff.), although he gave no indication that the working people would ever enjoy any benefits from the increasing value of their productivity. Eventually, the working class was expected to develop that most wonderful of all qualities, "a taste for labour" (ibid., 1:200, 202)—all as a result of a well-designed market.

According to Steuart's vision, this transformation would set in motion a broad process of capital accumulation. Over time, the variable capital per worker would increase with the subsidence of the household sector. The increasing mass of labor, as well as its heightened productivity, was supposed to allow capitalists to pay a larger wage bill. In addition, as more commodities come on the market, the problem that Rosenstein-Rodan described would recede.

Steuart, however, did not sense the full potential of capital. Like the Physiocrats, he still saw the world from the standpoint of the profit of capitalist farmers. In addition, Steuart overestimated capital's ability to control the Scottish Highlands at the time. For example, a half century later, the agent of the duke of Sutherland, in attempting to get textile entrepreneurs to invest in factories on his employer's property, spoke honestly of the tenants: "They have all some land—labour remarkably cheap" (cited in Ross 1973, 228). Yet profit-seeking businesspeople did not stake their money on Scottish Highland labor.

Steuart's work is invaluable in understanding the early stages of capital accumulation. Certainly, the other classical political economists have little to offer in helping us understand why industry was slow to emerge in the Highlands.

The point that Robert Urquhart (1996, 403) made about Steuart's approach certainly holds for his analysis of primitive accumulation: "Steuart's distinctive significance . . . is that he is the last major political economist to have a true theoretical commitment to complexity." Perhaps one of Steuart's contemporaries was able to see as far and clearly concerning the nature of early economic development as Steuart was, but if so, he covered up any evidence of that insight.

Steuart's Hostile Reception

Modern historians of political economy, a breed noted for its excellence in perusing the most obscure documents, have largely ignored Steuart. With few exceptions, such as S. R. Sen (1957), Paul Chamley (1965), Andrew Skinner (1981; 1993), and Michael Hudson (1992), scholars have scrupulously avoided the social content of Steuart's work (for a convenient bibliography of this sparse literature, see Akhtar 1979). A search of all economics journals collected in JSTOR (jstor.org) found the name Steuart mentioned a mere 83 times, compared to 1,669 for Adam Smith.

While few authors credit Steuart, many in the past have profited from his books without attribution. P. Dockes regards von Thünen as a mere derivative of Steuart. Indeed, Steuart (1767, 1:187 ff.) clearly anticipates von Thünen in describing the economic determination of the locations of gardens and fields. Since economists sometimes credit von Thünen with anticipating much of what became marginal analysis, conventional economic theory might well afford Steuart some of the honors usually poured on Smith for his occasional modernisms (Dockes 1969).

This neglect is astonishing considering that Steuart was the most important economist of his day. After all, he was the author of the first complete English treatise on political economy. Moreover, besides *The Wealth of Nations,* no other comparable works were published until Ricardo's *Principles.*

So why the thundering silence with respect to Steuart's achievements? In part, Steuart earned his neglect by adopting a different class perspective than most classical political economists. Unlike Adam Smith (1759, bk. 6, chap. 1), who mocked pretensions of the nobility and lauded prudence, Steuart pointed to the nobility as the appropriate source of future class leadership. For example, Steuart complained that the middle class held the nobility in contempt, except during wars. He insisted that in times of military crises, those same characteristics that impede the nobility's success in the humdrum world of bourgeois calculation suddenly become admirable (Steuart 1767, 1:83).

Steuart (ibid., 1:320) was not one to base his work on the airy fiction of a social contract. Instead, he wrote with a blunt honesty about the harsh nature of capitalist development, seeking out the real forces that impelled people to produce surplus value for others, especially the destruction of the self-sufficient household.

Whereas most of his contemporaries described historical evolution in terms of the romance of natural law, Steuart (ibid., 1:237) was willing to investigate the real forces that caused "men . . . to submit to labour." His sophisticated application of the classical theory of primitive accumulation made his work an embarrassment to the mainstream political economists who pretended that capitalist development was a voluntary affair. In this respect, he was far more truthful than the rest of the classical political economists combined.

From the first, Steuart understood the uniqueness of his efforts. He observed:

> No problems of political economy seem more obscure than those which influence the multiplication of the human species, and which determine the distribution and employment of them, so as best to advance the prosperity of each particular society. . . . I have nowhere found these matters treated to my wish, nor have I ever been able to satisfy myself concerning them. (ibid., 1:89)

Steuart was correct. He was unique among the central figures of political economy in his emphasis on the creation of a social division of labor. Yes, Malachy Postlethwayt (1751, 1:118) touched on the social division of labor in arguing that "prosperity of a trading nation to consist in the multiplying of the number of new trades; that is to say, in the multiplying of the different species of mechanics, artificers and manufactures," but he was a secondary figure at best.

Public acclaim eluded Steuart. Indeed, he seemed to realize that he was flying in the face of the prevailing fashion in political economy. He asked his readers, "Is it not of the greatest importance to examine with *candour*, the operations by which all of Europe has been engaged in a system of policy so generally declaimed against, and so contrary to that which we hear daily recommended as the best" (Steuart 1767, 1:xix; emphasis added).

Steuart recognized that he could have eliminated some of the resistance to his book by adopting a style that would "prevent certain expressions here and there interpreted, from making the slightest impression upon a reader of delicate sentiments," but:

> Nothing would have been so easy as to soften many passages, where the politician appears to have snatched the pen out of the hand of the private citizen; but as I write for such only who can follow a close reasoning, and attend to the general scope of the whole inquiry, I have, purposely, made no correction; but continued painting, in the strongest colours. (ibid., 1:xvii)

Steuart grossly misjudged the reaction of his readers. Despite the reviewers' obvious respect for Steuart's insights, they wanted to reject his conclusions. An anonymous reviewer in *Scots Magazine* admitted as much. Following a Smithian line of reasoning, the reviewer argued: "It is the common interest which is properly subject to laws; while the management of the particular interest of each individual, not interfering with that of the public, ought to be left to itself" (Review 1767b, 199).

Instead, this same reviewer charged that in Steuart's work, "we behold the dismal prospect of millions enslaved for the gratification of the few" (ibid.). Yet the same reviewer could not easily dismiss him:

> The observations he has made, and the intelligence he has acquired, during his residence in several parts of Europe have furnished him with the most authentic facts for the foundation of his reasoning; and a capacious philosophical genius which has been employed in producing a composition which cannot fail to be admired by all who are able to comprehend it. But whether this admiration may not, in some

> sort, resemble that which we bestow on a well-constructed instrument of war, calculated either to defend or to destroy, according to the hands that it falls into [is an open question]. (ibid.)

This astute reviewer was indeed correct. Steuart's work was "a well-constructed instrument of war." Neither this reviewer nor the reading public appreciated Steuart's bluntness about the role of government in stimulating economic development. Polite society preferred to pretend that economic progress was a neutral affair, guided by market forces.

Steuart's contemporary readers understood that he was a central figure. One particularly unsympathetic reviewer felt compelled to label Steuart a "penetrating genius" (Review 1767c, 125), and another still less sympathetic one termed his work "a code for future statesmen and ministers" (Review 1767a, 32). The latter of these two reviewers was typical in his attitude toward Steuart. He feigned surprise that the state had a major role in constructing the economy, claiming: "We have no idea of a statesman having any connection with the affair, and we believe that the superiority which England has at present over all the world in point of commerce is owning to her excluding statesmen from the executive part of commercial concerns" (ibid., 412). In fact, the East India Company solicited Steuart's advice and later gave him a diamond ring as a token of gratitude for his efforts (see Chalmers 1805, 381). Yet, for the most part, we hear little about Sir James Steuart.

One puzzle remains. Why was Steuart singled out for such rough treatment when David Hume said much the same thing in his essay "Of Commerce"?

Parallels between Hume and Steuart

Edward Gibbon once referred to David Hume as the Tacitus of Scotland (Pocock 1985, 125). Unlike Tacitus, who wrote his history of the conquest of foreign barbarians, Hume shared the nationality of the "uncivilized" peasants who fell under the heel of the modern Caesar—capital. He spoke with a broad Scottish accent, although he advised his friends to anglicize both their written and spoken language (Mossner 1954, 370–75).

Hume had the ability to write like both Steuart and Smith within the same paragraph, suggesting that the gulf between these supposedly polar opposites was not nearly as wide as it might seem. After all, in many ways, Steuart merely expressed truths that Smith preferred to shroud in silence.

Nonetheless, assessing Hume's relationship to Steuart is not a straightforward matter. Allegedly, Steuart had written the first part of his *Principles* by 1749, prior to the publication of Hume's famous essays. Hume did express approval of Steuart's *Principles* prior to its publication (Skinner 1993, 32).

Without access to the early version of Steuart's work, I am not sure how much of the similarity between Steuart and Hume is due to Hume's influence, and how much reflects their shared culture.

In his essay "Of Commerce," Hume (1752d, 256) explained that "the bulk of every state may be divided into *husbandmen* and *manufacturers*." He then went on, "Time and experience improve so much these arts, that the land may easily maintain a much greater of men, than those who are immediately employed in its culture, or who furnish the more necessary manufactures to such as are employed." As a result, society finds itself with "superfluous hands," who can either be used to produce luxuries or "the sovereign [may] lay claim to them, and employ them in fleets and armies, to encrease the domination of the state abroad, and spread its fame over distant nations" (ibid., 256).

Hume (ibid., 257) also observed, "A state is never greater than when all its superfluous hands are employed in the service of the public." Still, after posing the possibility of emulating Sparta, Hume (ibid., 259) concluded: "I answer, that it appears to me, almost impossible; and that because ancient policy was violent, and contrary to the more natural and usual course of things." At this point, Hume (ibid., 260–61) noted:

> Where manufactures and mechanic arts are not cultivated, the bulk of the people must apply themselves to agriculture; and if their skill and industry encrease, there must be a great superfluity from their labour beyond what suffices to maintain them. They have no temptation, therefore, to encrease their skill and industry; since they cannot exchange that superfluity for any commodities, which may serve either to their pleasure or vanity. A habit of indolence naturally prevails.

Then Hume (ibid., 261) penned his famous expression: "Everything in the world is purchased by labour; and our passions are the only causes of labour."

Like so many of his day, Hume (1752e, 300) taught that this passion could be turned to serve the interests of capital, suggesting: "There is no craving or demand of the human mind more constant and insatiable than that for exercize and employment; and this desire seems the foundation of most of our passions and pursuits."

Once labor is harnessed to these passions, farmers will produce a surplus, which they will then exchange for luxuries. In Hume's (1752d, 261) words: "When a nation abounds in manufactures and mechanic arts, the . . . [agricultural] superfluity, which arises from . . . labour is lost; but is exchanged with manufactures for those commodities, which men's luxury now makes them covet."

Hume's analysis of luxury differed from that of Smith. For Smith, the choice was between luxuries and goods that serve a mass market. Hume, in contrast, was concerned about putting the superfluous hands to work producing luxuries, rather than letting them fall into inactivity: "Luxury, when excessive, is the source of many ills; but is in general preferable to sloth and idleness" (ibid., 280).

Smith believed that mass production for the home market was the key to economic success, but Hume did not share that opinion. He speculated that "in most nations, foreign trade has preceded any refinement in home manufacturers, and given birth to domestic luxury" (ibid., 263).

Hume considered the same alternative with which Steuart toyed. He wrote:

> The greatness of the sovereign and the happiness of the state are, in great measure, united with regard to trade and manufacturers. It is a violent method, and in most cases impracticable, to oblige the labourer to toil, in order to raise from the land more than what subsists himself and family. Furnish him with manufactures and commodities, and he will do it of himself. Afterwards you will find it easy to seize some part of his superfluous labour, and employ it in the public service, without giving him his wonted return. Being accustomed to industry, he will find this less grievous, than if, at once, you obliged him to an augmentation of labour without any reward. (ibid., 262)

All in all, the flow of ideas is remarkably similar to that of Steuart. For example, Hume expressed concern about creating the proper mix of agriculture and industry. He noted that although manufactures are advantageous, "a too great disproportion among the citizens weakens any state" (ibid., 265).

Like both Steuart and Smith, Hume (1752f, 32–33) was distrustful of the masses, yet he understood that the state depended on their acquiescence: "Nothing appears more surprizing to those, who consider human affairs with a philosophical eye, than the easiness with which the many are governed by the few. . . . [A]s FORCE is always on the side of the governed, the governors have nothing to support them but [the] opinion [of the masses]."

Fearing the masses, Hume hoped to keep them ignorant enough to maintain their allegiance to the existing order of things. For example, in

discussing the execution of Charles II in his *History of England*, Hume
(n.d., 4:491) wrote:

> If ever, on any occasion, it were laudable to conceal truth from the
> populace, it must be confessed that the doctrine of resistance affords
> such an example, and that all speculative reasoners ought to observe,
> with regard to this principle, the same cautious silence, which the
> law in every species of government have ever prescribed to them-
> selves. Government is instituted in order to restrain the fury and
> injustice of the people, and is being always founded on opinion, not
> on force, it is dangerous to weaken, by these speculations, the rever-
> ence which the multitude owe to authority, and to instruct them
> beforehand that the case can ever happen when they may be freed
> from their duty of allegiance. Or should it be found impossible to
> restrain the licence of human disquisitions, it must be acknowledged
> that the doctrine of obedience ought alone to be *inculcated* and that
> exceptions, which are rare, ought never or seldom be mentioned in
> popular reasoning or discourses.

Like Steuart, Hume (1752b, 419–20) realized the necessity of creating a
social division of labor in order to jumpstart capitalist accumulation, asserting: "The most natural way, surely, of encouraging husbandry, is, first,
to excite other kinds of industry, and thereby afford the labourer a ready
market for his commodities, and a return of such goods as may contribute
to his pleasure and enjoyment. This method is infallible and universal."

Hume stood apart from Steuart in one respect: he put relatively less
reliance on primitive accumulation compared to capital accumulation. In
other respects, as we noted above, Hume was much closer to Steuart than
to Smith, yet contemporary students of classical political economy commonly speak of Smith and Hume in the same breath, while denigrating
Steuart as nothing more than a late mercantilist.

In truth, what separates Hume, Steuart, and Smith is a matter of style,
not substance. Smith set out to put the best possible face on capitalist
development. Steuart was more forthright and detailed in his analysis. As
a result, he never received a warm reception for his efforts.

The Circumvention of Steuart

Even those who shared Steuart's views on primitive accumulation seemed
to fear associating themselves with his name. For example, our old friend,
the Reverend Joseph Townsend (1786, 430), whom we have already met as
the "Well Wisher to Mankind," may well have been favorably referring to

Steuart when he wrote that "the best politicians in Europe" agreed with his own condemnation of the poor laws. According to Townsend (ibid.), that particular "nobleman, who stands foremost among the literati in the North of Britain, has more freely and more fully delivered his opinion." Indeed, the sixth section of his book, which discussed the role of a wise legislator and the need to "confirm the natural bonds of society," sounds more than a bit like Steuart (ibid., 406 ff.).

Occasionally, published works would refer to Steuart's views on money or other matters, but those whose interest in political economy was primarily theoretical were generally silent regarding Steuart in discussing abstract matters. Take the case of Jean-Baptiste Say (1880, 206), who misspelled Steuart's name when citing him as an authority. This reference merely lumps Smith and Steuart together "in thinking, that the labour of the slave is dearer and less productive than that of the freeman" (ibid.). When dealing with more important questions, he left any debt to Steuart unacknowledged. For instance, in a chapter in his *Cours Complet* titled "The Influence of Social Life on the Production of Riches," Say (1843, 253–58) scrupulously avoided mention of any conflict in creating a social division of labor. In the place of primitive accumulation, Say (ibid., 233) wrote of "a concert of wills." Once the matter of primitive accumulation was put aside, Say could then address the relationship between the division of labor and the social division of labor:

> I will not repeat here, Sirs, what I have said about the division of labor. . . . You have to recall that this prodigious growth of human power is principally due to the possibility of concluding exchanges. . . . The progress of industry establishes bonds, relations among men, by means of which they are at the same time each independent on his side, and yet obliged to manage himself reciprocally. (ibid., 234, 237)

Say, however, neglected to mention Steuart's name in this discussion.

Even Steuart's modern editor, a sympathetic scholar with wide-ranging knowledge of both Steuart and his milieu, departs from his usual detached attitude with respect to Steuart to insert the comment about Steuart's insights into the division of labor: "Statements of this kind are all that Steuart had to offer on the division of labour" (Steuart 1966, 1, 89n). Indeed!

Such remarks merely confirm the usual practice of relegating Steuart to the status of an obscure mercantilist. They would lead the casual reader to expect to have little to learn from what Steuart saw or said concerning the development of capital. They encourage the reader to turn from Steuart to the likes of Adam Smith, whose analysis might seem to represent a more scientific viewpoint.

Steuart and Smith

The public had to wait until almost a quarter century after Steuart's death, for a British author to offer a strongly positive opinion regarding Steuart. In a rather obscure work, Daniel Wakefield (1804, 3) judged Smith to be an "inferior copy" of Steuart, charging:

> Few writers have been under equal obligations to another, as Doctor Adam Smith to Sir James Steuart, and but few have been so entirely destitute of candour and gratitude, as in no place to acknowledge the debt, or to pay a tribute to the fame of their instructor. The style of the Wealth of Nations renders the work popular, though . . . obscurity frequently supplies the place of profundity. (ibid.; see also Marx 1859, 167–68)

Wakefield was the first of a series of writers to comment on the practice of plagiarizing Steuart, "that great MASTER of political science, to whose invaluable work, succeeding writers have had recourse, as to the grand storehouse of knowledge" (ibid., 3).

A couple of years later, an anonymous reviewer, whom Donald Winch (1966, 24–25) identified as James Mill, while praising Smith's virtues with respect to his great "mercantilist" rival, acknowledged the value of Steuart's emphasis on detail (Review 1806a, 231–32). This apparently disparaging remark bears some similarity to Marx's complementary evaluation of Steuart, to which I will turn in a moment.

Two years later, a reviewer of Steuart's collected works mentioned his writings concerning "the influence of political economy on civil government." He noted: "To this topic, also, Dr. Smith has only incidentally averted; and here, likewise, in the few observations he makes on it, we find him tread closely in the footsteps of his precursor" (Review 1806b, 115).

The next flash of recognition came from none other than Dugald Stewart, who may be best remembered as Smith's eulogist. Stewart (1855, 2:458) told his students:

> With respect to NATIONAL WEALTH, I have all along recommended, and must beg leave again to recommend, Mr. Smith's Inquiry, as the book with which the student may, with the most advantage, begin his researches on the subject; not only on account of the comprehensive outline it exhibits of its various parts, but as it is the Code which is now almost universally appealed to, over all Europe, as the highest authority which can be quoted in support of any political argument. The work of Sir James Steuart, too, besides some ingenious speculations of his own, contains a great mass of accurate details.

A few years later, Marx (1859, 167–68) also judged Smith's omission of Steuart harshly:

> Adam Smith records the results of Steuart's research as dead facts. The Scottish proverb ["Mony mickles mark a muckle"] that if one has gained a little it's often easy to gain much, but the difficulty is to gain a little, has been applied by Adam Smith to intellectual wealth as well, and with meticulous care he accordingly keeps the sources secret to which he is indebted for the little and turns it into much.

Unlike Steuart, Smith wrote what the reading public wanted to find. Smith expressed trust that the market alone was capable of bringing about economic development. In contrast to Steuart, who attributed the development of reciprocal obligations to the actions of statesmen, Smith (1978, VI.46, 348) credited this evolution to voluntary market relationships, asserting that a "bartering and trucking spirit is the cause of the separation of trades and improvements in arts."

Where Steuart credited the statesman with the power to do good, Smith's statesman was certain to do enormous harm. For Smith, the statesman was but a "crafty and insidious animal" (Smith 1976, IV.ii.39, 468). In the paragraph following his immortal metaphor of the invisible hand, Smith (ibid., IV.ii.10, 456) charged:

> The statesman, who should attempt to direct private people in what manner they ought to employ their capitals, would not only load himself with a most unnecessary attention, but assume an authority which could safely be trusted, not only to no single person, but to no council or senate whatever, and which would nowhere be so dangerous as in the hands of a man who had folly and presumption enough to fancy himself fit to exercise it.

Of course, Steuart never suggested that his statesman determine how people should deploy their capital. His statesman was more concerned about how people without capital should be deployed.

Steuart and Arthur Young

Indeed, Steuart seemed destined to appeal mostly to those whose interests were more practical than theoretical or ideological. We find one of the most remarkable echoes of Steuart is found in Arthur Young's *Travels in France.* In assessing the importance of Young, the longtime secretary of the British Board of Agriculture, keep in mind that almost none of the major figures of classical political economy except Steuart had much agri-

STEUART'S SECRET HISTORY 167

cultural experience. The one exception to this generalization was Richard Jones, an avid gardener, whom Harriet Martineau addressed as "My dear King of Roses" (cited in P. James 1979, 283), the same Richard Jones whose knowledge of growing plants supplied him with the penetrating insight with which he demolished classical rent theory.

Although Young is rarely counted among the significant classical economists, all of his contemporaries seemed ready to credit him as being a major authority on agricultural affairs. In late-eighteenth-century parliamentary debates concerning economic matters, Young's name came up far more rarely than that of Adam Smith (Kirk 1979, 510). In this sense, his response to Steuart represents a test of the practical value of Steuart's work by an individual who had little sympathy for matters of pure theory.

Young (1794, 366) described Steuart as "a genius of superior cast." Like Steuart, Young (ibid., 365) judged the success of an agricultural system by its contribution to the deepening of the social division of labor. After a long discussion of the subject, Young (ibid., 312) concluded: "The size of farms is most beneficial, in general, which secures the greatest produce in the market; or, in other words, converted into money"; although he later qualified this conclusion with the remark: "In the preceding observation, I have had rented farms only in view" (ibid., 315). However, Young was no great friend of self-provisioning. In a long passage that reflected the ideas of Steuart, although the latter's name was misspelled, Young (ibid., 427) wrote:

> It is a remarkable circumstance in the agriculture, or rather in the domestic economy of France, that the culture of hemp or flax, for home uses pervades every part of the kingdom. It is a curious question how far this is beneficial or not to the general interests of the national prosperity. On the one hand, in favour of this system it may be urged, that the national prosperity being nothing more than the united prosperity of single families, if any such article of economy be advantageous to individuals, it must be so to the nation at large; that it cannot fail of being beneficial to a poor man's family to have the women and children industriously employed on clothing the whole rather than forced to buy such articles at an expense of money which they may not be able to procure. By means of industry, thus exerted, a poor family is rendered as independent as its situation admits. All of them are likewise warmer, and more comfortably clothed, as far as linen is concerned, than if it were bought; for whatever demands money will be consumed with much more caution than if the result merely of labour. . . . A modern society flourishes by the mutual

exchange of the products of land for the manufactures of towns; a natural connection of one with another, and it may be remarked, that in proportion as the exchange is rapid from a great consumption, in such proportion will a people generally flourish. If every family in the country have a patch of flax or hemp for its own supply of all the manufactures founded on these materials, this beneficial intercourse of the country with the town, is so far cut off, and no circulation takes place. If the practice be good in flax, it is good in wool; and every family should have a sufficient number of sheep, to cloth [sic] themselves in woolens; and if every little village have its little tanner, the same supposition may be extended to leather. A patch of vines furnishes the beverage of the family; and thus, by simple domestic industry, all wants are supplied; and a poor family, as it would be improperly called, would have no occasion to resort to the market for any thing to buy. But with nothing to sell; . . . [A] minute division of the soil into small properties always attacks the existence of towns, that is to say, of what Sir James Stewart [sic] calls the free hands of a society. A countryman living on his own little property with his family industriously employed in manufacturing for all their own wants, without exchange, connection, or dependence on any one, offers, indeed, a spectacle of rural comfort, but a species absolutely inconsistent with the prosperity of a modern society.

In what sense was this spectacle of rural comfort inconsistent with the prosperity of modern society? Young (ibid., 27) estimated that French agriculture was able to deliver food to market at a very low cost: "Living is reckoned cheap here. . . . As I conceive the English to have made far greater advances in the useful arts, and in manufactures, than the French have done, England ought to be the cheaper country. What we meet with in France, is a cheap mode of living, which is quite another consideration." According to his detailed calculations, "The consumption of bread, and the price of labour [were] about 76 percent cheaper in France than in England" (ibid., 339–40), just as Steuart had predicted would be the case under such circumstances. The problem lay elsewhere. Primitive accumulation was a prerequisite for the development of the social relations of capitalist production.

Again, Young (ibid., 322) clearly revealed the logic of the early marketplace:

> The most industrious and hard labouring of our poor peasants, are not those who keep their little gardens in the best order and cultivation; but such, on the contrary as make inferior earnings, that mark some-

thing of debility. . . . No labour is so wretchedly performed, and so dear, as that of hired hands accustomed to labour for themselves; there is a disgust, and a listlessness, that cannot escape an intelligent observer; and nothing but real distress will drive such little proprietors to work at all for others; so that I have seen, in the operosely cultivated parts of France, labour comparatively dear, and ill performed, amidst swarms of half wild people. . . . Can anything be apparently so absurd, as a strong hearty man walking some miles, and losing a day's work which ought to be worth 15 or 20s. in order to sell a dozen of eggs, or a chicken, the value of which would not equal the labour of conveying it, were the people usefully employed? This ought to convince us, that these small occupations are a real loss of labour.

Just what did Young mean by a "real loss of labour"? Certainly, he did not mean that peasants who worked on their own account were lazy. Young himself had written, "Give a man the secure possession of a bleak rock, and he will turn it into a garden" (ibid., 45). With a revealing turn of a phrase, Young recalled, "I saw nothing respectable on small properties, except a most unremitting industry" (ibid., 316). After all, for Young, as for many of his contemporaries, unremitting work was not respectable unless it was performed for wages.

What of the time dissipated in carting insignificant quantities of produce to market? On several occasions, Young sneered at peasants who dissipated their energy in trifling transactions (see ibid., 81, 306). Yet he knew enough peasant life to realize that market day was not strictly an economic affair. It was a time for socializing by people who were often cut off from society. The peasant whom he met carrying two chickens to a market twenty-four miles away may not have been behaving economically, but we have no reason to believe that he or she was acting irrationally (ibid., 306). All in all, Steuart could not have asked for a more devoted disciple than Young.

Intellectual Primitive Accumulation

Steuart never realized that his work would eventually win modest appreciation. In the last year of his life, frustrated by the lack of public acceptance of his ideas, he wrote of his deceased dog, "Were I to write his life, it would be a work as voluminous as my *Political Oeconomy* and perhaps as little relished by the public" (cited in Skinner 1966, iv).

The reference to "dead dogs" brings up a curious coincidence. Marx

170

(1859, 167), writing of Steuart's eclipse, said: "Steuart remained even more of 'a dead dog' than Spinoza appeared to be Moses Mendelssohn in Lessing's time." On another occasion, Marx applied the very same metaphor to Hegel, whose work was also related to that of Steuart (see Marx to Kugelmann, 27 June 1870, in Marx and Engels 1975, 225).

Over the years, Hegel's reputation fared much better than Steuart's. To some extent, however, Steuart may have been responsible for the recognition that Hegel received.

In his youth, Hegel drew heavily on the unacknowledged Steuart, all the while praising Smith (see Chamley 1965, 142–47; Dickey 1987, 192). Indeed, Steuart's discussion of double competition bears considerable similarity to Hegel's dialectic.

Hegel would not have been alone in claiming Steuart's original research as his own. Malthus, for example, praised Steuart in private correspondence with Ricardo (see Ricardo 1951–1973, 6:33–35), yet we search his published work in vain looking for a reference to Steuart. Other writers (see Young 1794, 318; Steuart 1767, 4:315; Stewart 1855, 1:150–51), including even Adam Smith, fell to publishing Steuart's ideas as their own. In the words of Smith's pupil and lifelong friend, the earl of Buchan:

> As for the great work, the *Political Oeconomy*, it is needless to praise it, for the public will do ample justice to it, when it has thrown from its literary meal the high-seasoned cookeries of the plagiarists, who have obtruded Sir James's facts, principles, and reasoning, on the world, without acknowledging from whence they were derived. (cited in Chamley 1965, 26)

We might value the earl's words even more highly if they had not been lifted verbatim from those published earlier by Archibald Hamilton (ibid.).

In short, the same honesty that allowed Steuart to produce such an insightful theoretical system guaranteed his obscurity. Given this obscurity, political economists seemed to realize that taking credit for Steuart's work was relatively riskless. Moreover, to acknowledge Steuart would lend credence to his frank treatment of the process of capital accumulation. Thus Steuart, the greatest classical theorist of primitive accumulation, found himself the victim of a primitive accumulation of a literary sort. We are all the poorer for the lack of attention given to this seminal mind.

Obfuscation of Class

They were standing on a plank which had been laid across a tanning pit; the doctor, who was talking warmly on his favorite subject, the division of labor, forgetting the precarious ground on which he stood, plunged headlong into the nauseous pool. He was dragged out, stripped, and carried with blankets and conveyed home on a sedan chair.—*London Times*, 6 August 1790

Smith, The Unworldly Professor?

Smith's theory of primitive accumulation has heretofore passed unnoticed. Probably, Smith would have been pleased with the lack of attention to this aspect of his work. After all, he was so intent on minimizing the role of class conflict that bursts of harsh realism rarely intruded into Smith's presentation.

Perhaps Smith felt justified in taking this approach. In his early essay on the history of astronomy, he asserted that intellectual effort is nothing more than a response to the discomfort that the mind feels in the face of contradictory phenomena. As a result, he went so far as to identify science as an attempt to discover the underlying harmonies in order to "sooth[e] the imagination" (Smith 1790a, 46). Primitive accumulation is hardly a soothing subject.

In his efforts to calm, Adam Smith became a highly abstract writer who used charming prose to disarm his readers. He himself commended this tactic to his students, telling them that if they wanted to sway an unsympathetic audience, "we are not to shock them by affirming what we are satisfied is disagreeable, but are to conceal our design and beginning at a distance, bring them slowly on to the main point and having gained the more remote ones we get the nearer ones of consequence" (Smith 1762–63, 140–41). Just compare Smith's advice here with Steuart's description of his own uncompromising style.

In addition, Smith (1759, VII.iv.25, 336) himself described the weight that he placed on persuasion, writing, "The desire of being believed, the desire of persuading, of leading and directing other people, seems to me to be one of the strongest of all our natural desires. It is, perhaps, the instinct on which is founded the faculty of speech, the characteristic faculty of human nature."

Awareness of Smith's rhetorical practices helps solve a riddle that has troubled many of his readers: Why did Smith, who supposedly has so much to reveal about the nature of economic activity, have so little to say about the most significant contemporary developments in British economic society? This silence is most apparent in his discussion of the production process. Smith (see 1976, II.i.9, 280) made only passing reference to modern industry. Instead of textile mills, we hear of a pin factory, which Smith himself once deprecated as a "frivolous example" (1978, vi.34, 343). Thomas S. Ashton (1925, 281; see also Michl 1993, 331) wrote: "One may echo Dr. Clapham's regret 'that Adam Smith did not go a few miles from Kirkcaldy to the Carron Works to see them turning and boring their cannonades instead of his silly pin factory.' "

Charles Kindleberger (1976) attempted to explain this defect of *The Wealth of Nations* by writing off the author as an "unworldly" professor. Similarly, the usually perceptive Robert Coats (1962, 47; see also Seligman 1910, xi) explained Smith's lack of material on the specifics of commodity production by labeling Smith as an "economist . . . the domestic period." Such terminology does nothing to resolve the paradox of Smith, so long referred to as a scientific economist despite his great shortcomings. We would get no further by attributing his omissions and oversights to a lack of foresight, as Richard Koebner (1959) once argued.

What, then, could the Smith of Kindleberger, Coats, or Koebner possibly teach us about the wealth of nations? In truth, Smith was far from the unworldly professor that his commentators made him out to be. He won the close friendship of the wealthy merchants of Glasgow (Stewart 1811, 300). In fact, he owed his initial appointment as a professor, in part, to his close connections with them (Scott 1934, 46–48). Later in life, he became the intimate of some of the most powerful members of British society (Hartwell 1978, 130–35). Even the prime minister of England is said to have declared himself to be Smith's disciple (Rae 1895, 404), although we might note that this same illustrious disciple also wished to set pauper children to toil in workhouses to be known as "colleges of industry" (Pollard 1965, 192).

The supposedly unworldly Smith clearly understood the value of applied economics. He apparently began *The Wealth of Nations* in response to a request from Charles Townshend for material on "French finance, its administrative method, taxation and public borrowing" (Fay 1956, 151; see also Mossner and Ross 1977, 328n; 378n; Campbell and Ross 1981, 88;

but see Viner 1965, 86). His appointment as a commissioner of customs may well have been a reward for this aspect of his work (see Campbell and Ross 1981, 88). In addition, Smith seems to have played an active role in the banking controversies in Scotland (Gherity 1993).

Smith's association with practical economic affairs certainly influenced his book. For example, Smith also drew on his business friends, such as Alexander Cochrane, in preparing the original edition of his book (see Scott 1934, 81). One contemporary, a Sir T. Munroe, recalled:

> I remember about the time of the appearance of *The Wealth of Nations*, that the Glasgow merchants were as proud of the work as if they had written it themselves; and some of them said that it was no wonder that Adam Smith had written such a book, as he had the advantage of their society, in which the same doctrines were circulated with the punch every day. (cited in Hutchison 1988, 400)

Later, Smith's experience as a commissioner also left its mark in the 1784 revised third edition of *The Wealth of Nations* (see Campbell and Mossner and Ross 1977, 263–64, 266; Mossner and Ross 1981, 88).

Smith's Project

Why, then, would Smith, now reputed to be the premier political economist of his time, be so frequently interpreted as one who was out of touch with his own age? In answering this question, a comparison with Steuart is most instructive. Despite widespread praise for his detailed information, Steuart's basic message was swept aside, as we have seen. His grim advocacy of primitive accumulation was far too blunt, even for his contemporaries. Smith's cheerful optimism, in contrast, was just what polite society wanted to read: Curb the government, unleash the forces of the market, and all will be well. Unfortunately, Smith could present this vision only by substantially violating the truth.

While many people have commented on Smith's neglect of the emergent industrial system, fewer have taken note of Smith's treatment of the people who make up the economy. Joan Thirsk is an exception in this respect. She observed:

> [Smith] was not concerned with the personal lives led by individuals and could achieve the superb clarity of his exposition by detaching his theory from any sensitive consideration of the human beings whose labors created the wealth of the nation. Yet at every turn their lives obtruded themselves, insisting on inserting question marks at

the end of his confident expositions. For example, he had to explain
inequalities in the wages of labour. (Thirsk 1978, 152)

The defect to which Thirsk draws our attention is not the absence of fact or
detail in general, but rather the omission of fact or detail specifically when
dealing with the delicate question of conflict between classes. I suspect
that Thirsk saw what has escaped most historians of economic thought
because she was a distinguished agricultural historian. This background
allowed her to see through the fog of laissez-faire rhetoric to sense the
connection of Smith's work to primitive accumulation. I will return to
Thirsk's insight when examining the roots of Smith's *Wealth of Nations.*
For now, we need only to note that Smith's approach made *The Wealth of
Nations* extraordinarily uneven. It is at once full of detail and devoid of
much of the most important phenomena of the time.

Once we recognize that Smith designed his work for two different, and
even contradictory, purposes we will see that this unevenness appears all
but inevitable. On the one hand, Smith developed a handbook of practical
administration of the sort that Townshend requested (see Mossner and
Ross 1977, 328n). In this regard, we find an abundance of factual material.

On the other hand, Smith was the architect of a cleverly written revision of political economy and history in which he recast the harsh reality
of capitalist development in as favorable a light as possible. In this project,
Smith relied mostly on what his student Dugald Stewart termed "conjec-
tural history" (1855, 36; Stewart 1811, 450), an approach that Stewart
(1811, 449) defended by claiming that "in want of direct evidence, we are
under a necessity of supplying the place of fact by conjecture."

Smith's reliance on conjecture and anecdote is understandable. In his
revision of political economy, many facts—especially those concerning
existing economic realities—would have inconveniently contradicted
Smith's intended lesson: Economic progress should be explained in terms
of the increasing role of voluntary actions of mutually consenting individual producers and consumers in the marketplace.

Smith's casual approach to history, a subject that was not held in particularly high regard at the time, would not have shocked his contemporaries. Smith's colleague William Robertson (1781, 6) once described the
early period of Scottish history as "the region of pure fable and conjecture
and ought to be totally neglected or abandoned to the industry and credu-
lity of antiquaries."

I propose that we can think of *The Wealth of Nations* as two different
books: one concerns the ideology of political economy; the other is a
handbook for economic administrators. Although these two works are

not physically separated, we can roughly isolate them. We can read the book of practical administration by starting at the end of *The Wealth of Nations* and working backward. The ideological work begins on page 1 and continues forward as it gradually blends in with the book on political administration.

Despite its obvious deficiencies, Smith's ideological message was a step forward in some respects. He attempted to ground his work, for instance, in a materialistic theory of society that could "explain the origin and something of the progress of government . . . not as some writers imagine from any consent or agreement, but from the natural progress which men make in society" (Smith 1978, vi.19, 207; see also Meek 1977b).

Although Smith considered his application of this theory to the economy to be original, it clearly fell within a solid Scottish intellectual tradition. However, as we shall see, few were willing to accept this idea. Even Smith was prepared to abandon it in his own recommendations for administering economic affairs.

The Late Discovery of Smith's Economics

Even though his *Theory of Moral Sentiments* won him effusive praise, modern economists tend to overestimate Smith's importance. According to Karl Willis (1979, 510), during the eighteenth-century parliamentary debates, "the number of citations of Smith's is minute compared with . . . other writers," such as John Locke, Sir William Petty, David Hume, Gregory King, Charles Davenant, Sir Josiah Child, Dean Josiah Tucker, and Arthur Young. Willis reported, "Even twenty-five years after the publication of *The Wealth of Nations*, the Houses of Parliament were largely indifferent to its tenets, suspicious of its truth, and uncertain of its applicability" (ibid., 544). In addition, Willis (ibid., 528) observes that "Smith's influence on Townshend, Burke, and North was slight."

Charles James Fox made the first reference to *The Wealth of Nations* in Parliament on 11 November 1783, six years after the book first appeared (Rashid 1992, 493). However, Smith's economic ideas did not seem to have much of an impact at the time. In 1789, when Malthus signed out the 1784 edition of *The Wealth of Nations* from his college library, he was only the third person to do so (Waterman 1998, 295). The book went through five editions, but each of the first two sold only five hundred copies apiece (Waterman 1998b). Emma Rothschild notes with some irony that when Smith died in 1790, *The Annual Register* devoted twelve lines to him and sixty-five to Major Ray, a deputy quartermaster general with an interest in barometers. The *Scots Magazine* gave Smith a scant nine lines (Rothschild 1992, 74). Even up to 1800, only a few of the Cambridge colleges had acquired the book (Waterman 1998b).

Only after the beginning of the nineteenth century, when the *Edinburgh Review* began promoting Smith, did his economic theories become widely read. As Karl Willis (1979, 542) wrote: "It would not be until the generation of Canning (b. 1770), Liverpool (1770), Huskisson (1770), Brougham (1778), Robinson (1782), Palmerston (1784), Peel (1788), and Russell (1792) came to prominence that the ideas of political economy would achieve dominance in Parliament." By the turn of the century, most of the writers on political economy had ostensibly fallen in line with Smithian dogma (see Deane 1957, 88).

Why would the Tory government of Lord Liverpool, with its roots in the aristocracy rather than the immediate representatives of the capitalist class, take the lead in advocating Smith's ideas (Clarke 1988, 49)? The answer lies in the political rather than the economic climate of the period. The great fear arising out of the French Revolution suddenly gave the comforting message of Smith an urgency that it never had before.

How sincere this support for Smithian theory was is another matter. For example, Francis Horner, famous member of the Bullion Committee and editor of the *Edinburgh Review*, was requested to prepare a set of notes for a new edition of *The Wealth of Nations*. He explained his refusal in a letter to Thomas Thomson, written on 15 August 1803:

> I should be reluctant to expose S's errors before his work had operated its full effect. We owe much at present to the superstitious worship of S's name; and we must not impair that feeling, till the victory is more complete. . . . [U]ntil we can give a correct and precise theory of the origin of wealth, his popular and plausible and loose hypothesis is as good for the vulgar as any others. (cited in Horner 1843, 1:229)

The Appeal of Adam Smith

We can best understand the appeal of Adam Smith's *Wealth of Nations* against the backdrop of the work of Sir James Steuart. Although neither author won widespread acclaim from his contemporaries, Smith was by far the more popular from the outset.

Steuart's writing style put him at a severe disadvantage relative to Smith. Smith's prose is a joy to read, whereas Steuart's is heavy and dense. Their differences went far beyond style. Smith wrote of a familiar world. He began his now-famous book with: "The annual labour of every nation is the fund which originally supplies it with all the necessaries and conveniences of life" (Smith 1976, 10). In contrast, Steuart's (1767, 1:1) first words were "It is with great diffidence." He then went on to defend his project and apologize for his style. This defense carried little weight with the public, since the apology made the book no less difficult to read.

Joseph Schumpeter (1954, 176) once asserted:

> Steuart's work did not ride, like Smith's, on the wave of a single and simple policy that was rapidly conquering public opinion. . . . [O]ne cannot fail to be struck by the number of points that indicate more originality and deeper thought than does the *Wealth of Nations*. . . . In the theories of population, prices, money and taxation Steuart went much below the smooth surface on which A. Smith happily sailed his course.

Schumpeter went on to observe:

> Had he been more brilliant, he would have not been taken so seriously. Had he dug more deeply, had he unearthed more recondite truth, had he used difficult and ingenious methods, he would not have been understood. . . . [H]e disliked whatever went beyond plain common sense. . . . And it was Adam Smith's good fortune that he was thoroughly in sympathy with the humors of his time.

Although Steuart's prose was turgid, he was said to have been a persuasive speaker. Indeed, Smith himself acknowledged that he understood his rival's system better from their conversations than from reading Steuart's book (Rae 1895, 62; Chalmers 1805, 378). In Smith's case, frequent lapses of memory punctuated his conversation, whereas his book displayed an elegance of style.

The content of their respective books could hardly have been more dissimilar. With Smith, that part of history concerning the means by which the state reinforced the reign of capital falls from view. The litany about the lethargic nature of labor comes to an end, with the significant exception of Smith's (1976, 1.i.7, 18–19) portrayal of the small farmer who could afford to divide his time between farming and weaving.

As a result of his approach, Smith appears to be one of the most humanistic figures of classical political economy. Certainly, with the possible exception of John Stuart Mill, Smith was ostensibly more considerate of the interests of labor than any other political economist.

Finally, with Smith, we enjoy the diversion of charming anecdotes. With Steuart, we encounter the grim face of primitive accumulation.

Adam Smith versus Sir James Steuart

Although Smith was rather coy about his intentions, *The Wealth of Nations* was a direct challenge to Steuart's authority. Smith never once mentioned Steuart's name in his book, yet he probably aimed his heated denunciations of the mercantile school, at least in part, at Steuart. In his advertisement to the fourth edition, for example, Smith (1976, 9) attacked all previous works on the Bank of Amsterdam as "unintelligible." His modern editors point out that Steuart's perceptive work on that subject could hardly be liable to that charge (Smith 1976, 9n). They mention numerous other instances where notice of Steuart's work would have been appropriate.

Smith's silence concerning Steuart could not be charged to ignorance about him. After all, Smith attended the same Burgh School of Kirkcaldy where Sir James had earlier studied. Appropriately, Steuart, ever the aristocrat, acted the role of the king in a production of *Henry the Fourth* (Rae 1895, 5). By the time Smith wrote *The Wealth of Nations*, Steuart was the most eminent political economist of Scotland. Although Smith may not have personally known Steuart until the latter's long period of exile had ended, in later years, Smith and Steuart belonged to several of the same clubs (see Bell 1960).

In a private letter dated 3 September 1772, Smith wrote to William Pulteney: "I have the same opinion of Sir James Steuarts [*sic*] book that you have. Without mentioning it, I flatter myself that any fallacious principle in it will meet a clear and distinct confutation in mine" (Mossner and Ross 1977, 163–64; Rae 1895, 253–54). This letter is doubly interesting because it also concerned Smith's attempt to win an appointment to an East India Company committee that was to travel to India to investigate administrative malpractices. Fortunately for Smith's reputation as a stalwart opponent of entrenched monopolies, the mission was never completed, although Smith was selected as a member (Ambirajan 1977, 2–3).

Smith may well have been aware that the East India Company had already commissioned Steuart to analyze the state of the coinage in Bengal (see Steuart 1772). Smith's (1977, 164) reference to the views he shared with Pulteney on the "disorders of the coin of Bengal" suggests that the letter may have been intended to deprecate Steuart, both as author and consultant. Smith's basic thesis in his attempted refutation of Steuart was appealing: The interest of individuals might clash, but society as a whole, as well as the classes of which it is composed, have a common interest. Within Smith's presentation, primitive accumulation, a term that he inadvertently helped to coin, was an unnecessary, or even nonexistent, element in economic development.

Smith's first book, *The Theory of Moral Sentiments*, had won the lavish praise of Edmund Burke (1759, 488), who gushed that "a dry abstract of the system would convey no juster idea of it, then the skeleton of a departed beauty would of her form and allure when she was alive." Booksellers decorated their display windows with busts of the author (Viner 1965, 39–40). Steuart's book suffered a far different fate. One month before his death, he wrote to a correspondent that his "opinions . . . have little weight, they have long been printed, little read and less considered" (cited in Skinner 1966, lv). Despite Smith's commercial success, Steuart may have had more influence on the policy of the time.

Alas, the modern literature of economics has recorded neither the battle between Smith and Steuart, nor Steuart's subsequent defeat. Indeed, we hear little mention of Steuart, except that he was a trifle more modern than the run-of-the-mill mercantilist.

A publication titled *The Market and the State: Essays in Honour of Adam Smith* (Wilson and Skinner 1976) marked the obliteration of Steuart's contribution. This title suggests a detailed analysis of Smith's response to the question of state intervention. Although some of the contributions do bear titles that relate to his subject matter, a review of the body of the work proves disappointing.

One of the coeditors of this book had produced an earlier edition of Steuart's *Inquiry* and a number of valuable articles, yet not one mention of Steuart can be found in this volume. One contributor, W. Arthur Lewis (1976, 139), was irreverent enough to venture the opinion that "industrialization required government action," but that particular article was at variance with the Smithian theme of the title.

Although other scholars share Lewis's conclusion (Kroos and Gilbert 1972, 162; Kuznets 1965, 108), they are in the minority. Today, the majority of academic economists believe that market forces suffice to develop an economy. In contrast, until the time of Smith, economists almost universally accepted the necessity of government intervention (see Deane 1957, 89). Smith vainly attempted to dispute it.

Sociology of Class and Dependent Social Relations

Parallel to his oblique attack on Steuart, Smith launched a vigorous yet surreptitious ideological assault on the social and economic behaviors of all groups, except the particular strata of the middle class with which he identified. In a sense, Smith was not unusual in this regard; economists commonly single out a narrow group of society for special approbation.

Joseph Schumpeter (1950) lauded the entrepreneur while laying the blame for the imminent demise of capitalism on more fainthearted members of the middle class. John Maynard Keynes placed his faith in the well-educated elite while mocking both investors and businesspeople (Perelman 1988, chap. 1). Alfred Chandler's (1977) hero is the corporate administrator, who wrests control of business from less-talented investors.

The unifying feature of Smith's sociology is a strong advocacy of the values of the self-employed artisan, merchant, or professional. Smith expresses this attitude in his negative depiction of dependent social relations, which demean both the lower classes that find themselves dependent and the aristocracy that required others to be subservient.

This concern with dependency is a recurrent theme in all of Smith's mature works, from *The Theory of Moral Sentiments* to *The Wealth of Nations*. We should recognize that Smith was not antagonistic to all forms of dependency. He was more than tolerant of the dependency of those in the employ of another, when those employees were producing goods to be sold on the market. We shall discuss the limits of this tolerance later. We shall see that Smith's attitude toward dependency helps to explain his interpretation of productive and unproductive labor, as well as various policy issues.

Smith versus the Aristocracy

As an example of Smith's intemperance, consider his unrelenting hostility toward the aristocracy: "The nobility are the greatest opposers and oppressors of liberty that we can imagine. . . . The people can never have security of person or estate till the nobility be crushed" (1978, iv.165, 264).

Could Robespierre have been more shrill?

Smith often couched his antagonism toward the nobility in terms of the demeaning nature of personal dependency that they imposed on those who occupied lower stations in society. Throughout his writings, Smith (1976, III.iv.5, 413) expressed an abiding opposition toward the nobility for maintaining "a multitude of retainers and dependents." He aggressively condemned such dependency: "Nothing tends so much to corrupt and enervate and debase the mind as dependency, and nothing gives such noble and generous notions of probity as freedom and independency" (Smith 1978, vi.7, 333).

According to Smith (1976, III.iv.6, 414–15), "Such a proprietor feeds his servants and retainers at his own house. . . . [The servants'] subsistence . . .

is derived from his bounty, and its continuance depends upon his good pleasure." Such hospitality owed nothing to generosity. It was merely the result of the lords' inability to convert the produce of the land into exchange values. He explained that "the rich man has no way of spending the produce of his estate but by giving it away to others, and these become in this manner dependent upon him" (Smith 1978, iv.9, 202; see also ibid., 410; Hume 1752a, 291; S. Johnson 1774, 85).

Once the aristocracy obtained access to luxury goods, it abandoned its rustic hospitality. According to Smith:

> The arts which are now cultivated give him an opportunity of expending his whole stock on himself. . . . He gives nothing away gratuitously, for men are so selfish that when they have an opportunity of laying out on their own person what they possess, tho on things of no value, they will never think of giving it to be bestowed on the best purposes by those who stand in need of it. (1978, i.117, 50)

Smith's discussion of the Game Laws offers an additional instance of his antagonism toward the gentry. For Smith, the Game Laws were irrelevant to capital accumulation. Recall how he attributed these laws to the perverse nature of the gentry. In so doing, Smith hid the conflict between labor and capital behind two layers of assertions. To begin with, the gentry are ostensibly concerned with an intense exploitation of the people. Smith was undoubtedly correct here, but his silence conveys the suggestion that capital is disinterested in matters of primitive accumulation. Then Smith went on to assert that the gentry's claim to an interest in economic success was spurious, arguing that their real concern was an atavistic love of hunting and a drive to dominate their fellow human beings (Smith 1978, 192; 1976, III.ii.10, 388).

Here, as in the rest of his work, folly appears to be the most pervasive of all human faults. Conversely, rational thought (read "capitalism") would seem capable of excluding exploitation and misery from the world. Smith's avuncular posture makes for charming reading, but it is hardly satisfactory either as history or political economy.

Smith's attitude toward such personal dependency appears ironic, considering that he frequently found himself dependent on aristocrats for assistance in obtaining teaching positions. Consider John Rae's (1895, 30) description of Smith's circumstances:

> In returning to Scotland Smith's ideas were probably fixed from the first on a Scotch university chair as an eventual acquisition, but he thought in the meantime to obtain employment of the sort he after-

wards gave up his chair to take with the Duke of Buccleugh, a travel-
ing tutorship with a young man of rank and wealth. . . . While casting
about for a place of that kind he stayed at home with his mother in
Kirkcaldy . . . for two full years. . . . The appointment never came;
because from his absent manner and bad address, we are told, he
seemed to the ordinary parental mind a most unsuitable person to be
entrusted with the care of spirited and perhaps thoughtless young
gentlemen. But these visits he paid to Edinburgh in pursuit of this
work bore fruit.

The irony goes further. Smith's family, though not particularly wealthy,
had its own strong aristocratic roots. His mother was from the Douglas
family of Strathenry, a great-great-granddaughter of Sir William Douglas
of Lochleven, later earl of Morton, the laird who held Mary Queen of
Scots prisoner on an island in Lochleven (Scott 1934, 18). His father de-
scended from a family of Aberdeenshire lairds at one time identified with
Rothiebirsben and later with Inveramsay (ibid., 8).

Nonetheless, Smith's branch of the family had long been at odds with
traditional Scottish aristocratic values. According to Scott (ibid.), the
more wealthy branch was strongly Jacobite, and "the younger sons were
even more forceful on the other side." Scott mentioned that during the
revolution, many members of the family displayed a flair for administration and won high posts.

Dependency and Unproductive Labor

Smith's contemporaries commonly denounced particular occupations as
unproductive. For example, the Physiocrats deemed the labor of agricultural producers as the only productive labor. Smith, in contrast, distinguished labor as productive and unproductive according to the social relations of production. As a result, some workers in a particular occupation
might be classified as unproductive workers while others would be productive. Smith left no doubt that he related the question of dependency to
his theory of productive and unproductive labor.

Smith clearly associated unproductive labor with the demeaning social
relations characteristic of feudalism (Smith 1976, II.iii.9–12, 334–35).
Consider his comparison of the social relations of retainers and independent tradesmen:

When the great proprietors of land spend their rents in maintaining
their tenants and retainers, each of them maintains entirely all his
own tenants and all his own retainers. But when they spend them in

maintaining tradesmen and artificers, they may, all of them taken together, perhaps maintain as great, or on account of the waste which attends rustick hospitality, a greater number of people than before.... Each tradesman or artificer derives his subsistence from the employment, not of one, but of a hundred or a thousand customers. Though in some measure obliged to them all, therefore, he is not absolutely dependent upon any one of them. (Smith 1976, III.iv.12, 420)

In effect, Smith considered one sort of labor to be productive because he approved of the social relations of commodity production, while condemning another type as unproductive because it entailed social relations of (feudal) dependency. For example, he wrote:

A man of fortune, for example, may either spend his revenue in a profuse and sumptuous table, and in maintaining a great number of menial servants, and a multitude of dogs and horses; or contenting himself with a frugal table and a few attendants, he may lay out the greater part of it in adorning his house or his country villa....

The expense . . . that is laid out in durable commodities, gives maintenance, commonly, to a greater number of people than that which is employed in the most profuse hospitality. (ibid., II.iii.38, 41, 346, 348)

Smith offered no reason why durable commodities should employ more labor.

Elsewhere, he suggested that durability was an end in itself:

The labour of menial servants . . . consists in services which perish generally in the very instant of their performance, and does not fix or realize itself in any vendible commodity which can replace the value of their wages and maintenance. The labour, on the contrary, of artificers, manufacturers and merchants, does naturally fix and realize itself in some commodity. (ibid., IV.ix.31, 675)

Notice that the extension of the circuits of vendible commodities can widen and even intensify without a comparable accumulation of capital. Recall the Physiocratic analysis where manufacturing is identified with the labor of artisans who work with virtually no capital and earn only a subsistence wage. I am convinced that Smith's advocacy of accumulation was secondary to his desire for commercial social relations.

In fact, the only consistent explanation of Smith's treatment of unproductive labor is that unproductive laborers were dependent on the aristocracy, whereas productive labor is always embedded in market relations.

Smith believed that unproductive workers had personal characteristics of which he disapproved. In contrast, productive labor would be more likely to adopt the petty bourgeois values that Smith wished to see flourishing in his society.

In this spirit, Smith contrasted the energy of a commercial city with the idleness surrounding a society in which feudal retainers are common. He noted, "In mercantile and manufacturing towns where the inferior ranks of people are chiefly maintained by the employment of capital, they are in general industrious, sober and thriving" (ibid., II.iii.12, 335).

Smith's Hostility toward Self-Sufficient Farmers

Although Smith denounced the aristocracy for keeping rural people dependent, he showed little concern for the dependent people of the countryside beyond superficially bemoaning their dependency. Using language echoing the brutal analysis of Sir James Steuart, Smith followed his discussion of the degrading nature of dependency by acknowledging the legitimate need of modern, profit-maximizing farmers to rid the land of those people whom he dehumanized as "unnecessary mouths" (1976, III.iv.13, 420). He also commended "the diminution of cottagers, and other small occupiers of land; an event which has in every part of Europe been the immediate forerunner of improvement and better cultivation" (ibid., I.xi.1.10, 243).

Smith's image of the traditional farmer, who had not completely accepted the psychological values that Smith associated with the commercial stage of society, was just as unfavorable. He ridiculed their behavior:

> The habit of sauntering and of indolent careless application, which is naturally, or rather necessarily acquired by every country workman who is obliged to change his work and his tools every half hour . . . renders him always slothful and lazy, and incapable of any vigorous application even on the most pressing occasions. (ibid., I.i.7, 19)

This emotional outburst did not do Smith much credit. Joan Thirsk (1978, 151), a keen student of English rural life, described this passage as a "grotesque caricature." No wonder she found fault with Smith's purported psychological analysis. John Stuart Mill (1848, 2:126) also took issue with Smith on this passage: "This is surely an exaggerated description of the inefficiency of country labour. Few workmen change their tools oftener than a gardener; is he incapable of vigorous application?"

Why was Smith so hostile to the small producer? How could he assume that the "natural effort of every individual to better his own condition" was somehow foreign to the allegedly indolent and sauntering country weaver (Smith 1759, 508)?

Indeed, once he moved from the ideological to the administrative sections of his work, Smith (1976, V.i.a.15, 697) admitted that poor but independent small farmers worked very hard: "Those improvements in husbandry . . . which the progress of arts and manufactures necessarily introduces, leave the husbandman with as little leisure as the artificer."

Here Smith was addressing a practical problem. As we shall see, he was concerned that the demands on country folk were so great that they could not spare the time to form a militia. As a result, state had to spend more money for national defense.

Dependency and the Corruption of Cities

Smith's wide-ranging hostility extended to the working class as well. He feared the wrath of large masses of degraded workers huddled in large cities. In one justly famous denunciation of the dark side of the division of labor, he concluded:

> In the progress of the division of labour, the employment of the far greater part of those who live by labour . . . comes to be confined by a few very simple operations. . . . But the understandings of the greater part of men are necessarily formed by their ordinary employments. The man whose whole life is spent in performing a few simple operations, of which the effects too are, perhaps, always the same, or very nearly the same, has no occasion to exert his understanding, or to exercise his invention in finding out expedients for removing difficulties which never occur. He naturally . . . becomes as stupid and ignorant as it is possible for a human creature to become. . . . But *in every improved and civilized society this is the state into which the labouring poor, that is, the great body of the people, must necessarily fall, unless the government takes some pains to prevent it.* (ibid., V.i.f.50, 781–82; emphasis added)

Smith complained about "the gross ignorance and stupidity which, in a civilized society, seem so frequently to benumb the understanding of all inferior ranks of people" (ibid., V.i.f.61, 788). He continued, "A man, without the proper use of the intellectual faculties of a man, is, if possible, more contemptible than even a coward, and seems to be mutilated and deformed in a still more essential part of human nature" (ibid.).

Similarly, after telling his students about the benefits of the division of labor, Smith explained:

It is remarkable that in every commercial nation the low people are exceedingly stupid. The Dutch vulgar are eminently so. . . . the rule is general, in towns they are not so intelligent as in the country, nor in a rich country as in a poor one. (Smith 1978, 539)

According to Smith:

[When a worker] comes into a great city, he is sunk in obscurity and darkness. His conduct is observed and attended to by nobody, and he is very likely to neglect it himself, and to abandon himself to every sort of low profligacy and vice. (Smith 1976, V.i.g.12, 795)

These moral deficiencies threatened grave consequences for the rich, according to Smith (ibid., V.i.f.50, 781–82), who warned that "in the poor the hatred of labour and the love of present ease and enjoyment, are the passions which prompt to invade property, passions much more steady in their operation, and more universal in their influence." Given such attitudes, Smith was not well disposed toward the masses of urban workers. In fact, despite his low regard for independent farmers and farmworkers, Smith (ibid., I.x.c.24, 144; see also 1978, 539) held them in significantly higher esteem than unskilled urban workers. He exclaimed, "How much the lower ranks of the people in the country are really superior to those in the town, is well known to every man whom either business or curiosity has led to converse with both."

Social Relations and the Military in Smith's Work

The degradation of people who move from the countryside to large urban settlements posed a practical problem for Smith's vision of a commercial society. He knew that the bulwark of the traditional army consisted of the same small farmers who stood in the way of his desired commercial society.

These farmers made excellent soldiers. The rhythms of agrarian life were ideally suited to warfare, since peasants could participate in military campaigns during the off-season. Sweeping the majority of these small farmers off the land would transform them into landless farm workers or urban proletarians, who would be less suited to serve in the military.

While the economic failure of the farmers would weaken the military, the success of other occupations would limit the pool of willing and able soldiers. Specifically, Smith (1978, iv.170, 266) fretted that the minority of urban workers who succeed in commercial society would be disinclined to participate in the military: "The better sort of mechanicks could not get a sufficient compensation for the loss of their time [while on military duty]. An army composed of gentlemen has occasion for very little discipline."

In addition, employers would be loath to let their best workers participate in the military:

> In a state where arts, manufactures, and handicrafts are brought to perfection, . . . they cannot dispense with labourers in this manner without the total loss of business and destruction of the state. Every hour a smith or a weaver is absent from his loom or the anvil his work is at a stop, which is not the case with the flocks of a shepherd or the fields of the husbandman. (ibid., 230; see also Smith 1976, V.i.a.9, 694–95; Hume 1752b, 259–60)

The reluctance of the aspiring petty bourgeoisie to serve in the military would leave national defense in the hands of the two classes that represented the greatest threat, in Smith's view, to commercial society: the aristocracy and the unreformed workers, who resented the new society. Smith (1978, iv.170, 266) warned: "But when the army comes to be compos'd of the very meanest people, they must be forced into a standing army and a military discipline must be established."

Unfortunately, troops in these standing armies are "very much dependent" on their officers (ibid., iv.89, 234). Smith feared this arrangement would become a recipe for usurpation of power since "the temptation [to subvert the state] when offered is such as few men would be able to resist" (ibid., 236). Presumably, the greater threat is that neither the officers nor their men would display a sufficiently respectful attitude toward private property.

To make matters worse, Smith realized that the wealth of a commercial society would make it an inviting target for foreign powers. According to Smith, "An industrious, and upon that account a wealthy nation, is of all nations the most likely to be attacked. . . . [T]he natural habits of the people render them altogether incapable of defending themselves" (1976, V.i.a.15, 697–98).

Smith's Humanism and National Security

Craufurd Goodwin (1991, 23) once observed, "Classical political economy was forged on the anvil of war. The Seven Years' War barely ended when Smith published *The Wealth of Nations.*" Goodwin shows that the military was a significant element in Smith's thought. Smith (1776, V.i.a.14, 697) even proclaimed "the art of War . . . the noblest of all arts."

Smith's preoccupation with the military carried into his personal life in the sense that he, like Steuart, belonged to the Poker Club, of which the chief condition for membership was a zeal for the establishment of a militia (Pascal 1938, 169; Rendall 1978, 13). This concern for national security also led him to contradict much of the rest of his work. For example, in the context of national security, Smith abandoned his call to crush the nobility. Instead, Smith proclaimed that "the hereditary nobility is the great security of the people's liberty" (1978, 444; see also 1976, V.i.a.41, 706–77).

Again, considerations of national security prompted Smith to take note of the negative side of commercial society. For example, he complained in his *Lectures on Jurisprudence* that commerce erodes the military spirit of the people:

> Another bad effect of commerce is that it sinks the courage of mankind, and tends to extinguish martial spirit. In all commercial countries the division of labour is infinite, and every one's thoughts are employed on one particular thing. . . . The defence of the country is therefore committed to a certain set of men who have nothing else ado; and among the bulk of the people military courage diminishes. . . . they grow effeminate and dastardly. (Smith 1978, 540; see also 540; and 1976, V.i.a.15, 698)

Such anxiety prompted Smith to make one of his rare references to the social division of labor. Sounding very much like Sir James Steuart, Smith (1976, V.i.a.12, 697) concluded, "It is the wisdom of the state only which can render the trade of a soldier a particular trade separate and distinct from all others."

Smith's trepidation about the future of the military led him to advocate that the state offer prizes to encourage "military and gymnastic excersizes" so that the people would maintain a proper martial spirit (1976, V.i.f.58, 786). Given his fears about the discipline of both the military and the working class, Smith called for state intervention in the educational process. Hopefully, schooling could make the potentially unruly working class more accepting of both military discipline and property rights.

This concern led Smith (ibid., V.i.f.50, 781) to make his famous lament in the previously cited passage concerning the deleterious effects of the division of labor that began "In the progress of the division of labour, the employment of the far greater part of those who live by labour . . . comes to be confined by a few very simple operations."

Typically we find part of this citation offered as evidence of Smith's humanitarian concern for workers. The full citation suggests that workers may be stupid but the division of labor is responsible for their plight. It does seem to fly in the face of Thirsk's claim that Smith left out the human costs of his program.

Seen in a fuller context, we can see that Smith was not at all concerned about the conditions of the workers in this passage. Instead, he was troubled about threats to the welfare of the rich. Consider the ellipsis before the end of the citation about the harmful effects of the division of labor:

> [The typical individual] is incapable of defending his country in war. The uniformity of his stationary life naturally corrupts the courage of his mind, and makes him regard with abhorrence the irregular, uncertain, and adventurous life of a soldier. It corrupts even the activity of his body. . . . His dexterity at his own particular trade seems . . . to be acquired at the expence of his intellectual, social, and martial virtues. But in every improved and civilized society, this is the state into which the labouring poor, that is, the great body of the people, must necessarily fall, unless government takes some pains to prevent it. (Smith 1976, V.i.f.50, 782)

Adam Smith's reputation has flourished, not in a small part because of his supposed solicitude for the well being of the working classes. Modern authors often wheel out the preceding portion of the above citation to prove that Smith rose above his time, crying out for justice for the working class.

In reality, the continuation of the citation indicates nothing of the kind. Smith's attention was elsewhere at the time. Within a few brief words, he had forgotten about the welfare of the people and has returned again to the importance of creating a martial spirit to protect the property of the rich.

Smith's Hostility toward Workers' Traditional Norms

Smith did not attribute all of labor's negative attitudes to the corrupting influence of urban life. He was equally aghast at the continuing tradition of popular rural justice that displaced rural workers brought with them to the cities. For example, workers insisted that necessities should not sell above what they considered to be a just price. Edward P. Thompson (1971) referred to these traditional attitudes as the "moral economy."

Smith (1978, 197; see also 1976, IV.v.b.8, 527) was outraged that these lower-class cultural values made poor people feel justified in times of high prices when they "break open granaries and force the owners to sell at what they think a reasonable price." He countered that the corn merchants served a useful purpose:

> By raising the price he [the corn merchant] discourages the consumption, and puts every body more or less, but particularly the inferior ranks of people, upon thrift and good management. . . . When he foresees that provisions are likely to run short, he puts them upon short allowance. Though from excess of caution he should sometimes do this without any real necessity, yet all the inconveniences which his crew can thereby suffer are inconsiderable in comparison of the danger, misery, and ruin, to which they might sometimes be exposed by a less provident conduct. (Smith 1976, IV.v.a.3, 524)

Apparently, Smith, writing during a time of recurrent food shortages, thought that people should be grateful for their hunger as an educational experience.

Smith opposed every aspect of the moral economy. He was appalled that the government had once passed laws regulating the retail corn trade in order to mollify the populace, although much of this legislation was repealed in 1772 (Sklar 1988, 103). For Smith, such legislation was every bit as unjustified as the laws regarding religion (1976, IV.v.b.40, 539). He claimed that people's fear of forestalling was no more warranted than anxiety about witchcraft (ibid., IV.v.b.26, 534).

Smith's Fear of Working-Class Leveling

Smith (1976, V.i.b.2, 709) feared that the working classes were possessed by "passions which prompt [them] to invade property, passions much more steady in their operation, and much more universal in their influence." Consequently, government is necessary to protect the property of the rich (ibid., 670 ff.). Smith (1978, 208; see also 404) even went so far as to teach his students:

> Laws and government may be considered in . . . every case as a combination of the rich to oppress the poor, and preserve to themselves the inequality of the goods which would otherwise be soon destroyed by the attacks of the poor, who if not hindered by the government would soon reduce the others to an equality with themselves by open violence.

Smith repeatedly returned to the idea that the purpose of a legal structure was to protect the rich from the poor (ibid., 709 ff.; Smith 1978, 209, 338, 404). He also believed that market society would become increasingly egalitarian. As a result, he prophesied that over time, people would become more accepting of the social order:

> Civil government supposes a certain subordination. But as the necessity of civil government gradually grows up with the acquisition of valuable property, so the principle causes which naturally introduce subordination gradually grow up with the growth of that valuable property. (Smith 1976, V.i.b.3, 710)

Less developed regions, where acceptance of the rules of the market was not widespread, required considerably more protection of private property than was common at the time in England. For example, in a letter of 8 November 1799 discussing the poverty of Ireland, Smith observed:

> It is ill provided with [coal and] wood; two articles essentially necessary to the progress of Great Manufactures. It wants order, police, and a regular administration of justice both to protect and restrain the inferior ranks of people, articles more essential to the progress of Industry than both coal and wood put together. (cited in Mossner and Ross 1977, 243)

Smith (1759, VI.ii.1.21, 226; see also pt. 2, sec. 1) left no doubt about the priority of law and order. He claimed that, although "the relief and consolation of human misery depend upon our compassion for [the poor], the peace and order of society is of more importance than even the relief of the miserable." Smith (1978, 262) justified his position, in part, arguing that inequality was a necessary stimulant to commerce.

Smith and Working-Class Dependency

Although Smith enjoys an undeserved reputation as a friend of labor, he was, in fact, thoroughly antagonistic toward the vast majority of the working class. Smith did seem to come out squarely on the workers' side in commenting on the conflict over wages. Smith (1776, I.viii.48, 101) also charged that farmers, landlords, and masters alike prefer poor harvests and high prices because, under such conditions, they can "make better bargains with their servants . . . and find them more humble and dependent."

Certainly, Smith's rhetoric sounded more progressive than that of any other classical political economist. He ensured his reputation as a humanitarian by writing:

> Is this improvement in the circumstances of the lower ranks of society to be regarded as an advantage or as an inconveniency to society?

The answer seems at first sight abundantly plain. . . . But what improves the circumstances of the greater part can never be regarded as an inconveniency to the whole. No society can surely be flourishing and happy, of which the far greater part of the members are poor and miserable. It is but equity, besides, that they who feed, cloath and lodge the whole body of the people, should have such a share of the produce of their own labour as to be themselves tolerably well fed, cloathed and lodged. (ibid., I.viii.36, 96)

Nonetheless, Smith's well-known advocacy of high wages did not prove that he took the workers' side. Smith disapproved of low wages because they reinforced precapitalist norms of behavior. Smith was not usually explicit about such matters. Although he never unambiguously articulated his theory, we can deduce that he worried that low wages could lead to two sorts of outcomes, neither of which appealed to him. On the one hand, those workers who do feel humbled may then feel compelled to show an exaggerated deference to employers, re-creating the rural dependency that Smith despised. Such workers could easily fall under the sway of a demagogue. On the one hand, low wages could reinforce workers' tendency to assert themselves. These sort of workers are likely to follow the dictates of the moral economy and attack property or participate in other mob actions. In neither case would low-wage workers tend to conform to the values that Smith so prized.

Smith believed that big business made such class conflict more likely. To begin with, the opulence that goes with large enterprise would be more likely to stir up the mobs. In addition, the small capitalists, lacking the advantages of their larger counterparts, presumably would not be able to conspire to keep wages low.

Smith used his advocacy of high wages to suggest that the harmonious functioning of the market would serve the interests of workers. I will explore this element of Smith's work in more detail in chapter 10. He also hoped that high wages could somehow encourage workers to adopt middle-class aspirations and abandon their antagonism toward market society. He hypothesized:

The liberal reward of labour . . . encourages . . . the industry of the common people. The wages of labour are the encouragement of industry. . . . A plentiful subsistence increases . . . the comfortable hope of bettering his condition, and of ending his days perhaps in ease and plenty. . . . [I]t animates him to exert his strength to the utmost. (ibid., I.viii.44, 99)

Of course, not all workers were willing to adopt middle-class values. For those who took pride in their traditional working-class culture, Smith had nothing but scorn. Education, Smith proposed, might help redeem such people. Schools could teach them to accept their lot in a capitalist system and abandon the values associated with the "moral economy" that Smith opposed. He wrote:

> Though the state was to derive no advantage from the instruction of the inferior ranks of people, it would still deserve its attention that they should not be altogether uninstructed. The state, however, derives no inconsiderable advantage from their instruction. The more they are instructed, the less liable they are to the delusions of enthusiasm and superstition, which, among ignorant nations, frequently occasion the most dreadful disorders. An instructed and intelligent people besides, are more decent and orderly than an ignorant and stupid one. They feel themselves, each individually more respectable, and more likely to obtain the respect of their lawful superiors, and they are therefore more disposed to respect those superiors. They are more disposed to examine, and more capable of seeing through, the interested complaints of faction and sedition, and they are upon that account, less apt to be misled into any wanton or unnecessary opposition to the measures of government. (ibid., V.i.f.61, 788)

The above citation reflects the fact that Smith was a true son of his age, a period when intellectuals thought that the masses could be molded at will by appropriate instruction from their superiors (see Foucault 1979, pt. 3).

Smith's Hostility toward Government and Business

Not surprisingly, Smith spoke ill of government administrators, although he actively curried their support for his own position as a customs collector. Ironically, in his role as customs collector, he enforced government regulations just as energetically as he had previously denounced them in his books (see Tollison 1984; Anderson, Shugart, and Tollison 1985). However, since we popularly associate Adam Smith with a critique of government, we can let his views on that subject go without further comment.

Instead, we will now turn to the strangest entry in Smith's extensive catalog of villains—the capitalist. Many people are startled to learn that Adam Smith, the great defender of capitalism, had few good words for the capitalists. For example, in his exchange with Bentham, Smith favored the prudent, petit bourgeois artisan or small merchant, whereas Bentham lauded the entrepreneur who was willing to take risks (Pesciarelli 1989).

Indeed, Smith saved what may be his harshest criticisms for the wealthy capitalists themselves. Time and time again, he attributed the lofty position that the successful capitalist occupied to government favoritism, perhaps giving lie to his fable that capital had evolved naturally.

Smith even accused employers of behaving unfairly toward their workers. In addition, he charged that they also used the government to achieve their purposes. In Smith's (1976, I.viii.12, 83–84) words:

> It is not . . . difficult to foresee which of the two parties [employers and employees] must . . . have the advantage in the dispute (over wages), and force the other into a compliance with their terms. The masters, being fewer in number, can combine much more easily; and the law, besides, authorizes or at least does not prohibit their combinations, while it prohibits those of the workmen.

Even when they resorted to violence, Smith felt that workers would still be at a disadvantage vis-à-vis their employers. He concluded a page-long discussion of the advantages enjoyed by employers of labor with the comment:

> The workmen, accordingly, very seldom derive any advantage from the violence of those tumultuous combinations, which, partly from the interposition of the civil magistrate, partly from the superior steadiness of the masters, partly from necessity . . . generally end in nothing but the punishment or ruin of the ring-leaders. (ibid., I.viii.13, 85)

Although strikes may not promise much to workers, the market did not offer a particularly attractive prospect either. In the next paragraphs, Smith suggested that the lower bound to wages was set only by the minimum level of subsistence (1976, I.viii.15, 85).

Smith's hostile attitude toward the wealthy capitalists is ironic, since Smith himself had sought out the assistance of powerful merchants in obtaining his initial academic appointment. Most people credit Smith's antagonism toward business as further evidence of his egalitarianism, although one writer noted that Smith's attitude might reflect personal resentment: "Some part of the intensity of Smith's attacks on businessmen may be . . . explicable at a personal level. A general distaste for the everyday reality of commercial society was likely to be manifest in a reclusive intellectual of modest means" (Coleman 1988, 162).

William Baumol (1976) collected numerous extracts intended to "prove" that Smith was a friend of labor by demonstrating Smith's hostility toward business. In reality, with a single exception, Smith did not write any of Baumol's collection of citations for the support of labor. Instead, he was either attacking corporate business, which enjoyed exclusive privileges, or denouncing the anticompetitive behavior typical of entrenched business interests.

The only exception in Baumol's collection is a paragraph that concerns the tendency of business to criticize high wages while remaining silent about high profits (Smith 1976, I.ix.24, 115). Baumol's reference to this citation presents a puzzle. Edwin Cannan, editor of the edition that Baumol used for his references, pointed out an almost identical passage that occurs later in the book, although Baumol never cited it as evidence for his argument. The context of this second citation indicates that Smith again had in mind corporate business rather than business in general (ibid., IV.vii.c.29, 599).

My interpretation of Smith's attitude toward business is different. I will show that Smith did want higher wages as such. His underlying interest in this regard was his hope that higher wages would undermine working-class culture and make the workers more like the petit bourgeoisie.

CHAPTER 9

The Revisionist History
of Professor Adam Smith

Smith's Ideological Context

Just as Hobbes attempted to persuade his readers that a sovereign was necessary to maintain political harmony (see Macpherson 1962, 89), Smith proposed that the market would ensure economic harmony. Unlike Hobbes, Smith did nothing to show how this "harmony" of wage labor originated. Had he based his analysis on history, he would have had to confront the bloody process of primitive accumulation.

Smith ignored such matters. He merely assumed that capital had already forced labor into a situation in which most workers had to choose between accepting wage labor or starving. In that context, wage labor appeared to be a voluntary affair. Once capital no longer had to rely as extensively on the initial extramarket compulsion to create wage labor, Smith could argue that contrived measures to undermine the self-sufficient household were unnecessary. With the establishment of an epoch in which "the silent compulsion of economic relations" had become more effective (Marx 1977, 899), capital could pretend that workers were willing partners in a mutually rewarding transaction.

Smith's theory of harmony was at odds with the popular understanding of his time that the existence of wage labor was bound up with some means of coercion (see Wiles 1968 for some exceptions); however, around 1760, people first began to mention the possibility that the system could rely on the incentive of wages rather than external compulsion (Coats 1958, 35; conversely, see Hobsbawm 1974).

Real wages in England between 1770 and 1800 were falling or, at best, stagnant (Deane 1957, 92), perhaps indicating that primitive accumulation had set the stage for silent compulsion. Of course, employers still used coercive practices to control workers. As late as 1815, the British government prohibited skilled English workmen from emigrating (Marx 1977, 719), a matter of prime importance for employers of skilled labor. Josiah Wedgewood even wished to authorize the postmaster to open letters of "suspected persons" (cited in McKendrick 1961, 47). So pervasive was this selective reliance on market forces that no one saw anything unusual in proposals such as Wedgewood's.

Certainly, Smith is welcome to his illusions about the voluntary nature of the labor market; however, we have the obligation to scrutinize his falsification of the historical relation between labor and capital. In the course of this examination, we will see that Smith fashioned a marvelous fable of economic harmonies. Wordsworth (1802, 418) may have written of him as "the worst critic, David Hume excepted, that Scotland, a soil to which that sort of weed seems natural, has produced," but as a poet of economic harmony, Smith was second to none.

Smith's political economy, like most political economy at the time, was, first and foremost, an analysis of how people conducted their lives, especially insofar as this conduct reflected on morals and ethics (see Pocock 1971; Teichgraeber 1986). Indeed, part of Smith's charm was that he seemed to take a more personal, less abstract position in evaluating how people behave than others of his day.

Smith's actual goal was somewhat different from what most readers believe to have found in his work. At the very least, we have seen that he could hardly claim to be an "impartial spectator" of economic affairs. Instead, Smith's work represents a vigorous defense of the mores of one narrow segment of the population and an equally vigorous denunciation of all other values.

Smith's Bourgeois Role Models

Let us start with Smith's positive vision. Smith greatly admired the mores of the hardworking, but relatively unsuccessful members of the petit bourgeoisie. He knew that these people were not attractive to other sectors of society. In a rather strange passage that began with a discussion of fashionable tastes during the reign of Charles II, Smith (1759, V.2.3, 201) seemed to shift to a contemporary context:

> A liberal education . . . was connected, according to the notions of those times, with generosity, sincerity, magnanimity, loyalty, and proved that the person who acted in this manner was a gentleman and not a puritan. Severity of manners and regularity of conduct, on the other hand, were altogether unfashionable, and were connected, in the imagination of that age, with cant, cunning, hypocrisy, and low manners. To superficial minds the vices of the great seem at all times agreeable. They connect them . . . with many superior virtues which they ascribe to their superiors; with the spirit of freedom and independence,

with frankness, generosity, humanity, and politeness. The virtues of the inferior ranks of people, on the contrary, their parsimonious frugality, their painful industry, and rigid adherence to rules seem to them mean and disagreeable. They connect them both with the meanness of the station to which these qualities commonly belong, and with many great vices which, they suppose, usually accompany them—such as an abject, cowardly, ill-natured, lying, pilfering disposition.

Despite the unattractive features of petit bourgeois values, Smith hoped that by giving workers reasonably high wages, they would become socialized in their attempt to climb the ladder from artisan to small capitalist. In this sense, Smith saw the small capitalist and the prudent, hardworking artisan as part of a single bourgeois life cycle.

Smith, as usual, ran up against his confusion about wage labor. At times, he seemed to favor a world of petty commodity production, where nobody would be in the employ of another. For example, he wrote that "nothing can be more absurd, however, to imagine that men in general should work less when they work for themselves, than when they work for other people. A poor independent workman will generally be more industrious than even a journeyman who works by the piece" (Smith 1976, I.viii.48, 101). More frequently, Smith accepted that in a market society, "every man is rich or poor according to the . . . labour of other people . . . which he can command, or which he can afford to purchase" (ibid., I.v.1, 47). In this spirit, Smith noted that "the greater part of the workmen stand in need of a master to advance them the materials of their work, and their wages and maintenance" (ibid., I.viii.8, 83). Despite his antagonism to dependency, Smith enthusiastically accepted this impersonal form of command over labor. In this sense, he limited his opposition to dependency to the personal dependency typical of feudal relations.

We should note that, at this level of discussion, the notion of class is absent from Smith's analysis. Although wage labor was to be commonplace in Smith's ideal world, presumably all workers could be diligent enough that, sooner or later, they too would be independent or even capable of hiring their own workers. This idea might seem fanciful, by the nineteenth century it had gained wide acceptance (Foner 1970).

Smith's Petit Bourgeois Utopia

More agreement surrounds Smith than perhaps any other major economist, notwithstanding the controversial nature of his claims. Mainstream literature generally pictures Smith as a benign figure recommending greater reliance on the market. Even Marxist literature is usually charitable toward him, often taking comfort in Smith's description of the labor theory of value (see Meek 1963). What dissent there is, concerns the extent to which *The Wealth of Nations* represents an effort to promote free market ideology rather than objective economic analysis.

As we have seen, Smith is a far less attractive figure—one who was intolerant of all but a narrow swath of society. Smith expressed antagonism toward large capitalists, who in his view connive and conspire against workers. He called for the destruction of the nobility, and displayed an unpleasant contempt for the masses of workers and small farmers.

Only small capitalists and ambitious artisans won his unalloyed admiration. Smith (1978, 320) himself tells us that his ideal role models were "the bustling, spirited, active folks [or perhaps the better sort of mechanic], who can't brook oppression and are constantly endeavoring to advance themselves, [who] naturally join in with the democratical part of the constitution and favour the principle of utility only, that is, the Whig interest." This group would include skilled artisans, small merchants, and manufacturers, as well as supposedly self-made intellectuals like himself. Unlike the nobility who enjoyed rank and privilege as a birthright, or the poor who lacked the initiative to advance themselves, the petty bourgeoisie with whom Smith personally identified supposedly earned their status by dint of hard work.

Certainly the artisans and small merchants so well loved by Smith were not at all like Joseph Schumpeter's heroic entrepreneur. As Joseph Spengler (1959, 8) observes, "Smith's undertaker strikes one as a prudent, cautious, not overly imaginative fellow, who adjusts to circumstances rather than brings about their modification." With enough diligence and a little luck, these rather plodding, hardworking individuals, who carried out their trade in a commonly understood fashion, could accumulate a bit by saving, but they would be unlikely to achieve positions of prominence.

These artisans and small merchants represent the basis of what Bentham (1954, 442–43n) later called "practical equality—the sort of equality . . . which has place in the Anglo-American United States: meaning always those in which slave holding has no place." According to Smith's understanding of the British economy:

> In the middling and inferior stations of life, the road to virtue and that to fortune, to such fortune, at least, as men in such stations can reasonably expect to acquire, are, happily, in most cases, very nearly the same. In all the middling and inferior professions, real and solid professional abilities, joined to prudent, just, firm and temperate con-

duct, can very seldom fail of success. . . . The success of such people . . . almost always depends upon the favour and good opinion of their neighbours and equals; and without a tolerably regular conduct these can seldom be obtained. (Smith 1759, I.iii.3.5, 63)

We can well imagine that many of these upwardly bound, generally self-employed petit bourgeoisie experienced substantial difficulties. Where others could appeal to the good offices of a feudal lord or government official to assist in their enterprise, few of these petit bourgeois folks had influence in such quarters.

The Evolution of Smith's Stunted Utopia

In his disapproval of the direct social relations that characterized the associations among workers, and between the aristocracy and their dependents, Smith consoled himself that society naturally progressed through four stages, beginning with hunting and gathering and culminating in commercial society.

In the place of working-class and aristocratic behavioral patterns, a system of social relations based on the social distance of faceless contracting, as practiced among small merchants, would emerge. In this sense, Smith's denunciation of dependency blends in nicely with his notion of sympathy. As Jacob Viner (1972, 80) perceptively noted: "To understand the relationship of 'sympathy' of the 'sentiments,' to Adam Smith's economic view as expounded in *The Wealth of Nations* it is essential to appreciate the role Smith assigns in the operation of sympathy to what I will here call . . . 'distance,' in the spirit of the term 'social distance.'"

Smith (1759, ii, II, 3, 2, 86; see also Smith 1978, 539) offered a glimpse of the world that he wished to see, observing: "Society may subsist among different men as among different merchants, from a sense of its utility, without any mutual love or affection." In this world, personal relations count for little relative to market relations. For Smith (1976, I.ii.2, 26), "In civilized society, [man] stands at all times in need of the co-operation and assistance of great multitudes [by way of the market], while his whole life is scarce sufficient to gain the friendship of a few persons."

Smith assumed that once his cultural prescriptions became universally accepted, aristocrats and workers alike would conform to the norms of the "hustling, spirited, active folks" whom he admired. I should note that Smith's unyielding antagonism toward the mass of workers, especially in the cities, seems inconsistent with his four stages approach to human betterment, in which commercial society would inevitably improve the populace. But then, despite Smith's eloquence, the world did not conform to his desires. Workers stubbornly retained their working-class culture. The gentry refused to acknowledge the achievements of people such as Smith and those with whom he identified. Alas, the meek have yet to inherit the world.

Doux Commerce

Although Smith was disappointed that the majority of his society did not share his values, he seemed to believe that somehow history was on his side. The same forces that drove his four stages theory would inevitably sweep aside the basis of the agrarian society of feudalism (see Meek 1976). In the process, the changing economic relations that Smith envisioned would undermine the commanding position of the aristocracy relative to that of the petty bourgeoisie. With the consequent rise of a modern commercial society, petit bourgeois values would take hold and dependency would inevitably decline. Accordingly, Smith informed his students:

> Commerce is one great preventive of this custom [of dependency]. The manufactures give the poorer sort better wages than any master can afford. . . . The gentry of Scotland are no worse than those of England, but the common people being considerably more oppressed have much less of probity, liberality, and amiable qualities in their tempers than those of England. (1978, vi.8, 333)

Smith returned to this theme in *The Wealth of Nations* when he discussed how commerce contributed to the improvement of rural society. There he noted:

> Commerce and manufactures gradually introduced order and good government, and with them, the liberty and security of individuals, among the inhabitants of the country, who had before lived almost in a continual state of war with their neighbours, and of servile dependence upon their superiors. (Smith 1976, III.iv.4, 412)
> Smith continued:
> Foreign commerce and manufactures . . . gradually furnished the great proprietors with something for which they could exchange the whole surplus produce of their lands, and which they could consume themselves without sharing it either with tenants or retainers. All for ourselves, and nothing for the people, seems, in every age of the world to have been the vile maxim of the masters of mankind. As soon, therefore, as they could find a method of consuming the whole value

of their rents themselves, they had no disposition to share them with other persons. For a pair of diamond buckles perhaps, or for something as frivolous and useless, they exchanged the maintenance, or what is the same thing, the price of the maintenance of a thousand men for a year, and with it the whole weight and authority which it could give them. (ibid., III.iv.10, 418–19)

Samuel Johnson (1775, 94) made a similar point:

Money confounds subordination, by overpowering the distinctions of rank and birth, and weakens authority by supplying power of resistance, or expedients for escape. The feudal system is formed for a nation employed in agriculture, and has never long kept its hold where gold and silver have become common.

Certainly, the deteriorating relations between lord and tenant accelerated the demise of aristocratic authority. Smith observed, "When luxury came in, this gave him [the aristocrat] an opportunity of spending a great deal and he therefore was at pains to extort and squeeze high rents from them. This ruined his power over them" (1978, iv.159, 262). In Rome, as well, "the power of nobles declined very fast when either commerce or luxury were introduced," owing to the growing antagonism between slave and master (ibid., iv.72, 227). Smith (ibid., 538) explained to his students: "Whenever commerce is introduced into any country, probity and punctuality always accompany it. These virtues in a rude and barbarous country are almost unknown."

Curiously, Smith mentioned that Hume was the only other writer who had taken this position, although as his modern editors note, his great rival, Sir James Steuart, as well as Lord Kames, Adam Ferguson, and William Robertson, had also preceded him in connecting commerce and liberty (Smith 1976, III.iv.4, 412n). Moreover, at least at one point, Smith attributed the decline of the Scottish aristocracy to political rather than economic forces, arguing, "There was little trade or industry in Edinburgh before the union" (ibid., II.iii.12, 336). Consequently, he concluded, "By the union with England, the middling and inferior ranks of people in Scotland gained a compleat deliverance from the power of an aristocracy which had always before oppressed them" (ibid., V.iii.89, 944).

Smith and the Bizarre Heroism of the Petit Bourgeoisie

The people with whom Smith identified crave recognition for their exploits. Sadly, other classes were unlikely to appreciate their notions of success, which were so thoroughly bound up in petty bourgeois norms. In frustration, Smith directed his hostility toward all those who differed from himself, certain that somehow the future belonged to his sort of people.

Smith strongly resented the low regard that well-off people had for the mores of lower-middle-class people with whom he identified. He knew that those of noble rank, taught to admire heroic virtues, would be unlikely to admire the scrimping and saving of a humble artisan. To do so would be to acknowledge the superiority of commercial society and the inferiority of aristocratic culture.

Smith (1978, 784) complained that, unlike the middle class, the well-to-do had the opportunity to develop social graces, telling his students: "People of some rank and fortune . . . generally have a good deal of leisure, during which they may perfect themselves in every branch either of useful or ornamental knowledge of which they may have laid the foundation, or for which they may have acquired some taste in the earlier part of life."

Smith offered considerable insight into his perception of the distinction between lower-middle-class and aristocratic behavior in his *Theory of Moral Sentiments*. He devoted the last year of his life to rewriting this book (Smith 1759). The key materials cited here fall within the particular chapter that he revised most extensively. In this chapter, Smith (1759, 51) expressed his jealousy of his social betters, declaring:

> The man of rank and distinction, on the contrary is observed by all the world. Every body is eager to look at him, and to conceive, at least by sympathy, that joy and exultation with which his circumstances naturally inspire him. His actions are the objects of public care. Scarce a word, scarce a gesture, can fall from him that is altogether neglected. In a great assembly he is the person upon whom all direct their eyes.

Here Smith did not attribute the powers of the aristocracy to their material influence over tenants and retainers. Instead, he referred to "a natural disposition to respect them" and "a habitual state of deference to those to whom they have been accustomed to look up as their natural superiors" (ibid., 53). Smith (ibid., 52) speculated: Our obsequiousness to our superiors more frequently arises from our admiration for the advantage of their situation, than from any private expectations of benefit from their goodwill." Then Smith posed the rhetorical question, How, then, can "the man of inferior rank hope to distinguish himself" (ibid., 54)? He cannot do it by imitating the behavior of the aristocracy, since "the coxcomb, who imitates their manner, and affects to be eminent by the superior propriety of his ordinary behaviour, is rewarded with a double share of contempt for his folly and presumption" (ibid.). After all, Smith asked, "Why should the man, whom nobody thinks it is worth while to look at, be very anxious about the manner in which he holds up his head, or disposes of his arms, while he walks through a room"? This man must adopt a different tactic. Smith suggested that he must win recognition "by more important virtues." He continued:

> He must acquire dependents to balance the dependents of the great, and he has no other fund to pay them from but the labour of his body and the activity of his mind. He must cultivate these therefore: he must acquire superior knowledge in his profession, and superior industry in the exercise of it. He must be patient in labour, resolute in danger, and firm in distress. These talents he must bring into public view, by the difficulty, importance, and at the same time, good judgment of his undertakings, and by the severe and unrelenting application with which he pursues them. Probity and prudence, generosity and frankness, must characterize his behavior upon all ordinary occasion. (ibid., 55)

Notice that Smith commended the prudent man to take on dependents, but that this sort of dependency was somehow superior to the dependency associated with the despicable nobility. Perhaps Smith saw no other way. He accepted the reality that "prudence . . . commands a certain cold esteem, but seems not entitled to any ardent love or admiration" (ibid., 216). Nonetheless, Smith (ibid., 213) observed that "the desire of being the proper objects of this respect [of equals], of deserving and obtaining this credit and rank among our equals, is, perhaps, the strongest of all our desires."

How else could the prudent man win admiration except by taking on dependents? This change in Smith's attitude toward dependency pales in comparison with the remarkable, or should I say, "fantastic" reversal, which follows. Without warning, Smith somehow endowed the prudent man with the heroic virtues typically associated with the nobility, while he rebuked the aristocrat for cowardice:

> [The man without social stature] must at the same time, be forward to engage in all those situations, in which it requires the greatest talents and virtues to act with propriety, but in which the greatest applause is to be acquired by those who acquit themselves with honour. With what impatience does the man of spirit and ambition, who is depressed by his situation, look around for some great oppor-

tunity to distinguish himself? No circumstances, which can afford this, appear to him undesirable. He even looks forward to the prospect of foreign war, or civil dissension, and with secret transport and delight, sees through all the confusion and bloodshed which attend them, the probity of those wished-for occasions presenting themselves, in which he may draw upon himself the attention and admiration of mankind. The man of rank and distinction, on the contrary, whose whole glory consists in the propriety of his ordinary behaviour, who is contented with the humble renown which this can afford him, and has no talents to acquire any other, is unwilling to embarrass himself with what can be attended either with difficulty or distress. To figure at a ball is his greatest triumph, and to succeed in an intrigue of gallantry, his highest exploit. (ibid., 55)

Smith's strange reverie tells us that something was amiss with the good professor. How could it be that Adam Smith, who was typically disdainful of heroic virtues, could suddenly transform his petit bourgeois role model into a hero? Could Smith have seen himself as such a hero? At least on one occasion, he did seem to cast himself into a heroic role. In *The Wealth of Nations*, a work that he described in a letter to Andreas Holt of 26 October 1790 as "a very violent attack upon the whole commercial system of Great Britain" (Smith 1977, 251), Smith proclaimed:

[If any one opposes the monopolist,] and still more if he has authority enough to be able to thwart them, neither the most acknowledged probity, nor the highest rank, nor the greatest publick services, can protect him from the most infamous abuse and detraction, from personal insults, nor sometimes from real danger, arising from the insolent outrage of famous and disappointed monopolists. (1976, V.ii.43, 471)

The Tortured Vision of Adam Smith

Why was Smith so violent in his denunciation of behavioral patterns that differed from those of the petit bourgeoisie? A psychohistorian might be inclined to paint a picture of Smith as an unworldly academic, lacking in social graces, resentful at being beholden to his social betters. Michael Balint's perceptive essay, "On Love and Hate," may be relevant here. It reads, in part:

We hate people who, though very important to us, do *not* love us and refuse to become our cooperative partners despite our best efforts to win their affection. This stirs up in us all the bitter pains, sufferings, and anxieties of the past and we defend ourselves against their return by the *barrier of hatred*, by denying our need for those people and our dependence upon them. (Balint 1965, 128)

Smith's own psychological writings offer a further clue to his attitude. According to his interpretation of human nature, the need to be correct is so powerful that even economic behavior is subordinated to it. In Smith's (1978, 352) words:

If we should enquire into the principle in the human mind on which this disposition of trucking is founded, it is clearly the naturall inclination every one has to persuade. . . . Men always endeavour to persuade others to be of their opinion even when the matter is of no consequence to them. If one advances any thing concerning China or the more distant moon which contradicts what you imagine to be true, you immediately try to persuade him to alter his opinion. And in this manner every one is practicing oratory on others thro the whole of his life. You are uneasy whenever one differs from you.

This obsession with being in control is associated with an overriding urge to dominate others. Recall that Smith had earlier recommended that persons of inferior rank acquire dependents of their own. Later, he wrote that "the love of domination and authority over others . . . is naturall to mankind, a certain desire of having others below one, and the pleasure it gives to have some persons whom he can order to do his work rather than be obliged to persuade others to bargain with him" (ibid., 192; see also Smith 1976, III.ii.10, 388). Smith often dismissed the material hardships of poverty as unimportant, claiming that the real damage inflicted was the shame and mortification that it imposed on the poor. If correct, Smith's petit bourgeois heroes were truly impoverished.

Angry about the inability of the petit bourgeoisie to persuade the rest of society, Smith took his revenge in this brief literary flourish. In this flight of fancy, he transformed the resentment and envy of the petit bourgeois into a heroic spirit, although Smith normally acknowledged that most of the petit bourgeoisie were unsuited for military life (see chapter 8). Yet, as Smith (1978, 395–96) himself told us, "the disposition to anger, hatred, envy, malice, [and] revenge . . . renders a man . . . the object of hatred, and sometimes even of horror, to other people." He continued:

Envy is that passion which views with malignant dislike the superiority of those who are really entitled to all the superiority they pos-

sess. The man, however, who, in matters of consequence, tamely
suffers other people, who are entitled to no such superiority, to rise
above him or get before him, is justly condemned as mean-spirited. . . .
Such weakness, however, is commonly followed by much regret and
repentance. . . . In order to live comfortably in the world, it is upon all
occasions as necessary to defend our dignity and rank, as it is to defend
our life and our fortune. (ibid.)

Envy might have been stronger in Scotland than elsewhere, if we can
trust Samuel Johnson's (1774, 117) assessment:

The Scots, with a vigilance of jealousy which never goes to sleep,
always suspect that an Englishman despises them for their poverty,
and to convince him that they are no less rich than their neighbours,
are sure to tell him a price higher than the true. When Lesley, two
hundred years ago, related so punctiliously that a hundred hen eggs,
new laid were sold in the Islands for a penny, he supposed that no
inference could possibly follow, but that eggs were laid in great abundance. Posterity has since grown wiser; and having learned, that nominal and real value may differ, they now tell stories, lest the foreigner should happen to collect, not that eggs are many, but that
pence are few.

Smith, like many other aspiring Scottish intellectuals, took pains to speak
more like an English native (Muller 1993, 21–22). So, perhaps, Smith's
ethnic background may have played a role. Still, we should be careful
about pushing these ideas too far. As appealing as the individualistic explanation of Smith's motives might be, it is inadequate. Similar ideas repeatedly appear in the works of Hume and other writers. These thoughts
were intimately related to the revolution in human affairs that was occurring at the time. In the apt phrase of Elizabeth Fox-Genovese and Eugene
Genovese (1983, 98):

A traditional world view that subordinated the individual to the
community and justified him or her according to social function
yielded to a modern world view that subordinated society to the individual and justified social institutions as serving individual needs.
The rights of the group and the obligations of the individual gave way
to the obligations of the group and the rights of the individual.

Tocqueville (1945, 1:56) shrewdly noted one of the significant consequences of the new society that was evolving: "Democratic institutions

have a very strong tendency to promote the feeling of envy in the human heart."

Smith and Populism

The resentment that Smith expressed bears a strong resemblance to populism. In general, populism appeals to people who feel that they are neither capitalists nor wage earners. Like Smith, populists feel threatened both by those above and below them in social status and usually blame their problems on the machinations of powerful elite groups. Populists frequently reject complex analyses of the world in favor of more simplistic solutions. The most common populist nostrums are paper money schemes or the break up of monopolies. Although laissez-faire is not usually associated with populism, it probably should be. As Noel Thompson (1977; 1984) has shown, the purportedly Ricardian socialists should be considered populists, or even better, Smithian anarchists.

I suspect that Smith's work earned much of its popularity because he expressed so eloquently what others deeply felt. Unlike many of the less educated populists, Smith was usually able to sublimate his rage into his charming theory of the invisible hand, in which competition and even aggression is channeled into harmonious actions that better the world. Frequently, cracks appeared in this fantasy, and the harsh reality of the world around him intruded. At such times, we can catch a glimpse of Smith's theory of primitive accumulation.

Smith's vision of the bizarre heroism of the petit bourgeoisie seems to reflect his own rage at those who refused to adopt the values that were so dear to him. Even if Steuart's language was brutal, I suspect that society has more to fear from the repressed emotions of someone like Smith. His metaphor of the invisible hand may be relevant in this regard. We may equate friendship with an open, outstretched hand, but an invisible hand has something sinister about it. In this spirit, Macbeth requested that the darkness of night, "with thy bloody and invisible hand," cover up the crimes he was about to commit (*Macbeth* 2.2). Or we could turn to Friedrich Nietzsche's eerie discussion of the invisible hand:

> If I wanted to shake this tree with my hands I should not be able to do it. But the wind, which we do not see, tortures and bends it in whatever direction it pleases. It is by invisible hands that we are bent and tortured worst. . . . It is with man as it is with the tree. The more he aspires to height and light, the more strongly do his roots strive earthward, downward, into the dark, the deep—into evil.

Adam Smith's Socio-Psychological Theories of Harmony

ADAM SMITH'S DISCOVERY OF THE DIVISION OF LABOR

John Maynard Keynes (1938, 330) once remarked: "It is chiefly in the description of Adam Smith's intellectual progress and in the analysis of influences which went to make the *Wealth of Nations* that there may be room for something further." I suspect that Keynes was unaware of how much of an understatement he was making.

The section of Adam Smith's *Lectures on Jurisprudence* dealing with the subject of police gives us a most remarkable insight into his struggle to obscure the harsh reality of primitive accumulation, within the context of the theoretical structure of *The Wealth of Nations*. Smith (1978, 333) began this section by commenting that the state had an obligation to maintain the cheapness of commodities. He then went on to note that in spite of the rarity of some materials, advances in technology could make things much more affordable (ibid., 337). Such progress requires the enforcement of the law, which is necessary for the preservation of "that useful inequality in the fortunes of mankind" (ibid., 338). This unexceptional discussion seems to somehow have aroused Smith's curiosity about the equity of the law.

Are the poor merely victims of the law? Smith, as a social scientist, observed that laws were required to protect the rich from the poor (ibid., 208). This idea sat poorly with Smith, the ideologue.

Although Smith admitted to his Glasgow students of 1762–1763 that "the labour and time of the poor is in civilized countries sacrificed to the maintaining of the rich in ease and luxury," he apologized for this situation with the modest claim that the most disadvantaged members of society enjoy a far greater degree of "plenty and opulence" than they would in a "savage state" (ibid., 340, 338). In fact, he asserted, "An ordinary day labourer ... has more of the conveniences and luxuries than an Indian [presumably Native American] prince at the head of 1,000 naked savages" (ibid., 339).

Smith here went further than Locke (1698, 314–15), who had merely asserted that the English worker "feeds, lodges and is clad" better than an Indian prince. Smith may well have come to this thought by way of Bernard Mandeville (1723, 26), who wrote that "the very poor Liv'd better than the Rich before." He then turned to another thought of Mandeville, who had observed that the production of a fine crimson or scarlet cloth requires a multiplicity of trades working together in its manufacture (Mandeville 1723, 356–57). The democratic Smith used the example of a blue coat of a worker rather than a scarlet cloth, but the thought remained unchanged nonetheless.

The unfortunate masses huddled in great cities would likely not have agreed with Smith's assertion that they had "more of the conveniences and luxuries" than an Indian prince. Neither would the Ojibwas who visited London in the 1840s. They reportedly told the English who attempted to engage them in conversation:

> [We are] willing to talk with you if it can do any good for the hundreds and thousands of poor and hungry children we see in your streets every day. . . . We see hundreds of little children with their naked feet in the snow, and we pity them, for we know they are hungry. . . . [W]e have no such poor children among us. (cited in Tobias 1967, 86)

In general, Smith did not have much patience with such uncomfortable intrusions of reality. His goals were more ideological. Still, for some reason here, Smith let himself stray from his narrow ideological course. He returned to his idea of the relative affluence and comfort of his contemporaries, asking how the poor of his day could live better than a rich Indian prince? He mused:

> But that the poor day labourer or indigent farmer should be more at ease, notwithstanding all oppression and tyranny, should be more at his own ease than the savage, does not appear so probable. Amongst the savages there are no landlords nor usurers, no tax gatherers, so that every one has the full fruits of his own labours, and should therefore enjoy the greatest abundance; but the case is otherwise. (Smith 1978, 339–41)

So here is the key: The poor laborer has more commodities, but also less leisure than the savage. Smith was aware of the importance of leisure in primitive society. Nonetheless, he ended his lecture without speculating about why the laborer would rationally choose to substitute commodities for free time. Smith did not even raise the possibility that this transformation may not have been voluntary.

In his earlier works, Smith had addressed the role of class in the evolution of leisure. He even had attributed the excellent poetry of primitive cultures to the enormous amounts of leisure that they enjoyed (Smith 1762–63, Lecture 21, January 1763). In contrast, he noted that "In civilized nations, the inferior ranks of people have very little leisure, and the superior ranks have many other amusements" (Smith 1790b, 187; see also 1790a, 50). In any case, the elimination of his contemporaries' leisure does not seem to have aroused Smith's curiosity.

The next day Smith expanded upon his remarks from the previous lecture:

The labour and time of the poor is in civilized countries sacrificed to the maintaining of the rich in ease and luxury. The landlord is maintained in idleness and luxury by the labour of his tenants. The moneyed man is supported by his exactions from the industrious merchant and the needy who are obliged to support him in ease by a return for the use of his money. But every savage has the full enjoyment of the fruits of his own labours; there are no landlords, no usurers, no tax gatherers. . . . [T]he poor labourer . . . has all the inconveniences of the soil and season to struggle with, is continually exposed to the inclemency of the weather and the most severe labour at the same time. Thus he who as it were supports the whole frame of society and furnishes the means of the convenience and ease of all the rest is himself possessed of a very small share and is buried in obscurity. He bears on his shoulders the whole of mankind, and unable to sustain the weight of it is thrust down into the lowest parts of the earth from whence he supports the rest. In what manner then shall we account for the great share he and the lowest persons have of the conveniences of life? (Smith 1978, 340–41)

This last sentence is curious. In a prior lecture, Smith had asserted that the poor laborer was better fed, clothed, and housed than a savage. In this session, just as his students were hearing about the same laborer's "small share," Smith suddenly asked them to account for the "great share he [has] . . . in the conveniences of life."

What follows is just as remarkable. Smith seems to have unconsciously stumbled onto the classical theory of primitive accumulation. Recognizing that the unfortunate agricultural laborers, who represented the majority of the workers in his society, find themselves compelled to work long hours for a meager existence, Smith swiftly fled from that subject.

At this point, Smith found comfort in his early theory of the division of labor. His next words to his students were, "The division of labour amongst different hands can alone account for this" (ibid., 341). However, the division of labor was completely irrelevant to the question at hand, namely, the condition of the poor laborer.

Perhaps his blue coat reminded him of Mandeville, who had earlier written of the division of labor (see Mandeville 1723, 284). In any case, we hear nothing more about the effect of the increased working day. Instead, Smith turned the attention of his audience to what he called a "frivolous" example, the pin factory. No wonder Schumpeter could complain of the lack of attention given to Smith's use of the division of labor. Schumpeter

(1954, 187) emphasized, "Nobody, either before or after A. Smith, ever thought of putting such a burden upon division of labor."

In the concluding few lectures, we find a compressed version of *The Wealth of Nations* (see Stewart 1811, 275). In short, Smith seems to have developed his great work as an attempt to evade the logic of the classical theory of primitive accumulation.

Smith's Anthropology of Self-Betterment

Even in his imaginary account of the social division of labor, Smith fell into confusion regarding the forces that could overcome the inertia of traditional society. For example, he described a static state of affairs prior to primitive accumulation. He speculated that "in that rude state of society in which there is no division of labor, in which exchanges are seldom made, and in which every man provides enough for himself, it is not necessary that any stock [meaning capital] should be accumulated" (Smith 1976, II.3, 277; see also Marx 1967, 2:140n).

Smith seemed to suggest that this rude state could persist even well into modern times. For example, he noted that in "the Highlands of Scotland, every farmer must be a butcher, baker and brewer for his own family" (Smith 1976, I.iii.2, 31; see also Stewart 1855, 1:327–28).

Nonetheless, Smith speculated elsewhere that each society was inevitably bound to transcend the rude state because a social division of labor naturally evolves from agriculture. In this regard, he asserted:

> [When industry is not] introduced . . . by the violent operation . . . of the stocks of particular merchants or undertakers, who established them in imitation of some foreign manufactures . . . , manufactures for distant sale . . . grow up of their own accord, by the gradual refinement of those coarser manufactures. . . . Such manufactures are the offspring of agriculture. (Smith 1976, III.iii.19–20, 407–9)

Although Smith associated the social division of labor with a market society, he also taught that it preceded capital and market societies. He informed his students: "The compleat division of labour . . . is posteriour to the invention of agriculture. . . . The smith, . . . the carpenter, the weaver and the tailor soon find it in their interest not to trouble themselves with cultivating the land" (Smith 1978, 584). He contended that even precapitalist societies, such as the Hottentots, developed a social division of labor because of the economies associated with specialization (ibid., 583–84; see also Meek 1977a, 52). Thus Smith, the anthropologist, discovered a historical motivation for the social division of labor that was not "the effect of any human policy" but rather "the necessary consequence of a natural disposition . . . to truck, barter and exchange" (cited in Meek 1977a, 38; see also Smith 1976, 27n).

This sort of anthropological principle was not by any means novel. John Wheeler, in his 1601 *Treatise on Commerce*, had observed, "There was nothing in the world so ordinarie, and naturall unto men, as to contract, truck, merchandize, and traffike one with another" (cited in Appleby 1978, 94). Smith's merit was in pushing this principle further than anyone else.

Smith's Contradictory Anthropology of Class

On a more realistic level, Smith did not actually believe in the universality of his own anthropological principle. Instead, he held a contradictory anthropology based on class. For example, we have already seen that Smith posited one anthropology for the poor, when explaining the need to defend property against the passions of the working classes. Smith proposed another anthropology for the gentry, who remained aloof from the market by refusing to engage their savings in capitalistic ventures. Because the gentry did not share the middle-class passion for trucking and bartering, Smith launched a furious attack on them.

Smith was not unique in attacking the gentry for their disregard for market-oriented behavior. Indeed, as early as 1618, Francis Bacon had advised that prosperity requires that a nation not be overburdened by clergy or nobility, "for they bring nothing to stock" (cited in Appleby 1978, 115). Defoe (1724–26, 596), too, had charged that "the gentry have no genius to trade; 'tis a mechanism which they scorn; . . . they would not turn their hands toward business." Steuart (1767, 84) also felt that trading was beneath the gentry, although he was sympathetic to their behavior.

As we already noted, Smith attempted to provide a theoretical basis for his contempt of the gentry with his theory of unproductive labor. He contended that the creation of a shirt would only be considered productive if it were eventually purchased; if it came from the hands of a servant, the act of producing the shirt would be unproductive (Smith 1976, II.iii). Of course, poorer households that produced their own goods were also guilty of not engaging in productive labor.

By disconnecting his critiques of the gentry and the working classes from his anthropology of self-betterment, Smith managed to hide the class nature of his analysis of human society, thereby lending an illusion of universality of this principle. Smith could not consistently maintain this universalist fiction. When he addressed matters concerning the actual behavior of various groups, Smith switched to his class-based anthropologies, in effect refuting his pretension to a universalist anthropology.

In both of his anthropologies, Smith failed to make explicit the distribution of property. As Governor Pownall of Virginia explained to him, "Before a man can have the propensity to barter, he must have acquired something somewhat" (Pownall 1776, 338).

The Other Invisible Hand

Smith seemed to think that he could resolve the contradictions in his system by invoking a wonderful harmonizing property of the market. Accordingly, we read in *The Theory of Moral Sentiments* that "the rich . . . are led by an invisible hand to make nearly the same distribution of the necessaries of life which would have been made had the earth been divided into equal portions among all its inhabitants" (Smith 1769, 184–85).

Smith here said no more than Steuart (1767, 1:193), who had earlier written, "The most delicate liver in Paris will not put more of the earth's production into his belly than another: he may pick and choose, but he will always find that what he leaves will go to feed another." In fact, this version of the invisible hand leads to the same sort of equality that Steuart presumably envisioned when he dreamed of resurrecting the Spartan slave republic.

Smith's notion of the harmonious workings of the invisible hand does not resolve the confusion between his two anthropologies. To make this line of reasoning coherent, he should not have addressed the subject in terms of the "distribution of the necessaries of life," but rather with regard to the distribution of the means of production. After all, he himself had strongly emphasized the importance of "stock."

Even if Smith had been justified in ignoring the distribution of the means of production, he very well understood that consumption goods, in general, were not shared equally among all people. There, he acknowledged that although "the desire of food in every man is limited by the narrow capacity of the human stomach," other forms of consumption seem "to have no limit or certain boundary" (Smith 1976, I.xi.c.7, 181). He had observed that in spite of the invisible hand, "for one very rich man, there must be at least five hundred poor, and the affluence of the few supposes the indigence of the many" (Smith 1978, 670; see also Meek 1977c, 11).

Smith finally did shift his attention from consumption to production in *The Wealth of Nations.* Instead of ensuring a kind of justice in the sphere of consumption, in this book the invisible hand works in the sphere of production, where "private interests and passions naturally dispose . . . [people] to turn their stock toward the employments which in ordinary cases are most advantageous to society" (Smith 1976, IV.vii.c.88, 630).

Unfortunately, Smith's assertion that the distribution of stock is advantageous for society remains little more than meaningless cant without some analysis of the effect of the arrangement of the ownership of that stock on the distribution of income. After all, we have already seen that Smith (ibid., I.viii.36, 96) himself had observed: "No society can surely be flourishing and happy, of which the far greater part of the members are poor and miserable. It is but equity, besides, that they who feed, cloath and lodge the whole body of the people, should have such a share of the produce of their own labour as to be themselves tolerably well fed, cloathed and lodged."

Nonetheless, Smith's discussion of the invisible hand reveals a great deal about his method of analysis. On some level, he recognized the conflict between his class-based explanation of the evolution of the social division of labor and his alternative explanation framed in terms of market forces. Yet when dealing with class antagonisms, Smith continually muddied the issues rather than facing up to the full implications of class conflict.

The Political Economy of Vanity

In his effort to obscure further any disharmonious forces within capitalism, Adam Smith deployed a fascinating psychological analysis of wealth. In this context, he claimed not to value the accumulation of wealth on account of its contribution to prosperity. Consider how he dismissed the problem of poverty in *The Theory of Moral Sentiments*, where he speculated, "Avarice overrates the difference between poverty and riches" (Smith 1759, III.3.30, 149). Referring to the misfortunes that people suffer, Smith supposed that "the greater part of them have arisen from [people] not knowing when they were well, when it was proper for them to sit still and to be contented" (ibid., III.3.32, 150).

Smith counseled his readers to lead a life without luxury, even of the most modest sort:

> How many people ruin themselves by laying out money on trinkets of frivolous utility? . . . Power and riches appear then to be, what they are, enormous and operose machines contrived to produce a few trifling conveniences to the body, consisting of springs the most nice

and delicate, which must be kept in order with the most anxious attention and which in spite of all our care are every moment to burst into pieces, and to crush in their ruins their unfortunate possessor. They are immense fabrics, which it requires the labour of a life to raise, which threaten every moment to overwhelm the person that dwells in them, and which while they stand, though they may save him from some of the smaller inconveniences, can protect him from none of the severer inclemencies, can protect him from summer shower not the winter storm, but leave him always as much, and sometimes more exposed than before, to anxiety, to fear and to sorrow, to diseases, to danger, and to death. (ibid., IV.1.5–8, 180–83)

In short, people deceived themselves in working toward material success. In *The Theory of Moral Sentiments*, Smith (1759, I.iii.2.1, 50) wrote a chapter titled "Of the Origin of Ambition, and of the Distinction of the Ranks," beginning with the notion that "we pursue riches and avoid poverty" only to avoid the humiliation of poverty, although "the wages of the meanest labourer [can] supply the necessities of nature."

According to Smith, even the "meanest labourer" spends a "great part [of his wages] . . . upon conveniences, which may be regarded as superfluities, and that, upon extraordinary occasions, he can give something even to vanity and distinction" (ibid.). Again, in *The Wealth of Nations*, Smith reassured his readers that the wages of the English workmen were above this lowest possible rate (Smith 1976, I.viii.28, 91).

Despite the folly of chasing after material success, the vain desire for ostentation ultimately served a noble purpose:

And it is well that nature imposes upon us in this manner. It is this deception which rouses and keeps in continual motion the industry of mankind. It is this which first prompted them to cultivate the ground, to build houses, to found cities and commonwealths, and to invent and improve all the sciences and arts which enable and embellish human life; which have entirely changed the whole face of the globe, have turned rude forests into agreeable and fertile plains. (Smith 1759, IV.1.9, 183)

That the concluding words of the citation were identical to his translation of a passage from Rousseau's *Discours sur l'origine de l'inegalite*, published in Smith's "Letter to the Editors of the *Edinburgh Review*," hints at the ideological nature of Smith's approach (see Smith 1755–56, 250). There, he was disputing Rousseau's contention that the acquisition of private property caused inequality.

In the very same paragraph in *The Theory of Moral Sentiments* in which Smith repeated his words about changing rude forests, he proposed his previously cited theory that the invisible hand would miraculously eliminate inequality. Again, we arrive at the conclusion that Smith's concern with workers' welfare had nothing to do with their material circumstances. For Smith, what counted was their mental state, which he hoped would eventually conform to that of the petit bourgeoisie.

How Fast Does the Social Division of Labor Evolve?

Smith (1978, 88) acknowledged to his students that the exclusive privileges of corporations had been able "to bring about . . . the separation of trades sooner than the progress of society would naturally effect." This last point may be interpreted as an aside noted down by a diligent student. Certainly, we find nothing of the sort in *The Wealth of Nations* for it would have conceded much ground to the theory of Steuart.

Smith did observe in *The Wealth of Nations* that a "particular manufacture . . . may sometimes be acquired sooner" by virtue of encouragement (Smith 1976, IV.ii.13, 458); but he alleged that such actions slow down the overall process of accumulation, thereby hindering the "natural evolution" of the social division of labor. Even if we grant that market forces alone could have gradually worn away traditional society, Smith provides no information about the pace of this transition in the absence of primitive accumulation. We might infer, however, that since the division of labor precedes agriculture, the social division of labor evolves at glacial speeds.

In addition, by implying that (1) the contemporary social division of labor was the result of mutually advantageous adjustments and (2) that this process is a continuation of social behavior that stretches back into prehistoric times, Smith presented the misleading inference that the creation of the social division of labor was a natural process, devoid of conflict. We are left with his fable about hunters and artificers of bows and arrows specializing according to their particular skills.

Indeed, a social division of labor may be seen in preagricultural societies. Harmonious cooperation can even be found among the flora and fauna (Engels 1954, 402–5; see also Wynne-Edwards 1962); however, merely to analyze the social division of labor as a natural history is to sacrifice all hope of understanding the mechanism that governs its evolution in human society.

Clearer thinkers such as Marx (1977, 335) and Edward Gibbon Wakefield agreed that we should more properly seek the origins of the differ-

entiation among employments in slavery rather than purely technical explanations. One can even find such a suggestion in Smith's (1978, 196)
own work.

True, market forces could eventually lead to a more elaborate social
division of labor. A decline in self-sufficiency could create a home market
for mass-consumption goods; yet such a home market begins from a very
small base and could not reach a substantial size overnight. Are we to
believe that those who stood to profit from the growth of capitalism
would stand by and let the social division of labor precede at such a
slow pace?

The mercantile school, in particular, did not care to wait for the natural
maturation of a home market, preferring to tap the riches of world markets as soon as possible. To this end, they were willing to launch an
immediate attack on the self-sufficient household as a first step in stimulating the production of commodities for export (Marx 1967, 3:785). As a
result, the difference between the supposedly Smithian and mercantile
paths was substantial. As Marx (ibid.) noted:

> The characteristic feature of the interested merchants and manufac-
> turers of that period, which is in keeping with the stage of capitalist
> development represented by them, is that the transformation of feu-
> dal agricultural societies into industrial ones and the corresponding
> industrial struggle of nations on the world-market depends on an
> accelerated development of capital, which is not to be arrived at along
> the so-called natural path, but rather by means of coercive measures.
> It makes a tremendous difference whether national capital is gradu-
> ally and slowly transformed into industrial capital, or whether this
> development is accelerated by means of a tax which they impose
> through protective duties mainly upon landowners, middle and small
> peasants, and handicraftsmen, by way of accelerated expropriation of
> the independent direct producers, and through the violently acceler-
> ated accumulation and concentration of capital, in short by means of
> accelerated establishment of conditions of capitalist production. It
> simultaneously makes an enormous difference in the capitalist and
> industrial exploitation of the natural national productive power.

Arthur Young (1774, 298; cited in Deane 1957, 88; see also Young 1794,
436), the peripatetic agricultural writer who was unique in showing respect for Steuart, reflected the prevailing attitude when he characterized
"trade and manufactures of . . . sickly and difficult growth; if you do not
give them active encouragement they presently die."

Here again we confront the stark contrast between Steuart and Smith.

For Steuart, trade first begins with government support of luxury exports. Gradually, inland commerce takes on more significance (Steuart 1767, 1:347–49). Smith, by contrast, saw the acceleration of domestic exchanges as a consequence of the expansion of internal markets. He associated this tendency with "natural" progress as opposed to the contrived commerce that Steuart identified as the motor force (Smith 1976, III.i.8, 380). As a result, Smith wrote as if he would have preferred to wait for the household economy to atrophy on its own as the market withdrew economic energies away from traditional activities.

Smith believed that agricultural society would naturally transform itself into an urban commercial society in short order. In truth, even the towns, which were central to Smith's theory of economic development, began as artificial units that were granted special privileges by the state (see Merrington 1976, 180–82). Later capital shifted much of its activity to places, such as Leeds, Birmingham, Manchester, where it could be less encumbered by traditional labor regulations. In these rural sites workers no longer passed through apprenticeships, but remained as low-paid underlings (Ashton 1972, 15–16, 94). In the northern colonies of North America, however, towns did seem to develop more like Smith had envisioned the process (see Bidwell 1916, 256–62), but despite his best efforts, the preponderance of the colonial experience flew in the face of Smith's theory of harmonious economic development.

Was Smith merely being disingenuous in pretending that market forces were sufficient to cause accelerated economic development? After all, Britain had colonial rivals who could profit from any possible lethargy in British development. Rosa Luxemburg (1968, 370), discussing the course of the transformation of colonial expansion, noted:

> If capital were here to rely on the process of slow internal disintegration, the process might take centuries. To wait patiently until the most important means of production could be alienated by trading . . . [would be] tantamount to renouncing the production forces of these territories altogether.

Or was Smith once again providing ideological cover for the market society that he was witnessing?

The Natural Evolution of the Division of Labor

According to Smith, the progressive social division of labor should be understood exclusively in terms of the anthropological principle of the natural disposition of human beings. He counseled that we should prohibit any attempts to affect the division of labor through political action since such efforts were "evident violations of natural liberty" (Smith 1976, IV.v.b.16, 530). Consequently, they are "unjust and as impolitic as unjust" (ibid.).

On these grounds, Smith (ibid.) concluded, "It is in the interest of every society that things such as this kind [i.e., the creation of a new social division of labor] should never be forced or obstructed." Thus Smith (ibid., 466) also criticized drawbacks as destructive of "the natural division and distribution of labor in the society."

In 1749, Smith first presented the division of labor as unfolding naturally within the bosom of the countryside, claiming:

> Little else is requisite to carry a State to the highest degree of opulence from the lowest barbarism, but peace, easy taxes and a tolerable administration of justice; all the rest being brought about by the natural course of things. All governments which thwart this natural course, which force things into another channel, or which endeavour to arrest the progress of society at a particular point are unnatural and to support themselves are obliged to be oppressive and tyrannical. (cited in Stewart 1811, 322)

Again, in *The Wealth of Nations,* Smith (1976, IV.v.b.43, 540; see also II.iii.28, 341) repeated his claim that the "natural effort of every individual to better his own condition" was sufficient to guarantee economic development. According to Smith (1976, IV.v.b.43, 540), "This principle is so powerful . . . that it is alone, and without any assistance capable of carrying on the society of wealth and prosperity." Smith's theory of the orderly progress of society excluded the possibility that primitive accumulation may have played a role in economic development or that economic hardship for the masses may have been an expected outcome of economic progress.

Smith also theorized that the social division of labor could be understood in terms of the individual division of labor within the workshop; thus, the "separation of different trades and employments from one another seems to have taken place in consequences" of the advantages of the division of labor in the workshop (ibid., I.i.4, 15). This analogy formed the foundation of Smith's basic argument: Since within the workshop, a more refined division of labor is economical, surely people would choose to arrange their employments in a manner that would create a more progressive social division of labor.

Smith's theory of the natural evolution of the division of labor served a crucial purpose in his work. His teacher, Frances Hutcheson, had opposed the works of Bernard Mandeville at every opportunity. In one of Smith's early works, he followed his teacher's tradition, taking both Mandeville and Rousseau to task for "suppos[ing] that there is in man no powerful instinct which necessarily determines him to seek society for its own sake" (Smith 1755–56, 250).

Smith obstinately attempted to prove that capitalism would naturally evolve within a community of independent households. His hypothetical account of the history of the social division of labor is satisfactory as far as it goes. We can accept that petty commodity production could evolve from agriculture. Farmers can work on their own as shoemakers or weavers once their field work is done. Smith's reference to the division of labor in the workshop at first sounds even more substantial, but it substantially fails on one count: it never explains the sudden appearance of workshops where employers who own the means of production hire workers who have no capital of their own.

Unlike Steuart (1767, 1:109), who advocated extraeconomic measures to create "a free and perfect society which is a general tacit contract, from which reciprocal and proportional services result universally between all those who compose it," Smith was obliged to indicate how such a social division of labor would naturally evolve from market relations. Unfortunately, Smith failed miserably in this regard.

Stock and the Social Division of Labor

Smith did not consistently analyze the social division of labor in terms of the "separation of different trades and employments from one another." He also discovered a class-based principle to explain the phenomenon. This analysis centered on the concept of "stock" or, to be more precise, capital. In describing this second type of analysis, Smith (1976, II.intro.3, 277) boldly asserted, "The accumulation of stock must, in the nature of things, be previous to the division of labour." Within this context, people can no longer simply specialize in one or another occupation. Now a prior accumulation of stock is a precondition.

On its face, the assertion that stock (meaning capital) must exist prior to a division of labor seems to be utter nonsense. Smith (1978, 522) himself noted: "Til some stock be produced there can be no division of labour, and before a division of labor stock be produced there can be very little accumulation of stock." Are we to believe that people who were not engaged in market relations somehow plowed with their fingernails and cut wood with their teeth? As Mountiford Longfield (1834, 190) suggested: "Imagine a number of intelligent and industrious men, placed in a fertile country . . . utterly destitute of capital. With what difficulty could they eke out a miserable subsistence, possessing no tools except what they could fashion with their hands, and teeth, and nails." Of course, Smith could not have meant that people had no tools before the social division. For him, the term "stock" usually had a special meaning. It represented capital in particular, rather than tools and equipment in general. More specifically, Smith's stock referred to means of production held by a group of people who employed other people to use them.

Smith, however, is not consistent in this respect. In his lectures, he informed his students: "The number of hands employed in business depends on the stored stock in the kingdom. . . . Many goods produce nothing for a while. The grower, the spinner, the dresser of flax, have no immediate profit" (Smith 1978, 365). Since people produced flax and spun linen before capitalism, we can wonder how they were able to do so without stock. Yet, according to *The Wealth of Nations*, only an increase in capital was capable of bringing about an increase in production (Smith 1976, II.iii.32, 342).

Is Smith's confusion about the nature of stock here an isolated lapse? His friend, Turgot, whom nobody has to my knowledge accused of being an unworldly professor, used an almost identical line of reasoning in his *Reflections on the Formation and Distribution of Wealth*.

In the first two sections, Turgot indicated how diversity of land can lead to barter, but not wage labor. The institution of wage labor arises out of a natural history of commodities quite similar to Smith's. Wheat must pass from grain to flour to bread; cattle are raised, then their hides are tanned and made into shoes. "If the same man who cultivates on his own land these different articles, and who raises them to supply his wants was obliged to perform all the intermediate operations himself, it is certain he would succeed very badly" (Turgot 1766, 5). Consequently, "everyone profits" from a more refined social division of labor (ibid., 6). In the next paragraph, however, Turgot began by introducing us to a new individual, the "mere workman, who depends only on his hands and his industry . . . [who] has nothing but such part of his labour as he is able to dispose to others" (ibid., 7). Like Smith, Turgot neglected to explain exactly how the transition from an equal ownership of land with which he began his exposition to a situation in which some are reduced to the status of "mere workmen" is in the interests of these people. Such is the nature of political economy!

Jacob Viner (1965, 128–38) suggested that the parallelisms between Smith and Turgot may not have been coincidental, although Peter Groenewegen (1969) makes the case that they may have been. In any event, Smith went further than Turgot.

In conclusion, Smith's assertion about the priority of stock raised many questions. First, we might ask again, what then was the origin of this stock? Does it fall from the air? How do the means of production suddenly become stock? If it does not come from primitive accumulation, how is it that one group of people came to possess stock and another group has none? Unfortunately, Smith never offered any satisfactory answers.

The Origin of Stock

For Smith, the introduction of stock remained an unexplained event that somehow changed the entire nature of society. According to Smith, "As soon as a stock has accumulated in the hands of particular persons, some of them will naturally employ it in setting to work industrious people" (Smith 1976, I.v.5, 65).

We might ask, why do the industrious people need these particular persons to set them to work? Smith's (ibid., I.viii.8, 83) answer was that "the greater part of the workmen stand in need of a master to advance them the materials of their work, and their wages and maintenance." Smith had the good sense not to include capital goods in his account, since many workers owned their own tools at the time (see Ashton 1972, 217).

Smith wrote nothing to indicate how this new principle suddenly becomes dominant. Obviously, the introduction of stock changed the world. Instead of picturing a society in which workers voluntarily chose their occupations, Smith (ibid., III.v.12, 362) even lumped together "labouring cattle" and "productive labourers" in his description of a world dominated by stock.

Admittedly, the conflating of laborers and cattle was not unique, as we saw in discussing Mirabeau. In addition, John Locke (1698, 307) had written, "Thus the Grass my Horse has bit; the Turfs my Servant has cut; and the Ore I have digg'd . . . become my Property," but Smith went much further.

In fact, Smith attributed so much importance to stock that we are told "stock cultivates the land; stock employs labour" (Smith 1976, V.ii.f.6, 849). What would possess a thinker of the stature of Smith to resort to such ridiculous reasoning?

No wonder the dumbstruck Piercy Ravenstone (1824, 38–39) exclaimed:

> The word, capital, is sufficient to account for every thing. If nations grow populous, it is the effect of capital. If they direct their industry to the cultivation of their fields, it is capital lends them lands. . . . If they build cities, and encourage manufactures, it is still the effect of

capital. . . . Whence came the capital that creates all these prodigies?
Adam left none to his children. . . . Capital like all the productions of
man, has had a beginning; but how that which is the result of accumulation could act before accumulation took place, could be its
cause is a problem.

Smith indicated another dimension to his befuddlement in writing about
the origin of capital in his chapter on money in *The Wealth of Nations.*
Here, he began with a historical treatment of money as a unit of account
(Smith 1976, book 1, chap. 4). He seemed unable to move beyond that
point; after a long series of anecdotes about ancient money, he ventured to
promise to examine the rules that determine exchangeable value. Suddenly, he shifted to a paragraph on the difference between use values and
exchange values (ibid., I.iv.13, 44). What followed, however, was a disappointing introduction to his superficial treatment of value as the sum of
the component parts of wages, profits, and rent. Never once did he mention how he was able to justify his jump from the armor of Diomede to the
wages of labor (ibid., I.iv.4, 39).

In the end, Smith's confusion about the origins of capital seems to have
served a good purpose, since it put Marx on the track of his own theory of
the so-called primitive accumulation.

The Two Principles of the Social Division of Labor

If effect, Smith proposed two principles regarding the social division of
labor. In the first, occupational-based analysis, the social division of labor
evolves because people voluntarily choose specialized occupations. The
second, and contradictory principle regulating the social division of labor,
divides society into classes, one of which is defined by the ownership of
stock. Each principle has its own underlying anthropology. Each has its
own intended use.

The division of the social labor process into occupations was a useful
tactic to explain the harmony of the marketplace through the example of
the mutually beneficial nature of barter among independent workers. The
class-based analysis was conducive to recognizing conflict. Thus, for instance, the occupational-based analysis led Smith (ibid., 1.ii.2, 26–27) to
discover the socially desirable results of the self-interest of the butcher,
brewer, and baker. In contrast, Smith's class-based theory inclined him to
observe that the interest of capital in general "has not the same connexion
with the general interest of society" (ibid., I.xi.p.10., 266).

Within the class-based analysis, we can no longer explain capitalist social relations by a "natural disposition . . . to truck barter or exchange." Also, the second principle requires a different theory of value. As Edward Gibbon Wakefield (1835, 2:230–31n) noted in his commentary on Smith's chapter "On the Profits of Stock" in *The Wealth of Nations:*

> Treating labour as a commodity, and capital, the produce of labour, as another, then, if the value of these two commodities were regulated by equal quantities of labour, a given quantity of capital would, under all circumstances, exchange for that quantity of capital which had been produced by the same amount of labour; antecedent labour, as capital has been termed, would always exchange for the same amount of present labour.

On the whole, Smith's class-based theory was more consistent than his theory of occupational cooperation. Moreover, Smith presented the former as a system of administration to be implemented in practice, whereas he placed his occupational-based theory in the ideological sections of his famous work. Still, the contrast between an occupational-based and a class-based analysis of society, although not made wholly explicit by Smith, remains a great achievement.

Stock and the Transition to Wage Labor

Edmund Spenser (1591, 130) once wrote, "For why should he that is at libertie make himself bond? Sith then we are free borne, Let us all servile base subjection scorne." Had Smith dared to wrestle with Spenser's question, he would have written a greater book, but one that would have met the same fate as Steuart's work. Instead, Smith laid the groundwork for modern economic theory by focusing on exchanges.

Exchanges, in and of themselves, could not explain such a fundamental modification of the economic system as occurred with the introduction of stock (Marx 1967, 3:325–27). Yet Smith was unable to come to grips with the transition from the self-sufficient household to the capitalist mode of production. He could only come as close as barter, or even simple commodity production, but the leap to wage labor was beyond him.

Smith gave no indication that he in any way comprehended the move from the "rude state" to one in which people who were once able to live without "stock" now found themselves "stand[ing] in need of those particular persons," the capitalists, who are able to claim a reward for their "stock." He might have suggested that with population growth, the division and subdivision of farms leaves some people dependent on wage labor. Many historians might even be satisfied with such an explanation, but this force would be too slow to cause the rapid economic changes that were occurring. Besides, in Smith's laboratory, the Scottish Highlands, depopulation was the order of the day.

In any case, Smith never squarely faced the issue of the change in the mode of production, as the self-sufficient household gave way to wage labor. He presumably left his analysis of the specifics of the transition vague because he assumed that the institution of wage labor somehow came into existence prior to the initiation of the process of development.

Indeed, Smith frequently fell into confusion because he consistently failed to distinguish between the creation of petty commodity production, in which individuals produced goods on their own account for sale on the market, and the introduction of capitalism, where capitalists hired workers to do wage labor. Because Smith could not distinguish between these two phenomena, he often regaled his readers with contradictory assertions about the nature of the social division of labor. For example, we have just seen that in explaining the evolution of petty commodity production, the division of labor naturally evolved out of the rude state of society in which no stock existed. Yet, within the other theory, stock is the principal motor force.

Nowhere do we find Smith addressing the question, What changes could make people in the Scottish Highlands suddenly find it in their interest to abandon their self-sufficiency in order to accept wage labor? Even if such incentives did exist, how do we know that they would create a labor force fast enough to satisfy those who wanted to profit by hiring wage labor?

In short, Smith's theory of a natural evolution of the social division of labor was wholly inadequate. Rather than explaining the origin of stock, Smith would have us believe that capital somehow appeared from nowhere to demand a profit on its stock. The central question remains: How, then, do some people find themselves in the employ of others? Here, Smith fell silent, although a dramatic form of primitive accumulation was uprooting masses of people in Smith's own Scotland at the time. These people had no choice but to adopt a new occupation, often in far-off lands.

Taking Stock of Smith

Smith's assertion about the precedence of stock is relevant to our study of primitive accumulation. As mentioned earlier, Marx's English translators retranslated part of Marx's German translation of Smith's original accumulation into the phrase "primitive accumulation." In this passage,

Smith had no intention of explaining primitive accumulation. Instead, he was emphasizing the importance of the division of labor in creating economic progress, although strictly speaking, Smith was referring to the social division of labor at this point.

No wonder Marx (1977, 486n) felt moved to charge that Smith did less "to bring out the capitalist character of the division of labor" than earlier writers such as William Petty and the anonymous author of *Advantages of the East-India Trade* (on the authorship of this tract, see Barber 1975, 57n; see also Cannan 1929, 96–100; Rodbertus 1899, 78–79).

Among all the other later commentators, only Edward Gibbon Wakefield seems to have divined Smith's intentions. Wakefield (1835, 1:v) noted that Smith "appears to be composing, not a theory, but a history of national wealth." Wakefield correctly chided Smith for confounding the division of labor with the social division of labor (ibid., 30). He even insinuated that Smith was "not thoroughly acquainted with . . . this subject" (ibid., 21).

Smith was not as unacquainted with his subject as Wakefield charged. In fact, at times, Smith even seemed to be on the verge of coming to grips, perhaps unconsciously, with the concept of surplus value. Unfortunately, on such occasions, he plucked out his offending eye in a primitive ritual whereby the category of stock was deified.

In all fairness, Smith was not alone is confusing petty commodity production with wage labor. No major figure in classical political economy successfully distinguished between these two forms of production. Early commentators on political economy also generally overlooked the theoretical challenge posed by the transition to wage labor. Perhaps the closest to a recognition came from the question that von Thünen posed: "How has the worker been able to pass from being the master of capital—as its creator—to being its slave?" (cited in Dempsey 1960, 335; see also Marx 1977, 772n).

An anonymous Swedish pamphleteer with an eye for realism also noted, "Freedom of enterprise would lead to disastrous misfortune; all the small masters would be ruined because all would like to be masters and nobody a servant, all subordination and order will disappear" (cited in Magnusson 1987, 423). Such flashes of insight concerning the nature of primitive accumulation were rare. As Walter Bagehot (1880, 419) charged, "Political Economy does not recognize that there is a vital distinction between the main mode in which capital grows in England now, and the mode in which countries grew at first."

In addition, Bagehot (ibid., 361) observed:

> The main part of modern commerce is carried on in a very different manner; it begins and ends at a different point. The fundamental point is the same: the determining producer—the person on whose volition it depends whether the object should be produced or not—goes on so long as he is satisfied. . . . But the determining producer is now not a laborer but a capitalist.

In other words, considering that Smith was engaged in producing a history of wage labor, he should have to account for the forces that would induce self-sufficient households to exchange labor power for wages. He never did.

Whatever his defects, at least Smith had the merit of pointing toward both the class-based and occupation-based theories of the social division of labor. Even so, Smith was primarily interested in creating a theory in which the role of class conflict could be obscured by a fable of harmonies. As a result, *The Wealth of Nations* emerged as an epic poem of a strange world where "things are in the saddle and ride mankind" (Emerson 1940).

CHAPTER 10

Adam Smith and the
Ideological Role of the Colonies

The differences of circumstance between this and the old countries of Europe,
furnish differences of fact whereon to reason, in questions of political economy,
and will consequently produce sometimes a difference of result.—Thomas Jefferson, 1 February 1804 letter

Adam Smith's North American Laboratory

As we have seen, Adam Smith advocated high wages for the practical
reason that he hoped that greater remuneration would convert workers to
petty bourgeois values. His call for high wages also served the ideological
purpose of proving that the interests of capital and labor were not at odds.
In this theoretical effort, Smith relied heavily on evidence from his study of
labor markets in the North American colonies (see Skinner 1976, 78). Conditions there appeared to be ideally suited to support Smith's purposes.

From Smith's perspective, the experience of the colonies demonstrated
how high wages could help capital to prosper. If Smith were correct in this
respect, he could resolve significant contradictions in his theory. Specifically, he could show how a market society could develop harmoniously
without the need for harsh measures, such as primitive accumulation.

Smith (1976, IV.vii.b.3, 565) claimed that profits in the North American
colonies were "commonly very great." He concluded that people in the
colonies prospered there because they enjoyed more natural liberty than
did the people of Britain. In the colonies, high wages and high profits
supposedly coexisted, presumably because that society was free of the
feudal fetters that had held back British development (ibid., III.iv.19, 423–
24). According to Smith (ibid., IV.vii.b.2, 565), "Every colonist gets more
land than he can possibly cultivate. He has no rent and scarcely any taxes
to pay. No landlord shares with him in his produce, and the share of the
sovereign is commonly but a trifle."

Despite the paucity of data, Smith wrote about the colonies with unwavering conviction. Although he criticized the absence of distributive
equity in the British wage system relative to that of North America, for

example, the wages of skilled labor were actually approximately equal in both Britain and North America (see Habakkuk 1967; Cole 1968, 64). In this spirit, he declared, "The plenty and cheapness of good land are such powerful causes of prosperity, . . . the very worst government is scarce capable of checking the efficiency of their operation" (Smith 1976, IV.vii.b.12, 570; see also IV.vii.b.2, 564–5; IV.vii.b.17, 572).

Smith's Theory of Colonial Development

For Adam Smith to make his case that colonial conditions pointed the way for British development, he had to go beyond merely demonstrating that high wages promoted prosperity in a far-off land. The colonial experience might be nothing more than a curiosity if the colonies were simply an agricultural backwater with little in common with England.

To convince his readers that the colonial experience had any relevance to the British, Smith had to somehow explain how the colonies would go on to develop a sophisticated capitalist economy. In this respect, Smith faced a serious contradiction. Although the likelihood of an industrial future in the colonies would further his ideology, in reality, he wanted the colonists to remain backward by specializing in providing raw materials for the British to work up into finished goods. According to Smith's vision, the British would then export these finished goods to the colonies.

Here we come up against another contradiction in Smith's works: Even though Britain was to abandon much of its agricultural pursuits to the colonies, Smith maintained a strong Physiocratic bent that made him look favorably on agriculture. He taught that agriculture was "of all the arts the most beneficial to society" (Smith 1978, 522). He also insisted that agriculture "adds much greater value to the annual produce of the land and labour of the country, to the real wealth and revenue of its inhabitants" (1976, II.v.12, 364). He concluded, "Of all the ways in which a capital can be employed, it is by far the most advantageous to the society" (ibid., II.v.12, 364).

Despite the allegedly great advantages of agriculture, we might expect that Smith would have supported protection for agriculture in England, but he was not a firm defender of British agriculture. Instead, he predicted that "even the free importation of foreign corn could very little affect the interest of the farmer of Great Britain" (ibid., IV.ii.20, 461). England was too advanced to devote considerable energy to agriculture.

As a general principle, Smith insisted that nations with limited capital should always specialize in agriculture (see, for example, Smith 1976, II.v.11 and 12, 363). He declared:

Agriculture is the proper business of all new colonies; a business which the cheapness of land renders more advantageous than any other. . . . In new colonies, agriculture either draws hands from other employments, or keeps them from going to any other employments. There are few hands to spare for the necessary, and none for the ornamental manufactures. The greater part of the manufactures of both kinds, they find it cheaper to purchase of other countries' than to make it themselves. (Smith 1976, IV.vii.c.51, 609)

Smith contended that such agricultural specialization benefited the colonies. He went so far as to claim that because colonial "wealth is founded altogether in agriculture" (ibid., III.iv.19, 423; see also III.v.21, 366), the colonies were enjoying an extremely rapid increase in prosperity (ibid., III.v.21, 366–67; III.iv.19, 422–23).

Smith's optimistic prognosis for the colonies seemed to fly in the face of his own theory of the division of labor. After all, the first sentence of *The Wealth of Nations* read: "The greatest improvements in the productive powers of labour . . . seem to be the effects of the division of labour" (ibid., 11). A few pages later, he added, "The nature of agriculture . . . does not admit of so many subdivisions . . . as manufactures" (ibid., I.i.4, 16).

Still, Smith (ibid., III.v.12, 363) suggested that agricultural specialization allowed the colonial economy to prosper since the "capital employed in agriculture . . . not only puts into motion a greater quantity of productive labour than any equal capital employed in manufactures, but in proportion to the quantity of productive labour it employs." He reasoned that "land is still so cheap, and consequently, labour so dear among them, that they can import from the mother country, almost all the more refined and more advanced manufactures cheaper than they could make them for themselves" (Smith 1976, IV.vii.b.44, 582). Smith (ibid., III.i.7, 379) believed the colonists to be fortunate in this respect, claiming:

If the society has not acquired sufficient capital to cultivate all its lands, and to manufacture in the completest manner the whole of its rude produce, there is even a considerable advantage that the rude produce should be exported by a foreign capital, in order that the whole stock of the society may be employed in more useful purposes.

According to Smith's logic, where capital is scarce, society should specialize in agriculture, which is less capital-intensive than industry since a unit of capital in agriculture can set more workers in motion than a comparable unit in industry. Yet individual agricultural workers will not be as productive as industrial workers given that agriculture will have a less developed division of labor. Even so, agricultural development will still make sense because it will employ a greater mass of workers.

Unfortunately, for the colonial experience to lend support to Smith's ideology, he would have had to show how the natural course of development in the colonies would allow them to converge with the British economy. He never really broached that subject beyond his four stages theory, which asserted that agricultural economies would naturally evolve into commercial economies.

If the colonies were to industrialize, where would Britain obtain her raw materials? Did Smith expect that the transformation of the colonies into commercial society would cause Britain to revive some of its agrarian past?

The Free Trade Imperialism of Adam Smith

Reading Smith, one could almost believe at times that the colonists were getting the better of the British, who were left to shoulder the burden of the carrying trade (Smith, 1976, III.v.21, 366–67; see also III.i.6, 379). Since the British took care of such a capital-intensive endeavor, the Americans were free to specialize in agricultural production. Smith maintained:

> Were the Americans, either by combination or by any other sort of violence, to stop the importation of European manufactures, and by thus giving a monopoly to such of their own countrymen, . . . [and to] divert any considerable part of their capital into this employment, they would retard instead of accelerating the further increase in the value of their annual produce. (ibid., II.v.21, 367)

Elsewhere, Smith (ibid., IV.ix.37, 677) admitted that under this arrangement, England would prosper, since "a small quantity of manufactured produce purchases a great quantity of rude produce . . . while . . . a country without trade and manufactures is generally obliged to purchase, at the expense of a great part of its rude produce, a very small part of the manufactured produce of other countries." Smith (ibid., IV.ix.41, 680–81) linked this same idea to the benefits that foreign markets bring for the development of economies of scale in manufacturing, without associating this thought with the teachings of either Sir James Steuart or Josiah Tucker.

Instead, Smith appeared oblivious to the possibility that such economies of scale could set off a cumulative process in which the manufacturing prowess of the industrial economy becomes increasingly entrenched. Smith's silence in this regard is surprising. After all, his close friend, David Hume, had engaged in a strong debate with Josiah Tucker, who had maintained that such trade would allow Britain to develop an insurmountable industrial lead (Hudson 1992, 69 ff.). Hume responded that cheap wages would permit the less advanced economies to converge with the more advanced.

Perhaps simply because Smith was attempting to make the case that wages would be high in the colonies, he let the matter pass in silence. Michael Hudson proposed another possibility. Hudson (1992) observed that Steuart as well as Tucker maintained that the less developed economies would be left in a state of permanent backwardness if they left their fate to the market. Hudson charged that Smith framed his work to evade as far possible the ideas of his rivals, who foresaw a polarized world economy.

In addition, Smith should have benefited from his experience in Scotland, which remained a supplier of raw materials even in the absence of mercantile prohibitions of native industry, such as those that had crippled Ireland. More than fifty years after Defoe (1724–26, 634–37) first criticized Scotland's position as a mere supplier of raw materials, James Anderson (1777, 395–97) found it necessary to repeat the same idea.

So little had changed that Defoe and Anderson produced an almost identical list of imports. Other than some textiles, Scotland was said to export no manufactured goods to England. Much of its imports were manufactured. Anderson (ibid., 397) complained that the situation in Scotland was, if anything, a more extreme dependence than that found in the United States: "An equal number of the inhabitants of North America, who hardly take any other articles from England but cloathing and hardwares, cannot consume more English manufactures than an equal number of the Scots do."

Unlike Defoe and Anderson, Smith did not see dependence in the Scottish economy. Among Smith's contemporaries, however, almost everyone believed that Scottish development would have to be administered. Smith's own patron, Lord Kames, was a leading member of the Board of Trustees for Fisheries, Manufactures, and Improvements in Scotland, set up to rescue the "Highlands from its archaic backwardness" (Rendall 1978, 11).

Robert Wallace (1809, 159) advocated a scheme to create a fishing village along the Scottish coast to promote the exploitation of the fishing resources. Earlier, Steuart (1767, 2:194) had also supported this project. Smith and Bentham appear to have been virtually alone in their opposition to this proposal (Mossner and Ross 1977, 327; Rae 1895, 409). At least the industrious Jacob Viner (1965, 92) could find no other indication of dissent.

Smith recognized no structural reason for the primitive conditions that he saw in Scotland. He attributed the lack of development in the Highlands to the absence of a division of labor. He complained that the highland farmer had not yet adapted to the modern division of labor. Instead, the farmer still doubled as "butcher, baker and brewer." As a result, the highlanders were not yet dependent on purchased commodities. Nonetheless, Smith had faith in the future of the Highlands. He speculated that improved roads alone would seem to be sufficient to modernize the area (Smith 1976, I.i.3, 32–33). However, Smith gave no indication that the Highlands could ever rival Britain as a manufacturing center. In fact, the region seemed destined to remain forever a dependent supplier of raw materials for British industry.

In light of his tacit approval of the economic dependence that he saw in the Highlands as well as the colonies, we might well credit Adam Smith, the teacher of economic administrators, with being the first theorist of free trade imperialism, although Dean Tucker might justifiably lay claim to this distinction (see Schuyler 1931, 35–36). Even so, in reviewing our analysis of Smith in this section, we find that Smith was more or less consistent. An economy would supposedly best develop through a regime of specialization under free trade, eventually leading to prosperity.

Unfortunately, with Smith nothing is as simple as it first appears. To begin with, Smith had taken issue with Steuart, who identified foreign trade as the locus of development. In contrast, Smith held that the home market was central to economic development. According to this logic, the colonies should have aimed for self-sufficiency.

In addition, so long as the colonies adhered to Smith's recommendations, their military capacity would also be limited, since as Smith (1976, IV.i.30, 445; 1978, 196–97) noted, the financing of warfare through the export of raw materials is always inconvenient. Thus the colonies would remain a de facto appendage to England.

The Economics of Underdevelopment

Many farmers in the colonies achieved a degree of self-sufficiency, comparable to what Smith saw in the Scottish Highlands (see Bidwell and Falconer 1941, 126–31, 162–63; see also Peffer 1891; cited in Luxemburg 1968, 396–98); yet Smith insisted that even in the absence of government intervention, capitalism was perfectly capable of developing out of the local initiative and enterprise of the countryside.

Smith offered a confused account of the evolution of such an agrarian society. He proposed his four stages theory, according to which societies naturally evolve from hunting and gathering, to herding, then to agriculture, and finally to a commercial society but did not explain why this evolution was inevitable. Smith seemed to sense that this development came at a cost. For example, just before a discussion about the role of the colonies in the international division of labor, Smith went to some lengths to describe the "beauty," "tranquility," and "charm" of a rural lifestyle (1776, III.i.3, 378).

After noting that "man . . . seems . . . to retain a predilection for this primitive employment," Smith's next paragraph abruptly begins with the idea that a social division of labor that includes industry is required for an efficient agriculture. One might be led to believe that the humanitarian British were about to sacrifice their idyllic existence so that the fortunate colonists might be allowed to live in harmony with nature. In any case, Smith offered no explanation of why people would voluntarily abandon their agricultural life. Instead, Smith merely dismissed the difficulty of developing an economy, offering even less than he did when he suggested that the provision of roads be sufficient to induce development in the Scottish Highlands.

On other occasions, Smith acknowledged that agricultural profits might not be high after all. Low profits, of course, would impede the transition to an industrial society. Smith (ibid., I.x.c.21, 142) himself wrote:

> That the industry which is carried on in towns, is every-where in Europe more advantageous than that which is carried on in the country, without entering into any nice computations, we may satisfy ourselves by one very simple and obvious observation. In every country of Europe we find great fortunes from small beginnings by trade and manufactures, the industry which properly belongs to towns, for one who has done so by that which properly belongs to the country, the raising of rude produce by the improvement and cultivation of the land. Industry, therefore, must be better rewarded, the wages of labour and the profits of stock must evidently be greater in one situation than the other.

If profits are highest in the commercial and industrial activities that occur in the towns, presumably economies that specialize in such activities will have the potential to develop at a faster rate than agrarian societies. This phenomenon may help to explain the persistent backwardness that Smith found in the Scottish Highlands.

Additionally, Smith's theory of the division of labor suggests that the development of nonagricultural professions should accelerate the rate of productivity, even in the agriculture of advanced societies. Smith himself never took note of this factor, although we might read it into his work where he observed, "Without the assistance of some artificers, indeed, the cultivation of the land cannot be carried on but with great inconvenience

236

and continual interruption. . . . The inhabitants of the town and the country are mutually the servants of one another" (ibid., III.i.4, 378). As a result, even agriculture might advance faster in more developed economies.

Smith (ibid., II.v.37, 374) also understood that agriculture was not the quickest path to personal affluence:

> The profits of agriculture, however, seem to have no superiority over those of other employments in any part of Europe. Projectors, indeed, in every corner of it, have within these few years amused the public with most magnificent accounts of the profits to be made by cultivation and improvement of the land. Without entering into any particular discussion of their calculations, a very simple observation may satisfy us that the result of them must be false. We see every day the most splendid manufactures, frequently from a very small capital, sometimes from no capital. A single instance of such a fortune acquired by agriculture in the same time, and from such a capital, has not, perhaps occurred in Europe during the course of the present century. In all the great countries of Europe, however, much good land remains uncultivated, and the greater part of what is cultivated is far from being improved to the degree of which it is capable.

Alex de Tocqueville (1848, 551–53) observed a similar phenomenon during his sojourn in the United States:

> Agriculture is perhaps, of all the useful arts, the one which improves most slowly in democratic nations. . . . To cultivate the ground promises an almost certain reward . . . but a slow one. In that way you only grow rich by little and with toil. Agriculture only suits the wealthy, who already have a great superfluity, or the poor, who only want to live. . . . [T]he great fortunes . . . are almost always of commercial origin.

The same phenomenon struck observers in situations as far away as nineteenth-century Japan (see Thomas Smith 1966, 66).

Moreover, where high profits do exist in agricultural societies, they accrue to commercial ventures, not agricultural proper. If agricultural societies were to break out of their backwardness, presumably those who reap profits outside of farming would have to invest in nonagricultural activities, which would eventually also modernize agriculture. However, in less developed economies, those who profit from doing business with farmers rarely invest in farming themselves.

Finally, the sort of development based on self-sufficiency tends to restrict capitalism to luxury markets (see Melotti 1977, 109). England developed its strong industrial base precisely because it was so successful in carrying out the process of primitive accumulation. With so many people left dependent on the market for their basic needs, British industry had a far greater mass market at hand than any other country. This advantage was crucial for the success of the Industrial Revolution in England.

In short, successful agrarian economies would have to follow a different course than Smith suggested.

Adam Smith's Mercantilism

In reality, to the extent that the colonies flourished, they did not do so because of free labor and voluntary commercial transactions. Instead, the key to economic growth in the colonies was the combination of unfree labor together with the advantages of a vast array of natural resources obtained through primitive accumulation on a continental scale. Smith himself never took account of the advantages of either unfree labor or primitive accumulation.

Nor did Smith acknowledge the significance of the measures that Britain took to impede development through the prohibition of important manufacturing activities and restrictions of imports. Instead, he took the position that the colonies proved that economic freedom was the surest route to progress.

Here we come to still another major contradiction in Smith's work: Although modern readers identify him with laissez-faire, Adam Smith, the theorist of economic administration, was not nearly the doctrinaire free trader that he is generally thought to be. He warned that "freedom of trade should be restored only by slow gradations" (Smith 1976, IV.ii.40, 469).

In financial matters, Smith also saw the need for government regulation. He called for the prohibition of the issue of small denominations of bank notes (ibid., II.ii.91, 323; II.ii.106, 329). In fact, Smith earned a strong rebuke from Bentham (1787a and 1790) for his acceptance of laws to prohibit usury (Smith 1976, II.iv.14–15, 356–57).

Smith was also in favor of using various devices to promote industry in Britain. Although he recognized that some duties were justified to counterbalance taxes levied on domestic producers (ibid., IV.ii.30, 464), he favored duty-free importation of raw materials as an encouragement to industry. However, Smith often looked favorably on restrictions of the export of raw materials. To cite one instance, he criticized the low duty on linen yarn on the grounds that the work of spinners made up four-fifths of the labor used in the production of sailcloth (ibid., IV.viii, 4, 644). He did not make the case, as he might have, that spinning could have helped such people carry on their agricultural pursuits. Instead, he relied on a mercantilistic allusion to the creation of employment. Similar reasoning led to his recommendation of duties on the export of wool (ibid., IV.viii.26, 653). In addition, Smith advocated that "Premiums [be] given by the publick to artists and manufacturers who excel their particular occupations" (ibid., IV.v.w.39, 523).

In fact, Smith's actual prescription for administration was very much at odds with his supposed ideology. Like any red-blooded mercantilist, Smith proclaimed, "the great object of political economy of any country is to increase the riches and power of that country" (ibid., II.v.31, 372). Not surprisingly, we find Smith's assertion about riches and power in the very same chapter of *The Wealth of Nations* where Smith recommended agricultural pursuits to the colonists.

Piecing together Smith's remarks suggests a pattern consistent with the thesis that he favored a system in which the colonies were to produce raw materials for the mother country to work up into finished products. In this light, Smith's plan for the colonies appears to be nothing more than a sophisticated brand of mercantilism.

In summary, Smith took a distinctly pragmatic approach to laissez-faire policies. In spite of his philosophical ruminations about the psychology of wealth and accumulation, Smith was an advocate of economic realpolitik. With respect to his work on international trade and development, Smith's interest lay as much with the nations of wealth as *The Wealth of Nations*. In this regard, T. Perronet Thompson, before departing to Africa as a colonial governor, wrote to his fiancée, "I am beginning my course of study for the time being of Adam Smith on the *Wealth of Nations*, as fitting a subject I guess for the Sierra Leone as can be devised" (Thompson 1808, 33). Quite so!

Smith's Theory of Harmonious Economic Development

We began by noting that Adam Smith had two objectives in analyzing the colonies. His practical program aimed at keeping the colonies as a supplier of raw materials for Britain. On a theoretical level, he intended to demonstrate that the coexistence of high wages and high profits in the colonies proved that the interests of capital and labor were identical.

Only one difficulty stood in the way of Smith's theory of the harmony of wage labor in the colonies. Assuming that profits in the colonies were high, Smith (1976, IV.vii. b.3, 565–66) observed, "This great profit cannot be made without employing the labour of other people in clearing and cultivating the land." This notion brings us back to the central puzzle that

Smith refused to confront: Where would farmers find the help that they needed? Why would people accept a position as a farm worker producing a surplus for an employer when the same people could just as easily work on their own and enjoy all the fruits of their labor?

Smith, of course, never answered such questions. To do so would have required that he confront the harsh reality of primitive accumulation. Instead, he only asserts that in view of the scarce supply of labor, the employer "does not, therefore, dispute about wages, but is willing to employ labour at any price" (ibid.). In addition, because of the scarcity of labor, "the interest of the two superior orders obliges them to treat the inferior one with more generosity and humanity" (Smith 1976, IV.vii.b.3, 565).

The reference to the "generosity and humanity" of employers is not particularly informative. At first glance, it might seem to support Smith's contention about the harmony of classes; however, readers of his recently discovered *Lectures on Jurisprudence* can also learn that "the slaves in the American colonies on the continent are treated with great humanity, and used in a very gentle manner" (Smith 1978, 183), suggesting a very loose interpretation of the concept of humanity.

According to Smith, only where slave owners' wealth had progressed to the level of the lords of the sugar islands would slavery degenerate to a barbaric relation (ibid., 183–87). Following this line of reasoning, we could just as well use Smith's reading of colonial conditions to assert the essential harmony between slave and master.

Smith (1776, I.ix.11, 109; IV.vii.c.51, 609) did note the ease with which workers could gain access to land. At one point, he even admitted that the conditions in North America were incompatible with wage labor:

> In our North American colonies, where uncultivated land is still to be had for easy terms, no manufactures for distant sale have yet been established in any of their towns. When an artificer has acquired a little more stock than is necessary for carrying on his own business in supplying the neighbouring country, he does not in North America, attempt to establish it with manufacture for distant sale, but employs it in the purchase and improvement of uncultivated land. From artificer he becomes planter, and neither the large wages nor the easy subsistence which that country affords to artificers, can bribe him to work for other people than for himself. He feels that an artificer is the servant of his customers . . . , but that a planter . . . is really a master, and independent of all the world. (ibid., III.i.5, 378–79; see also IV, vii.b.44, 582)

The colonial employers themselves certainly did not appreciate the environment of "generosity and humanity." Gabriel Thomas (1698, 33–34) wrote from Pennsylvania:

> The chief reason why Wages of Servants of all sorts is much higher here than there, arises from the great Fertility and Produce of the Place; besides if these large stipends were refused them, they would quickly set up for themselves, for they can have Provision very cheap, and Land for a very small matter, or next to nothing in comparison of the Purchase of Land in England.

Indeed, high wages were a constant lament in that part of the world (see, for example, Dorfman 1966a, 1:44–47, 63–64, 117, 214; Bogart and Thompson 1927, 67, 82).

Not only was wage labor expensive, it was impermanent as well. The more wages that capital paid out to its workers, the sooner they accumulated enough money to become independent farmers. Even in England, Smith (1976, I.viii.46, 101) claimed that "in years of plenty, servants frequently leave their masters, and trust their subsistence to what they can make by their own industry." In the northern American colonies, the situation was much more serious.

As late as the mid–nineteenth century when the United States had become far more developed, two or three years of farm labor were said to be sufficient for a penniless worker to save enough to acquire the land and equipment needed to begin farming (see S. Williams 1809; Ogg 1906; cited in Bidwell and Falconer 1941, 118, 163), although Clarence Danhof (1941) estimates that more time might have been required.

In Smith's day, wage labor was the exception rather than the rule in the colonies. The majority of workers were unfree, being either slaves or indentured servants. Those who had their freedom might be able to farm on their own after working for a short time. In that case, we come up against the substitution of household labor for wage labor, the very opposite of the movement that initially Smith set out to explain. Finally, those who did not care to accept wage labor, even temporarily, could subsist from hunting and trapping.

In short, Smith provided no insight into what forces might cause people to voluntarily choose wage labor. Certainly, he was unsuccessful in attempting to resolve his theoretical contradictions about wage labor with evidence from the colonies, where wage labor was the exception rather than the rule. Instead, his analysis of the colonial economy was pertinent to a discussion of self-provisioning or petty commodity production, but not an analysis of wage labor.

The Reaction to Smith

THE AMERICAN RECEPTION OF SMITHIAN ECONOMICS

Time and time again, Smith had held out the market-oriented economy of the northern colonies as the prime example for the still partially mercantile English economy to follow. We might reason that, since Smith's theory was meant to praise the conditions in these colonies, the people who resided there would embrace Smith's work.

Indeed, much of Smith's perspective had been anticipated by his illustrious namesake, Captain John Smith, a century and a half before the appearance of *The Wealth of Nations*. The earlier Smith (1616, 195–96) had written of New England:

> And here are no hard landlords to racke vs with their many disputations to Ivstice. . . . here every man may be master and owner of his owne labour; or the greatest part in a small time. If hee have nothing but his hands he may set vp trade; and by industrie quickly grow rich.

However, the colonists never accepted the views of Adam Smith. In point of fact, although the English public largely ignored Steuart, his work was more popular in North America than Smith's. In describing the influence of Smith's book, Arthur Schlessinger (1986, 220) noted, "Though read and admired, it did not at once persuade." Joseph Dorfman (1966a, 1:242), whose monumental study of economic thought in the United States is unsurpassed, concluded: "All seemed to know Sir James Steuart. Adam Smith's *An Inquiry into the Nature and Causes of the Wealth of Nations* would often be cited along with Steuart, but always within the framework of that variant of mercantilism to which the author adhered." Symbolically perhaps, the first American edition of *The Wealth of Nations* did not appear until 1789, eight years after Steuart's work (M. O'Connor 1944, 22).

I attribute Steuart's warm reception in North America to the continuing importance of nonmarket activities in the colonies. In general, Steuart's book was popular where capital had not yet matured. The Irish, French, and German editions all fared rather well (Sen 1957, 13). Similarly, English conditions explained Smith's eventual popularity in England, a nation where capital had already risen to ascendancy and the household economy had become less of a competitor than a useful complement in the eyes of capital. Smith offered a convenient justification for the prevailing path of economic development.

Admittedly, Smith might have exercised a wider influence in North America had he not classified the clergy as unproductive labor. Since the churches ran the schools and colleges in the colonies, academic admin-

istrators took offense at Smith's assessment of their clerical status. However, the schools were largely irrelevant, since their economic teaching
was notoriously out of touch with the real business world (see O'Connor
1944).

The 1821 translation of Jean-Baptiste Say's *Treatise* helped win an
eventual academic acceptance of Smith's ideas. This book, the first consciously composed textbook in economic theory (see Spiegel 1960, 65; see
also James 1965), omitted any mention of Smith's offending passages.
More important, the successful application of primitive accumulation
made the eastern seaboard of the United States become more like England.

Friedrich List, a vocal opponent of laissez-faire, for example, in a speech
at the dinner given in his honor by the Pennsylvania Society for the Promotion of Manufacturers in 1827, expressed regret that he found Say's
book "in the hands of every pupil" (cited in M. O'Connor 1944, 34). We
should note that, although Say (1880, xlx) did follow Smith in many respects, he saw himself as going beyond Smith. Say told his readers, "We
are, however, not yet in possession of an established textbook on the
science of political economy, . . . a work in which . . . results are so
complete and well arranged as to afford each other mutual support, and
that may everywhere, and at all times, be studied with advantage."

Political Leaders' Reading of Smithian Economics

The people charged with the responsibility of administering the colonies
did not seem to have been well-disposed toward Smith's abstract ideas,
which offered little help in solving the real problems that they faced. After
all, the reality there was not as simple as either Captain Smith or Adam
Smith suggested. In this spirit, Governor Pownall (1766) of Virginia provided Smith with an insightful critique of *The Wealth of Nations*.

Pownall, anticipating the language of Marx and Charles Fourier, understood that the object of economics was to analyze "those laws of
motion . . . which are the source of, and give direction to, the labour of
man in the individual; which form that reciprocation of wants and inter-
communion of mutual supply that becomes the creating cause of community" (ibid., 337; also see Marx 1977, 92; Anikin 1975, 353). The parallel
with Steuart is striking as well, although Pownall gave no indication of
any familiarity with Steuart's work. As mentioned already, Pownall rejected Smith's reliance on speculative anthropology.

Pownall (ibid., 343) also recognized the relationship between the social
division of labor and the "division of objects," that is, property. Finally, he
emphasized the advantages of using administrative means to speed up the

creation of markets and the accumulation of capital (ibid., 371). Pownall, however, was an administrator, and consequently, might have been instinctively more attuned to the doctrines of Steuart than those of Smith.

Still, Pownall was a representative of a nation engaged in profiting from mercantile policies vis-à-vis the colonies. What was the attitude of those who supported the revolution supposedly directed against the mercantile interests of England? Should not they be likely disciples of Smith?

True, Warren Nutter (1976) goes so far as to credit Smith with bringing Benjamin Franklin into the liberal fold, but as we shall see in the next chapter, this claim is questionable. Jefferson (1950–, 111) praised *The Wealth of Nations* as "the best book extant," although by 1817, he felt that Say's presentation was superior (Jefferson 1817). James Madison (1962–, 6:86) recommended to Jefferson that Congress purchase the works of both Steuart and Smith. In John Adams's (1819, 384–85) opinion, "the pith and marrow of science" were contained in . . . the great works of Sir James Stuart [*sic*], and of Adam Smith."

This weak testimony to the influence of Smith, cited above, must be taken with a grain of salt. After all, Adams was not an accomplished student of political economy. In the same letter in which he recommended the works of Steuart and Smith, Adams confessed himself unable to understand the Physiocratic school. Jefferson predicted that Ricardo's "muddy reasoning . . . could not stand the test of time" (cited in Spengler 1968, 7).

William Appleman Williams (1966, 145) judges Madison to have been greatly affected by Sir James Steuart. Madison (1962–, 502) himself lamented "the present anarchy of our commerce." To remedy the situation, he relied on the authority of Steuart's "anti-quantity theory of money" as a means of improving the organization of economic activity (Dorfman 1966a, 1:221).

A more accurate verdict on the perceived merits of Smith came from Fisher Ames (1854, 49; cited in Nutter 1976, 16), who remarked in 1789: "The principles of the [*Wealth of Nations*] are excellent, but the application of them to America requires caution."

Alexander Hamilton and Smith

Of all the founding fathers, Hamilton was most inclined toward the mindset of political economy. Scholars have noted certain parallelisms between the work of Hamilton and *The Wealth of Nations* (Gourne 1894; Mitchell 1957–62, 2:144, 146, 149; the editorial notes in A. Hamilton 1961, 10:1–240). William Grampp (1965, 134–36) even suggests that a reading of *The Wealth of Nations* was sufficient to wean Hamilton of his earlier mercantilist leanings. Smith's unimportant role in the development of Hamilton's thought is suggested by one source, who noted that Hamilton had actually prepared a critique of *The Wealth of Nations* during his term in the Continental Congress (Hamilton 1961, 10:i; J. Hamilton 1879, 2:514).

In fact, Hamilton's ideas were remarkably close to those of Steuart. Both thought that institutions other than the market were required to integrate the economy. Hamilton (1961, 7:70) approved of Steuart's popular monetary theories because they would "cement more closely the union of states." Indeed, Steuart used the same metaphor, calling upon statesmen to "cement" their society (1767, 2:191). Elsewhere, Hamilton (1961, 2:635, 402; see also 3:4, 29) praised debt and the army as cement for the union. In an address delivered in support of the proposed United States Constitution to the New York ratifying convention in 1788, Hamilton sounded almost like an echo of Steuart, proposing:

> Men will pursue their interests. It is as easy to change human nature, as to oppose the strong current of the selfish passions. A wise legislator will gently divert the channel, and direct it, if possible, to the public good. (Hamilton 1961, 5:85; also cited in Cooke 1982)

Steuart's influence was readily apparent in Hamilton's *Report on the Establishment of a Mint*, which drew heavily on the work of his master (Hamilton 1961, 10:462). Although Hamilton did not explicitly acknowledge Steuart, an early draft did allude to him as "an English writer of reputation who appears to have investigated the point with great accuracy and care and who accompanies his calculations with their data which are confirmed by other authority" (ibid., 482).

In his most systematic study of the limits of the market, Hamilton (ibid., 3:76; see also 15:467) lashed out at those "who maintain that trade will regulate itself. He continued: "Such persons assume that there is no need of a common directing power. This is one of those wildly speculative paradoxes, which have grown into credit among us, contrary to the practice and sense of the most enlightened nations."

Hamilton's most noteworthy contribution to economic theory proper was his *Report on the Subject of Manufacturers* (ibid., 10:1–340). In spite of admittedly frequent appropriations of Smith's thought, the intent of the document was decidedly unsmithian (ibid., 7; see also Cooke 1967, 81). Hamilton (1961, 249) wrote of the division of labor, but his division of labor was Steuart's, not Smith's. He began with the assertion:

It has just been observed, that there is scarcely anything of greater moment in the economy of a nation, than the proper division of labour. The separation of occupations causes each to be carried to a much greater perfection, than it could possibly acquire, if they were blended.

To create an appropriate social division of labor, Hamilton (ibid., 251) called for the "separation of the occupation of the cultivator, from that of the Artificer," by "diverting a part of its population from Tillage to Manufactures . . . leaving the farmer free to pursue exclusively the cultivation of his land and enabling him to procure with its products the manufactured supplies requisite either to his wants or to his enjoyments" (ibid., 10:251, 216, 261–62).

Hamilton (ibid., 280) recommended that the state enact a continual tax that would act as "a Motive to *greater exertion* in any occupation." Like Steuart, he saw industry as engaging those "willing to devote the leisure resulting from the intermissions of their ordinary pursuits to collateral labours" (ibid., 253). In short, Hamilton (ibid., 266) rejected "the proposition, that Industry, if left to itself will naturally find its way to the most useful and profitable employment: whence it is inferred that manufacturers without the aid of government will grow up as soon and as fast, as the natural state of things and the interest of the community may require." Steuart could not have said it better.

The Practical Rejection of Adam Smith's Theory

Even when they proclaimed their adherence to their master's theory, Adam Smith's professed disciples often went to elaborate lengths to support the manipulation of the institutions of society so as to foster the growth of markets and the elimination of remnants of the preexisting mode of production (see Samuels 1966, 22–23; see also Samuels 1973; E. Thompson 1963, 82). Perhaps nowhere do we see this contradictory role more clearly than in the elaborate projects of Jeremy Bentham, especially his Panopticon (see Foucault 1979, pt. 3).

In the American colonies, Adam Smith indicated that something akin to a state of natural liberties might have existed. According to many accounts circulating in England, nature was exceedingly generous in the colonies. Thomas Hariot (1588, 1:343) estimated that "one man may prepare and husband so much grounde . . . with less than foure and twenty hours, as will yield him his victuall for a twelve month" on twenty-five square yards of ground. The author of a similar description of Virginia also reported grapes so plentiful that a single vine could fill a London cart, potatoes as thick as a child's thigh, and frogs large enough to feed six Frenchmen (see Marx 1964, 75–80).

A more reliable source, George Bancroft (1854, 1:234) wrote: "Labour was valuable; land was cheap; competence promptly followed industry. There was no need of a scramble; abundance gushed from the earth for all. . . . It was 'the best poor man's country' in the world." The practical men of affairs were unwilling to stake their future on the market in the best poor man's country. Instead, they relied on a long-standing tradition of economic control to turn the tide in favor of employers.

A century earlier, the Massachusetts Bay Company had attempted to enforce wage ceilings (Bailyn 1955, 32). The colonial government had also limited landholdings of the poor in the Massachusetts Bay Colony, partly for the purpose of preventing what Governor Winthrop termed the "neglect of the trades" (cited in Goodrich and Davison 1935, 168). In seventeenth-century Virginia, the same object was achieved by the extensive claims staked by earlier settlers (see Morgan 1975, 218–23).

Given the independent spirit of workers in the colonies, capital understood that great profits required the use of unfree labor. Indeed, some Americans made great fortunes on the triangular trade that hinged on the sale of slaves. British leaders also realized that slaves created a strong market for English goods. In 1766, Pennsylvania was able to import 500,000 pounds worth of British goods while exporting only 40,000 back to Britain. Benjamin Franklin (1959–, 13:133) told Parliament that the balance was made good through exports from the North American colonies to the West Indies.

Even in the northern colonies, the workers were mostly in a state of bondage, either as slaves or as indentured servants (Herrick 1926; A. E. Smith 1927, chap. 2). Moreover, much of the profits earned in the northern states were derived from the surplus originating on the southern plantations (North 1966, esp. 6, 68, 105). Northern capitalists profited from a host of other activities, such as sales, financial services, and shipping, all of which were directly related to the cotton trade. Almost all the wealthy families of the Northeast owed their fortunes to such lines of business (see Pessen 1973, chap. 4).

Some have suggested that this so-called cotton-thesis is too strong (see Rattner, Soltow, and Sylla 1979, 223–26). For example, a few authors dismiss the importance of plantations in explaining the prosperity that northern and western farmers owed to southern food deficits, since much of the produce arriving in the South was destined for New Orleans and other large cities (see Lee and Passell 1979, 146–51). Of course, such cities were also part of the cotton system. Moreover, workers in these southern cities were part of a complex set of linkages with the plantation economy.

Cliff Leslie once offered an ironic commentary on the dependence of slavery on the demands of "free enterprise." Although he intended a very different lesson, his ambiguous words can be read as a summary of my position:

> It is said, indeed, that we owed to slavery the produce which supplies the principal manufacture of Britain. But the whole of this production was in truth credited to free industry. . . . The possibility of the profitable growth of so much cotton was caused by the commerce and invention of liberty. (Leslie 1888, 17)

Or, as Marx (1977, 925) bluntly observed, "The veiled slavery of the wage-workers in Europe needed the unqualified slavery of the New World as its pedestal."

Smith refused to acknowledge the mutualism between slavery and wage labor, simply assuming that the latter was clearly superior to the former. He should have realized that slavery neatly fits into the supply and demand analysis that he advocated so eloquently. When labor is scarce and the price it can command for its services is high, capital has good reason to prefer slavery (Domar 1970). The same logic explains the second serfdom in eastern Europe, which was characterized by the re-institution of old feudal obligations following the period of labor scarcity after the Thirty Years' War (Dobb 1963, 57).

Instead, Smith merely asserted that the colonies provided proof of the success of "free labor." His account was subject to numerous objections, foremost of which was the centrality of unfree labor.

Smith never bothered to acknowledge these objections, since he was too zealous in promoting his ideology. In fact, he may have been more deceptive in his discussion of slavery than in any other aspect of his writing.

Adam Smith and Colonial Slavery

Smith recognized that the slave plantations made great profits. He commented, "It is commonly said, that a sugar planter expects that the rum and the molasses should defray the whole expense of his cultivation, and that his sugar should be clear profit" (Smith 1976, I.xi.b.32, 173).

Characteristically, Smith did not mention that such profits reflected either the efficiency of slavery or the exploitation of slaves. Instead, according to Smith (1976, I.xi.b.32, 173–74; III.ii.12, 389), a combination of price supports and temporary shortages in the European markets explained the high profits that sugar planters earned. Indeed, Smith (1976, III.ii.9, 387; I.vii.44, 99; Millar 1806, 261–82) generally went out of his way to diminish the benefits of slavery, which he described as "the dearest of any" system of production relations.

Yet Smith once seemed to infer by his own remarks that southern slavery also may have been profitable in spite of his theory about the costly nature of slave labor. He wryly observed that "the late resolution of the Quakers in Pennsylvania to set at liberty all their Negro slaves, may satisfy us that their number cannot have been very great" (Smith 1976, III.ii.10, 388). Here Smith demonstrated a clear grasp of the logic of commodities, adding, "Had they made any considerable part of their property, such a resolution could have never been agreed to" (ibid.).

In reality, slaves were an inconsequential part of the labor force in Pennsylvania only because typical smallholders did not possess enough cash to purchase a slave for life; instead, they had to content themselves with indentured servants, whose labor could be obtained with a much lower initial outlay (see Kalm 1770–71, 1:388; *America* 1775, 121–22; see also Tully 1973; Main 1965, 33).

Thus, only two years after the publication of *The Wealth of Nations*, a suggestion to free the indentured servants of Pennsylvania elicited stern response from the legislature, which insisted that "all apprentices and servants are the property of their masters and mistresses, and every mode of depriving such masters and mistresses of their Property is a Violation of the Rights of Mankind" (cited in T. Hughes 1976, 111).

In fact, "apart from the Puritan migration to the northeastern colonies, something between a half and two-thirds of all white emigrants to the Colonies were convicts, indentured servants or redemptions" (Rich 1967, 342). The benefits of convict labor were obvious at the time. Edward Gibbon Wakefield (1829, 127) cited an American author who pleaded in 1824, "Place us on an equal footing with New South Wales, by giving us a share of the benefits which must, more or less, accrue from . . . convict labour" (*Suggestions*).

Only a fool could have expected property owners in the South, where slaves made up a substantial proportion of the wealth (Wright 1978, 35), to have willingly shown more humanity. Planters in Georgia, the only southern state founded on the concept of "free labor," soon pleaded a hopeless inability to recruit enough wage labor. They insisted that "it is clear as light itself, that Negroes are as essentially necessary to the cultivation of Georgia, as axes, hoes or any other utensil of agriculture" (cited in P. Taylor 1972).

After the Civil War in the United States, slave labor became unavailable

for all (see Ransom and Sutch 1977, 44–46). Partially because of a preference for leisure, and, also because black families profited from devoting
much of their female labor to subsistence production (G. Wright 1978, 62),
cotton production fell precipitously. This experience again demonstrated
the narrowness of Smith's doctrine of wage labor.

Eventually, Smithian ideology actually resulted in major changes in
social relations in one part of the world, the West Indies, the last bastion
of British colonial slavery. Although slavery was officially abolished in
1834, blacks were kept in a state of virtual slavery for four additional
years. John R. McCulloch (1845, 341) charged the British with hypocrisy
on this count: Why officially abolish sugar slavery when British industry
continued to depend on cotton slavery?

Even so, the British approached abolition quite cautiously, and with far
more concern for the slave owners than for the slaves. For example, the
government spent seven million pounds for famine relief in Ireland compared to twenty million to compensate slave owners for their loss of property. The Gladstone family alone received over 80,000 pounds for their
2,000 slaves (Newsinger 1996, 13).

The eventual implementation of an antislavery policy after 1838 had
disastrous consequences for the slave-possessing classes. Marx (1974,
325–26) reported that *The Times* of November 1857 printed a cry of outrage by a planter that the freed slaves preferred self-provisioning to wage
labor. As a result, sugar production plummeted. Annual production in the
period 1839–46 was 36 percent below what it had been during the period
1824–33 (Temperley 1977; see also Harris 1988).

Smith's Distortion of the Political Economy of Slavery

Ironically, as Smith was asserting that slavery was uneconomical, Scottish salters and miners were still being held in a state of virtual slavery,
even to the point of having to wear collars engraved with their master's
name (Mantoux 1961, 74; Millar 1806, 289–92; Duckham 1969). Thomas
Ashton noted that iron founders in South Wales were also tied to their
employers for life (Ashton 1948, 112).

In keeping with his practice of maintaining almost absolute silence on
the subject of rural poverty in Scotland in *The Wealth of Nations*, except
for the hardships that stubborn cotters were supposed to have brought on
themselves (Viner 1965, 101), Smith never once mentioned the existence
of slavery in Scotland. He did cite Montesquieu's comparison of the Hun-
garian mines worked by wage labor with the inefficient Turkish mines
worked by slaves (Smith 1976, IV.ix.47, 684).

Smith did compare the wages of colliers in Scotland and England without commenting on the unfree status of the Scottish miners, estimating that these workers earned approximately three times as much as common labor (ibid., I.x.b.14, 121). In addition, he estimated that the Scottish slave earned more than a British worker in comparable occupations (ibid., I.x.b.14, 121n), although this estimate is open to the complex objections that make most comparisons of this kind questionable (see E. Thompson 1963, chap. 6). Later scholars found that the Scottish mines did pay less (Nef 1932.2:190; Viner 1965, 115).

Recall that Smith (1978, 339) justified wage labor because the hired worker "has more of the conveniences and luxuries" than those outside of the labor markets. Indeed, Smith could have used this same argument to rationalize slavery as opposed to wage labor, just as Southern defenders of slavery frequently did.

Instead, Smith observed that Scottish slaves escaped to seek employment as wage workers in British mines in spite of supposedly lower earnings. For this reason, Smith concluded that the institution of wage labor for these Scottish workers would benefit all parties.

What could explain the existence of slavery in Scotland? According to Smith, it was, like the Game Laws, merely a vestige of earlier times—one that served no economic function. It was the result of the "love of domination and authority over others, which I am afraid is naturall to mankind" (Smith 1978, 192). However, in 1765, only a few years after Smith's lectures, British masters endeavored to turn the British system of "a yearly bond into a slavery as gross as that which was . . . in Scotland" (Hammond and Hammond 1919, 12–13).

Smith's reluctance to address the question of the status of the Scottish miners was surprising. The subject was a matter of considerable public interest at the time. In 1774, while Smith was busily at work on *The Wealth of Nations*, the Lord Advocate of Scotland, Sir Alexander Gilmore, prepared a bill at the instigation of the Earl of Abercorn and other coal masters (Arnot 1955, 8). The primary reason for its introduction was given in its preamble: "There are not a sufficient number of colliers, coal-bearers, and salters, in Scotland, for working the quantity of coal and salt necessarily wanted" (cited in ibid., 8). As a secondary consideration, it intended to "remove the reproach of allowing such a state of servitude to exist in a free country" (ibid.).

For some time, the law proved itself highly ineffective in freeing the slaves, although the old system of bondage eventually lost much of its potency. Pitmen enlisted in the navy, or restricted their work to three or four days per week (ibid., 10). Even so, not until 1799 did the Scottish slaves officially receive their full freedom.

The immediate consequences of emancipation were not exactly what Smith had predicted. After 1799, wages steadily rose until the beginnings of the Napoleonic Wars. Only after the shock of demobilization occurred, coming on top of a strong influx of Irish immigrants, did the wage level sink back, falling to somewhere between 45 and 70 percent of its peak (Smout 1969, 434–35).

We might also have expected some discussion of slavery with respect to the tobacco trade. However, Smith never mentioned that the tobacco merchants' trade was based on slave labor.

Smith discussed tobacco on occasion, but he never hinted that the prosperity of his friends and patrons, the Glasgow merchants, depended on their monopoly of the trade (Smith 1976, II.v.32, 372–73; Smout 1969). In fact, the tobacco merchants became the chief partners of the first Glasgow banks, established in 1750. Between 1754 and 1764 tobacco imports doubled to 11,500 tons per annum (Soltow 1959).

Although Smith observed that the trade of Glasgow was said to have doubled in the fifteen years following the founding of the banks, he did so only to indicate the beneficial effect of such financial institutions (Smith 1976, II.ii.41, 297). After 1776, when the Glasgow merchants lost their access to tobacco, the town fell on hard times (Kindleberger 1976, 12), but Smith did not inform his readers of this situation in later editions of his book.

Smith's presentation was devious in one other respect. The leading authority on the subject of Scottish banks at the time was most likely Steuart, whose modern editor noted an "interesting" absence of reference to him at this point in *The Wealth of Nations* (Skinner 1966, xlii; see also Steuart 1966, bk. 4, pt. 2).

The Eclipse of Smith

We must make a distinction between Smith's role as an ideologist and his contributions to economic theory. In spite of the enthusiastic reception that Smith's ideology enjoyed, his revision of history proved to be an unworkable basis for the development of economic policy.

The one area where Smith may have exercised influence on policy earned him little credit. Specifically, some later commentators believe that Smith's recommendations on colonial taxation were responsible for the import duties that helped to spark the American Revolution (Fay

1956, 116; Smith 1977, letter 302; Winch 1978, chap. 7). For example, according to Jacob Viner (1965; see also Willis 1979, 522), "Smith's main activity during his stay in London . . . (November 1766) was work with Townshend on his disastrous taxation project."

In fact, the behavior of governments over the years seems to lend support to the thesis that the more they praise the ideals of Smith, the more apt they are to use their powers to intervene in the interests of capital. For example, in the period following Smith's ideological ascendancy, the British ruling classes passed a string of repressive legislation that ran counter to the Smithian values that the government espoused. These measures include the Combination Acts of 1799 and 1800, repeal of the justices' power to fix wages in 1813, the apprenticeship clauses in 1814, as well as the Poor Law Amendment Act of 1834. All of these acts stand as irrefutable testimony of the use of the state to further the interests of capital (see Pollard 1978, 151).

The repeal of the Combination Act in 1824 was the most telling exception to the anti-Smithian legislative stance of the time. Parliament passed this law to reduce economic protests (see Hollis 1973, 102–15; Marx 1847, 170) and prove the correctness of the Wages Fund Theory to the working class (see Wallas 1919; Halevy 1956, 204–8). By 1830, Nassau Senior was ready to reestablish these restrictions on labor in an apparent admission of the failure of this unique experiment (see S. Levy 1970, 71–73).

By 1830, political economy had openly embraced Edward Gibbon Wakefield's theories, which directly contradicted those of Smith (see chapter 13). Indeed, except for a brief period when Smith's ideas flourished, political economy, reaching back from the theoretical prehistory of the mercantilist epoch to the triumph of the Wakefield school, was a continuous affirmation of the need for government action to sustain the interests of capital.

Adam Smith: A Recapitulation

Smith's ideas about colonies are useful in comparing his works with those of Steuart. Sir James's ideas are shocking to a modern reader. Smith's appear benign. Yet this appearance of benevolence is dangerous, since it deadens our critical facilities. The occasional references to the conflict between labor and capital throw us further off guard. Although we can read in Smith (1976, I.viii.8, 83) that the interests of labor and capital are "by no means the same," we are within only a couple of pages of the story of labor in North America. This touch of realism makes us even more credulous by the time we reach the tale of the harmonious conditions of labor and capital in North America. Nothing could be more subtle.

From a broader perspective, in spite of Smith's obvious talents, his *Wealth of Nations* can be counted as less than a total success. All too often, he became entangled in his own ideology.

Concerns with both ideology and good government led Smith to call for a regime of laissez-faire; however, this accord was achieved only by ignoring reality. A lesser mind could have put together a flat, yet consistent story. Smith could not—perhaps because, on some level, he recognized the underlying reality he was trying to deny. He also failed as a result of the contrary nature of his conflicting objectives. On the one hand, he attempted to put together an ideology of class harmony; on the other hand, his theory of political and economic administration required an explicit analysis of class conflict.

Generally, his ideological perspective conflicted with his administrative principles. The one case where his two approaches to economics seemed to coincide was in his analysis of the colonies of North America (for a conventional view of Smith's analysis of the colonies, see Stevens 1975). Even there, as we have seen, Smith could not successfully meld his ideology with his practical recommendations.

Smith himself proposed numerous violations of laissez-faire theory, as we have seen (see Viner 1927, 229). Certainly, Jacob Viner (1928, 230) was correct in noting that Smith "displayed a fine tolerance for a generous measure of inconsistency."

I might also add that Smith's own life was not altogether free of contradictions. Did he sense the irony of the patron saint of free trade collecting a pension from a nobleman or a salary as a commissioner of customs? Did he feel a tinge of hypocrisy when he sought the appointment to the committee of the East India Company?

To see these inconsistencies in Smith's life does not prove that he was attempting to deceive his readers. As Peter Berger (1963, 109), a student of such mentality, has observed: "Deliberate deception requires a degree of psychological self-control that few people are capable of. . . . It is much easier to deceive oneself."

The Wealth of Nations is not merely a product of self-deception. It is a great book. Its greatness rests, in part, on Smith's treatment of his own contradictions, "which he does not solve, but which he reveals by contradicting himself" (Marx 1963–1971, pt. 2, 151). At times, his work becomes so absurd that it alerts us that we have come on a matter of importance.

CHAPTER 11   Benjamin Franklin and the

Smithian Ideology of Slavery and Wage Labor

That few in public affairs act from a mere view of the good of their country, whatever they may pretend; and tho' their actings being real good to their country, yet
men primarily considered their own and their country's interest was united and did
not act from a principle of benevolence.—Benjamin Franklin, "Observations on My
Reading History in the Library"

Benjamin Franklin and North America

The subject of North America fascinated Europeans during the period of
classical political economy (see Whitney 1924, 370). Certainly, while
Smith was writing *The Wealth of Nations*, North American colonial affairs were very much in the minds of the English. Between 1720 and 1784,
about 10 percent of all books, pamphlets, maps, and prints published in
London concerned these colonies (Bonwick 1977, 35; citing T. Adams
1971). Similarly, from 1774 to 1779, about 20 percent of all books and
pamphlets printed in England were related to the colonies of North America (ibid.; see also Adams 1969).

   In part, Europeans considered the North American colonies to be important because they represented a vision of their own past. "In the beginning all the world was America," wrote John Locke (1698, 319; see also
Hobbes 1651, chap. 13; Meek 1976, 66–67, 136–45; Meek 1977b, 30). In
the words of William Robertson (1777, 50–54; cited in Rendall 1978, 190–
91), in his *History of America:*

> Much discovery of the New World . . . presented nations to our view, in
> stages of their progress, much less advanced than those wherein they
> have been observed in our continent. In America, man had to subsist
> under the rudest norm in which we can conceive him to subsist. We
> behold communities just beginning to unite, and may examine the
> sentiments and actions of human beings in the infancy of social life.

Even Tocqueville saw Tacitus's Germans in the Native Americans
(Tocqueville 1848, 328; see also 32).

Not surprisingly, Adam Smith also took a lively interest in North America. Lois Whitney (1924, 370) pointed out that Smith owned at least thirty books on travel and collections of voyages to exotic regions. Like many others, Smith (1976, V.i.a.2, 689–90) saw Native Americans as living in a society that approximated the "rude state." Besides the numerous examples from the lives of the Native Americans in his *Lectures on Jurisprudence*, Smith speculated that the ancient Scots must have been like that people (Smith 1978, 239).

Of all the sources of information on colonial affairs, the most famous was Benjamin Franklin, whose opinions on this subject were said to be "a degree of credit little short of proofs of holy writ" (Knox 1769, 111; cited in Benians 1926, 252). After all, who in English society could match his knowledge (real or imagined) about primitive life?

Not surprisingly, Franklin had great influence. He was able to convince William Petty's son-in-law, Lord Shelburne, the powerful president of the British Board of Trade and later Prime Minister of England, that he was "one of the [three] best authorities for anything related to America" (Franklin 1959–, 14:325; see also the editor's cautionary note).

Benjamin Franklin's Opportunism

We are all familiar with Franklin's persona—a genial man of great wit and inventiveness. In real life, he was a much more complex character than the hagiographies of Americana would have us believe. No political economist, with the possible exception of Petty, was either as mercurial or as engaging as Franklin. Consequently, some biographical material will be useful in gaining a perspective on his prolific writings on political economy.

Franklin (1959–, 14:76–86) made his debut as a political economist in 1729, while still in his early twenties, with a splendid "application" of William Petty's *Treatise of Taxes and Contributions* (1662). Franklin seems to have been originally drawn to the subject of paper money by William Rawle's pamphlet on the same topic, which Franklin had printed in 1725 (see Fetter 1943, 472n). Whole paragraphs of Franklin's pamphlet on paper money appear to be lifted directly from Petty (see Wetzel 1895). Indeed, John Davis (1803, 2:25–36) alleged that, throughout his career, Franklin borrowed without proper attribution many of the words for which he was to become most famous.

The relative weights of Franklin's various works are difficult to assess because he used his pen more often to further his own interests rather than the truth. For instance, shortly after his first pamphlet appeared, the state of Pennsylvania rewarded him with a contract for printing the paper money, which he had so ably advocated in that work (Franklin 1964, 124). In later years, Franklin continued to write to advance his position in society rather than any principles.

Because of the shifting political winds, after the appearance of his pamphlet on paper money, Franklin expressed so many contradictory opinions that one scholar compared him to a chameleon (Eiselen 1928, 29). For example, he wrote pamphlets to argue against smuggling and for the maintenance of low wage rates, apparently with the hope of winning himself a more lucrative position with the British government (see Conner 1965, 37; Franklin 1959–, 15:14–16, 159–64; 16:162). During the late colonial period, he railed against restrictions on manufacturing in the colonies, with an eye to winning the favor of powerful British interests. Later, he promoted self-sufficiency for the newly emerging republic. Even his writings about the noble savage, which we will discuss later, served his own self-interest.

The difficulties of evaluating Franklin's activities are so pervasive that even his commitment to the colonial cause has been brought into question. According to Dennys DeBerdt, colonial agent for Massachusetts, Franklin "stood entirely neuter [with regard to the Revolution] till he saw which way the cause would be carried, and then he broke out fiercely on the side of America" (cited in Currey 1965, 148). A more hostile interpreter charged that Franklin's opportunism and greed led him to work as a double agent for the British during the Revolutionary War (Currey 1972). Whether or not we accept such a damning verdict, Franklin was an undeniable master of saying whatever would accrue to his own advantage.

Despite doubts about Franklin's intentions, as well as Joseph Schumpeter's (1954, 192) undoubtedly correct verdict that Franklin's work offers "little to commend for purely analytic features," Franklin still has an important place in the story of primitive accumulation as it developed within the context of classical political economy.

The Source of Adam Smith's Information on the Colonies

Given Smith's strong interest in North America and Franklin's reputation as an expert in the subject, we should not be surprised to find that Smith relied heavily on Franklin in his analysis of the colonies. We should expect that Smith would have been especially interested in what Franklin would have had to say concerning the indigenous people of the New World. Reading *The Wealth of Nations*, we find too much of a love of anecdotes from both ancient and classical sources to believe that Smith would not have questioned a visitor with so much firsthand information about the rude state of society. Whether the implications of such stories as Franklin had to offer concerning the colonies would register was another matter.

Even so, the proof of Franklin's influence is not conclusive. His name does not appear in *The Wealth of Nations*, but then neither does that of Steuart, whom Smith was challenging, nor that of Turgot, whose work was embarrassingly similar to Smith's own (see Viner 1965, 128–38). Smith (1976, I.viii.23, 88 and III.iv.19, 423) did repeat statements similar to those made in Franklin's essays suggesting that the population of North America had doubled in twenty or twenty-five years. The most likely written source for such estimates would be Franklin's (1751) essays, *Observations Concerning the Increase of Mankind* (Franklin 1959–, 4:227–34) and the 1760 *The Interest of Great Britain Considered* (Franklin 1959–, 9:47–100), both of which Smith possessed.

In fact, Smith's own analysis of the prosperity of the North American colonies commenced with this discussion of population growth. Thus, both pamphlets are particularly relevant because of their possible role in shaping Smith's opinions concerning the relations between labor and capital in the economic development of North America.

Smith's editor, Edwin Cannan, overlooked Franklin as the source of Smith's estimate of North American population growth, proposing instead Richard Price as the source (see Smith 1937, 70, 393). Later editors, as well as Lewis Carey (1928, 126), dismissed Price on the basis of a letter written by Smith (1976, 88n): "Price's speculations cannot fail to sink into the neglect that they always deserved. I have always considered him a factious citizen, a most superficial Philosopher and by no means an able calculator."

We should not dismiss Price's significance just on the basis of this letter. After all, we know from our consideration of the relationship between Smith and Steuart that we should not be unduly hasty in taking Smith's statements at face value. In addition, since the judgment on Price is dated twelve years after the appearance of *The Wealth of Nations*, the ever-controversial Price could have fallen from grace long after 1773.

Cannan suggested a second possible source of Smith's information; namely Dr. John Mitchell's (1767), *Agriculture, Population, Trade, and Manufactures* (Smith 1937, 70n). An equally likely candidate would have been *American Husbandry*, believed by some to have also been written by Dr. Mitchell (American 1775; see also Review 1776; Carrier 1918, 48, 52–53, 123).

The strongest claim for Franklin's role in the development of political economy can be traced to Franklin himself. A Mrs. Logan, widow of one of Franklin's friends wrote:

Dr. Franklin once told my husband that the celebrated Adam Smith, when writing his *Wealth of Nations*, was in the habit of bringing chapter after chapter, as he composed it, to himself, Dr. Price and other literati of that day, with whom he was intimate; patiently hearing their observations, and profiting by their discussions and criticisms. . . . Nay, that he has sometimes reversed his positions and rewritten whole chapters, after hearing what they had to remark on the subject before them. (cited in Carey 1928, 126)

Franklin's Contribution to "The Wealth of Nations"

Franklin and Smith met for the first time in Edinburgh in 1759 (Carey 1928, 115). As Lewis Carey (ibid.; see also Viner 1965, 42–45) pointed out, Franklin, as well as Richard Price, was indeed in London during the period 1773–75, while Smith was there working on his book. Franklin, Smith, and Price were all members of the Royal Society of London (Carey 1928, 118). Finally, both Franklin and Smith were both very close to Strahan, the publisher of *The Theory of Moral Sentiments* and a member of the firm that first published *The Wealth of Nations* (Fay 1956, chap. 9).

Although Smith had begun his book long before the period in question, Carey noted that Franklin would have good reason to be unaware of its extended period of gestation (Carey 1928, 119); moreover, the subjects upon which Smith was working during 1773–75 included the chapter "Of Colonies," written in October 1773, and the passages on American wages in the chapter, "Of the Wages of Labour" (ibid., 120).

By the early 1760s, Smith had already begun an early draft of *The Wealth of Nations*, in which he asserted that Pennsylvania and some of the New England colonies were wealthier than Virginia (Scott 1965, 363). Also, Smith used the Native Americans as an example of a society with an underdeveloped social division of labor. Unless these thoughts occurred only after meeting Franklin in 1759, we might expect that Smith would have been eager to take advantage of the eminent visitor's expertise.

We do get a hint, however, that, in spite of the cordial correspondence between Franklin, on the one hand, and Lord Kames and Hume, on the other, something may have gone amiss during this visit. In reminiscing about the natural tendency to avoid disputation, Franklin (1964, 60) listed as exceptions: "Lawyers, University Men, and Men of all sorts that have been bred at Edinborough."

We have no direct evidence of Smith's esteem for Franklin; however, the opinion of his closest friend, Hume, may be indicative. In 1762, a few years after first meeting Franklin, Hume praised him lavishly: "America has sent us many good things: gold, silver, sugar, tobacco, indigo, etc.; but you are the first philosopher, and indeed the first great man of letters for whom we are beholden to her" (Franklin 1959–, 10:81–82). By 1774, Hume's attitude had changed. He asked Smith:

> Pray what strange account are these we hear of Franklin's conduct? I am very slow in believing that he has been guilty in the extreme degree that is pretended, tho' I have always known him to be a very factious man, and Faction next to Fanaticism is of all the passions the most destructive of morality. (cited in Rae 1895, 267)

The incident to which Hume refers probably is the theft of the letters of the governor and lieutenant-governor of Massachusetts in which Franklin was implicated. Apparently, the colonists were beginning to doubt if Franklin was vigorous enough in the colonial cause to justify his pay as their agent in Britain. As a result of this scandal, Solicitor-General Alexander Wedderburn, a former student under Smith and a friend of Hume's, required Franklin to appear for examination before the Privy Council on 29 January 1774 (Carey 1928, 117). Franklin's actions in this affair may have cut short Smith's association with him, but probably not before he had the opportunity to supply Smith with much information on the impact of plentiful lands and high wages characteristic of the northern colonies of America (see Carey 1928, 123–25).

The material on the colonies is crucial to Smith's project in *The Wealth of Nations* because it is the only concrete example that Smith offered in his attempt to prove that labor could prosper without seemingly damaging the interests of capital. Consequently, it played an essential role in the creation of the Smithian ideology of the noncoercive nature of wage labor. Accordingly, we proceed carefully in evaluating Franklin's contribution.

Notice that Smith judged Price to be guilty of the same sin as Franklin; Smith's use of the concept of Factiousness was highly subjective. As he wrote to Lord Shelburne, "For tho' a little faction now and then gives spirit to the nation, the continuance of it obstructs all public business and puts it out of the power of [the] best Minister to do much good" (Mossner and Ross 1977, 28).

The tone of a letter that Franklin (1905–7, 8:8) addressed to Price on 6 February 1780 implied that the two may have suffered a common ostracism stemming from their methods of supporting the cause of the colonists: "Your Writings, after all the Abuse you and they have met with begin to make serious Impressions on those who at first rejected the Counsels you gave; and they will acquire new Weight every day and be in high Esteem when the Cavils against them are dead and forgotten."

Despite the numerous hints and claims, the extent to which Franklin actually influenced Smith remains a subject of vague speculation. We will see that Franklin had his own theory of economic development, one which Smith failed to appreciate enough to incorporate into his own work.

Smith and the Ideology of the Colonial Relationship

Despite the probable correctness of Franklin's claim of influence on Smith, broad theoretical divergences separated the two authors. To begin with, Franklin had merely alleged that the English had no need to legislate against the development of colonial manufactures; Smith insisted that the English had no need of any colonial relationship whatsoever. For Smith, colonial ties placed an unnecessary burden on England, since the colonies would necessarily remain within the British orbit, with or without the formalities of colonial bonds, directly contradicting his previously discussed theory of colonial development. In this respect, he stood shoulder to shoulder with Dean Tucker (1776b, 30–31), although Smith's analysis was more devious. While Tucker believed that less advanced nations would remain economically backward, Smith maintained that the neocolonial arrangement would somehow be in the best interest of all parties (Hudson 1992).

Moreover, Smith, the ideologist, sought evidence for the harmonious coexistence of the factors of production in North America. He contended that the colonies offered proof that capital could flourish in the face of high wages. Franklin, in contrast, emphasized conflict between labor and capital, as expressed by the desire of workers to become independent farmers. In addition, Franklin's call for colonial independence was not necessarily intended to leave the colonies as an appendage to the British economy.

How are we to understand the differences between Smith and Franklin? We saw that Smith knew Franklin personally and was in possession of some of his writings. On one occasion, he criticized a scientific work of Franklin's that was bound together with the same two pamphlets of Franklin, which we have been discussing (Carey 1928, 122).

Smith would have difficulty in misunderstanding Franklin's meaning in these pamphlets. Although the wily American frequently contradicted himself, these particular pamphlets were unambiguous. Smith's own contradiction of Franklin's description might be explained by the Scotsman's recurrent confusions. For example, we discussed Smith's embarrassing bewilderment in analyzing his treatment of the noncoercive origins of wage labor.

The same symptoms of befuddlement pervade his discussion of the colonies. We have already alluded to this confusion in the section in which Smith recognized the necessity of wage labor as a prerequisite for earning great profits in colonial agriculture (Smith 1976, IV.vii.b.3, 565–66. Smith interpreted the high wages that the proprietors were forced to pay to be consistent with rapid capitalist development because they encouraged "population and improvement" (ibid.).

Of course, the population increase would require a long time. At least, such was the message of Franklin's pamphlets. Even the most optimistic observers of the North American colonies understood that wage labor would be restricted to those few industries in which employers could afford to pay high wages because of the special advantages of abundant resources or labor-saving technologies (see Hamilton 1961, 10:272 for one of the most favorable views of American circumstances; see also Raymond 1823, 242; McCulloch 1825, 136). Smith himself concurred. He saw the colonies as advancing only within the sphere of dependency—at least for the foreseeable future.

Smith's ideological analysis required him to explain why workers would willingly engage in wage labor. The first side of his dual formula of "population and improvement" suggested that wage labor would take hold as a result of Malthusian pressures, which would eliminate the very phenomenon of prosperity that he set out to explain. He seemed to rule out the other side in his recommendation that the colonies confine themselves to the production of raw materials, since the farmers that Smith envisioned would likely be self-employed rather than working for wages.

British Colonial Domination outside North America

Unlike Smith, Franklin was sharply critical of British colonial relations with lands closer to the mother country. In response to an English gentleman who wondered why North America did not rival Ireland in the export of beef, butter, and linen, Franklin (1959–, 19:22) snapped back that "the Reason might be, Our People eat Beef and Butter every Day, and wear Shirts themselves."

Franklin may well have also shared his disdain for the Irish system with liberal friends, such as Smith and Hume. This hypothesis is all the more likely, since Franklin's fervent hopes for success in speculating on Ohio Valley lands were checked, in part, by powerful Irish landowners.

Following Josiah Child (1751, 134), who in his *New Discourse of Trade* argued against plantations by writing "that lands (tho' excellent) without hands proportional, will not enrich any kingdom," the English landowners wanted labor to be kept in the mother country, expecting that economic losses would result from the migration of their tenants to the American West. In particular, the president of the British Board of Trade, Lord Hillsborough, feared that further immigration from Ireland would reduce the profitability of his extensive Irish holdings (Franklin 1959–, 13:414; Currey 1965, 221; Alvord 1917, 2:121; Plath 1939, 231).

By contrast, the Scottish gentry welcomed the exodus of their "free hands." Because the Scottish crofters had only recently lost their traditional rights to the use of the land (see S. Johnson 1774, 97), the lairds saw immigration as a means of solidifying their property rights to their grazing land, at least until the rate of emigration reached a point that threatened them with a shortage of workers (see Franklin 1959–, 20:522–28). The greater tolerance for emigration in Scotland may also be partially explained by the less labor-intensive cropping system used there.

At the same time, the less thorough British conquest of Scotland gave the British less cause to concern themselves with the retention of the population. Unlike the case in Ireland, where the British divided the land amongst themselves, in Scotland, the British left ownership of the land in the hands of the traditional lairds.

Another major difference between the two cases may well have been the disposition of firearms (see Pettengill 1981). As Defoe (1724–26, 667) noted, "The Highlanders not only have all of them fire-arms, but they are all excellent marksmen." Guns were not as common among the Irish poor.

In hindsight, we now know that the British were far more successful in subduing the Highlanders than the Irish. However, many of the most defiant Highlanders moved to the Appalachian and Allegheny regions of North America, where they engaged in numerous rebellions.

In contrast to Franklin, Smith never acknowledged the hardships that Britain imposed on the peoples of Ireland and Scotland. Recall that he attributed the poverty in Scotland to a stubborn adherence to traditional ways, thereby holding both the poor and the lairds culpable.

In Ireland, Smith was more generous to the gentry. There, he attributed the impoverished conditions of the populace to their rebelliousness. As he wrote to Lord Carlisle:

> [Ireland] is ill provided with (coal and) wood; two articles essentially necessary to the progress of Great Manufactures. It wants order, police, and a regular administration of justice both to protect and restrain the inferior ranks of people, articles more essential to the progress of Industry than both coal and wood put together. (cited in Mossner and Ross 1977, 243)

Smith never elaborated on the role of force in the colonies. We have already discussed Smith's belief in a strong legal system to protect the property of the rich. We cannot be sure whether he believed that his recommendation for Ireland was a reflection of this general concern for the protection of property or if somehow Ireland was unique.

In sum, Smith's use of Franklin's writings was very selective. Some of what Franklin wrote about the North American colonies was consistent with Smith's theory of the harmonious relationship between capital and labor in the colonies. Franklin, however, displayed far more awareness of the depth of colonial conflict than Smith, except when referring to the North American colonies. Certainly, Franklin's imagery differs from what Smith proposed in making his case for the voluntary evolution of the social division of labor.

Franklin and the Bleak Prospects for Colonial Industry

Despite similarities between Smith's works and those of Franklin, they differed in significant respects. Consider the case of Franklin's *Observations*. This pamphlet was a masterful brief on behalf of colonial industry, calculated to win favor from both the English and the colonists. John R. McCulloch (1845, 253) saw this remarkable piece of argumentation as an "excellent specimen of the penetrating sagacity and compressed and clear style" of Franklin. Thomas Robert Malthus (1803, 8) hailed it as a forerunner of his own work, although it was not what we might consider Malthusian. Franklin even expressed a wish for an increase in the numbers of the "Body of White People on the Face of the Earth" (Franklin 1959–, 4:234).

Franklin penned this work in response to the British Act of 1750, which prohibited the erection of additional slitting and rolling mills, plating forges, and steel furnaces in the American colonies (ibid., 4:225–26). At the time, some people had already noted the strategic importance of a strong British settlement, considering the ongoing struggle between France and England for control of the Continent (ibid., 4:224). Yet to argue for the potential vitality of the colonial economy solely on such political grounds would play to the worst fears of those who wished to nip their colonial competitors' potential in the bud.

Franklin did not question the right of the English to frame such legislation. Instead, he deftly sought to resolve the contradictory interests of Britain and the colonies by proving that the economic future of the colonies would be complementary to that of Britain. In this sense, his objective ran parallel to that of Smith. According to Franklin, the mother country had no need to impede industrial development in the colonies. The economy of North America would grow, but its growth would necessarily be agricultural. In this sense, his framework was Smithian, although Franklin went beyond Smith.

In contrast to Smith, who asserted that colonial regimes would naturally progress beyond the agricultural state, Franklin assured his English readers that the abundance of land would impose a natural handicap on the use of both slave and wage labor in the colonies, forestalling industrial development into the indefinite future.

Franklin's argument was internally consistent concerning the threat of colonial competition. The English were said to have nothing to lose and everything to gain from the granting of more freedom to the colonial economy. Still, one might question why colonists should be concerned about laws that compelled them to do what they would have done in the absence of any such legislation. To raise such a question would be to apply a standard that was foreign to such pamphlet literature. Franklin's intent was merely to dispel the immediate English fears about the colonial economy.

The same idea about colonial development recurs in Franklin's *Interest of Britain Considered*, written in 1760. The issue at hand was whether the English should claim Canada or Guadeloupe in consequence of the French surrender at Montreal in 1759. The debate was heated. Prime Minister William Pitt was in a quandary, wondering, "some are for keeping Canada; some Guadeloupe; who will tell me which I shall be hanged for not keeping?" (Alvord 1917, 1:19).

Franklin's contribution was again an exceedingly clever brief prepared on behalf of the American interests. To appear more convincing, he posed as an English writer, maintaining that Guadeloupe had little demand for English wares, since the majority of its inhabitants were slaves. In contrast, Canada would serve the English purposes much better by providing a ready market for Britain.

To reinforce his case, Franklin stressed the complementary, rather than the competitive, characteristics of the colonial mainland. Here we have another instance of Franklin adopting whatever measures were required to win a point.

Franklin consistently seemed determined to lull the English into complacency about the strength of the colonial economy for some time. For example, in 1766, after the British requested that the colonial governors supply them with a summary of their colony's industrial strength, Franklin advised his son, whom he had arranged to be appointed governor of New Jersey, to shade the truth. Franklin (1959–, 15:77) wrote, "You have only to report a glass-house for coarse window glass and bottles, and some domestic manufactures of linen and woolen for family use that do not clothe half the inhabitants, all the finer goods coming from England and the like."

His son complied almost to the letter. Other governors followed suit. Similarly, Governor Moore of New York replied with a long description of the difficulty of retaining the employment of workmen who took up farming as soon as possible (see Rabbeno 1895, 73). Only North Carolina boasted of its fifty sawmills on a single river (ibid.), but that industry was hardly a threat to Britain.

Of course, colonial industry had not taken hold to any great extent by that time. The question was, would it do so in the future?

Franklin, Smith, and Slavery

In reality, the northern colonies were not nearly as idyllic as Smith's ideological presentation implied, but they still had many attractive features compared with the economies of western Europe. Even so, unfree labor was essential to the colonial prosperity, so much admired by both Smith and Franklin. Unfortunately, neither Smith nor Franklin alerted their readers of the contribution of the coercive relations of slavery to rapid colonial development.

Both agreed that slavery could never be efficient. In Franklin's (1959–, 4:229) words, "Labour of Slaves can never be so cheap here as the Labour of working men is in Britain." Although this citation was in an admittedly unscientific pamphlet, it does reflect greater consistency concerning alternative modes of production than *The Wealth of Nations,* which it seems to have influenced. Whereas Smith argued that slaves were more costly to use than wage labor without reference to any particular historical situation, Franklin made the far more modest claim that slave labor in the colonies could not be so cheap as wage labor in Britain.

Even so, at least Franklin demonstrated that he understood that slaves could be advantageous in the colonial economy. He wrote: "Why then will Americans purchase Slaves? Because Slaves may be kept as long as a Man pleases, or has Occasion for their Labour; while hired Men are continually leaving their Master (often in the midst of his Business), and setting up for themselves" (Franklin 1959–, 4:230).

This unusual lapse of realism concerning slavery did not come near to confronting the extent of unfree labor in the colonies. Although slavery did not exist to a great extent in the Northeast, indentured servitude was common. In addition, many in that region derived great profits from the slave trade. In addition, when manufacturing did mature there, it often found its markets in the regions in which slavery flourished.

In Franklin's adopted home of Pennsylvania, it was "white servitude" that planted in its "fertile soil . . . the seeds of a great industrial future" (Herrick 1926, 76). Was Franklin or Smith so naive as to believe that slavery and indentured servitude were irrelevant to the development of the American colonies?

Franklin found slavery in Smith's Scotland; Smith could only discover it in history or in the far-off Turkey of his day. Neither addressed the role of the temporary servitude of indentured labor, let alone the harsher lot that fell to the blacks, who suffered a lifetime of slavery in North America.

For example, Franklin's (1959–, 4:227–34; see also Viner 1965, 113–14) "Conversation on Slavery," published in the *London Public Advertiser* in 1770, seems to have played a significant role in preparing for the emancipation of the Scottish bondsmen who lived in a state of virtual slavery. Addressing himself to a hypothetical Scotsman, he wrote, "Sir, as to your observation, that if we had a real love of liberty, we should not suffer such a thing as slavery among us, I am a little surprised to hear this from you . . . in whose own country, Scotland, slavery still subsists" (cited in Viner 1965, 114).

Unlike Smith, Franklin expressed racist sentiments in *Observations*, although in later life he appeared to be unalterably opposed to the institution of slavery (see Carey 1928, chap. 4; Mellon 1969, pt. 1). In a later edition of that work, he had the good sense to alter the phrase "almost every Slave being by Nature a Thief" to "almost every Slave being from the nature of slavery a Thief" (Franklin 1959–, 4:239n).

Even though Franklin had a low opinion of slavery, before 1770 he gave few indications that North American producers could bridge the gap between household manufactures and industry based on wage labor. Franklin's antislavery position was politic in Quaker Pennsylvania at the time, yet he continued to hold it long after he could expect much gain from local political conditions. His later opposition to slavery may be the only example of a strongly held ethical position in his life.

Smith's silence on the subject of slavery is especially troubling, since he obtained much of his information about the colonies from the Glasgow tobacco merchants and planters who had returned from the colonies (Fay 1956, 264–66). Of course, Smith may have been disinterested in southern conditions, but he still should have understood the importance of the plantation for the rest of the economy.

Instead of trying to reconcile his contradictory assertions about slavery in *The Wealth of Nations*, Smith (1976, IV.vii.b.3, 565–66) irrelevantly interjected his opinion that "the progress of many of the ancient Greek colonies toward wealth and greatness, seems accordingly to have been very rapid." Edward Gibbon Wakefield (1834, 236; see also Wakefield 1829, 154) was quick to respond to that dodge: "In no Greek colony did anyone ever sell his labour; or anyone pay wages, high or low. . . . [The work was] performed exclusively by slaves."

Smith's allusion to slavery seems to reflect a subconscious recognition of the force required to ensure that workers allow employers to extract surplus value. Smith the ideologue never gave full expression to this semi-repressed insight. Had he done so, *The Wealth of Nations* might well have conformed more closely to Benjamin Franklin's more realistic interpretation of colonial development.

Franklin on Wage Labor in the Colonies

Franklin's contention that manufacturing could not develop easily in the colonies rested on the idea that the abundance of land would preclude the ability to hire many workers. In Franklin's (1959–, 4:228) words, "Land being thus plenty in America, and so cheap as that a labouring Man, that understands Husbandry, can in a short Time save Money enough to purchase a Piece of new Land sufficient for a Plantation, whereon he may subsist a Family," manufacturing based on wage labor would be uncompetitive in the foreseeable future.

Wages were sufficient for workers to establish themselves as farmers. According to Franklin (1782, 607–8):

> Land being cheap in that Country, . . . hearty young Labouring men, who understand the Husbandry of Corn and Cattle, . . . may easily establish themselves there. A little Money sav'd of the good Wages they receive there while they work for others, enables them to buy the Land and being their Plantation.

Similarly, in writing about Guadeloupe, Franklin maintained:

> [Until the colonies become more populous] this nation [Britain] must necessarily supply them with the manufactures they consume, because the new settlers will be employ'd in agriculture, and the new settlements will so continually draw off the spare hands from the old, that our present colonies will not . . . find themselves in a condition to manufacture even for their own inhabitants . . . much less for those who are settling behind them. (1959–, 9:78)

At still another point, Franklin (ibid., 9:73) was even more emphatic about the hurdles that manufacturing faced in the colonies:

No man acquainted with political and commercial history can doubt [that] Manufactures are founded in poverty. It is the multitude of poor without land in a country, and who must work for others at low wages or starve, that enables undertakers to carry on a manufacture, and afford it cheap enough to prevent the importation of the same kind from abroad, and to bear the expense of its exportation. But no man who can have a piece of land of his own, sufficient by his labour to subsist his family in plenty, is poor enough to be a manufacture and work for a master. Hence while there is land enough in America for our people, there can never be manufactures to any amount of value.

In a promotional tract entitled *Information For Those Who Would Remove to America*, written in 1782, Franklin took a position much like that advocated by Smith. He stated that, when the state does subsidize individual industries:

It has rarely succeeded, so as to establish a Manufacture, which the Country was not so ripe for as to encourage private Persons to set it up. Labor being generally too dear there and Hands difficult to be kept together, every one desiring to be a Master, and the Cheapness of Lands inclining many to leave trades for Agriculture. (Franklin 1782, 610)

Franklin continued, "Some indeed have met with Success, and are carried on to Advantage; but they are generally such as require only a few Hands, or wherein the great Part of the Work is performed by Machines" (ibid.). In short, Franklin generally took the position that the colonies would have to remain agrarian until the time would arrive when the crush of population became too great to allow the common worker to become an independent farmer. The English, thus, had no reason to fear competition from the colonies.

In 1769, when Franklin (1959–, 16:209; see also Coxe 1794, 442–43) communicated his approval of the colonial Resolutions of Non-Importation, he rationalized the reliance on agriculture in the colonies:

For their Earth and their Sea, the true Sources of Wealth and Plenty, will go on producing; and if they receive the annual Increase, and do not waste it as heretofore on Gegaws of this Country (i.e., England), but employ their spare time in manufacturing Necessaries for themselves, they must soon be out of debt, they must soon be easy and comfortable in their circumstances, and even wealthy.

Franklin's espousal of the Physiocratic doctrine at this period sat well with his intense involvement in land speculation (Currey 1965, 89).

In conclusion, Franklin's ideas about wage labor were less confused than those of Smith. Both recognized that the availability of cheap land would impede the development of wage labor. Where Smith seemed to suggest that the colonies could prosper through a gradual transition from the production of raw materials to manufactures, Franklin appeared to understand that societies do not easily move to a new mode of production. He realized that independent farmers would not gladly adopt the role of low-paid factory workers.

Franklin on the Economy of High Wages

After the colonies won their independence, Franklin changed his analysis once again. Using data from *The Wealth of Nations*, Franklin (1783, 440) maintained that workers in the United States earned considerably more than in England. Perhaps echoing Adam Smith, he proclaimed that a "community cannot be pronounced happy, in which, from the lowness and insufficiency of wages, the labor class procure [sic] so scanty a subsistence, that, they have not the means of marrying and rearing a family" (ibid., 436).

In spite of his earlier theory that high wages would be detrimental to the development of modern industry, Franklin did not see high wages as a cause for alarm at this time. Nor did he find a conflict between happiness and competitiveness, arguing, "It is not the wages of the workmen, but the price of the merchandise, that should be lowered" (ibid., 437). For example, an increasingly refined division of labor can offset the high price of labor (ibid., 436).

Franklin (ibid., 438–39) did admit that "the high price of wages is . . . one of the reasons for the opinion . . . that it will be many years before the manufactures of the United States can rival those of Europe." However, here he rejected that perspective. In fact, high wages offered an economic advantage. According to Franklin: "High wages attract the most skillful and industrious workmen. . . . A good workman spoils fewer tools, wastes less material, and works faster than one of inferior skills. . . . The perfection of machinery in all the arts is owing, to a large degree, to the workmen" (1783, 439). Franklin predicted that high wages would provide a permanent advantage, since for the newly independent colonists emigration would equalize wages across the Atlantic. In addition, prosperity in the new nation would raise demand for imports from Britain.

Franklin's Ideas Were in the Air

Franklin was not unique in understanding the relationship between lack of access to land and economic development. His *Observations* was published in 1755. The following year, Mirabeau published similar views on the importance of land scarcity in *L'Ami des hommes*. Mirabeau's brother was the governor of Guadeloupe, despite his objection to slavery (D. Davis 1966, 428). Whether or not Mirabeau received the idea from his brother or from Franklin is a matter of conjecture. Such ideas were certainly in the air.

Likewise, Adam Smith's contemporary, the anonymous author of *American Husbandry*, observed two decades later: "When land is difficult to be had or not good, owing to the extension of the settlements or to the monopolies of the country, the poor must be driven to other employments than those which depend on the land; manufacturing, commerce, fisheries, etc., must thrive in the natural course of things" (American 1775, 525). The leaders of the United States generally seemed to accept Franklin's verdict that the economic future of colonial manufacturing was modest. As Jefferson (1788, 260) wrote:

> It is impossible that manufactures should succeed in America from the high price of labour. This is occasioned by the great demand of labour for agriculture. A manufacturer from Europe will turn to labour of other kinds if he finds more can be got by it, and he finds some emploiments [*sic*] so profitable that he can lay up enough money to buy fifty acres of land to the culture of which he is irresistibly tempted by the independence in which it places him.

John Adams (1780, 255) concurred:

> Among men of reflection the sentiment is generally . . . that no power in Europe has anything to fear from America. The principal interest of America for many centuries to come will be landed, and her chief occupation agriculture. Manufactures and commerce will be but secondary objects and subservient to the other. America will be the country to produce the raw materials for manufactures; but Europe will be the country of manufactures, and the commerce of America will never increase but in a certain proportion to the growth of agriculture, until its whole territory of land is filled up with inhabitants, which will not be in hundreds of years.

A few years later, Madison (1787, 98–99) predicted that the extent and fertility of the western soil would, for a long time, give to agriculture a preference over manufactures.

Of course, Jefferson and Madison wrote as politicians rather than political economists. They feared an industrial future with a multitude of workers massed in large urban areas, steeped in lofty, revolutionary slogans about liberty and freedom.

Happy Mediocrity

Franklin's ideas were similar to those of Jefferson and many other revolutionary leaders in another respect. Many of his revolutionary contemporaries were also highly critical of class relations in England. In marginal comments on an anonymous pamphlet, *The True Constitutional Meaning*, Franklin (1959–, 16:290) offered some private thoughts on this subject: "And ought the Rich in Britain, who have such numbers of Poor by engrossing all the small Divisions of Land; and who keep the Labourers and working People Poor by limiting their wages; ought these Gentry to complain of the Burthen of maintaining the Poor that have work'd for them at unreasonably low rates all their Lives?" Many observers in the United States agreed that European manufactures depended on dangerous concentrations of impoverished masses in the cities. Given this perspective, Franklin suggested that manufacturing would not take root until the country became more populated. He initially predicted that population would not become dense enough until the distant future.

A few decades later, in a 1799 tract titled *The Internal State of America*, Franklin speculated that North America had already reached the point where manufacturing might take hold. Reading the pamphlet in question, we can easily find suggestions that would have appealed to the author of *The Wealth of Nations*. He observed:

> Whoever has travelled thro' the various parts of Europe, and observed how small is the Proportion of People in Affluence or easy Circumstances there, compared with those in Poverty and Misery; the few rich and haughty Landlords, the multitude of poor, abject, and rack'd Tenants, and the half-paid and half-starv'd ragged Labourers; and view here the happy Mediocrity, that so generally prevails throughout these States, where the Cultivator works for himself, and supports his Family in decent Plenty, will . . . be convinc'd that no Nation that is known to us enjoys a greater share of human Felicity. (Franklin 1905–7, 10:120)

Similarly, in his promotional tract, *Information for Those Who Would Remove to America*, Franklin (1782, 604) asserted: "The Truth is, that though there are in that Country few People so miserable as the Poor of

Europe, there are also very few that in Europe would be called rich; it is rather a general happy Mediocrity that prevails. There are few great Proprietors of the Soil, and few Tenants; most People cultivate their own Lands, or follow some Handicraft or Merchandise." According to Franklin (1905–7, 10:117), "The great Business of the Continent is Agriculture." Yet in the earlier tract, he concluded, "In short, America is the Land of Labour" (Franklin 1782, 607).

Other authors wrote in terms that sounded like Franklin. One contemporary writer commented, "Each man owns the house he lives in and the land with which he cultivates, and everyone appears to be in a happy state of mediocrity" (Weld 1800, 170). Similarly, Richard Price (1783; see also de Crèvecoeur 1782, 40, 58, 89) asked: "Where do the inhabitants live most on an equality, and most at their ease? Is it not in those inland parts where agriculture gives health and plenty, and trade is scarcely known? Where, on the contrary, are the inhabitants most selfishly luxurious, loose and vicious; and at the same time most unhappy? Is it not along the sea-coasts, and in the great towns, where trade flourishes and merchants abound?" Franklin's contribution was more important for what it omitted rather than what it appeared to say. In presenting the advantages of the state of "happy mediocrity" in which workers could earn relatively high wages while capital profited, Franklin, along with Smith, painted a picture of relative harmony between labor and capital. In reading Franklin, however, we must always consider the context of his work.

Unfortunately, Franklin's celebration of happy mediocrity came at a time when this egalitarian age was quickly coming to an end. The period in which Smith was completing his *Wealth of Nations* witnessed a significant increase in the concentration of wealth in the northern colonies (Williamson and Lindert 1977). Although the prerevolutionary farmers in the North may have been relatively prosperous (see Sachs 1953), between 1700 and 1736 the number of landless whites had already risen from 5 to 12 percent (Mayer and Fay 1977, 44). The average size of landholdings per adult male had declined from approximately 150 acres in the early seventeenth century to 43 acres in 1786 (ibid.).

In short, like Smith, Franklin was engaged in an ideological project, albeit less a theoretical endeavor than that of Smith. Specifically, Franklin was aiming his later theory of economic development at consoling those who were disturbed by the growing disparity between conditions of the urban wealthy and the masses of farmers in the countryside.

Even though the growth of luxury was incompatible with a state of happy mediocrity, Franklin (1905–7, 10:121) counseled his readers not to be alarmed, since "upon the whole there is a continual accumulation."

Franklin also saw advantages in the finer things in life despite his famous advocacy of Spartan simplicity (McCoy 1980, 75). In a 26 July 1784 letter, Franklin (1905–7, 9:244) asked Benjamin Vaughan: "May not Luxury, therefore, produce more than it consumes, if without such a Spur People would be as they are naturally enough inclined to be, lazy and indolent?" He then told a story to illustrate his point:

> The skipper of a shallop employed between Cape May and Phila-delphia, had done us some small service for which he refused to be paid. My wife understanding that he had a daughter, sent her a pres-ent of a new-fashioned cap. Three years after, this skipper being at my house with an old farmer of Cape May, his passenger, he mentioned the cap, and how much his daughter had been pleased with it. "But," he said, "it proved a dear cap to our congregation." "How so?" "When my daughter appeared with it at meeting, it was so much admired, that all the girls resolved to get such caps from Philadelphia; and my wife and I computed that the whole could not have cost less than a hundred pounds." "True," said the farmer, "but you do not tell all the story. I think the cap was nevertheless an advantage to us; for it was the first thing that put our girls upon knitting worsted mittens for sale at Philadelphia, that they might have wherewithal to buy caps and ribbons there; and you know that industry has continued, and is likely to continue and increase to a much greater value, and answer better purposes." (ibid., 243–44)

Commercialization

The transition from Franklin's happy mediocrity (of free workers) to an increasing commercialization of agriculture was especially powerful in the regions that served large urban areas. For example, in southeastern Pennsylvania, the region Franklin knew best, the typical farm of 1790 was already marketing about 40 percent of its produce (Lemon 1967, 69). Franklin (1905–7, 10:118) himself noted that farmers still had little need for imported goods, but they found themselves with a surplus of goods to market.

Franklin (ibid.) expressed certainty that farmers were doing well, writ-ing: "Never was the Farmer better paid for the Part he can spare Com-merce.... The Lands he possesses are also continually rising in value with the Increase of Population; and, on the whole, he is enabled to give such good Wages . . . that . . . in no Part are the labouring Poor so well fed and well cloth'd, and well paid as in the United States of America." Franklin gave no hint of the worsening distribution of income that accompanied these signs of prosperity. Rather, he insisted that the population as a whole shared in a general bounty, observing, "If we enter the Cities, we find, that, since the Revolution, the Owners of Houses and Lots of Ground have had their interest vastly augmented in value; Rents have risen to astonishing Height" (ibid.).

Franklin had always realized that commercialization would eventually lead to manufactures. As early as 1769, he had suggested to Lord Kames, Smith's patron (Rae 1895, 31), that the true value of manufactures was to concentrate value so that "Provisions may be more easily carried to a foreign market" (Franklin 1959–, 16:109). Elsewhere, he made use of a biblical allusion (John 6:12) to recommend manufactures on account of their ability to "gather up fragments (of time) that nothing may be lost" (Franklin 1959–, 15:52; repeated in 21:173).

These transitional conditions explain how Franklin (ibid., 16:295), in 1769, in the paragraph following his comments on part-time domestic manufacturing in the aforementioned marginal notes on *The True Constitutional Meaning*, maintained: "But some Manufacturers may be more advantageous to some Persons than the Cultivation of the Land." Franklin expanded on the meaning of his note in an earlier discussion with Gottfried Achenwall, professor of jurisprudence at the University of Gottinger. According to Achenwall's (1767, 354) account, Franklin stated: "There is land enough for the rich and poor, and the former prefer the larger profits from trade to the small return from the land."

These citations indicate that Franklin believed manufacturing would remain a part-time adjunct to the independent farm, just as the proto-Marxian model of primitive accumulation suggests. In his marginal notes to "The Constitutional Means for Putting an End to the Disputes between Great Britain and American Colonies," he remarked, "There is no Necessity for their leaving their Plantations; they can manufacture in their Families at spare Times" (Franklin 1959–, 16:295; see also Coxe 1794, 442).

Franklin (ibid., 20:442–45) also observed that families who practice this sort of economy were the healthiest in the nation. Unless these jottings were meant to prepare Franklin for a public encounter, they probably represented his true beliefs.

Workers were also supposed to be doing well in this state of affairs. Franklin (1782, 608) wrote: "There is a continual Demand for more Artisans of all the necessary and useful kinds, to supply those Cultivators of the Earth with Houses, and with Furniture and Utensils of the grosser sorts, which cannot so well be brought from Europe."

In this economy, Franklin (1905–7, 10:118–19) took the position:

"These Workmen all demand and obtain much higher Wages than any other Part of the World would afford them, and are paid in ready money." However, Franklin did not publicly express the belief that America had developed enough to begin large-scale manufacturing. As late as 1782, he explained: "Great Establishments of Manufacture require great Numbers of Poor to do the Work for Small Wages; these Poor are to be found in Europe, but will not be found in America, till all the Lands are taken up and cultivated, and the Excess of People, who cannot get Land, want Employment" (Franklin 1782, 611). In unpublished notes, Franklin indicated both less favorable conditions for workers as well as a brighter future for manufacturing. For example, he left a marginal comment on *The True Constitutional Meaning* that alluded to the declining welfare of the independent farmer: "No Farmer of America, in fact, makes 5 percent on his Money. His Profit is only being paid for by his own Labour and that of his Children" (Franklin 1959–, 16:294).

As the social division of labor became more elaborate, the opportunities for self-employment became less common, despite Franklin's contention that workers could easily become independent farmers. Franklin saw this evolution well before Smith had published his *Wealth of Nations*.

Thus, with rising land values and relatively low returns to subsistence farming, we are but a short distance from the institution of wage labor. To say as much does not indicate that Franklin saw America as replicating English conditions. Indeed, he took pride in the uniqueness of the colonial experience. Nonetheless, his analysis of commercialization is far closer to Steuart's than Smith's.

Franklin's Comparative Sociology of Wage Labor

At times, Franklin did express doubts that everybody would willingly participate in the process of commercialization. The Native Americans, for instance, were, for Franklin, proof of the "proneness of human Nature to a life of ease, of freedom from care and labour." He added that, although they understood the advantages that "Arts, Sciences, and compact Society procure . . . they have never shown any Inclination to change their manner of life" (Franklin 1959–, 4:479).

Not only the Native Americans who were educated in white society, but even whites taken prisoner by the Indians inevitably drifted back to the "primitive" society in preference to the civilized one (ibid.). On this same score, Madison fretted that American society as a whole might fall back into the "savage state" of the indigenous people (see Branson 1979, 241; see also de Crèvecoeur 1782, 52; Morgan 1975, 65–66).

In a letter to Joshua Babcock, Franklin (1959–, 19:6–7) wrote: "Had I never been in the American colonies, but was to form my judgement of Civil Society by what I have lately seen [in the British Isles], I should never advise a Nation of Savages to admit of Civilization. . . . the Effect of this kind of Civil Society seems only to be, depressing the Multitudes below the Savage State that a few may be rais'd above it." Franklin seems to have been so pleased with this anthropological flourish that he repeated it in another letter written on the same day (ibid., 19:16–24).

Yet Franklin generally expressed a fondness for the values of the Native American (see, for example, ibid., 148–57), which contrasted sharply with his impatience with any white who would not labor diligently. He explained the happiness of the Native Americans by their few natural wants, which were easily supplied; whereas, the civilized community had "infinite Artificial wants, no less craving than those of Nature, and much more difficult to satisfy" (ibid., 4:482).

Likewise, Franklin applauded the simplicity of other precapitalist cultures. Two members of Captain James Cook's crew related to Franklin in 1771 that the inhabitants of New Zealand refused to accept Cook's presents, presumably because they would be unable to create them on their own. Franklin termed those people "brave and sensible" and exclaimed, "Behold a Nation of Philosophers! Such as him [meaning Socrates] we celebrate as he went thro' a Fair, How many things there are in the World that I don't want" (ibid., 18:210).

Cook himself wrote that:

> they live in a warm and fine Climate and enjoy a very wholesome Air, so that they have very little need of Clothing and this they seem to be fully sensible of, for many to whome we gave Cloth &c to, left it carelessly upon the Sea beach and in the woods as a thing they had no manner of use for. In short they seem'd to set no Value upon any thing we gave them, nor would they ever part with any thing of their own for any one article we could offer them; this in my opinion argues that they think themselves provided with all the necessarys of Life and that they have no superfluities. (cited in Beaglehole 1955–67, 399)

In contrast, when missionaries distributed European goods to the Yir Yoront group in Queensland, Australia, the aboriginals accepted the gifts and soon lost their knowledge about their own traditional technology (Diener 1991, 77–78).

Despite his professed admiration for traditional societies, Franklin later took an active part in a proposed project to carry the benefits of civilization to New Zealand (Franklin 1959–, 20:522–28).

Fortunately, so far as Franklin was concerned, not everybody would resist engaging in a commercial society. In his pamphlet *The Internal State of America*, he asserted that "there seems to be in every nation a greater proportion of Industry and Frugality, which tend to enrich, than Idleness and Prodigality, which occasion Poverty; so that upon the whole there is continued accumulation" (Franklin 1905–7, 10:121). This notion would surely have appealed to Smith, of whom it has been said that he believed "there was a Scotchman inside every man" (Bagehot 1880, 343).

Franklin, however, had not always showed such confidence in the industry of the populace. In a valuable letter written to Peter Collison, he observed that when British workers came to the colonies, where "Labour is much better paid than in England, their Industry seems to diminish in equal proportion" (Franklin 1959–, 4:479). Noting that the same did not hold true of the German immigrants, Franklin supposed that the variation had to be traced to the "Institution" (ibid.). The institution to which he referred was the Poor Laws, which lent support to the unfortunate.

Given this perspective, not just poverty, but grinding poverty would be required to ensure the accumulation of capital. Despite all the pious sentiments about the naturalness of a liberal wage rate, the hard-liners would seem to be correct after all, at least so far as Franklin was concerned.

In the very same letter in which he heaped lavish praise upon the Native Americans for their simple ways, Franklin called for the erection of workhouses, where the indigent would be "obliged to work at the pleasure of others for a bare subsistence and that too under confinement" (Franklin 1959–, 15:148–57). Or, in the words of his alter ego, Poor Richard, "a fat kitchen, a lean will" (ibid., 1:315).

In conclusion, although the relatively egalitarian society of the northern colonies provided a welcome comparison with England, Franklin realized that a certain degree of poverty was required to establish wage labor. He appreciated that the American wage rate was coming closer to the ideal of a "normal" or "natural" rate or wages under which capital could prosper without driving labor into utter destitution (see Thompson 1977). Smith, no doubt, shared a similar appreciation of colonial conditions.

Franklin versus Smith

Smith attempted to use the experience of the New World as an object lesson in the virtues of laissez-faire. Although Franklin often wrote as if he were in league with Smith, the wise Pennsylvanian actually instructed the New World to follow a course much more in tune with Steuart than with Smith. On closer inspection, Smith (1976, IV.vii.b.3, 566) would have been hard-pressed to find a vindication of his doctrine of "population and improvement" in Franklin's works. In other words, despite these suggestions of rustic tranquility, the United States was destined to follow the course of development that Steuart, rather than Smith, charted. As Franklin (1959–, 18:82) concluded:

> Every Manufacturer encouraged in our Country, makes part of Market for Provisions within ourselves, and saves so much Money to the Country as must otherwise be exported to pay for the manufactures he supplies. Here in England it is well known and understood that whenever a Manufacture is established which employs a number of Hands, it raises the Value of Lands in the neighbouring Country all around it; partly by the greater Demand near at hand for the Produce of the Land; and partly from the Plenty of Money drawn by the Manufactures to that Part of the Country. It seems therefore, in the Interest of all our Farmers and owners of Lands, to encourage our young Manufacturers.

In fact, Smith's eulogist, Dugald Stewart cited Franklin's Smithian-sounding story of the gift of the cap in describing Steuart's analysis of economic development. Stewart introduced the citation with the comment that Franklin's "trifling anecdote . . . places the whole of this natural process in a stronger light than I can possibly do by any general observations" (Stewart 1855, 2:154).

Like Steuart, Franklin saw industry as beginning as an adjunct to agriculture, then evolving toward a separation between agricultural and manufacturing pursuits, as the use of time became more intensive. Given the different conditions in which they lived, we should not be surprised that Steuart was somewhat more favorably inclined toward manufactures than was Franklin.

Despite Franklin's similarities with Steuart, some recent authors still place Franklin closer to Smith than Steuart. For example, Patricia James (1979, 106) recently speculated that Steuart's claim about the wholesomeness of cities was, in fact, a direct response to Franklin. Franklin, however, understood as well as Steuart, that an increasing population could push labor into accepting full-time employment in manufacturing. Otherwise, Franklin's work was decidedly inferior to Steuart's.

William Grampp (1979) and Warren Nutter (1976) both stress Smith's influence on Franklin. Although we might find echoes of Smith in Franklin's later work, we have no evidence that Franklin ever seriously studied *The Wealth of Nations*, even though he did own the book, Smith's message, like many of Franklin's, was in the air at the time. We can safely conclude that Franklin's evolution was influenced less by Smith than by the conditions of the society in which he lived.

True, Franklin occasionally expressed sentiments that sounded Smithian, but we must always be on guard against taking Franklin at face value. In short, the case for Smith's influence on Franklin is slim to say the least.

For example, Franklin's contribution to Whateley's pamphlet "Principles of Trade" indicates a militant free-trading spirit (Franklin 1959-, 21:169-77). However, industry was more firmly rooted by 1774, when that work was written, than was the case when Franklin wrote his *Observations* and the *Interest of Great Britain Considered.* More importantly, the doctrine of free trade lent support to the colonial cause. Although this pamphlet was published pseudonymously, people soon learned who wrote such works.

Franklin's infatuation with a system of happy mediocrity was appropriate to the early stage of the accumulation process. It was comparable to Steuart's analysis of domestic industry. Later, as a satisfactory labor supply seemed to be put in place, Franklin supported a more conventional theory in which markets, utility, and luxury have more prominence. Even in this late period, Franklin's work still bore a marked similarity to Steuart's.

We know that Franklin did study Steuart. He made several pages of notes on chapter 11 of book 2 of Steuart's *Principles* (reprinted in Carey 1928, 144-46). (Unfortunately, the otherwise thorough editors of Franklin's works omitted these notes. One of the editors has assured me that they will be printed in a subsequent volume.) The choice of this chapter of Steuart's book is significant, since it contains Steuart's most coherent analysis of the transition to capitalist social relations from a system of self-sufficiency.

Smith gave no indication that he recognized this aspect of Franklin's work; however, Smith himself did all that he could to downplay the analysis of this transition. His selective appropriation of Franklin's analysis of North American development lends further credence to the thesis that Smith falsified the political economy of the wage relationship, a relationship that appears clearly in the writings of Franklin and Steuart.

CHAPTER 12

The Classics as Cossacks: Classical
Political Economy versus the Working Class

The head of the new school, Mr. Ricardo, has, they say, declared himself that there
are no more than twenty-five people in England that had understood his book.
Perhaps he had cultivated obscurity, so that those who understood him . . . had
become a sect of adepts with a new language.—Sismondi, *Nouveaux principles
d'economie politique*

The Scotland of Steuart and Owen

Robert Owen was a successful cotton spinner. Like others of his trade, he
discovered that the creation of a capitalist society in Scotland, or elsewhere, was no easy task. Workers generally resisted "the supervision of
labour; fines; bells and clocks; money incentives; preaching and schooling; the suppression of fairs and sports" associated with industrial discipline (E. Thompson 1967, 90). This opposition was especially strong in
Scotland. In Owen's (1857, 58) words, the "regularly trained Scotch peasant disdained the idea of working early and late, day after day, within
cotton mills."

According to Sidney Pollard (1965, 261), "The Highlander," it was said,
"never sits at ease at a loom; it is like putting a deer in a plough." He
pointed out that "in Scotland, significantly, people referred to factories as
'public works,' revealing a mental association with workhouses, and migration to factory districts was likened to transportation" (Pollard 1965,
194; see also Kuczynski 1967, 70). Marx pointed out that even Adam
Smith interchangeably used the terms "manufactory" and "workhouse"
(808n). The feeling against factories ran so strong that the father of Richard Oastler, a famous industrialist, sold his business rather than employ
the "machine [which] symbolized the encroachment of the factory system," machines that he regarded as "a means of oppression on the part of
the rich and of corresponding degradation and misery to the poor" (cited in
Thompson 1963, 548, 549).

Given the widespread revulsion created by factory work, employers had
to go to great lengths to snatch labor from the depths of the urban centers.

For example, children were sometimes bound to the factory by indentures of apprenticeship for at least seven years and usually until they were twenty-one (Mantoux 1961, 410). "Lots of fifty, eighty or a hundred children were supplied [by the Poor Law authorities] and sent like cattle where they remained imprisoned for many years" (ibid., 411).

Prospective employers had to be quick to take advantage of fortuitous events. David Dale, a famous Scottish cotton lord and future father-in-law of Robert Owen, on hearing of two hundred emigrants shipwrecked on a nearby coast, rushed off to recruit them (Pollard 1965, 261). Dale, like other cotton magnates, eventually found it expedient to create entire villages in order to maintain a labor force (A. Robertson 1971, 150–51; Pollard 1965, 231–42; Collier 1930). Dale's village, located in Lanark County, home of Sir James Steuart, eventually passed into the hands of Owen.

Realizing that opportunities, such as the occasional shipwreck, would be insufficient to staff a modern textile industry, Robert Owen concluded: "Two modes then only remained of obtaining these labourers, the one to procure children from the various public charities of the country, and the other to induce families to settle around the works" (Owen 1813, 26).

In order to reconcile his workers to their condition, Owen established a nursery school for young children and night schools for older ones. He also developed a support fund to take care of the injured, sick, and aged. In addition, workers enjoyed the services of a company-owned savings bank and stores that undersold private dealers (on this latter point, see Ricardo 1951–73, 5:218).

Perhaps because of his enlightened policies, Owen's business was extremely profitable, but his partners were upset that Owen was spending too much on the welfare of his workers. As James Mill wrote to Jeremy Bentham on 3 December 1813, the partners "had in general got soured with him on account of his endeavours (to which they were averse) to improve the population of the mills" (reprinted in Conway 1988, 31–32). Owen then turned to a group of new investors, including Jeremy Bentham (see Bowring 1962, 466–67).

Soon the relationship between these two unlikely partners also degenerated. By 25 March 1815, Bentham wrote to Owen to request money back from his investment (Conway 1988, 451–52). In a later conversation, Bentham described Owen in unflattering terms: "Robert Owen begins in a vapour, and ends in smoke. He is a great braggadocio. His mind is a maze of confusion, and he avoids coming to particulars. He is always the same— says the same things over and over again. He built some small houses; and people, who had no houses of their own, went to live in those houses—and he calls this success" (Bowring 1962, 10, 570). Owen (1857, 95–96) reciprocated, describing Bentham as a recluse, whose only contact with the real world was through his books and a handful of trusted friends. He claimed that Bentham's friends told him that the investment in New Lanark was Bentham's only successful venture (ibid., 96).

Certainly, Bentham's view of Owen's establishment was in a distinct minority. New Lanark won the admiration of people around the world. Owen's workers seemed to enjoy a better life than the urban proletariat, even though he paid them below the going rate. More important, his factory earned a healthy, but not unusual profit (A. Robertson 1971, 147–48).

Thomas Robert Malthus offered a different dissenting report of Owen's works. In 1810, he entered into his diary, "About fifteen hundred people are employed at the cotton mill, and great debauchery prevails among them" (Malthus 1966, 233); however, his next sentence describes the thirteen-hour, six-day-per-week schedule. Unfortunately, Malthus supplied no details about the debauchery, which must have been confined to the Sabbath.

Robert Owen's Model of a Humane Economy

Although Owen's community had many progressive features, the workers themselves complained about the paternalism: "We view it a grievance of considerable magnitude to be compelled by Mr. Owen to adopt what measures so ever he may be pleased to suggest to us on matters that entirely belong to us. Such a course of procedure is most repugnant to our minds as men, and degrading to our characters" (cited in Robertson 1971, 150).

One need only follow the course of development of company towns to see the potential for abuse. We can begin with Francis Cabot Lowell, who had originally attempted to re-create what he saw at New Lanark in his Massachusetts textile towns (Dillard 1967, 328–29; Marx 1967, 2:516), including the emphasis on discipline (see Ware 1924, 78–79).

Next we can turn to the town that bears George Pullman's name. The company designed this community to "attract and retain a superior type of workingman, who would in turn be elevated and refined" by the physical setting (cited in Harvey 1976, 283). We could complete our tour with the grotesque system engineered by Henry Ford, with a "staff of over thirty investigators . . . [who] visited workers' homes gathering information and giving advice on intimate details of the family budget, diet, living arrangements, recreation, social outlook and morality" (Flink, 1975, 89; see also Sward 1972, 228–29; Harvey 1976, 277).

To his credit, Owen understood the shortcomings of his village. He attempted to create alternative communities with more self-governance, although the *Black Dwarf*, a radical newspaper, perceptively denounced his paternalistically planned community as a "nursery for men" (cited in Hollis 1973, 31).

Owen's involvement with the cotton industry educated him in many respects. He recognized that labor was being driven from the countryside much more rapidly than it could be absorbed in the factories. In this regard, Owen seems also to have been influenced by Thomas Spence, whose call for land reform was discussed earlier (Rudkin 1966, 191 ff.); however, with Owen, the Spencian demands for collective ownership of the land were softened. Rather, he had hoped that the wealthy, including the royal family, would help him in establishing villages that could set labor back to work on the land.

Like Steuart and Spence, Owen realized that the social division of labor in food production was a vital element in the determination of the level of real wages. In a letter dated 25 July 1817, and published in the London newspapers five days later, Owen (1857, 74) declared, "Value must be restored to manual labour, and this cannot be done except by employment on the land."

Owen designed a plan for villages based on labor-intensive agriculture. He stressed the social, rather than the technical advantages of his plan, calling on the wealthy, and even the government, to invest with him in a program to correct the imbalances in the social division of labor.

Although most of the attempts to put Owen's ideas into practice met with failure, the Ralahine community in County Clare, Ireland, was, in fact, quite successful, even on purely monetary grounds, until its owner gambled away his fortune (Garnett 1971, 47–52; see also Bray 1841, 2:580–85). Some members of the royal family were duly impressed.

Of course, a good deal of Owen's idea was by no means novel. Owen himself discovered later that John Bellers, who appeared in chapter 3, had already proposed much of his analysis, as well as much of his solution. Bellers, considered by Marx (1977, 619) to be "a veritable phenomenon in the history of political economy," advocated that capitalists invest in colleges of industry that could educate the poor, teach them industry, and shelter them from earthly cares, although he shrewdly observed that "the labour of the poor . . . [is] the mine of the rich" (Bellers 1696, 164).

And why was profit necessary? Bellers (ibid., 177) answered simply, "Because the rich have no other way of living but by the labour of others." This naive philanthropist hoped to benefit all humanity by virtue of an improved social division of labor in which the cooperation of concentrations of labor would result in a tremendous expansion of productivity. In Bellers's (ibid., 176) words: "As one man cannot and ten must strain to lift a ton weight, yet one hundred men can do it only by the strength of each of them." Bellers may have been the first person to suggest something akin to the modern notion of an efficiency wage, arguing that a decent life for the poor was compatible with a wholesome rate of profit for the rich.

Political economy recoiled from Owen's plan. After all, Owen intended to raise the demand for labor. As Steuart (1767, 1:175) had recognized earlier, increasing the mass of people employed in self-sufficient farming would reduce the number available for the production of the surplus. Steuart had fretted that profits would suffer as a result of a return to spade husbandry. Such honesty was nowhere to be found in later classical political economy. Instead, later political economists lashed out at Owen's scheme as nothing less than an assault on civilization.

A Brief Digression on Land Reform

Subsequent calls for land reform echoed Owen's ideas. In Britain and the United States, workers were in the forefront of the struggle for land reform, even though they might not ever get the opportunity to work the land themselves (E. Thompson 1963, 231, 295; P. Foner 1975, 44–45). The Chartists, for example, even bought up land during the 1840s to lease back to their members (see Engels 1847; Tsuzuki 1971, 18–19). According to Feargus O'Connor in the 7 June 1845 issue of the *Northern Star:*

> The first use the land would be to them was to ease the labour market of its surplus; the second was to create a certainty of work for the people; and the third was to create a natural rate of wages in the artificial market; for so long as there was a surplus to fall back on, or a warehouse from which to procure labour, so long would work be uncertain and wages low. (cited in Prothero 1969, 99)

O'Connor (1845, 307) had intended that workers could be drawn off into agriculture in such a way that "the number working at each trade (could be adjusted) to the amount of produce required from each as to ensure a healthy settlement of demand and supply."

Unfortunately, O'Connor's perspective was limited. He denounced "communism" as "a fascinating theory [that] . . . opens a wide field for indulgence of the wildest of visionaries" (O'Connor 1848b, 55). He wanted "to make idleness a crime" (ibid., 56). More important, O'Connor looked backward to a system of petty commodity production. In any event, the Chartists's plan failed and the capitalist system continued; so did its intended "screwing and grinding" (Spence 1807; cited in E. Thompson 1963, 805).

Not surprisingly, the left wing of the Chartist movement, as well as Marx and Engels, could not support O'Connor's project, just as they could not endorse Hermann Kriege's land reform activities in the United States (see Draper 1978, 411, 420–25); however, Engels did recognize that a program to give peasants land could be progressive in the context of less advanced economic conditions, such as were found in Germany (see Marx and Engels 1846b, 351–55).

The Chartist plan might have worked to raise the wages of labor in the short run. The case of Mr. R. F. Powell, hired by wealthy philanthropists as superintendent of the Philadelphia Vacant Lots Cultivation Association, illustrates this point (Dudden 1971, 36). As a follower of Henry George, Powell was keenly aware of the extent of vacant land held for speculative purposes in his city, which he estimated to have amounted to one-quarter of the urban area (see Kelley 1906, 306). Mr. Powell helped set almost one thousand families to work raising gardens on these lots. For the especially needy, Mr. Powell would hire them as gardeners at only twelve and a half cents per hour, although the organization would not have suffered a loss, even if the wages had been raised as high as forty cents per hour.

Why were wages set at the lower level? The board of directors of the association, composed of wealthy businessmen, would not allow a higher wage. Powell informed Florence Kelley, the translator of the American edition of Engels's *Conditions of the Working Class:* "It would make no end of trouble . . . if these people were to find that they could earn as much as that they would either leave the factories or demand as much pay there" (ibid., 306).

David Ricardo

Owen's schemes stirred up a great deal of controversy. Classical political economy was drawn into the fray. This dispute is crucial for what it reveals about the attitude of classical political economy with respect to the social division of labor and self-provisioning.

David Ricardo, for one, became a reluctant participant in this wrangling. No one should have expected Ricardo to offer much support to Owen's plan. Although modern commentators often cite Ricardo's words of sympathy for the poor, this sentiment was rather abstract, if not hollow. Ricardo was not at all critical of the attempts of employers "to keep down the recompense to the labourer to the lowest rate" (1951–73, 9:54). In his very first speech to Parliament, he warned his fellow members against being overly tender to the children of the poor, lest such actions encourage the poor to breed more offspring (ibid., 5:1).

In 1818 Ricardo (ibid., 7:359–60) refused to send James Mill a donation for the Westminster Infant School because the children were to be given some dinner:

> If it is part of the establishment . . . to feed as well as to take care of and educate the children of three years of age, and upwards, belonging to the poor, I see the most serious objections to the plan, and I should be exceedingly inconsistent if I gave my countenance to it. I have invariably objected to the poor laws, and to every system which should give encouragement to excess of population. If you are to feed, clothe, and educate all the children of the poor, you will be giving a great stimulus to a principle already too active.

Even so, while attending a meeting of the Owenites, along with Robert Torrens, Ricardo succumbed to pressure to join a committee to study Owen's proposal. From the beginning, Ricardo was skeptical that the scheme could be administered in the socialistic form envisioned by Owen. As he wrote to his friend, Trower: "Can any reasonable person believe with Owen, that a society, such as he projects, will flourish and produce more than has ever yet been produced by an equal number of men, if they are to be stimulated to their private interest? Is not the experience of ages against him?" (Ricardo 1951–73, 8:46).

Ricardo's objections were not limited to philosophical speculations on human nature. He charged Owen with the grave error of building "a theory inconsistent with the principles of political economy, and . . . calculated to produce infinite mischief to the community" (ibid., 5:30).

While both Ricardo and Owen argued that the then existing social division was brought about by matters of individual self-interest, Owen interpreted the result to be detrimental to the well-being of labor. Ricardo reasoned on a different basis, assuming that if labor-intensive technologies were beneficial to society, then they would turn out to be more profitable. Consequently, he told Parliament that "as soon as the farmer knew that it was in his interest to pursue a different system, he would adopt it as a matter of course" (ibid., 6:31n).

Given this position, Ricardo could accept some of Owen's diagnosis, but certainly not his remedy. Ricardo was only willing to go so far as to ascertain if spade husbandry would be more profitable. The market could take care of the rest.

In this spirit, Ricardo (ibid., 5:31) responded to his own rhetorical question: "For what did the country want at the present moment? A demand for labour. If the facts stated of spade husbandry were true, it was a beneficial course, as affording that demand."

Later, Ricardo routinely equated charity with Owenism. For example, in 1819, Ricardo was nominated to a parliamentary committee of inquiry into the Poor Laws headed by William Sturges-Bourne, who proposed to eliminate all poor relief to destitute parents of large families, but advocated providing relief to hungry children on the condition that they be placed in workhouses. Ricardo dissented from this bill, contending that assuring parents "that an asylum would be provided for their children, in which they would be treated with humanity and tenderness . . . was only the plan of Mr Owen, in a worse shape and carried to a greater extent" (ibid., 1, 7).

Ricardo on Horses and Machinery

Despite his outwardly confident attitude about the market, Ricardo was intellectually honest enough to feel the pangs of skepticism. He eventually granted some credence to Owen's concerns in his unpublished *Notes on Malthus*. There, Ricardo explicitly recognized that an alternative agricultural technology might very well improve the position of the working class, even though it would not necessarily be more profitable to individual farmers:

> It might be possible to do almost all the work performed by men with horses, would the substitution of horses in such case, even if attended with a greater produce, be advantageous to the working classes, would it not on the contrary very materially diminish the demand for labour? All I mean to say is that it *might* happen with a cheaper mode of cultivation the demand for labour *might* diminish, and with a dearer it might decrease. (Ricardo 1951–73, 2:239)

Two comments are relevant to Ricardo's (ibid., 2:238) position here. First, Ricardo had already recognized in an earlier note that "diminished [net] production is, in fact, compatible with an increased consumption, by human beings." In terms of agriculture, the sum of the grain consumed directly by the farm workers plus the farmers' profits, measured in grain, might also be higher with spade husbandry than when horses are used, even though profits could be higher when farmers substituted horses for human labor. The fact that Ricardo even stopped to reflect on the possibility of diminished consumption indicates that he sensed something amiss in the marketplace.

Second, Ricardo wrote and then deleted the thought: "This is perhaps the only case in which the substitution of labour for fixed capital, if horses can be so called, is not attended with advantage to the capitalist yet is nevertheless beneficial to the working class" (ibid., 2:239n). In other words, the possibility of detrimental effects from the introduction of fixed capital is limited to the case of substituting horses for human labor.

In opposition to Piero Sraffa (1951, 1:lix), Samuel Hollander (1971; 1979; see also Maital and Haswell 1977) took the position that a concern about the effect of horses on the demand for agricultural labor did not necessarily lead to Ricardo's later idea that machinery, in general, could operate to the detriment of labor. Hollander's stance has merit for several reasons.

To begin with, a number of writers besides Owen noted the detrimental aspects of horse husbandry. At the time, one horse performed work roughly equivalent to five men (Daunton 1995, 46). Horses also consumed an enormous amount of food that might have otherwise fed farm workers. A single horse typically required an estimated three pecks of oats and a gallon of beans daily in addition to its hay (Ashton 1972, 55). One writer referred to the horse as "the most dangerous moth in the whole web of agricultural economy" (Tatham 1799, 412). We can even find an allusion to this phenomenon in Richard Cantillon (1755, 63).

Other economists found fault with horse husbandry without generalizing their objections to investment in machinery. Perhaps Nassau Senior (1868, 2:43) offers the best example of this phenomenon. Senior suggested that the use of horses might be excessive. However, despite Senior's doubts about horse husbandry, he never accepted the later Ricardian position on machinery. He wrote, "I do not believe that there exists upon record a single instance in which the whole annual produce has been diminished by the use of *inanimate* machinery" (Senior 1831, 39–40; emphasis in original).

Thus, even though Ricardo seems to have adopted his ideas on machinery only a few months after he made his observations on horse husbandry, we cannot say for certain that one necessarily led to the other. Nor can we ever know with certainty if Ricardo's discussion of machinery was somehow related to Owen's scheme. Ricardo presented his analysis in the form of an abstract principle, absolutely unrelated to any particular point of policy. He claimed to be "not aware that I have ever published anything respecting machinery which it is necessary for me to retract" (Ricardo 1951–73, 1:386). Still, he added what might be an admission that he had not treated Owen altogether fairly: "yet I have in other ways given my support to doctrines which I now think erroneous" (ibid.). Could he have had his earlier critique of Owenism in mind?

Horses as a Special Case

Modern economists tend to sweep aside even modest speculations, such as Ricardo's qualms about horses. They presume that the supply of food is not an issue. New employment will come on line naturally, because the superior technology from horse husbandry will drop food prices, thereby expanding aggregate purchasing power. Since the augmentation of purchasing power will increase the demand for labor, labor replaced by horses will merely shift to new jobs. Any reference to the competition between horses and people for food would seem to be irrelevant. This optimistic perspective makes sense only if the displaced workers find alternative employment and earn enough to purchase comparable amounts of food. The experience of modern times does not give much cause for such optimism.

In contrast, classical political economists could regard horses as a special case for two reasons. First, a special model of agriculture colored their perception of the effect of horses. They often built simplified models of agriculture in which the input—grain—and the output—food—are more or less identical (De Vivo 1985).

Where grain is both the input and the output, the explanation that technical change will benefit the workers was not as convincing, especially because classical political economy assumed that wages ultimately depended on a fund, which employers presumably set aside to nourish workers. Moreover, that fund often seemed to consist of the real goods that workers consume. Since horses consumed food that workers might otherwise eat, horses could rightfully be said to diminish the fund.

Second, many people associated the substitution of horses for people with the enclosure movement. The enclosures were part and parcel of a momentous change in the mode of production, whereas the adoption of machinery in general took place within the capitalist mode of production. Thus, the case of horse husbandry may have been assumed to be unique, even though most political economists held that in spite of the suffering engendered by the initiation of market relations, the development of the market would make life better for all in the long run.

We should resist the temptation to add a third reason why Ricardo's discussion of horses might be considered unique: agriculture often seems to be an extremely labor-intensive business compared to the image of the modern textile works that were spreading through the British Isles during the Industrial Revolution. In reality, this impression is misleading—at least Ricardo thought so. He told Parliament on 9 May 1822 that he doubted that agriculture was less capital-intensive than industry (Ricardo 1951–73, 5:77–78; see also Gordon 1976, 139–40). In fact, industry in late-eighteenth-century England was not very capital-intensive at all. The nation spent more money on horseshoeing than was invested in capital in the entire textile industry, even though textile production was the core sector during the Industrial Revolution (Crouzet 1972, 22).

Thus, the uniqueness of the agricultural sector, with grain seen as both an input and an output, might have left Ricardo free to see horses and agriculture as a special case without much relevance for manufacturing.

Economists still debate whether Ricardo was mistaken or not in his machinery chapter. I suspect that part of the reason that this subject has caused so much confusion is Ricardo's inadequate treatment of the depreciation of machinery. Paul Samuelson (1989) gave one of the better readings of this chapter. Perhaps because Samuelson used horses as his example of machinery, he had an advantage over those who thought in terms of machines proper. As a result, Samuelson was able to steer clear of some of the more common errors in interpreting Ricardo theory of machinery.

Ricardo and Depreciation

Ricardo's theory of fixed capital might also explain why he did not consider his theory of horses to be comparable to his theory of machinery. As a background to this speculation, we should note that Ricardo's peculiar notion of capital created a serious flaw in his chapter "On Machinery." Like most economists of his day, Ricardo generally assumed that fixed capital does not depreciate. Instead, he treated fixed capital as permanently productive so long as sufficient maintenance would be performed to keep it intact (Chatfield 1977, 102; Brief 1965).

Yes, I know that sections 3 through 5 of Ricardo's first chapter of his *Principles* are filled with considerations about the durability of capital, but by the time we get to the chapter on machinery, all concern with durability has fallen by the wayside. Ricardo (1951–73, 8:388) almost admits as much in an 18 June 1821 letter to McCulloch, confessing, "If I have not said whether the machine was to last one, ten, or a hundred years I have not been so explicit as I ought to have been."

We should also note that elsewhere in the *Principles* Ricardo did allude at times to technological improvements that could cause machines to depreciate through obsolescence. For example, he discussed the case . . . of a man who has erected machinery in his manufactory at a great expense, machinery which is afterwards so much improved upon by more modern inventions, that the commodities manufactured by him very much sink in value. It would be entirely a matter of calculation with him whether he should abandon the old machinery, and erect the more perfect, losing all the value of the old, or continue to avail himself of its comparatively feeble powers. (1951–73, 1:271)

Even so, in the chapter on machinery, Ricardo treated machinery as if it had infinite durability. We should not judge Ricardo too harshly for this shortcoming in his analysis. In the first place, he was merely following standard accounting practices of his day. Indeed, the fashion at the time was to treat all overhead costs, such as the original cost of a machine, as unproductive labor (Chatfield 1977, 102). According to one historian of account thought, Richard Brief (1965, 14–15):

> The oldest assumption on which accounting practices were based implies that the value of fixed tangible assets remains constant if they are maintained in working order. . . . Under replacement accounting, all expenditures on maintenance, repairs and renewals were charged directly to expense. Expenditures on additions and betterments, i.e., capital expenditures, made with funds provided from the proceeds of stock and bond issues were capitalized. . . . the recognition of depreciation associated with the original plant is delayed until those assets are replaced.

Given this perspective, Ricardo and his contemporaries saw no need to take account of depreciation when discussing machinery; however, this neglect of depreciation significantly weakens Ricardo's treatment of machinery.

In the absence of depreciation, Ricardo's machinery, like his land, somehow becomes endowed with an imagined productivity that lasts indefinitely. Consequently, Ricardo did not count the labor used to produce the machinery as part of the value of the final output in that chapter, since the machinery itself is unchanged in the course of production. Given that setup, Ricardo only had to take the labor used to maintain the machine as a cost.

Why would Ricardo, the premier economic theorist of his day, fail to go beyond the crude capital theory of his day in his chapter on machinery? Why wouldn't he have integrated his observations about technological obsolescence into his more theoretical analysis?

Although there is no way to know Ricardo's thoughts on this matter, let me offer a conjecture. Ricardo's inconsistent capital theory may not be an indication of confusion on his part. Instead, it may reflect the depth of his understanding of capital theory.

Ricardo's allusions to the need to take account of the depreciation of capital suggest that he saw the deficiencies of the naive capital theory of his day. At the same time, Ricardo's sophistication might well have made him aware of the impossibility of a precise theory of depreciation within the context of economic models.

If Ricardo had attempted to come to grips with the concept of depreciation, he would have been swamped by the complexity of the subject. In fact, no economic model has ever introduced an even remotely realistic treatment of depreciation. The reason is not hard to fathom.

The rules of thumb that accountants use are inadequate for a theory of economics that purports to show how profit maximizing outcomes arise. Depreciation, however, requires that the theory confront the unknowable future.

For example, the depreciation of a capital good depends, among other things, upon the economic lifetime of that equipment. Most firms do not discard capital goods because they wear out. Instead, conditions change, making the good uneconomical. If the firm scraps the good in a year, it will have to depreciate it completely within that period. If the good lasts ten years, then the depreciation will be more gradual.

Each subsequent replacement will be affected by the expectation of later replacements in the still more distant future. A profit maximizing investor will generally require foreknowledge of the date of the introduction of the next generation of capital before making that replacement decision. As Joseph Schumpeter (1950, 98) once wrote:

> Frequently, if not in most cases, a going concern does not simply face the question whether or not to adopt a definite new method of production that is the best thing out. . . . A new type of machine is in general but a link in a chain of improvements and may presently become obsolete. In this case it would obviously not be rational to follow the chain link by link regardless of the capital loss to be suffered each time. (1950, 98)

Economists briefly looked at the incredibly difficult requirements for a realistic theory of the economic lifetime of capital toward the end of the Great Depression (see Preinreich 1940), but the demands of such a theory were so great that nobody dared to take up the challenge. Since depreciation depends on the economic lifetime of a capital good, analysis of depreciation requires a parallel analysis of expectations. Economists still have no adequate theory for expectations.

Just as Adam Smith built his theory to show that the market created a harmony of interests between the small masters, their workers, and the rest of society, modern economists construct their theory to show why market forces lead to the most efficient possible outcome. As a result, they avoid the theory of depreciation. This practice is part of a larger tendency to deny that accidents, ignorance, or anything else except intrusive government could cause an economy to wander off a path of maximum efficiency. Realism in such matters is a trivial consideration.

To have expected a Ricardo to have mastered the intricacy of a theory of depreciation a century and a half ago is wildly unrealistic. Ricardo was, above all, a master of making his models analytically tractable. Just consider how cleverly he eliminated any consideration of rent from his value theory. So while realistic comments about the realities of depreciation crept into his book, Ricardo was careful to avoid any examination of depreciation when it could threaten to garble the message of his theory of machinery.

Here we see that horses differ from Ricardian machinery in still another sense. The idea of an undepreciating horse is utter nonsense. Horses are not immortal. Despite the best care and maintenance, all horses eventually succumb to injury, disease, or old age. Thus, "horse capital" falls somewhere between Ricardo's notions of fixed and circulating capital, although a large enough farmer could theoretically have an undepreciating herd of horses—at least in an actuarial sense.

Ricardo and Machinery

The core of Ricardo's famous chapter analyzed conditions by which the introduction of labor-saving techniques in industry could harm labor. He even went so far as to speculate in a letter to John R. McCulloch that "if machinery could do all the work that labour now does, there would be no demand for labour" (Ricardo 1951–73, 8:399–400). Under this assumption, "Nobody would be entitled to consume who was not a capitalist, and who could not buy or rent a machine" (ibid.).

Ricardo offered the observation that "the labouring class have no small interest in which the net income of the country is expended, although it should, in all cases, be expended for the gratification and enjoyments of those who are fairly entitled to it" (ibid., 1:392). A few paragraphs later, Ricardo (ibid., 394) noted that wages could fall with the cessation of war if the wealthy people devoted their funds for "the purchase of wine, furniture, or other luxuries." In effect, he seems to have given labor the implicit right to have some say in how the wealthy classes spend their money, although he gives no indication that the working classes have any comparable right to question the distribution of wealth.

What do the consumption patterns of the wealthy have to do with the policy issues raised by the machinery model? After all, the substantial dislocations following the end of the Napoleonic Wars were too great to be explained by excessive purchases of luxuries. The mere mention of this period, however, seems to suggest an important policy dimension to the model.

In the next paragraph, Ricardo (ibid., 394) returned to the possible detrimental effect of the use of horses, again suggesting that his model was intended to be more than an abstract exercise:

> There is one other case . . . the possibility of an increase in the net revenue of a country, and even of its gross revenue, with a diminution in the demand for labour, and that is, when the labour of horses is substituted for that of man. . . . to substitute the horses for the men . . . would not be for the interest of the men, and . . . it is evident that the population would become redundant and the labourer's condition would sink.

In other words, while machinery in general may be harmful to labor, the effect is far more dramatic in the case of horse husbandry because gross output and labor demand can fall together.

Rather than continue with this line of reasoning, Ricardo undercut any policy implications of his model in the following paragraph. He pointed out that his model only referred to the *sudden* improvement of machinery, whereas in reality, technical change is gradual (ibid., 395). Of course, sudden improvements in technology are inconsistent with Ricardo's static theory of value.

Ricardo further downplayed the relevance of his finding by implicitly arguing that machinery could not do a great deal of harm to workers, since the introduction of machinery would not be economical unless wages are high. Even high wages would not necessarily lead to the widespread introduction of machinery. For example, according to Ricardo, machinery was not economical in American agriculture because land was so abundant there (ibid., 395). Of course, the intensive use of agricultural machinery was soon to become a hallmark of agriculture in the United States.

The Corn Laws in England

Even if Owen's proposal were peripheral to Ricardo's theoretical activities, the question of labor-intensive agriculture was a hot political topic at the time. Parliament was actively enforcing a controversial policy that was discouraging labor-intensive agriculture: namely, the infamous Corn Laws.

In the first half of the eighteenth century, Britain was the granary to a large part of Europe, exporting an amount sufficient to feed one-quarter of the British population (B. Thomas 1985, 140–41). With the combination of population growth coupled with the process of primitive accumulation, the British economy became increasingly dependent on imported grain. In this respect, Hussain Athar and Keith Tribe (1981, 28) observed: "One may note that it was in Britain—the country with no peasantry and a country with a developed capitalist economy—that the largest contraction in cultivated area as a result of international competition occurred."

At the time, most economists attributed this trend to comparative advantage—the idea that Britain could specialize in manufacturing, leaving food production to the periphery. However, more recent history has shown that industrialized nations can also be major food exporters. In this light, the weakening of the traditional system of food production (including the greater concentration on livestock), associated with the process of primitive accumulation, was probably the major cause of the contraction of British grain production.

According to the conventional wisdom, the Corn Laws should have increased the demand for agricultural labor. Boyd Hilton (1977, 120) even insists that the Corn Laws expanded the demand for labor in general. He reasons that even if higher bread prices had restricted the demand for industrial labor, prior to the 1820s, this diminution would have been more than offset by the greater amount of labor employed in agriculture.

Following this reasoning, the Corn Laws increased domestic agricultural production because they impeded access to imported produce. In addition, the labor demands per bushel of domestically produced grain were supposed to be high on marginal lands. In effect, Ricardo himself appealed to the higher labor costs on marginal soil in constructing his theory of comparative advantage, which he used to argue against the Corn Laws (Ricardo 1951–73, 1:chap. 7). Some defenders of the Corn Laws also pointed to the extra employment that import restrictions offered to justify their opposition to the repeal of the Corn Laws (B. Hilton 1977, 125). The *Northern Star* repeated this line as late as 1840 (see Hollis 1973, 280–81).

In truth, this argument is not necessarily valid. Judging from the experience of the United States, many agricultural economists have claimed that price supports can actually result in lower long-run prices. The initially attractive investment climate stimulates the long-term technical change that can eventually bring about substantial cost reductions for those with adequate access to capital (see Nelson and Cochrane 1976). Indeed, James Anderson and some of the supporters of the earlier Corn Laws had justified the legislation in similar terms (see Anderson 1777a; Hollander 1979, Appendix C), as did the British government in 1815 (B. Hilton 1977, 112).

We should also take account of the type of farmers who were attracted to the highly capital-intensive project of draining marshland for agricultural purposes. In the case of these improvements, Ricardo's interpretation of capital as permanently productive, which is generally inappropriate, might be partially justified. Once these investments were in place, much of the previously marginal land could remain highly productive. These operations would not necessarily use more labor than the typical, less-capitalized wheat farm. In fact, many of these farmers were in the forefront of agricultural improvement. The abolition of the Corn Laws might well reduce the domestic acreage used for grain, but many, if not most of these improved lands were likely to remain in production.

In terms of elementary economics, the sequence of introduction and repeal of the Corn Laws probably shifted the agriculture supply curve to the right. Consequently, these farms may have actually used less labor than the average wheat farm. Accordingly, the Corn Laws would not create as much employment as might be expected.

In fact, I suspect that the Corn Laws actually reduced the demand for agricultural labor because of their negative effect on labor-intensive farming. Of course, the demand for (agricultural) labor and the vigor of labor-intensive agriculture are not identical. I will argue that, by reducing the viability of small-scale farming, the Corn Laws increased the amount of labor working for wages while expanding the extent of unemployment.

The Corn Laws and Small Farmers

The Corn Laws had a negative effect on agricultural employment in one significant respect. Grain uses relatively little labor compared to most crops. In addition, grain farming requires much more seasonal labor than most small-scale farming does, especially since the typical small-scale farmer adopted a system that included several crops in order to spread labor over as long a period as possible. Although the Corn Laws may have increased employment in grain production, a complete measure of the impact of the Corn Laws must include the consequences for more labor-intensive crops as well as grain.

Labor-intensive agriculture was significant in the early days of classical political economy. Market gardening grew rapidly in the late sixteenth century (Thirsk 1967b, 196). By 1649, members of the London Gardeners Company employed 1,500 people and 400 apprentices, an average of 6 employees and 1 or 2 apprentices apiece (Thick 1985, 514). Wealthy people also had their own private gardens (ibid., 504). Gregory King estimated that the English ate more fruit and vegetables than the Dutch. Others thought that they also consumed more than the French (ibid., 508).

By the early eighteenth century, England had developed an advanced system of labor-intensive farming and gardening. English public houses served vegetables, such as broccoli, at a time when they were rare in France (George 1953, 80). Although France had a reputation as the leader in market gardening, England seems to have been ahead of France in such techniques as forcing cauliflower and asparagus under bell glasses.

During the early Corn Law debates, market gardening usually was a small-scale, but often successful enterprise. Most observers at the time understood that small-scale farmers had a competitive advantage in such vegetables and dairy products, whereas larger farmers tended to be more competitive in the production of grain (H. Levy 1966, 6–7).

For the most part, large farmers had no interest in producing specialty crops. As primitive accumulation accelerated, many small farmers disappeared. As a result, according to Nathaniel Kent: "Formerly they [the laborers] could buy milk, butter, and many other small articles in every parish, in whatever quantity they wanted. But since small farms have decreased in number, no such articles are to be had; for the great farmers have no idea of retailing such small commodities, and those who do retail them carry them to town" (1775, 238; see also 213–14). In addition, the imposition of duties made grain far more lucrative relative to fruits, vegetables, and livestock (Kautsky 1899, 149; Marshall 1920, 162; Senior 1928, 1:243). Consequently, the tariff on grain shifted production toward grain and away from meat, dairy products, fruits, and vegetables (Athar and Tribe 1981, 40).

The decline in the production of specialty crops occurred even though the English climate was particularly well suited to activities, such as dairy and vegetable production (see Senior 1928; 1:243). Conversely, with the later fall in grain prices after the abolition of the Corn Laws, England witnessed an acceleration in the rate at which resources were channeled into the market gardening industry (Bearington 1975, 39). However, this later English market gardening differed from the earlier variant. It tended to operate on a rather large scale. It also relied heavily on migrant labor (Bearington 1975; Samuel 1973).

The Corn Laws were doubly effective in turning the terms of trade against small-scale production. First, this legislation directly encouraged grain production, contributing to economies of scale in farming. Second, because the typical small-scale farmer had to purchase grain for personal consumption, the Corn Laws directly struck at the economy of small-scale agricultural production.

We can see this dependence of small-scale agriculture on cheap grain in France, where wine growers often rioted over the high price of grain (see Rude 1980, 64). Flanders offers an even more striking example. There, purchases of grain allowed farmers to devote a maximum of land and time to the higher-priced crops. B. H. Slicher van Bath (1960, 136–37) estimated that a nineteenth-century Flemish family could sustain itself with a mere one and a half acres of flax. The output of such a farm was not insignificant. Alexander Hamilton once observed that in a good year, one-half acre of flax land could supply the needs of the entire state of Connecticut at the time that the greatest quantity of flax was being used (Cole 1968; see also Tyron 1917, 207). Nonetheless, such enterprises still required cheap grain in order to make ends meet.

Consequently, the Corn Laws turned the terms of trade against the small-scale farmer, possibly encouraging, we might add infractions against the Game Laws. Moreover, by raising the cost of hiring labor during the harvest or planting season, the Corn Laws either reduced the profits of farmers or forced them to adopt labor-saving technologies.

Even with the Corn Laws, British agriculture did remain labor-intensive enough that many British farmers continued to use sickles instead of scythes, despite the fact that the sickle required much more labor (Collins 1969). Still, British agriculture was far less labor-intensive than that of the Low Lands of Europe.

Students of southern agriculture in the United States after the Civil War discovered a similar phenomenon. As the average size of farms began to shrink, small farmers had no choice but to grow cotton instead of corn. Although cotton production entailed much more risk, farmers could hope to survive only by adopting a strategy of buying corn in order to have more resources to devote to their cash crop (see Wright 1978, 169). Consequently, higher corn prices would tend to work to the disadvantage of those farms that were too small to market grain.

In conclusion, the higher grain prices worked against many parts of the English agricultural system. In this regard, Hussain Athar and Keith Tribe wrote: "That the benefits for grain duty were very unevenly distributed was widely recognized and not just by agronomists. For instance Count Hohenlohe stated in 1895 that holdings under 12 hectares (i.e. 87 per cent of holdings according to the 1895 agricultural census) had no corn to sell, and in a large number of cases they were even net buyers of corn" (Athar and Tribe 1981, 32; referring to Ashley 1920, 62). Except for a brief comment by Marx (1845, 289), in which he noted that the effect of the Corn Laws was "to convert the peasants into the very poorest proletarians through high rents and factory methods of exploiting landed property," economists seemed to be oblivious to the connection between the Corn Laws and the scale of farming. Instead, they treated agriculture as if it produced a homogeneous output of wheat. Similarly, they failed to recognize the different economies of large- and small-scale agriculture. Robert Torrens appears to have been the only classical political economist even to mention the importance of the terms of trade within agriculture. He remarked:

> The moors of Lancashire could not have originally have been made to grow corn, because the quantity of corn consumed by the labourers reclaiming and cultivating them, would have exceeded the quantity they were capable of producing. But cheap corn was brought from Ireland and other places; increasing wealth and population created an intense and extensive demand for these agricultural luxuries, which, not entering into the subsistence of farm labourers, are not expended in reproducing themselves; and the consequence has been that what was the barren moor, now bears crops of great value, and pays higher rents than the most fertile corn lands in England. (Torrens 1835, 279; cited in Robbins 1958, 47)

Torrens was evidently satisfied with himself in having made this theoretical advance beyond Ricardianism. He repeated it word for word in his *Three Letters to the Marquis of Chandos on the Effects of the Corn Law on the Budget* (1839) and in *The Budget* (1842) (see Robbins 1958, 47). A somewhat similar line of reasoning is found in a letter he wrote to the *Bolton Chronicle* (Torrens 1833, 33). However, neither Torrens nor any of his colleagues bothered to take it any further.

In conclusion, we could interpret the Corn Laws as a measure primarily designed to help the larger farmers who marketed the majority of their produce at the expense of small ones. As a result, the shift to grain production probably meant a fall in aggregate agricultural employment.

Someone familiar with the literature of classical political economy might be tempted to interject here, "Wait a minute! Didn't the classical political economists oppose the Corn Laws?" I would have to respond, "Not exactly."

Only after the Corn Laws had served their purpose in manipulating the domestic labor market, did the British economists abandon them in the name of freedom of the market. Two strategic concerns caused this shift. First, now that British manufacturing had taken hold, they thought that the acceptance of imported grain would help to convince other nations to accept British manufactured goods, creating a more favorable international social division of labor, as we saw in chapter 4. Second, they thought that manufacturing would benefit from cheap food. As we shall see in the case of David Ricardo, however, this interest in cheap food was conditional.

Luxury Crops for the Rich

Given the unfavorable economic conditions for small-scale agricultural production under the Corn Laws, many specialty crops appeared to be in short supply in Britain during the period of classical political economy. For example, some Scandinavians complained to the vacationing Malthus (1966, 106) of the scarcity of cream in England. Sismondi (1827, 195–97; see also Escher 1814, 31) reported that England had become dependent upon eggs from France; in addition, butter and vegetables were difficult for him to find when he visited Britain.

Ironically, many affluent Britons of the time still managed to consume fruits, since most of the upper class, perhaps even including some Ricardians, owned their own greenhouses (see Escher 1814, 50; Thick 1985, 504–5). Here is Adam Smith (1976, I.xi.b.25, 169) on the differing pursuit of small-scale farming by the rich and the poor:

> The crop too, at least in the hop and the fruit garden, is more precarious. Its price, therefore, besides compensating all occasional losses, must afford something like the profit of insurance. The circumstances of gardeners, generally mean, and always moderate, may satisfy us that their great ingenuity is not commonly over-compensated. Their delightful art is practiced by so many rich people for amusement, that little advantage is to be made by those that practice it for profit; because the persons who should normally be their best customers supply themselves with their most precious productions.

In other words, the wealthy joined the peasantry in the obstinate pursuit of uneconomical small-scale agriculture, the very same activity that political economy denounced so vehemently. Of course, the practice of small-scale agriculture by the elite was governed by the laws of aesthetics, not economics.

We already saw a similar phenomenon in our discussion of the deer parks in chapter 3. Hunting, which was deemed to be an improper activity for the poor, was a prestigious recreation for the wealthy. Certainly, Samuel Johnson was in a distinct minority of wealthy Englishmen in asserting that "the best garden . . . produced most roots and fruits, and that water was to be prized that contained most fish. . . . As if one could fill one's belly with hearing soft murmurs, or looking at rough cascades" (cited in Ketton-Cremer 1965, 71).

The Corn Laws and Labor Supply

The foregoing reveals that the overall effect of the Corn Laws on the supply of labor could have been substantial. The number of small farms fell. Their places were taken by still smaller operations that were used to supplement nonfarm wages in accordance with the classical theory of primitive accumulation (see Wordie 1974).

John Barton, whose study is sometimes credited with prompting Ricardo's changed stand on machinery, associated poverty with a falling price of corn, which he took to be an indication of a higher demand for agricultural labor. He deserves much credit for bringing some attention to the appalling poverty of agricultural labor during the early nineteenth century (Barton 1817 and 1833). However, his analysis is not consistent with the idea presented here.

Indeed, without the Corn Laws, the falling demand for some types of agricultural labor would be more than compensated for by other, less seasonal farm labor demands. The resulting glut of agricultural labor would spill over into industrial labor markets, providing an increased supply of unskilled labor without helping to meet the demands for particular skills that were in high demand. To the extent that real wages fell as a result of the Corn Laws, this legislation would also serve to help establish labor discipline.

Between 1799 and 1815, grain prices rose, although as noted earlier, the conditions for a future price decline might have been set in motion by the growing rewards of potential productivity increases. In contrast to Ricardo, who theorized that the Corn Laws should have led to a rise in the real cost of wages and a fall in profits, Malthus recognized that as conditions for labor grew more unfavorable, employers were able to lengthen the working day (Marx 1977, 665–66). Although nominal wages rose, real wages actually fell and surplus value increased (ibid.). No doubt the contribution of the Corn Laws to the process of primitive accumulation in Britain assisted employers in this respect.

To make matters worse, the shift from manufacturing to agriculture, which one should expect to occur as a result of the Corn Laws, might have tended to make capital more scarce in industry. Recall that Ricardo thought that agriculture was more, not less, capital-intensive than industry. Assuming that Ricardo were correct, the artificial stimulation of grain production might increase the ratio of profits to wages by intensifying both the demand for capital and the supply of labor. This result would hold, even if we disregard the undermining of small-scale, labor-intensive farming.

After a while, a good number of the small farmers had been converted into industrial workers, and many industrial workers had come to accept the norms of factory work. At that point, a lower cost of food would result in a higher rate of surplus value. Since the continued existence of the Corn Laws might no longer be beneficial to capital, they could conveniently be abolished.

Yes, we have previously suggested that the Corn Laws may have actually decreased the price of grain; however, this factor did not enter into the logic of the repeal of the Corn Laws since few classical political economists perceived this benefit. In addition, farmers may have already exhausted the most efficient techniques for increasing the productivity of the land.

My understanding of the Corn Laws parallels a related thesis proposed by Nenri Nallet and Claude Servolin (1978), who have interpreted the persistence of relatively small-scale agriculture as an essential feature of capitalist development. Although the farmer's Janus-like appearance— half-capitalist, half-worker—frequently is seen as inconsistent with capitalist development, in fact, this arrangement is quite efficient in providing cheap food and raw materials.

The government allows this system of petty producers to feel a constant level of stress to spur them on. At the same time, the government provides a certain degree of protection to this seemingly archaic system of production, knowing full well that agriculture organized on a more strictly capitalist basis could prove to be substantially more costly. Nallet and Servolin argue their case on the basis of the French experience, but my own research on the U.S. system seems to bear them out (Perelman 1985).

The majority of the political economists of that time generally presented themselves as firm opponents of the Corn Laws. Accordingly, they would seem to be blameless for the hardships created by these measures.

In reality, however, Ricardo was far less doctrinaire in this matter than he was in his opposition to Owen (see Hollander 1979, chap. 2). Rather than calling for their immediate abolition, he recommended that the Corn Laws be gradually eliminated over a decade (Ricardo 1951–73, 4:243–44, 263–64).

Ricardo was not unique in this respect. In fact, none of the major figures of classical political economy called for outright repeal (see Grampp 1960, chap. 2). Nonetheless, the eventual abolition of the Corn Laws would have been slight consolation for those small producers without the means to wait until the repeal made cheaper food available.

This analysis of the Corn Laws runs counter to the common discussion of this legislation, which generally depicts it in terms of a struggle between business and landed interests. Certainly, more was involved than a simple question of large- versus small-scale farming; nonetheless, we still need to address the relationship between Ricardo and the state of the largely self-sufficient household or petty commodity producer.

In this respect, Barry Gordon (1976, 231; see also Johnson 1909, 122–23) correctly observed that Ricardian political economy was a continuation of those policies that "favored those agriculturalists who had access to capital without the need to mortgage estates." Ricardo's alliance with this class of farmers went deeper than the Corn Laws. According to Gordon (ibid., 153), Ricardo's deflationist policies generally favored "the interest of the rentier . . . which included the wealthier land owning aristocrats but took little cognizance of the needs of the entrepreneur," and one should add, the small-scale farmer. Given his importance in framing the attitude of classical political economy toward agriculture, Ricardo should be counted among the foremost influences in the development of primitive accumulation at the time.

Ricardo's silence about the differential impact of the Corn Laws was far from unique. Classical political economists never discussed the Corn Laws in terms of their impact on the small farmer. Given the level of economic sophistication found in the better works of English political economy, we can only ascribe the almost universal absence of comment on this effect of the Corn Laws either to an insensitivity to the conditions of the small producer or to a practice of obscuring the nature of their mission.

Ricardo on Ireland

Ricardo made his hostility toward small-scale agriculture especially evident in his private correspondence, but this hostility was not universal. Although he recommended large farms and cheap food for England, he

advocated small farms and expensive food for Ireland. We can only resolve this apparent contradiction if we read Ricardo in terms of primitive
accumulation.

In response to the suggestion of his friend, Trower, that "no permanent
or substantial good [in Ireland] can be done until all small farms and small
tenancies are got rid of" (Ricardo 1951–73, 9:145), Ricardo agreed with
the ultimate goal of eliminating small-scale agriculture in Ireland (ibid.,
9:153); however, he believed small farms were an effect rather than a
cause of conditions in Ireland.

Ricardo added that he understood that small farms reduced the cost of
food in Ireland. In words almost indistinguishable from those of Malthus,
he wrote to Francis Place: "The evil of which the Irish ought to complain
is the small value of food of the people compared with the value of other
objects of their consumption, and the small desire they have of possessing
other objects. Cheap food is not an evil, but a good, *if it not be accompanied by an insensibility to the comforts and decencies of life*" (ibid.,
9:56; emphasis added). Ricardo's (ibid., 7:48) fear of cheap food in Ireland
was so great that he maintained: "The evil they (the Irish) experience
proceeds from the indolence and vice of the people, not from their inability to procure necessaries. By reducing their population, you reduce
food in perhaps a larger proportion, and rather aggravate rather than remove their misery."

In the first edition of his *Principles*, he repeated the idea that the population of Ireland might be insufficiently large to encourage people to work
enough: "The facility with which the wants of the Irish are supplied per-
mits that people to pass a greater part of their time in indolence; if the
population were diminished, this evil would increase, because wages
would rise, and therefore the labourer would be enabled in exchange for a
still less portion of his labour, to obtain all that his moderate wants require" (Ricardo 1951–73, 1:100; see also 7:334). This section is worth
examining in more detail. The relevant portion began:

> In those countries where there is abundance of fertile land, but where
> from ignorance, indolence, and barbarism of the inhabitants, they are
> exposed to all the evils of want and famine, and where it has been said
> that the population presses against the means of subsistence, a very
> different remedy should be applied from that which is necessary in
> long settled countries, where from the diminishing rate of the supply
> of raw produce, all the evils of a crowded population are experienced.
> (ibid., 1:99)

The first edition continued, "In the one case, misery proceeds from the inactivity of the people. To be made happier, they need only to be stimulated to exertion" (ibid.). This passage reads much like something from the mercantilist literature, or even Joseph Townsend. Ricardo (ibid., 100) continued:

> In some countries of Europe, and many of Asia, as well as in the islands in the South Seas, the people are miserable, either from a vicious government or from habits of indolence, which make them prefer present ease and inactivity, though without security against want. . . . By diminishing their population, no relief would be afforded, for productions would diminish in as great, or even in a greater proportion. The remedy for the evils under which Poland and Ireland suffer, which are similar to those experienced in the South Seas, is to stimulate exertion, to create new wants, and to implant new tastes. . . . The facility with which the wants of the Irish are supplied, permits that people to pass a great part of their time in idleness: if the population were diminished, this evil would increase, because wages would rise, and therefore the labourer would be enabled in exchange for a still less portion of his labour, to obtain all that his moderate wants require. Give to the Irish labourer a taste for the comforts and enjoyments which habit has made essential to the English labourer, and he would be content to devote a further portion of his time to industry, that he might be enabled to obtain them. Not only would all the food now produced be obtained, but a vast additional value in those other commodities, to the production of which the now unemployed labour of the country might be directed.

George Ensor roundly attacked Ricardo for these words. He pointed out that the English labourer "is no object of admiration." Then he asked: "How are these tastes to be excited in Irish labourers? Is it supposed that they are not like other human creatures? but that they make choice of privations?" (Ensor 1818, 106; cited in Ricardo 1951–73, 1:100n). After the section came under the critical scrutiny of Ensor, Ricardo changed its tone, but not its meaning. He wrote, "To be made happier, they require only to be better governed and instructed, as the augmentation of capital, beyond the augmentation of people would be the inevitable result" (Ricardo 1951–73, 1:100).

Although food was cheap in Ireland, so too was life. British observers commonly denounced the Irish for their laziness, noting at times their excessive number of holidays (Mokyr 1983, 218, 222). Yet, for all the talk of indolence, the people had to go to great lengths to survive. The Irish collected and dried seaweed for manure. Irish children had to search for horse droppings on the roads in an effort to coax a few more crops from the soil (McGregor 1992, 479).

Primitive Accumulation in the Irish Breadbasket

Under conditions such as Ricardo saw in Ireland, workers chose leisure rather than wage labor. They had no desire to exchange many hours of wage labor for a few hours' worth of consumer goods. Thus, measures to eliminate indolence directly were of the utmost necessity for capital. Nonetheless, Ricardo only specifically mentioned increasing a taste for luxury. If the workers could be harnessed to wage labor, "a vast additional value in . . . other commodities would be produced" (Ricardo 1951–73, 1:100). Presumably, only a portion of these would do to satisfy the new-found tastes of the Irish workers.

Ricardo understood who was to benefit from the more intensive work that he advocated. In a private letter to Malthus, he admitted that the workers might even be behaving perfectly rationally in preferring leisure to increased consumption: "Happiness is the object to be desired, and we cannot be quite sure that provided he is equally well fed, a man might not be happier in the enjoyment of the luxury of idleness, than in the enjoyment of a neat cottage, and good clothes. And after all we do not know if these would fall to his share. *His labour might only increase the enjoyments of his employer*" (Ricardo 1951–73, 7:184; emphasis added). We should also note that, in his unpublished *Notes on Malthus*, Ricardo (ibid., 2:334–35, 339–41, 286–87 nn. 223, 226, 237) repeatedly dismissed Malthus's concern about the ease with which food can be obtained; but there he made his case only on the formal grounds that the examples Malthus used were inapplicable to England, which had "a dense population, abounding in capital, skill, commerce, and manufacturing industry, and with tastes for every enjoyment that nature, art or science will procure" (ibid., 344). However, Malthus did not have England in mind, but Ireland.

Ricardo's first edition of his *Principles* contained all the essential elements of the classical theory of primitive accumulation. Although he altered the tone of his discussion of Ireland in later editions, the substance remained unchanged. He inserted his oft-cited idea: "The friends of humanity cannot but wish that in all countries the labouring classes should have a taste for comforts and enjoyments" (ibid., 1:100). This version, which is often used as evidence of Ricardo's humanitarianism, merely served to soften his insistence that the natural process is for wages to fall.

We might expect that Ricardo took an active interest in the conditions of the mass of Irish people. After all, Ricardo sat in Parliament as their representative, even though he had purchased his seat and did not once set foot in his constituency of Portlarington.

In exploring the Irish problem with its attendant poverty, Ricardo fell silent about the great wealth flowing from Ireland. Instead, like so many of his contemporaries, he viewed that troubled isle as England's "most formidable" agricultural rival (ibid., 8:369). Indeed, the Irish agricultural potential was seen as virtually unlimited at that time (B. Hilton 1977, 4, 11, 23, 278). In 1794–96, Ireland supplied 44 percent of Britain's imports of grain, meat, and butter. From 1800–1814, no less than 35 percent of all British imports of grain, meal, and flour came from Ireland. Ireland shipped more than 5.5 million quarters of oats and almost 1.5 quarters of wheat (B. Thomas 1985, 142–43; see also Pollard 1978).

The extraction of Irish foodstuffs as a counterbalance to the claims of Irish rent recipients was thought to be unconnected to Irish poverty. One Irish writer, John Mitchel (1847, iv; cited in Boylan and Foley 1992), observed: "English Professors of political economy have, by perverting and misapplying the principles of that science, endeavored to prove to us, that to part with our bread and our cattle is profitable 'commerce' and that intercourse with their country enriches us immensely whatever the ignorant and starving Irish nay say and feel to the contrary." Jonathan Swift (1723–24, 132), writing in *The Drapers Letters*, summed up the situation succinctly, "Poor Ireland maketh many rich."

The fault with the Irish economy, according to the classical political economists, fell at the feet of the wretched peasantry itself. In general, these economists expressed impatience with the Irish culture (Boylan and Foley 1992). They wrote off Irish civilization as barbaric, while they condoned the barbaric measures of the English in the name of civilization.

In Ireland, classical political economy confronted a people not yet subdued by capital. Recall Smith's concern about the want of order in Ireland. Rather than recognize this resistance to capital as a normal reaction to highly exploitative conditions, early economists were prone to attribute it to a racial defect. As Nassau Senior (1928: i, 233) told his students of 1847–48: "Races which like the Celts, have neither docility nor intelligence must be governed by fear." Consequently, simple market solutions were not sufficient to govern Ireland.

Although Ricardo was less extreme in his attitude toward Ireland than

Senior, his call for further population growth there shows how casually laissez-faire ideology was cast aside when it ran up against barriers. One type of market force could potentially integrate the Irish into the market without external coercion. Specifically, all classical political economists agreed that if the Irish people learned to desire more luxuries, to be purchased by means of the proceeds of wage labor, they might become more tame (see Black 1960).

Ricardo's performance as a theorist of primitive accumulation does not diminish his brilliance as an economic theorist. If anything, it highlights his work as a dazzling exhibition of sleight of hand. Here we have a phenomenal display of intellectual achievement in the form of his value theory. Alongside this masterpiece, we find a practical refutation of the relevance of this theory in the form of his cynical policy recommendations for Ireland. In theory, cheap food is good. In Ireland, it is bad.

Certainly, Ricardo the political economist clearly understood the nature of the substantial difference between the Irish economy and that of England. Ireland was distinguished by the vigor with which people resisted capital. By contrast, England appeared to have reached the point at which it could rely on "silent compulsion," which becomes effective only after the "advance of capitalist production develops a working class which by education, tradition and habit looks upon the requirements of that mode of production as self-evident natural laws" (Marx 1977, 899–900).

Ricardo's Victory

Histories of political economy have not done justice to Ricardo's politics. They portray his fight against the Corn Laws as a struggle against irrational regulation of market forces. Some remember his staunch battle against inflation. His doubts about the effect of machinery stand as proof of his lack of ideological animus toward the working class.

In truth, Ricardo's legacy was even more ideological than Smith's. Ricardo merely managed to sanitize political economy. More than any other individual, he transformed political economy into economics—an abstract, deductive sort of logic that supposedly stands above the narrow interests of any individual group.

John Maynard Keynes (1936, 32–33) perhaps summed up Ricardo's victory as well as was humanly possible, writing:

> The completeness of the Ricardian victory . . . must have been due
> to a complex of suitabilities in the doctrine to the environment in
> which it was projected. That it reached conclusions quite different

from what the ordinary uninstructed person would expect, added, I suppose, to its intellectual prestige. That its teaching, translated into practice, was austere and unpalatable, lent it virtue. That it was adapted to carry a vast and consistent logical superstructure, gave it beauty. That it could explain much social injustice and apparent cruelty as an inevitable incident in the scheme of progress, and the attempt to change such things as likely to do more harm than good, commended it to authority. That it offered a measure of justification to the free activities of the individual capitalist, attracted to it the support of the dominant social force behind authority.

McCulloch and Primitive Accumulation

John Ramsay McCulloch, one of Ricardo's two most important disciples, continued to espouse self-provisioning as the primary cause of Ireland's poverty. Like most classical political economists, McCulloch was certain that, to be successful, agriculture had to be organized as capitalist agriculture. He generalized, "wherever an improved plan of agriculture is practised, or where it is carried on by persons of considerable capital farming for a profit, skill and attention are alike indispensable" (McCulloch 1864, 446). He added: "An individual possessed of capital will not engage in farming unless he expects to realise, over and above a remuneration for his trouble in superintending the business, ordinary profits on his capital" (ibid., 446).

McCulloch had no difficulty justifying the absentee control of Irish agriculture, both on historical and commercial grounds. In terms of history, he speculated: "The English noblemen and gentlemen who acquired large masses of confiscated property in Ireland, found their estates in the possession of a crowd of poor, uncivilised, and disorderly occupiers, whom it was impossible to eject, and of whose customs and mode of occupancy they were wholly ignorant. Such persons had no recourse but to let their estates to adventurers, who were ready to meet such a state of things, and to make the most of it" (McCulloch 1853, 245). In terms of the economic impact of absentee agriculture, he calculated: "Were the absentees to return to Ireland, there would be an increased demand for commodities, or labour, or both, in the home market, to the extent of four, or four and a half, millions. But it is plain that this increase of demand in the home market, would be balanced by an equal diminution in the foreign market" (ibid., 225). McCulloch (1825, 833) even alleged that restrictions on subdividing agricultural land were beneficial to the working class: "It has been extremely advantageous to the labouring class. By preventing the splitting of farms once joined together, it has tended to occasion cultivation by means of large farms, and . . . so that there has not been that facility of obtaining slips of land and the means of support which there had been in Ireland."

The process of subdivision reached a peak in Ireland, where "large tracts were parceled out into patches of the size of potato-gardens, occupied by the merest beggars" (McCulloch 1864, 446). In this spirit, he informed a parliamentary committee on Ireland: "I consider the combination of manufacturing and agricultural pursuits to be a proof of the barbarism of every country in which it exists. . . . I consider that the more labour is subdivided, the greater will be the quantity of produce obtained by each individual labourer. When you combine in the same family, the trades of manufacture and farmer, neither the one nor the other can be well carried out" (McCulloch 1825, 812). According to McCulloch, as a result of such subdivision of the land, "the country is overspread with a redundant and wretched population; so to in the end, rents are not paid, and the whole produce of the land become barely sufficient for the support of its occupiers" (McCulloch 1864, 446).

A Parliamentary questioner pressed McCulloch on this point: "Do you think that the condition of the labouring class is better, in consequence of their not being able to obtain land?" McCulloch responded, "Certainly, that is my clear opinion (1825, 833).

For McCulloch, the separation of workers from the land was justified in the name of progress. He denounced the security associated with the ownership of small plots of land as being "uniformly associated with poverty, frequently degenerating into destitution; it gives use to the most revolting of all combinations, that of penury, pride, and laziness; and instead of expanding, contracts and benumbs every faculty. . . . The happiness of peasant proprietors seems very much akin to that of the oyster—they are ignorant and satisfied" (McCulloch 1848, 89–90; cited in Coats 1971, 159–60). McCulloch's shrill advocacy of primitive accumulation offers a stunning commentary on the classical contribution to the analysis of satisficing!

Malthus on Economic Policy

Compared to Malthus, Ricardo appeared to be sympathetic to the poor. How else could we explain Malthus' bizarre assertion:

> To act consistently, therefore, we should facilitate . . . the operations
> of nature in producing this mortality. . . . Instead of recommending

cleanliness to the poor, we should encourage contrary habits. In our towns we should make the streets narrower, crowd more people into the houses, and court the return of the plague. In the country, we should build our villages near stagnant pools, and particularly encourage settlements in all marshy and unwholesome situations. But above all we should reprobate specific remedies for ravaging diseases; and those benevolent, but much mistaken men, who have thought they were doing a service to mankind by projecting schemes for the total extirpation of particular disorders. . . . The necessary mortality must come, in some form or other, and the extirpation of one disease will only be the signal for the birth of another perhaps more fatal. We cannot lower the waters of misery by passing them down in different places, which must necessarily make them rise somewhere else; the only way in which we can hope to effect our purpose is by drawing them off. (Malthus 1803, 236)

Once a parliamentary committee asked Malthus: "Do you not admit, that with mere reference to the wealth of the country that the demise of those [unemployable] labourers would not be attended with any loss?" Malthus responded: "Rather a gain certainly" (cited in Grampp 1974, 283).

According to Malthus (1820, 381–82), to allow people the means to produce for their own needs would generate a widespread pattern of indolence among the masses. Where food could be produced with little effort, he observed:

We ought always to find a small portion of the population engaged in agriculture, and a large proportion administering to the other wants of society. . . . But in examining the state of unimproved countries what do we really see?—almost invariably, a much larger portion of the whole people employed on the land than in those countries where the increase of population has occasioned the necessity of resorting to poor soils; and less time instead of more devoted to the production of conveniences and luxuries. (ibid., 334, 380)

Malthus did prefer a smaller scale of agriculture, reasoning that, with small-scale agriculture, more people would be elevated to the status of property owners (see, for example, Malthus 1976, 115; see also 1820, 385–89). He recognized that property owners would be likely to serve as a conservative political force. Thus, Malthus appreciated the modest prosperity of the Scandinavian smallholders (Malthus 1966, 145), but he opposed holdings as small as were found in France (Malthus 1836, 378). Reflecting the classical theory of primitive accumulation, he insisted that "all the great results in political economy, respecting wealth, depend upon proportions" (ibid., 376).

Not surprisingly, Malthus was skeptical of Owen's plan that envisioned masses of people engaging in self-provisioning rather than participating in labor markets. In a letter of 21 November 1819 to Arthur Young, he asked:

> Pray can you tell me in what small work I can obtain the best information respecting spade husbandry which has been lately talked of? I should also like to know what you think of it, and whether you are not of the opinion, that independently of the object of employing Parish Poor, our wastes are not likely to be cultivated by saving labour on the land, rather than increasing it. The great obstacle to the cultivation of Wastes is surely that the produce does not pay the expense of procuring it; and that this difficulty it appears to me is only to be overcome by skill and prices—not mere labour. (cited in P. James 1979, 325)

In fact, Malthus proved himself to be an irreconcilable foe of all sorts of measures that might improve the ability of the poor to maintain themselves, including even the very means that could help them follow Malthus's own advice—birth control. He warned, "Prudential habits among the labouring classes of a country mainly depending upon manufactures and commerce might ruin it," "although the greatest resource of the labouring classes for their own happiness must be in those prudential habits" (Malthus 1820, 221, 291; Malthus 1836, 261).

Only the purist, Jean-Baptiste Say (1821, 30), seemed to notice the anomaly between this position and the famous principle of population. In his opposition to Malthus, Say was not particularly interested in people's welfare. Instead, he appealed to the logic of the classical model of primitive accumulation. According to Say, since a celibate worker needs less to maintain a household, wages would be certain to fall (Say 1880, 333).

In addition, Malthus was a stout advocate of the Corn Laws. Over and above his support for these measures, he opposed providing families with plots of land for cows or gardens; he even favored the tearing down of rural cottages (Cowherd 1977, 7, 32, 50, 162).

Malthus generally went much further than Ricardo on the subject of self-provisioning because of one major difference between their respective interpretations of English society. Each took a different mode of production for his frame of reference. Malthus was not convinced that enough British workers had accepted wage labor.

In contrast, Ricardo felt that England had already reached the point where household economy was no longer a serious problem for capital. For him, the time had almost arrived to increase the relative surplus value through the importation of inexpensive grain. For Malthus, British capital needed a still stronger dose of primitive accumulation.

Malthus on Ireland

We might think of Ireland as the litmus test for an interest in primitive accumulation. In Ireland, the question of the household economy was not merely ideological or theoretical. It had quite practical implications. In Ireland, self-provisioning was still an extremely potent force and capitalism proper still had to be fostered. Consequently, Ricardo stood alongside Malthus when the discussion turned to Ireland.

Malthus (1836, 348) complained that in a country such as Ireland, "where the necessary food is obtained with so little labour, it is perhaps impossible that the time not devoted to the production of food should create a proportionate quantity of wealth, without a decided taste for conveniences and wealth among the lower classes of society." Malthus chided the Irish for having too few wants. Like Ricardo, he wished that the Irish would somehow develop a greater preference for commodities such as "ribands, lace and velvets" relative to leisure (ibid., 314; see also Berkeley 1740, 423; Hume 1752d; for earlier variants on this theme, see Appleby 1976, 505 ff.), but this recommendation rang hollow. As Sismondi (1827, 106; see also 127; Edmonds 1833, chap. 7) emphasized, luxuries become attractive only when they are bought with the labor of others.

Perhaps the Reverend Malthus should have adopted the practice later followed in the colonies. There, missionaries assisted capital by instructing people in a proper devotion to commodities as well as to God (see Magubane 1979, 60). More recently, the responsibility to inculcate a deeper respect for commodities has fallen on the shoulders of development advisers who labor to instill a taste for luxuries among the natives (Moser 1966, 34).

Besides having failed to develop a sufficient taste for luxuries, Malthus (1836, 349) charged that the Irish were also guilty of the further offense of "supplying [their wants] principally at home." In a 17 August 1817 letter to Ricardo he even went so far as to claim, echoing Steuart, that the basic problem in Ireland was production "with a view to support rather than sale" (reprinted in Ricardo 1951–73, 7:175). Malthus offered further insight into his attitude toward the Irish smallholders during a parliamentary examination by a member of the 1826–27 Committee on Emigration, who asked him if it were not true that "if a thousand [Irish] labourers . . . were to die, the wealth of the country would not be diminished by their decrease?" Malthus answered affirmatively (cited in Inglis 1971, 233).

We might dismiss as downright ridiculous Malthus's suggestion that the Irish workers should concern themselves with luxuries, although they were lacking the basic necessities. In fact, we should take his words seriously in the sense that the British used such sentiments to justify harsh measures against the Irish people.

Indeed, since the working class seemed disinclined to exchange an excessive amount of labor time in return for commodities of relatively little value, Malthus was willing to allow for extraeconomic pressures on the poor. Although he did not elaborate on how he wished to accomplish his objective, he opposed the use of the potato in Ireland on the grounds that it allowed the poor to survive with less effort (Malthus 1820, 344–45).

In all seriousness, Malthus saw water as an even greater threat to workers' discipline than the potato. In particular, he expressed serious misgivings about the work of Count Rumford, whose soups were said to be capable of feeding the poor for slightly more than one-quarter penny per day (Rumford 1795, 187). Rumford, whose scientific stature was considerably more solid than his political reputation, alleged that water was the major source of nutrients in his famous soups (ibid., 172). Although Malthus (1803, 298) admitted that Rumford's soups might be "excellent inventions for the public institution," he hoped that they "should not be adopted as the general food of the common people."

Malthus's ostensible concern was that cheap food resulted in low wages, but it did not take him more than a page to get from Rumford's soups to the dreaded indolence that threatened to plague capital.

Malthus's Evolution

In later years, Malthus anticipated the sort of underconsumption problems the Atlantic economies faced during the 1930s. His position won him the endearment of Keynes.

The evolution of Malthus's attitude smacked of opportunism. For most of his life, he expressed a growing confidence in the market, as primitive accumulation brought more and more workers under control. The earliest edition of his *Essay on the Principle of Population* was meant to forestall any plans to ameliorate workers' standard of living. Their lot, he believed, was hopeless in the long run. In 1798, when he wrote it, he explicitly stated that "The consumable commodities of silk, laces, trinkets are . . . the revenue only of the rich, and not of society in general" (Malthus 1976, 112).

The workers' only hope was a temporary increase in their consumption of necessities. This improvement could not be permanent because an increase in the consumption of food would necessarily result in population growth, which would eventually undermine the improved standard of living.

Malthus continued to revise the *Essay* to address other problems. He ceased arguing for the futility of charity for the victims of primitive accumulation; instead, he was developing the position that the poor could share in the prosperity of capitalism, provided that they worked hard. In the third edition of the *Essay*, he was arguing, "The condition of the labouring poor . . . cannot be essentially improved but by giving them a greater command over the means of subsistence" (cited in Gilbert 1980, 92). By the fifth edition, he suggested that "the comforts of the lower classes do not depend solely upon food, nor even upon strict necessaries" (ibid.).

Toward the end of his life, Malthus observed that untrammeled growth by itself need not necessarily worsen the lot of the poor (see Gilbert 1980). Rather, his concern turned to imbalances between sectors. The depression following the demobilization of the British economy subsequent to the Napoleonic Wars focused his attention on the consequences of imbalances.

In light of this depression, Malthus recognized that supply and demand were inadequate guides for economic action. Underlying his concern was the realization that, should the economic situation deteriorate too much, workers would be likely to raise a political challenge to the system—a challenge that even the promise of a future of ribbons, lace, and trinkets would be inadequate to prevent workers from raising a political challenge. Consequently, the government had the responsibility to ensure a proper balance of agriculture and industry lest high levels of unemployment threaten political stability.

Robert Torrens

Because Robert Torrens was Irish, Irish poverty was a preoccupation with him (Robbins 1958, 145). In addition, he was an officer in the marines, promoted to the rank of colonel as a reward for his gallantry in the defense of Anholt, an island in the Kattegat (ibid., 3). This background colored his economics.

Torrens wrote a strong article in which he denounced Owen's project as a particularly serious menace to capitalist society. William Thweatt (1974) argues that McCulloch had a hand in the article; however, O'Brien and Darnell (1978) have made a powerful case for dismissing that contention and attributing the work to Torrens. Instead of giving the unemployed access to land, Torrens felt that society should manage unemployment through emigration.

In the article, Torrens (1817; cited in Robbins 1958, 149) denounced Owen's plan as "nothing more than a Spencian project in disguise." This heresy had to be eliminated root and branch. Torrens complained, "Inasmuch as his plans extend to make villages consume within themselves whatever they produce, the division of labor, whether territorial or mechanical, will be superseded" (1817, 453–77). If Owen's scheme were put into effect, Torrens (ibid., 515–16) predicted that "the whole net revenue would be required to supply the merely animal wants of the people: that art, literature, and science, would be abandoned; a more than Gothic ignorance prevailed." Although Ricardo was a personal friend of Owen (1857), he expressed approval of Torrens's position (Ricardo 1951–73, 8:159).

Although the market could be counted upon to take care of certain matters, Torrens called on the government to play an activist role in some crucial respects. Just as Steuart wanted farmers to rid the land of "superfluous mouths," Torrens wanted the nation to deposit its excess labor in the colonies. Alongside his proposed efforts to export unemployment, Torrens favored restrictions on the export of machinery. Torrens thought that imperialism offered a positive solution to the problems that Owen tried to solve through spade husbandry. In fact, Torrens was the most realistic theorist of imperialism among those who are usually recognized as major classical political economists.

In his first work, *The Economists Refuted,* Torrens (1808, 14–15; cited in Robbins 1958, 20) wrote of the territorial division of labor. He emphasized that England's proper role was to trade finished products for the raw materials of the less developed countries. Torrens (1833, 56) informed his constituents: "It is not to France—it is the countries comprising the Russian empire, to the two continents of America, to our colonial possessions, to India, and to China, that we must look for new and extending markets. The measure which should be adopted, in order to open these vast regions to our commerce, must, however, be the subjects of future communications." Torrens warned that colonies would most likely suffer from their relationship with imperial England, at least in the short run. He wrote, "unless timely and energetic measures of precaution be adopted, Ireland, in advancing towards wealth and prosperity, must necessarily pass through a period of the most aggravated and intolerable distress" (Torrens 1828, 39–42; cited in Robbins 1958, 151).

We do not often find such realism in the annals of classical political economy. William Petty, knowing only an early sort of imperialism, never rose beyond the rank of cabin boy in the ship of state, whereas Torrens spoke like a true colonel in the Royal Marines.

Nassau Senior and Primitive Accumulation in Ireland

The 1840s brought ample confirmation of Torrens's previously cited prediction of "aggravated and intolerable distress" in Ireland. George Poulett Scrope and John Stuart Mill both called for land reform as a means of invigorating the devastated Irish economy, but they were in a distinct minority. For most, the catastrophe of the Irish potato famine was further evidence of the need for a stronger dose of primitive accumulation. The consensus was that only fully developed capitalism could save the Irish.

No one addressed this thesis more eloquently than Nassau William Senior, although he vehemently denied that the Irish were as poor as had been claimed. He deduced that since the population had been growing, he had solid grounds to doubt "that the great majority of the inhabitants of Ireland are in the state of destitution which is popularly ascribed to them" (Senior 1832, 6).

In his *Journals, Conversations, and Essays Relating to Ireland,* Senior collected information, just as if he were organizing one of the many government reports he had prepared. Most informants were given the opportunity to read over Senior's transcriptions of their conversations. Just enough personal detail was left to give an appearance of spontaneity to his carefully crafted work.

We have already met with Senior's opinion of the Irish people. He knew that "ribands, lace and velvets" could do little to change their ways. An unnamed Englishman told him: "They are less industrious than the English, less cleanly, less decent, and less comfortable, but they do not feel the want of comfort, or decency, or cleanliness" (cited in Senior 1868, 1:163).

Senior placed great hope in education. In his opinion, "the political economy of the poor" appeals to the uneducated because "though it is in the power of human institutions to make everyone poor, they cannot make everybody rich; . . . they can diffuse misery, but not happiness" (Senior 1871, 1:150).

In this same spirit, Senior longed to convince the Irish to abandon their antagonism toward market relations. He visited schools, observed the classes, and even questioned the children about their knowledge of political economy:

318

> I repeated the question which I have proposed in other schools [see ibid., 2:125]—"What would be the consequence of every man's being able to do four times as much as he can now?"
>
> "To make all the working people," they said, "poor for there would be no demand for their work."
>
> "Would not," I said, "the things which they consumed be much more abundant?"
>
> "Perhaps so," they said, "But they would have no money to buy them."
>
> "Why so?"
>
> "Because only rich people have enough now, and would employ one-fourth of them."
>
> This must be the obvious opinion, for I have always met with it. The poor seem to be unaware of the indefinite variety and extent of men's wants. (ibid., 2:137)

Senior hoped that the Irish would reject their political economy of class conflict, once Irish society as a whole changed. As proof, he noted that the Irish became excellent workers once they reached the United States (Senior 1928, 2:348).

Senior and his friends were acutely aware of the dimensions of their project of remaking Irish society. Although the poor people in the countryside did not actually own the land that they worked, the reorganization of Ireland amounted to something akin to primitive accumulation. A revealing conversation between Senior and a Dr. G. is worth citing in detail in this respect. Dr. G. began by explaining the beneficial impact of the recent famine:

> Before the famine, the tenant had no creditor except his landlord. He sold only to pay his rent, and he bought nothing; he depended on his potatoes, his pig, and (when he was prosperous) his cow. . . .
>
> Though he had an abundance of leisure, he seldom sought to work for wages. Indeed, he worked little even for himself, as the state of his fences and his copious crops of weeks showed. . . . He no longer depends for everything on his land; he feels—what he never knew before—that a man may starve with his land, and may live without it. (Senior 1868, 2:274)

Then Dr. G. offered Senior a wonderfully concise description of the program of the classical theory of primitive accumulation:

> "I believe," continued Dr. G., "that the struggle now going on in Ireland between cottiers and farmers, between agriculture on a large

scale, takes place in almost every country that has been feudal, and is therefore in the hands of large proprietors—at a certain stage of its improvement. When there is little capital, and therefore few manufactures, the bulk of the population are tillers of the ground. There are few cattle or sheep. Meat is little used. The best soils only are cultivated, and, by profuse labour, a large gross produce, though a small surplus produce, of grain is produced. "Much food," says Solomon, "is in the tillage of the poor: but there is that which is destroyed by want of judgement." As wealth increases, and with it the demand for cattle and sheep, landlords find it profitable to substitute pasture for arable, and large farms for small ones. There is more surplus produce, more rent, and less trouble.

The first result of every such change is, at the same time, to turn the small farmer and cottier into an agricultural labourer, and also much to diminish the demand for labour. The existing occupants of the land suffer in every way. They lose the freedom and the apparent security of their former state. They must obey a master, keep his hours, give up the frequent holiday of the wake and the fair, and work for wages which a sudden supply of labourers must render low. . . .

No friend to Ireland can wish the war to be prolonged—still less, that it should end by the victory of the tenants; for that would replunge Ireland into barbarism, worse than that of the last century. The sooner it is over—the sooner Ireland becomes a grazing country, with the comparatively thin population which a grazing country requires—the better for all classes. (ibid., 2:264–66)

In 1832, before the famine, Senior had addressed the question of Irish agriculture. He recognized that the Irish worker produced a surplus—"for every bushel that the Irish labourer consumes, he enables more than a bushel to be gathered" (Senior 1832, 48)—yet this inveterate advocate of the market saw greater profits resulting from a shift to wage labor. He recommended the "extension of farm, and the consequent conversion of cottiers into hired labourers . . . which may be assisted by Government, if money is advanced . . . to facilitate by emigration the consolidation of farms" (ibid., 20). This call for public funds to be spent to encourage larger farms is found in a work largely intended to warn the government of the dangers created by expending money to provide work for the impoverished Irish.

Senior's response to Dr. G. was more circumspect. He restricted himself to restating the doctor's case in positive terms consistent both with the tenets of classical political economy as well as the words of his informant:

> "The suffering of England," I said, "gradually and slowly wore away, as the surplus agricultural population was absorbed by the spread of manufactures, and the increase of towns. The absorption of the surplus population of the Highlands of Scotland . . . was assisted by a large emigration, and in the case of Sutherlandshire—one of the largest and *most beneficient* clearings on record. . . .
>
> "But in Ireland, there are scarcely any manufactures, except at Belfast. The trades-unions have destroyed them, or prevented their existence everywhere." (ibid., 266; emphasis added)

Senior's prescription for the ills of Ireland was fairly simple. He called for legislation to "enable the establishment of manufactures, by freeing the manufacturing population from the tyranny of the trades-unions" (ibid., 266). With these words, the enormities of English policy took on the mantle of liberty: Crush unions in the name of freedom. Political economy, even in Ireland, maintained the posture of laissez-faire no matter how brutal its policies actually were.

Senior was far more sympathetic to Irish small producers when he was speaking in his own voice. In his *Edinburgh Review* article of 1844, republished in his *Journals*, he wrote:

> The Material evils are the want of Capital, and the want of small Proprietors. A people, indeed, ill-provided with capital cannot enjoy much division of labour. Its labour, therefore, cannot be productive, its manufactures must be few and rude; the bulk of its members must be agricultural. . . . A middle class is the creature of capital. But though without a middle class, and without the diffusion of moral and intellectual cultivation which a middle class produces, such a population, if it consists of proprietors, may be happy. . . .
>
> On the other hand, in a country possessing abundant capital, the absence of small proprietors of land, though attended by considerable political inconvenience and danger—inconvenience and danger, perhaps, outweighing its economical advantages—is not inconsistent with general comfort and prosperity; and perhaps is a condition necessary to the greatest productiveness of labour, and to the greatest accumulation of wealth. (ibid., 2:22 ff.)

In conclusion, a study of Senior not only shows how classical political economists analyzed primitive accumulation, it also clearly demonstrates the manner in which they attempted to avoid responsibility for what they wrote.

The discovery of America . . . by opening a new and inexhaustible market to all the commodities of Europe . . . gave occasion to new divisions of labour and improvements of art, which, in the narrow circle of the ancient commerce, could never have taken place for want of a market to take off the greater part of their produce. The productive powers of labour were improved, and its produce increased in all the different countries of Europe, and together with it the real revenue and wealth of the inhabitants. The commodities of Europe were almost all new to America, and many of those of America were new to Europe. A new set of exchanges, therefore, began to take place which had never been thought of before, and which should naturally have proved as advantageous to the new, as it certainly did to the old continent. The savage injustice of the Europeans rendered an event, which ought to have been beneficial to all, ruinous and destructive to several of those unfortunate countries.—Adam Smith, *An Inquiry into the Nature and Causes of the Wealth of Nations*

Robert Gourlay

Robert Gourlay was not a political economist. He does not even seem to have read much political economy. Still, he managed to have provoked others to read Smith in a new light, perhaps because of his experience in agriculture. He recalled:

> When a young man, having time and money at command, I travelled over England for fifteen months together as an agriculturist, and during that time became acquainted with the late secretary to the Board of Agriculture [Arthur Young]. One day, in conversation with him, we hit upon a subject to which each of us had devoted peculiar attention. My father, and indeed my grandfather, had been in the habit of letting out small portions of land on a kind of perpetual lease, called in Scotland a feu, to labouring people, whereon each man might build a dwelling house, and enjoy the convenience of a garden. I had marked the wonderful influence which the possession of such a little property had upon the characters of the people . . . I had noticed with what

serene delight a labourer, especially of the sedentary class, would occupy himself in his garden at hours not devoted to his trade, and I had calculated what an addition, as well to individual as to national wealth and happiness, such economical arrangements, generally adopted, might produce. (Gourlay 1822, 83–84)

Arthur Young wanted to amend the general enclosure law so that "a portion of land sufficient to keep a cow should be secured to each man in lieu of his ancient right of pasturage." Young asked Gourlay to go to the "counties of Rutland and Lincoln, where the practice prevailed of letting the poor have land and cows" (ibid., 84).

During his travels Gourlay discovered the powerful impact of primitive accumulation on rural society. He recalled: "Year after year, at this place and that, the poor, seeing themselves unjustly deprived of advantages which they had inherited from time immemorial, grumbled, rioted, and were put down. The process of stealing gradually on, the strength of the mass was subdued piecemeal; and, finally, a change was effected, in the condition of English labourers, through a variety and succession of causes, but little reflected on or noticed by political economists" (ibid., 86). Gourlay was far from radical in his vision. Expressing "an absolute abhorrence of the spade husbandry, as proposed by the benevolent Mr. Owen," he wanted the distribution of land to be tied to the interests of employers (ibid., 156). Recall the long citation in chapter 5, where Gourlay (1822, 145–46), noted: "It is not the intention to make labourers professional gardeners or farmers! It is intended to confine them to bare convenience."

As Gourlay "despaired of seeing anything effectual accomplished by the Board of Agriculture, he insisted that "impressions as to the necessity of changing somehow the system of the poor laws became more and more riveted in my mind" (ibid., 86). The Poor Laws, he charged were "the greatest evil which overshadows the fate of England" (ibid., 83). How did he come upon this revelation? Gourlay (ibid., 87) reported that he was struck by the marked difference between the conditions of agricultural laborers in England and Scotland: "In the one [Scotland], labourers were independent and improving their condition, even in the face of growing taxation: in the other they were verging to extreme poverty and degradation, while all was flourishing around them. In Scotland it was more generally the custom to accommodate farm labourers with cows than in England, but this was far from constituting the difference." Although Gourlay was certain that the poor laws lay at the root of Britain's troubles, he did not join in the familiar lamentation about the excessive burden of the poor rates. Instead, he pointed out that the poor laws were meant to serve the interest of farmers: "Farmers had chiefly in view to hold down . . . wages of single men. . . . Thus, while the statute laws have been framed to prevent manufacturing labourers from combining to raise their pay, a most powerful combination . . . was at work to keep down husbandry labour below its proper level; and thus it was that I could hire an English ploughman for 12 pounds per annum, while I could not hire a Scotch ploughman of the same appearance at less than 18 pounds" (ibid., 109). By the time Gourlay was ready to publish his work, Scottish wages had fallen from twelve to nine pounds per year, while English plowmen continued to earn the same wage as before (ibid., 104). The superior wages earned in England were not a cause for rejoicing. In such times, we should at least hope that the fall in wages would be moderated so that both worker and employer would share in the losses that hard times bring.

Gourlay had a plan to rid England of its Poor Laws. It should unburden itself of its poor by having them emigrate to Canada. Thus taxes in Britain could be lower. Only one difficulty stood in the way of the Canadian economy being able to enjoy the benefit of this new supply of labor. Canada was cursed with an excess of cheap land. Gourlay (ibid., 414, 385) insisted:

> It should never be forgotten that wild land is the chief bane of this country, and no fair means should be left unemployed to lessen it. . . . Land in America is the very lubber-fiend which checks its own improvement. Could nine-tenths of it be sunk into the sea, and afterwards emerge by tenths, gradually, as it became absolutely necessary for the wants of mankind, there would be infinite gain in every way. The people of the States are wasting their strength by spreading too rapidly over their wide domain.

He complained that the average Ontario farmer owned 237 acres, of which only 38 were cultivated (ibid., 415). Land should not be granted freely; nor should it be held tax free.

I confess that I have made Gourlay's argument considerably more coherent than he did. It is full of bile and incentive, with matters pertaining to his economic program randomly scattered about. In the middle of the book Gourlay burst out, "I have exhibited my case . . . : produced documents: stated what course I was pursuing, and was about to pursue for redress" (ibid., 317).

His writing style was no more bizarre than his personal life, which had brought him into disrepute. In fact, Gourlay's economics and his personal behavior were intimately connected. Like many other early economists, including Petty, Steuart, and the subject to whom we will next turn, Edward Gibbon Wakefield, Gourlay attempted to write about the econ-

324

omy to restore his tattered reputation, which had suffered from his repeated lack of self-restraint. For example, when Henry Brougham neglected to respond to one of his letters, Gourlay horsewhipped him (Mills
1915, 136). Gourlay's willingness to antagonize powerful people led to
frequent incarcerations.

Although Gourlay's economic reasoning may seem rather commonplace, its influence turned out to be profound as it worked its way through
the world of political economy.

Edward Gibbon Wakefield

One of the handful of people who paid some tribute to Gourlay was Edward Wakefield Sr. Wakefield was land agent to David Ricardo and brother
of Daniel, the first author whom I know to have credited Steuart with
superiority over Smith. Regarding an early work of Gourlay's, Wakefield
Sr. wrote: "From my personal knowledge of that gentleman, I am inclined
to pay very great attention to his opinion, for few have seen so much of
England in a practical way as this intelligent North Briton" (Wakefield
1812; cited in Gourlay 1822, 89).

Some years later, Wakefield's son, Edward Gibbon Wakefield, seems to
have drawn some inspiration from Gourlay, although the younger Wakefield never gave much public acknowledgment to what Mills (1915, 139)
had called his "obvious debt to Gourlay." In fact, his endorsement of
Gourlay's book was lukewarm. In an article for the *Spectator*, Wakefield
wrote: "The author . . . has mixed up with much valuable statistical information an account of his own pre-eminent misfortunes and a picture of
his own mental sufferings, so distressing, or so annoying, to the reader,
that it becomes difficult to extract from his book those parts which are
merely useful" (Wakefield, 1831a; cited in Mills 1915, 136). Aside from
citing Gourlay in his pamphlet, "A Statement of the Principles and Objects of a Proposed National Society for the Cure and Prevention of Pau-
perism," which he published in 1830 (see Mills 1915, 136), and printing a
few extracts from Gourlay in the appendix to his *England and America*
(Wakefield 1834, 351–56), Wakefield generally refrained from mentioning
Gourlay. According to Gourlay—not necessarily a particularly reliable
source—Wakefield readily acknowledged his debt in private when they
met in Canada in 1838. Gourlay claimed:

> He introduced himself—Mr. Wakefield (the same who had been an-
> nounced in the newspapers as accompanying Lord Durham, to in-
> struct as to the settling of the wild lands of Canada). He told me that

he was the writer of letters which appeared in the *London Spectator*, ["Letters from P."], some seven years ago, regarding me. I called to mind the letters: they were highly complimentary, and intended to draw towards me the notice of the Grey Ministry. Never before having known to whom I was thus obliged I thanked Mr. Wakefield. . . . He then went on to say that he was also the author of a pamphlet on Colonization ["A Statement . . ." cited above], which was sent to me, soon after, under the frank of Lord Howick. . . . Mr. Wakefield said he had taken his ideas on colonization from my book. I replied that it gave a very imperfect view of my projects: . . . Mr. Wakefield added, "Nevertheless, Government has established a colony on your principles in Australia." (cited in Mills, 1915, 139)

Although Gourlay never made much of a stir, the importance of Wakefield's work cannot be overestimated. As Lionel Robbins (1958, 154) has written, "The arrival [of Wakefield] on the scene may be compared to the descent of some gorgeous tropical bird among the sober denizens of a respectable farmyard." To translate this metaphor into more understandable terms, the challenge of Edward Gibbon Wakefield ended the triumph of Smithian ideology in England—at least in terms of policy considerations.

Wakefield was a most unlikely person to have effected such a revolution in economic thought. Certainly, his early years were none too promising. His mother had long despaired of him ever putting his bright mind to good use. Later, the state confined Wakefield in Newgate prison for the abduction of a wealthy schoolgirl. While in prison, Wakefield came into contact with many candidates for transportation to Australia.

As might be expected, travel books were quite popular in Newgate (see Tobias 1967, 66). Wakefield wrote, "Whilst in Newgate, I had occasion to read with care every book concerning New South Wales and Van Dieman's Land, as well as a long series of newspapers published in these colonies" (Wakefield 1831a, 266). On the basis of such books, newspapers, and probably information gleaned from other prisoners, Wakefield wrote a book that purported to be the product of an English colonist in Australia.

Wakefield's Colonies

Surprisingly, from his jail cell, Wakefield (1829) succeeded in reconstructing the social relations of labor and capital in a very realistic fashion. He scoffed at the notion that the social division of labor was the product of voluntary consent. Its creation required authority, hierarchy, and, generally, slavery (Wakefield 1835, 1:46–47).

Wakefield was not as hesitant to embrace slavery as was Steuart. In his words, "Slavery appears to have been the step by which nations have emerged from poverty and moved toward wealth and civilization" (Wakefield 1841, 4:333; cited in Robbins 1958, 160; see also Engels 1894, 217).

In his pretended letter from Australia, after bemoaning the scarcity of labor, Wakefield (1829, 112) cried out:

> How often, in my presumption, had I cursed the memory of Las Casas, for bribing the first planters of Hispaniola to spare the inhabitants of that island, by suggesting that they might obtain slaves from Africa! How scornfully, in my ignorance of cause and effect, had I abused the Democrats of North America for cherishing the horrors of slavery! In moments of weakness, how I had sighed, and even shed tears of compassion and anger, at the damnable cruelties which I saw inflicted upon Blacks at the Cape of Good Hope! And yet, in spite of my reason and every better feeling of my nature, I brought myself to find excuses for the Spaniards, Americans, and Dutch; aye, even to think that a few thousand Negroes would be a great acquisition to New South Wales! So they would; and they would conduce to the wealth, and—deny it who will—even to the civilization of these colonial landowners.

Wakefield insisted that the importance of slavery had not disappeared, even in his day. He predicted that if slavery were abolished in the United States, the great cities of the North "would sink into insignificance" (Wakefield 1836, 11:2; cited in Winch 1967, 97n).

By extension, England itself was dependent on slavery. Herman Merivale, an Oxford professor and a disciple of Wakefield, delivered a set of lectures between 1839 and 1841 on the subject of colonizations and colonies, which won him an appointment as undersecretary for India. There, he explained to his fellow Britons, whose sensibilities were too delicate to accept the morality of slavery:

> What raised Liverpool and Manchester from provincial towns to great cities? What maintains now their ever active industry and their rapid accumulation of wealth? The exchange of their produce with that raised by American slaves and their present opulence is as really owing to the toil and suffering of the Negro as if his hands had excavated their docks and fabricated their steam engines. [Everyone connected with the commerce between Britain and the United States] . . . is in his very own way an upholder of slavery: And I do not see how any consumer who drinks coffee or wears cotton can escape from

the same sweeping charge. (Merivale 1841, 295; see also McCulloch 1845, 341)

Merivale (1841, 262; cited by Marx 1977, 937) instructed his Oxford students: "In the old civilized countries, the worker, although free, is by a law of nature dependent upon the capitalist. [In the colonies] it is of the highest importance to find some artificial substitute for the slave and convict labour, by which our colonies have been hitherto rendered productive."

Lessons from America

Although few were as open about the need for "artificial substitutes" as Wakefield, the problem of labor leaving for more accessible lands in the colonies was a fairly common theme in British mercantile literature after 1600 (see Appleby 1978, 135). Remember that Franklin's plans to colonize the Ohio Valley came to naught because of the resistance of Lord Hillsborough and other Irish landlords.

The Revolutionary War did not end British concern about the lure of cheap land in the United States (Herrick 1926, 156–59). As Daniel Webster (1879, 43–44; see also Fite and Reese 1965, 30–33; Harris 1953; and a similar assertion by Sir Robert Peel cited in Tuttle 1967, 221) noted, in New England, where settlers were "nearly on a general level in respect to property . . . their situation demanded a parcelling out of the land."

Employers resented the effects of cheap land. According to an eighteenth-century French ambassador, a group of influential Americans wished that Spain would close the Mississippi River to stop people from being able to live relatively unattached to commercial society (see Morgan 1976, 111). Later, politicians attempted to maintain a restrictive land policy, especially in the West (see Zahler 1941). The situation in New England was so unfavorable to would-be employers of wage labor that parents had to take measures to prevent their sons from moving away. The most common technique was to threaten to disinherit them unless they delayed marriage (see Folbre 1980, 6–7).

Politicians, such as ex-president John Quincy Adams and Senator Foote of Connecticut, were especially vocal in calling for restrictions on the availability of public lands (see Schlesinger 1945, 347). This debate remained a major policy issue in the United States. Readers of political economy could learn of it from Thomas Cooper (Cooper 1833, 107; cited in M. O'Conner 1944, 220), who denounced "the cunning and selfish management of the manufactures . . . [that] discourages the low price of western lands, that the door of emigration may be closed on their slavish operatives."

The threat of cheap land in the United States reached as far as Great Britain. High wages in the United States intensified the demand for machinery. As a result, employers in the United States were willing to pay a premium for machine-oriented skills. As late as 1814, skilled mechanics employed in the British machine-making industry were prohibited from emigrating on pain of severe punishment (see Marx 1977, 719–21). In 1816, some Britons were urging their government to stop migration to the United States, although the rationale was to stifle development in the New World (*Colonial* 1816, 62).

True, the ease of access to land in the United States was highly exaggerated. Even so, western land remained cheap by international standards. The relative accessibility to land in Britain and the former colonies is reflected in the following comparison: In 1830 a British farm worker could purchase about one-tenth acre of land with his annual wage; an Illinois farm worker could afford 800 times that area (Gates 1960, 276; see also Shireff 1835, 466).

Wakefield's Lessons from America

Drawing upon the American experience, as well as information from Australia, Wakefield argued that, where access to land was easy, capital would have to resort to coercion. According to his interpretation of history, "cheapness of land [was] ... the cause of slavery" (Wakefield 1834, 152; see also Domar 1970).

As proof of this proposition, Wakefield offered the example of Virginia, which never was the best rich man's country. Indeed, the struggle between the poorer Virginian farmers and the wealthy plantation owners in 1676 was "the greatest social conflict of pre-revolutionary North America" (Brenner 1977, 89). The rich Virginia planters never found an adequate supply of wage labor. Only slavery "saved" Virginia insisted Wakefield (Wakefield 1834, 201–23; see also Morgan 1975).

Wakefield and his school recognized that the key to maintaining dependent labor was the high price of land; for where land is to be had cheaply, workers "cease to be labourers for hire; they . . . become independent landowners (ibid., 1834, 203; Wakefield 1849, 347). Much of the power of Wakefield's system stems from his awareness that his self-evident observation contradicted the sacred laws of political economy: "At length the true light broke upon me. The scarcity of labourers was an insuperable bar to any mode of cultivation that requires the employment of many hands! I profess my self to be little versed in the laws of political economy; but the fact was self evident" (Wakefield 1829, 108). According to Wakefield's (ibid., 156) interpretation of the North American colonies, "the doctrine of Adam Smith concerning the effect of cheap land and dear labour, in producing national wealth has been refuted by the safest of all arguments—an ample experiment." An experiment, I should add, of Smith's own choosing, as we saw in chapter 10.

In Australia in contrast, "During forty years we have combined the fire and water of political economy—dear land and cheap labor" (ibid., 127). Wakefield expressed pride in the novelty of his ideas, although in reality, they were anything but novel (see Marx 1977, 932). Even in Locke, we find vague hints of Wakefield's theory (Locke 1698, 316). Hobbes also displayed some striking similarities (see Hobbes 1651, chap. 30, 387).

In the time of Locke and Hobbes, however, the working class was unaware of the doctrines of political economy. When Adam Smith was writing, the threat of working-class uprisings no longer seemed far-fetched (E. Thompson 1963). The French Revolution made the classical political economists put a premium on discretion. As a result, the classical political economists extolled the virtues of the freedom of market relations, even as nonmarket pressures on workers and peasants intensified.

Recall that the classical political economists were concerned about the difficulty that employers had in finding enough tractable workers. Those economists were intent of corralling workers into wage labor. Only Steuart and Malthus in his later works indicated an awareness that an excessive amount of labor could present a problem.

Writing at a time, however, when labor was temporarily in surplus, Wakefield had no particular reason to express concerns about induced labor shortages in England. Landholders had to contribute to the poor rates to support the unemployed workers. In this environment, practical economists were concerned to find a way to dispose of the excess supply of labor.

Always attuned to the needs of capital, Nassau Senior agreed with Wakefield in this respect. Senior believed that the reduced poor rates would more than pay for the cost of removing workers from England (Senior 1831, xvi). Also, Senior felt that emigration promised to reduce the pressure for social revolution (see S. Levy 1970, 70).

Wakefield, then, did no more than to bring a well-established practice into the discourse of economic theory. He dared to speak openly of such matters only because his program promised huge dividends at home and abroad. In the process, Wakefield gave lie to the laissez-faire pretensions of classical political economy. With Wakefield, we no longer hear of Smith's natural liberty; instead, Wakefield proposes the concept of natural slavery, going even beyond the language of Sir James Steuart.

Wakefield and Natural Slavery

Much of the emigration to Australia was hardly voluntary. The British routinely sent convicts there. Many of these people were guilty of the heinous crime of poaching (see Wakefield 1829, 105). The removal of the poachers eliminated those who were most likely to resist the demands of capital in England.

Emigration provided an additional benefit. It permitted the substitution of seasonal workers from Ireland for the more expensive permanent employees, who were to be removed to the colonies (Cowherd 1977, 158; Pollard 1978, 112). Yet for the Australian employers, labor was still too dear.

Wakefield's remedy for this situation was merely to make land artificially scarce by putting a sufficient price on it, thereby removing workers' opportunity to become self-sufficient farmers. This program, which he dubbed "systematic colonization," was clearly designed to limit access to land. He recommended these measures on account of their encouragement of "natural slavery . . . that natural subordination in which the greater part of mankind always has been and probably always will be" (cited in Semmel 1970, 111). Wakefield (1835, 1:46) was convinced that slavery, whether "natural" or enforced, had the advantage of allowing a more advanced division of labor. As a result, his system could also lead to an expansion of social productivity.

Unlike Steuart, Wakefield preferred natural slavery to its more direct variant. He argued that systematic colonization promised higher profits as well as a better standard of living than the free market could offer. Wakefield even called on English workers to join with him in a program to restrict access to land in the colonies.

The combination of expensive land and wage labor would allow a great influx of labor to be absorbed. The more English labor was drawn to the colonies to avail itself of the cheap resources, the better the condition of the remaining workers should be, disregarding numerous other contradictory impacts. Wakefield (1834, 130) claimed: "In order to raise wages immediately, the field for employment of English capital and labour must be enlarged." Consequently, he advised workers that their self-interest required that capital be granted satisfactory conditions in the colonies. He never explained how they would benefit from restrictions to labor.

Wakefield (1835, 51 ff.) played down the effect of the artificial glutting of colonial labor markets by invoking Bellers's principle: that concentration of workers can make enough of an addition to the total product to allow for increased benefits to both labor and capital. Of course, this same line of reasoning suggests that British workers would improve their situation by restricting the flow of both labor and capital abroad.

In spite of his supposed concern for the working class, Wakefield's essential message was that, where workers found alternatives to wage labor, capital would even resort to slavery. Thus Smith's optimistic evaluation of wage labor had to be amended. According to the calculations of the Wakefield school, "slave labour is dearer than free wherever abundance of free labour can be procured" (Merivale 1841, 256). In short, capital would submit itself to the rules of the marketplace only after labor had been made to submit itself to capital.

We might also note that, in Wakefield's program, the rights of indigenous people did not merit even a trifle of concern.

Wakefield, Australia, and the Game Laws

In 1830, England was abuzz with the concern about the occurrence of widespread incendiarism in the countryside. Wakefield associated the leadership with the struggles surrounding the Game Laws (see also Hobsbawm and Rude 1968, 63, 99, and 287). He charged:

> the privileged classes . . . inclose the commons. They stop footpaths. They wall in their parks. They set spring-guns and man-traps. They spend on the keep of high bred dogs what would support half as many children, yet they prosecute the labouring man for owning one. . . . They breed game in profusion for their own amusement, and having thus tempted the poor man to knock down a hare for his pot, they send him to the treadmills, or the antipodes, for that inexpiable offence. They make new crimes and new punishments for the poor.
>
> Even in church, where some of them solemnly preach that all are equal, they sit on cushions, in pews . . . sheltered by curtains from the wind and the vulgar gaze. . . . Every where they are ostentatious. (Wakefield 1831b, 14–15)

The gentry bred resentment as well as game. In Wakefield's words, "they entertain toward their oppressors feelings of rancorous hatred such as we have no account in the history of rural discontent" (ibid., 18). The response of the poor was more or less predictable. "Impelled by want of food, clothes and warmth, for themselves and their families, they become poachers whenever game abounds" (ibid., 12).

According to Wakefield (ibid., 9, 11, 12), two kinds of people took part in the actions: "[A] defective being, with calfless legs and stooping shoulders,

weak in mind and body, inert, pusillanimous, and stupid, whose prema-
ture wrinkles and furtive glance tell of misery and degradation. That is an
English pauper. . . . [The other has] large muscles, upright mien, and a
quick perception. . . . The bolder sort of husbandry labourers, by engaging
in murderous conflicts with gamekeepers and preventative men, become
accustomed to deeds of violence."

Wakefield's recommendations are less trenchant than his diagnosis. He
warned that raising wages would only impoverish manufacturing, transferring the problem to the cities (ibid., 41–42). In the short run, the rich
could subdue the poor by force. He proclaimed, "*Send troops into the
blazing districts; proclaim martial law; shoot, cut down, and hang the
peasants wholesale, and without discrimination*" (ibid., 43; emphasis in
original).

Wakefield admitted that such measures could not succeed for long. The
elimination of poverty is required, but he does not explain how to accomplish this end. One would expect a strong plea for emigration at this point,
but it is not forthcoming. More likely, Wakefield would have liked to
banish the strong rebels to a far-off colony, while leaving the paupers to
languish in a state of natural slavery.

Wakefield's Reception within Classical Political Economy

By suggesting that wage labor developed out of slavery or, even worse, that
the prosperity of England continued to be dependent, even in part, on
slavery, the Wakefield school undermined any humane pretensions of
political economy. Yet Wakefield's ideas won him the support of virtually
every major economist of his day, with the sole exception of McCulloch
(Winch 1965, 128–35; Semmel, 1970). Wakefield's influence extended
into the political realm. He became the major influence in the settlement
of New Zealand, the land to which Franklin had earlier proposed introducing the benefits of capitalist civilization.

In the United States, academic thought thoroughly assimilated Wakefield's interpretation of North American history, as it has been passed
down from Achille Loria through Frederick Jackson Turner (Benson 1950).

After reading *England and America* (1834), George Poulett Scrope wrote
to the author, "I cannot remember reading any work with greater interest,
or more thoroughly going along with any author in his views, opinions,
and sentiments" (cited in Mills 1915, 87–88). Nassau Senior (1928, 351–
52), always an outspoken foe of the working class, announced: "It is a
remarkable instance of the slowness with which political knowledge advances that though colonization has been vigorously carried on for about

3,000 years . . . the mode of affecting it in the manner most beneficial to the mother country and to the colony was discovered only twenty-five years ago. The discoverer was Edward Gibbon Wakefield." We might expect to find a clear exposition of Wakefield's theories in the work of his avowed disciple, John Stuart Mill; however, Mill felt compelled to dress up his master's ideas to make them more presentable. Accordingly, he introduced Wakefield to generations of students with a curious fable. Mill (1848, 2:119) asked his readers to "suppose that a company of artificers provided with tools, and with food sufficient to maintain them for a year, arrive and establish themselves in the midst of" a population of self-sufficient households. Consequently, he noted, "The economical position of the landed population is now materially altered. They have an opportunity given them of acquiring comforts and luxuries" (ibid.).

Just in case his readers missed his point, Mill (ibid., 121), the colonial administrator, shifted ground to recommend that "the best chance for an early development of the productive resources of India consists in the rapid growth of its exports of agricultural produce (cotton, indigo, sugar, coffee, etc.) to the markets of Europe."

Mill's effort is remarkable. In the first place, although political economy found Wakefield to be novel, a fable similar to Mill's appears in Steuart (1767, 1:254–62). Second, Mill attempted to take the sting out of Wakefield's program by allowing a Smithian extension of the division of labor. But where did he look? To India! India had never been used to translate Smith's ideology into practice; indeed, India's British administrators had always been congenial to the mercantilist conception of development. Finally, in Mill's fable, it would seem that wealth flowed from Britain, the home of the "company of artificers," to India. Repatriation of profits was not mentioned.

In discussing Mill's fable, we might also mention Marx's (1981, 3:445, 449–50) contention that the mode of production cannot be transformed merely by the actions of merchant capital. Nonetheless, stripped of its fantasies, Mill's fable smacks of Wakefield pure and simple: "The influence exercised on production by the separation of employments, is more fundamental than, from the mode in which the subject is usually treated, a reader might be induced to suppose. . . . The truth is much beyond this. Without some separation of employment, very few things would be produced at all" (Mill 1848, 2:118). Remember that this fable came from the pen of John Stuart Mill, who advocated a polite sort of socialism.

Marx reserved his last chapter of the first volume of *Capital* for Wakefield. He was not so much concerned with Wakefield's discovery of colonization. He had found those ideas more than a half century earlier in

Mirabeau, as mentioned before (Marx 1977, 932). He could have also looked to Franklin and numerous other Americans. What then was the significance of Wakefield?

Recall Smith's failed attempt to discover the nature of the British economy in the colonies of North America. Wakefield, who attempted to refute Smith, was more successful on this account. In Marx's (1977, 932) words, "he discovered, not something new about the colonies but in the colonies, the truth about capitalist relations in the mother country."

Wakefield's Reception by Modern Economists

In spite of such fulsome praise, Wakefield is generally passed over in silence today. Even Joseph Schumpeter's (1954) encyclopedic *History of Economic Analysis*, which brings together a discussion of the most obscure texts, fails to give Wakefield a single mention.

The major exception to the general neglect of Wakefield was Lionel Robbins (1958, 154n), who reluctantly accepted Wakefield's importance: "This judgement is a complete reversal of a view which I expressed some thirty years ago when, in the course of controversy about some Marxian theorems, I reproached my opponent, Mr. Maurice Dobb, with paying too much attention to Wakefield's propositions."

Robbins, while recognizing Wakefield, was still not willing to accept the lesson Marx drew from his work. Robbins chided Marx (1974, 940) for misrepresenting Wakefield in the final line of the first volume of *Capital*: "The capitalist mode of production and . . . capitalist private property have for their fundamental condition the annihilation of that private property which rests on the labour of the individual himself; in other words, expropriation of the worker." Robbins (1958, 163) cited Wakefield's *Letter to the South Australian Commissioners* (334) to prove his case against Marx: "Let it be clearly understood, that the object in putting a price on public land is not to prevent labourers for hire from ever becoming landowners. On the contrary, every one wishes that all the labourers taken out should be able to obtain land and servants of their own, after, and by means of, a few years of labour for hire. . . . In my own calculations . . . I have supposed that three years would be long enough for the capitalist and short enough for the labourer." Wakefield's key assumption in this work was the requirement that the stream of immigrants would be sufficiently large that the expanding population of employers could continue to have a satisfactory supply of labor. Such a condition would be rather unlikely.

Consider the case of the United States. Many observers estimated that frontier laborers could save enough to become independent within the three-year period that Wakefield recommended, but Wakefield regarded the resident of the frontier with displeasure. He described the frontiersman as "grossly ignorant, dirty, unsocial, delighting in rum and tobacco, attached to nothing but his rifle, adventurous, restless, more than half-savage (Wakefield 1834, 196). Thus, one must take his supposed support for easy access to land with a grain of salt.

Although an adequate labor force might have been theoretically maintained in the United States when people could obtain land within three years, in England, even with the proximity of Ireland, obviously too few immigrants were arriving to supply enough wage labor to satisfy employers. Labor had to be shaken loose from the countryside. In this sense, Wakefield demonstrated the need for the sort of primitive accumulation that actually occurred in England.

If Robbins wished to find fault with Marx's words, he could have pointed to the fact that capital can actually benefit from the workings of household production, as we learned from our analysis of the Classical Theory of Primitive Accumulation. Wakefield himself, however, made comparatively few direct comments on the English economy proper.

Wakefield and Primitive Accumulation

Perhaps Wakefield owed his relative originality to his thorough grounding in Irish affairs. Although he was not Irish, he was closely associated in his writings with his father, author of *Ireland, Statistical and Political*, which was considered to be the best work of that period on the subject of Ireland. Pitt supposedly consulted his father on Irish affairs (Lee 1879, 449).

Werner Stark (1944, 49n) once remarked on the importance of the Irish perspective in later British economic thought: "The apostles of historicism in England . . . were Irishmen. This is certainly no mere chance." We might also mention parenthetically that Torrens also was Irish. However, we must not let an overemphasis on Wakefield's Irish interests lull us into forgetting his critical exposure to the working classes at Newgate prison.

The crucial point here is that intensification of labor is a natural consequence of a regime of capital. Recall Smith's (1976, I.i.8, 18–19) criticism of "the habit of sauntering and indolent and careless application [that] . . . renders [the peasant] almost always lazy and slothful." Wakefield concurred. He attributed the lesser performance of the Irish peasant to what he cites McCulloch as calling "the apathy and languor that exist in a rude state of society" (Wakefield 1835, 1:76).

We need not belabor the point: Wakefield did not see the opportunities for exchange naturally evolving out of the abstract higgling and haggling

336

of the marketplace. True, like Steuart, Wakefield (1835, 1:77) attributed the unenthusiastic labors of the Irish peasant to the lack of opportunities for exchange. But, like Steuart, he attempted to encourage nonmarket forces to create the appropriate opportunities.

What concerned Wakefield most was the opportunity for the employer to exchange wages for labor power. Given the alternative of producing for itself, the peasant household displayed a marked aversion toward wage labor. The household members valued their chance to avoid exchanging many hours of labor for the equivalent of the value of fewer hours. Moreover, even when wage labor offered pecuniary advantages, workers still frequently chose the independence of a less regimented life (Pollard 1965, 166, 173). Wakefield (1835, 1:32) seemed to have much more to say on the subject, but he remained judiciously silent: "It must be confessed, that the power of exchanging has not been thoroughly analyzed by any writer on the subject. Of what element is that complex power composed, and by what circumstances it is apt to be increased or diminished; these are questions which would occupy much space in political economy." Moreover, Wakefield (1834, 25) recognized that this question of the social division of labor represented a theoretical challenge to political economy: "One cannot use capital merely by wishing to use it, nor can a single workman practice 'division of labour,' but the capital and the 'division of labour' arise from some anterior improvement."

Wakefield's insight into the political economy of wage labor might seem to be so self-evident as to be judged unworthy of consideration as theoretical analysis. Yet the same matter has often perplexed first-rate economists. For example, Ricardo (1951–73, 1:395), toward the end of his chapter on machinery, theorized that because of cheap food in America "there is not nearly such great temptation to employ machinery." If workers in both locations earned the same real wage, Ricardo might have found himself on solid ground.

More recently, Peter Temin (1971; see also David 1975, 19–91), who excels at the application of economic tools to historical material, has argued that extensive supplies of land should not have made industry in the United States more intensively mechanized than in England. Temin qualified his position by noting that industry in the United States would be more capital-intensive if interest rates were higher than in England (for a useful rectification of other aspects of Temin's work, see Clarke and Summers 1980, 129–39). The high proportion of farmers, traditionally debtors, did serve to push interest rates up. Although he based his conclusion on different premises, Friedrich List (1841, 332) proposed as a general rule that interest will always be higher in agricultural societies.

In reality, by restricting the growth of the industrial reserve army, the homestead was a great threat to profits. Had all workers been wage earners, the equations used to develop the argument might have been more sensible; however, even on the eve of the U.S. Civil War, a mere 28 percent of the northern labor force was estimated to have worked for wages (de Canio and Mokyr 1977). Wakefield (1834, 30), who was far more realistic in this matter, realized that only 10 percent of the labor force in the northern states earned wages.

Those economists who do correctly apprehend the conditions of employers in the early United States cannot resist obscuring the matter in a haze of neoclassical jargon. Heywood Fleisig (1976), for example, does not interpret the situation in terms of labor's opportunity to secure employment outside the wage nexus; rather, he pictures potential employers being denied outlets for their supply of entrepreneurial expertise.

Wakefield, in this sense, truly represents a high point in the study of wage labor. Political economy did not rouse itself to follow up on his insights until the appearance of *Capital*, exactly one hundred years after the publication of Steuart's *Inquiry*. Unfortunately, it fell back into a comfortable slumber shortly thereafter.

Wakefield and the British Economy

In Wakefield's opinion, Smith (1976, II.iv.8, 352; see also I.x.c.26, 144) was correct to teach that "as capitals increase in any country, the profits that can be made by employing them necessarily diminish." Wakefield (1835, 1:254) allowed for two means of improving the situation of capital: "Colonization and the importation of Food." Cheap imported food obviously implies that the same monetary wage would exchange for a greater use value. Wage labor could consequently become slightly less abhorrent compared to the alternative of petty commodity production controlled by merchant capital.

Colonization is another matter. Here Wakefield, in anticipation of Lenin, recognized that the export of capital can improve the rate of profit, providing the proper climate for colonization exists—namely, the absence of access to cheap land. Beyond this point, Wakefield was very evasive about what he found within the English economy.

Wakefield seems to have understood a reality that eluded Steuart: an honest exposition of the workings of the domestic economy would have made his theories too embarrassing for political economy to embrace. In describing his manner of presentation, he explained, "By dwelling altogether on the former question [of the distribution of shares], we make bad blood between the two classes; . . . by examining the latter question [of the total product], we may prove that masters and servants have one and the same interest" (Wakefield 1834, 83).

In his commentary to *The Wealth of Nations* we read: "When a body of men raise more food than they want, and employ that surplus food as capital, paying it in wages to other labourers, those other labourers act in concert or combination with those capitalists" (Wakefield 1835, 1:29).

We have no need to go further. Despite Wakefield's brutal clarity in dealing with colonial economies, he carefully obfuscates the cleavage between those who employ labor and those who labor when dealing with the British economy. Once he has gone that far, he can simply slide into the technical advantages of the division of labor. Such a contrived performance teaches us more about Wakefield than about political economy.

When Wakefield did come close to the truth, he presented it as nonsense, perhaps to make it more palatable. For example, after asking himself, "Why does *any man ever* produce of anything more than he himself can consume," he satisfied himself with the Smithian fantasy: "Solely because he expects that some other man will take from him that portion of his labours which he does not want, giving him in exchange something which he wants" (Wakefield 1834, 242; emphasis added).

Where Wakefield did attempt to justify the relationship between labor and capital, he became even more ridiculous. He repeated a variant of Locke's (1698, 320) naive fable about the social compact. Accordingly, we are told, "Mankind has adopted a simple contrivance for promoting the division of labour: they have divided themselves into owners of capital and owners of labour" (Wakefield 1834, 26). Wakefield even went so far as to propose that these two groups complemented each other's psychological needs: The capitalists are happy to save because they can expect to have workers to employ, and the workers are happy to spend because they can expect to find employment (ibid., 26).

At one point, immediately after picturing the English farmworker as "a miserable wretch," Wakefield (ibid., 29) suggested that "the agricultural class seems to have come to an understanding with the other classes, to separate its employment from the manufacturer and dealer." Were we not to know better, we might be led to believe that Wakefield was echoing Rousseau, who sarcastically wrote: "I will allow you," says the capitalist, "to have the honour of serving me, on the condition that, in return for the pains I take in commanding you, you give me the little that remains to you" (cited in Marx 1977, 909).

When push came to shove, Wakefield would be likely to have no part in voluntarism. What if the smallholders had refused to enter into a "voluntary" agreement? Would Wakefield (1835, 1:38), who charged that "a monotonous people are necessarily dull and ignorant" have been willing to abide by their choice?

We do know that Wakefield violently opposed Owen's plan. He charged that, if Owen's ideas were put into practice, "All the people would be . . . precisely like another" (ibid.). Wakefield ridiculed Owen's vision of a voluntaristic division of labor in which one is found "now digging, then trading, then mending a shoe" (ibid., 1:42).

Certainly, Wakefield was easily able to recognize that where small, self-contained households predominated, leisure would take precedence over production. Thus he asserted that "the labor of an Irish coal-heaver or pavior in London, whose labour, when he was without the means of exchanging, did just suffice to maintain his family, produced enough for the maintenance of perhaps a half-dozen families" (ibid., 1:77). We do not have to accept that the standard of living of the coal-heaver was so elevated even when compared to the impoverished Irish peasant, except in terms of monetary income.

At least, Wakefield signaled us when we could take him seriously. Consequently, we can separate the wheat from the chaff without much effort. Moreover, Wakefield's importance did not depend on his analytical gifts, but rather on his ability, generally, to keep from getting confused by the ideology around him, including his own.

John Rae: Preliminaries

Another frontal attack on Smith's theories came from the remarkable John Rae, namesake of both Smith's famous biographer and the no less renowned Arctic explorer. Such fame eluded this John Rae, although he was a political economist, as well as a doctor of medicine and a magistrate in Hawai'i, who made significant contributions in the fields of geology and linguistics.

Rae was even less recognized in his own lifetime. True, John Stuart Mill (1848) quoted from him extensively; Irving Fisher was also generous toward Rae, even dedicating his *Theory to Interest* to the memory of Rae and Eugen Boehm-Bawerk (see R. James 1965, 182). Acknowledgment from other quarters has been virtually nonexistent.

John Rae's assault on Smithian economics was even more significant than that of Wakefield, who never had any real pretensions as an economic theorist. By contrast, Rae was quite sophisticated. In addition, Rae knew about economic development, by virtue of his long experience living on the Canadian frontier, where he could study the meaning of primitive accumulation firsthand.

Rae does not seem to have owed anything to Wakefield, but he may have been indebted to Gourlay. In fact, their personal lives bore some similarity. Each wrote the bulk of his work in Canada. Both men seemed to embark on long journeys as an escape from private troubles (see Goodwin 1961, 7; James 1965, 14–15). Rae's proposal for dealing with the land set aside to finance the Canadian clergy had much in common with Gourlay's recommendations (see James 1965, 28). Finally, we might note Rae's appraisal of Gourlay's work was quite close to that of Wakefield.

In 1840, after Rae's only major work on political economy had appeared, Rae published a prospectus of another book that he intended to complete. In comparing his proposed book with earlier works, Rae wrote:

> It is believed that no work approaching in plan to the present, has been published by anyone personally acquainted with the country, with the exception of Dr. Dunlop's *Backwoodsman*, and Gourlay, Bouchette and Rolph's volumes. . . . With regard to the other books it may be remarked that Mr. Gourlay's book was published under very unfavorable circumstances that the talent which portions of it evidently display, lies buried under a heterogeneous mass of uninteresting matter. (cited in R. James 1965, 71)

Biographical Considerations

Rae is a difficult figure to approach. In some ways, his work is strikingly modern. He anticipated Boehm-Bawerk's capital theory, as well as Thorstein Veblen's notion of conspicuous consumption. Indeed, on two different occasions, he even described consumption as "conspicuous" (see Rae 1834, 287, 310). In another respect, he was almost a medieval thinker, ostensibly deriving his economics from an explicit theory of morality.

How might a writer as important as Rae get caught up in narrow-minded disputes over morality? In 1820, the North West Company was merged with the Hudson Bay Company. Montreal, in the process, lost its dominant role in the fur trade and its traditional mercantilist powers eroded. These new conditions opened the way for the merchant families of Montreal to increase their strength and influence in the economic life of the region (see R. James 1965, 134–35).

Rae, like the Montreal merchants, was a Scotch Presbyterian. He "was intimately associated with the Montreal merchants and their friends and in due course was to become one of their philosophers and publicists" (ibid., 134). His sister ran a boarding school that catered to the well-to-do merchant families. Her husband and brother-in-law were both successful merchants (ibid.).

The majority of the population in the region was Catholic and French. Dissimilar language, religion, and social customs among classes are familiar ingredients of violent turmoil. Canada was no exception. By 1837, armed conflict had broken out.

Rae became active in the movement that called for subsidies for the Protestant Church. According to Rae, the church had a legitimate claim on the one-seventh of Lower Canada, which was set aside "for the support and maintenance of a Protestant clergy" (31 Geo., c. 31, sec. 36). The Church of England held the position that the Presbyterian Church was not intended to be included in the phrase cited above. Rae's involvement in this controversy seems to have helped shape his economic theories, as we shall see.

Apparently, Rae's moral sensibilities had already put him in conflict with the theories of Smith while he was still young. In 1819, the Scottish public favored a reduction of the duties levied on alcohol. Rae recalled: "Almost everyone thought that great good would result from such a change of system and laughed at the fears which few entertained of its bad effects on the general morals of people. The authority of Adam Smith was cited as decisive on the question, and the measure was carried through amid a general acclaim of approbation. I own that I was among the doubters. . . . Time has now shown that I was not far wrong" (cited in R. James 1965, 13). We might note that Smith himself recommended taxes on alcohol (Smith 1976, V.ii.k.7); however, we have already seen that the people who invoke the authority of Smith are often more extreme than the great master.

The Durability of Capital

One would not expect a person with Rae's parochial mind-set to contribute much to a deeper understanding of the market, but Rae did. Rather than merely railing against the market as an amoral institution, he analyzed economic activity as a subset of morality. To understand his method, recall Gourlay's concern about the Canadian farmers' excess land. In the same vein, Rae (1834, 206; see also *American* 1775, 54) challenged his readers to ask a farmer:

> Why, instead of stone fences around his fields, which decay, or hedges which require constant trimming and dress, he does not put iron

railings, he will answer, "it does not pay." Ask the house-builder, why this is not cut stone, instead of brick, that oak instead of pine, this again iron, instead of oak or that copper instead of iron, and consequently the whole fabric doubly durable.

He will also reply, "it will not pay." In all these cases, and a thousand others that ought to be put, the answer is abundantly sufficient as regards the individual, but is no answer at all as regards the society.

Rae's observations were not unique. A few years earlier, Thomas Cooper (1830, 131) had used a similar image of a stone fence to illustrate the advantages of improvements in agriculture relative to industry on account of the less durable nature of investments in manufacturing. Even earlier, John Taylor (1818, 311) had written:

> Let us suppose that dead wood fencing will consume 10 per centum of a farmer's time, which supposition devotes about 36 days in the year to that object. It would cost him 5 whole days in 50. If his farm afforded stone, and his force could in 1 whole year make his enclosures of that lasting material, he would save 4 whole years by this more perfect operation; exclusive of the benefits gained by a longer life, or transmitted to his posterity. . . . It seems to me that the time necessary to rear and repair live fences, is less than one tenth of that consumed by those of dead wood.

Rae's comments were aimed as much at those farmers who had recently come from the British Isles as native-born Canadian farmers. Even though a farmer may initially look with disdain on the farming methods of the New World, the logic of profit maximization will force the adoption of the techniques that Rae (1834, 207) decried: "His neighbors will tell him, indeed, from the first, that if he expects the same profit as they have, he must have less dead stock on his hands, and he must give more activity to his capital; but he is slow of believing them."

Elementary economics predicts just such a result. The New World was short of capital. Thus, farmers as well as other businesses would be wise to ration capital very sparingly. Again, many other observers had noticed the same phenomena as Rae (see, for example, Morgan 1975, 141; Boserup 1965, 63; Grigg 1977, 63, 70; Kalm 1770–71).

We can also point to McCulloch (1824, 123n), who noted that British farmers who visited Flanders resolved to farm as carefully as the Flemish, but "a few years' experience . . . throws them back by a kind of necessity into their former habits; a falling off which they attribute to indolence or the incapacity of those whom they employ."

Rae, however, in analyzing this rationing, went further than anyone else would venture for another half century. Indeed, Rae himself seems to have inspired those subsequent developments. I cannot resist comparing the performance of McCulloch and Rae at this point. McCulloch came within a hair's breadth of stumbling onto Rae's brilliant insights. Instead, he attributed the failure of Flemish-style agriculture in England to the availability of land at a low rent. Thus he did not push his observation beyond the agricultural sector. In contrast, Rae used the same idea to develop sophisticated theories of both capital and the social division of labor.

Rae on the Division of Labor

Rae's theory of the social division of labor evolved out what he called "dead stock." In a society made up of identical, self-sufficient households, each one would have a complete outfit of the means of production. If some were to specialize in a particular trade, then society could economize on the total capital requirements (see Rae 1834, chap. 8):

> The exercise of the arts of the weaver, the blacksmith, the carpenter, the farmer, implies the existence of a great variety of tools with which they may be carried on. But, as a man can do only one thing at once, if any man had all the tools which these several occupations require, at least three fourths of them would constantly lie idle and useless. (ibid., 164)

> It is not perhaps likely, that this was the manner in which that division of occupations with which we are now familiar was originally produced, but it must evidently have been produced in this way . . . that even now it is thus brought to pass in the progress of settlements in North America. In such situations, every man is at first probably obliged to be his own carpenter, glazier, tanner, cobbler, and perhaps to a certain extent his own blacksmith. As the settlement fills up, and the population becomes sufficiently dense, he gives us this multifarious industry, and takes to some particular branch. (ibid., 165)

This idea was not entirely new. We can find it in Turgot (1766); still, nobody else seems to have given it much thought.

With Rae, the division of labor is merely a passive factor in economic development. This interpretation put him in direct conflict with Smith, who portrayed the division of labor as the principal motor of economic development. Rae (1834, 353) boldly challenged him in this regard: "In the

Wealth of Nations, the division of labor is considered the great generator of invention and improvement, and so of the accumulation of capital. In the view I have given it is represented chiefly as proceeding from the antecedent progress of invention."

Rae (1825, 196) hypothesized: "Among a people chiefly agricultural, in the early stages of human society, some persons, more ingenious than the rest, make discoveries and improve the natural products in a variety of modes, whence gradually arise the division of labour, the difference of professions, and a new distribution of wealth among mankind." By emphasizing science, Rae implicitly refused to credit those who displayed business acumen as being significant agents of progress, since he separated scientific from business pursuits.

Efficiency and the Durability of Capital

Rae's seemingly casual remarks about the techniques used by Canadian farmers evolved into a theory that eventually formed the core of the modern neoclassical analysis of capital. We can outline this theory of capital without much difficulty.

Let us return to the case of a farmer, who could use either wood or iron in constructing a fence. The initial outlay for the wooden fence would be cheaper, but the fence would be less durable. A profit-maximizing farmer would have to weigh the relative costs.

Imagine that the iron fence was produced in two stages. First, a wooden fence would be created. Then some additional work could somehow give the fence the durability of iron. Profit maximization would require that the extra expense of purchasing the durability be weighed against the cost of tying up the extra capital required to produce that durability. Where the rate of interest would be high, investors would be reluctant to tie up much of their investment in durability. The discounted cost of future maintenance or replacement would be relatively low because of the high rate of discount.

Rae seems to have been the first political economist to have given this idea any thought. Had he gone no further, he would have earned himself a place of honor. In fact, he did not stop there. He noted that, other things being equal: "Every individual endeavors to exhaust, as speedily as he can, the capacity of the instruments which he possesses. By rapidly exhausting the capacity of any instrument, the returns yielded by it are not lessened, but quickened" (Rae 1834, 164).

In order to be able to compare technologies with widely differing characteristics, Rae made some simplifying assumptions. To begin with, he supposed that each piece of equipment lasted for a specific period of time. Next, he expressed their capacity in terms of how much labor would be required to do an equivalent amount of work. Then, he proposed to measure how much time would have to elapse before an implement yields a quantity of work double that required to build in the first place. Finally, he implicitly assumed that those technologies that produce an effect equal to twice the original effort expended in their production in the shortest period of time will be the least durable. In other words, the least durable method of production will have the highest rate of return. Nonetheless, as was the case with his example of the iron fence, those techniques that yield the highest rate of return are the least efficient.

I am using the term "efficient" in a special sense to reflect Rae's perspective. Efficient investments require the least labor over the long run. For instance, suppose that the iron fence requires ten times more labor to install than the wooden one. The iron fence has a lifetime of fifty years and requires no maintenance. The wood fence lasts only three years. After thirty years, the average annual labor input per unit of fencing becomes higher for the wooden fence. Over an even longer time horizon, the advantage of the iron fence will become even greater.

In effect, Rae favored a society with a system of values that created a low discount rate in which durable technology such as iron fences would be adopted instead of more short-lived technologies such as wooden fences.

Rae's Racial Theory of Capital Accumulation

By this point, Rae had come close to Boehm-Bawerk's theory of capital by identifying more efficient techniques with a lengthening of the lapse of time before investments repay themselves. The high interest rates that prevailed in Rae's Canada reflected a shortage of capital. Restricting investment to those techniques that yielded a high rate of return indicated a sensible rationing of scarce capital resources.

In reality, Rae could not accept the logic of modern economics. He believed that capital was not scarce because of the natural conditions in which Canadian settlers found themselves, but because of a moral and ethical failure on the part of the people of Canada. According to Rae, people who adopted technologies that were not durable were more like primitive than civilized people.

For Rae, primitive people do not use simpler tools as a rational adaptation to economic conditions. Instead, they resort to such technologies because they have too little regard for the future. In Rae's (ibid., chap. 8) words, such people have an insufficient "effective desire of accumulation." At times, this moral defect was explained in environmental terms. For example, Rae supposed: "The life of the hunter seems unfavorable to the perfect development of the accumulative principle . . . [and] necessarily improvident. . . . [T]he future presents nothing, which can be with certainty either foreseen, or governed . . . every member of such a community thinks of nothing but whether the supply of game will be plentiful, or scanty" (ibid., 131). Thus the resulting "naturally low degree of strength of the accumulative principle among nations of hunters, prevents them . . . from forming instruments of sufficiently slow return" (ibid., 147). Accordingly, Rae assumed: "Circumstances have given to every community a peculiar character; the moral and intellectual powers of every people have received different degrees of development" (ibid., 162).

Rae never explained how a community might advance to a higher level, but instead attributed the capacity to progress to racial causes. He argued that those who saw parallels between European civilizations and the aboriginal peoples of America were mistaken. The Europeans were not hunters. Rae (ibid., 148) admitted that "it is our business to inquire how he [the hunter] could be induced to adopt" the ways of the pastoralist.

This line of reasoning led him to contradict his other theory—that science was the cause of development. He suggested that only if people had a sufficiently advanced effective desire of accumulation would they put new technologies into use. He noted: "[The] possession of flocks and herds, implies a considerable degree of care and foresight both in protecting, and making provision for them, and in avoiding to consume too great a number of them. It also implies the existence of private property to a large amount, and, consequently, of strength in the ties binding families together" (ibid., 143). Yet Rae offered no explanation, other than race, to indicate why the Europeans had come to practice animal husbandry (ibid., 144). He also saw race as the cause of the poverty of the Chinese, a people whom he depicted as "abandoned to gross sensuality, to drunkenness, and degrading licentiousness" (ibid., 151). As proof, he cited testimony of travelers who described the simple instruments used by the Chinese (ibid., 152). Although the intricate system of terraces and water works were evidence of long and hard work, Rae insisted that such projects were not indicative of "effective desire of accumulation" on the part of the Chinese because the irrigation works owed their existence to public officials rather than to individual choice (ibid., 284).

Not having the benefit of the recent work of Joseph Needham (1969),

Rae accepted the prevailing European view that Chinese science was inferior to that of Europe (ibid., 156). Although Chinese science had slowed down for a couple of centuries (Mokyr 1990, 218–19), "China came within a hair's breadth of industrializing in the fourteenth century" (Jones 1988). In his ignorance, Rae concluded: "It will I think be admitted as a fact, that Europeans in general far exceed Asiatics both in vigor of intellect, and in strength of moral feeling" (1834, 155).

Bad as the Chinese were, their "effective desire of accumulation [was] . . . greater than that of other Asiatics" (ibid., 151). Rae (1834, 166) offered the non sequitur: "Where, as in Hindostan, the loom is merely a few sticks, it would save one individual very little to employ another to weave for him. It is accordingly, in countries where the population is most dense, the facility of communication greatest, and instruments wrought up to the more slowly returning orders, that employments are most divided." Based on his theory of racial defects, he deduced: "We should, therefore, a priori, suppose that the instruments formed by them must be of orders of quicker return, and embracing a less compass of materials, than those constructed by European nations; but of slower return . . . than those to which the strength of the accumulative principle carries the other nations of Asia" (ibid., 151). Late in life, Rae (1862, 370) went so far as to claim that the "succession of race to race seems to have been one of the main causes of the progress of mankind."

Even so, race was not the only determinant of the effective desire of accumulation for Rae. He singled out environmental conditions for the changed behavior of the English farmers who migrated to Canada. In addition, like many other classical political economists, Rae attributed the same values to lower classes that he attributed to supposedly inferior races.

Not surprisingly, Rae criticized the lower classes for a failure to give sufficient attention to the future. He was convinced that improvidence kept the poor in a state of poverty (Rae 1834, 200). The small quantity of household utensils in the working-class homes was proof for him that such people had an inadequate desire of accumulation (ibid., 202). He complained that the poor squandered their funds on alcohol and tea instead of better pots and pans, which could have allowed them to reduce the amount of food that they waste (ibid., 202–4).

Those who are inclined to psychologizing might ponder on Rae's criticism of the lower classes. His own consumption of alcohol may have played a part in his dismissal as a teacher (see R. James 1965, 95). Rae often identified an effective desire of accumulation with a desire for offspring, yet Rae seems to have had no children of his own.

John Rae and the Moral Value of Primitive Accumulation

According to Rae, the condition of self-sufficiency and independence, as it was found in Canada, was characteristic of "the most simple state of society, when art is so rude, and accumulation so little advanced, that each individual forms almost all the instruments he himself or his family exhaust (Rae 1834, 173). Rae complained:

> In most communities where the population is scattered and the internal communications are bad, many trades are practiced in the farmers' houses and by their own families. In this way it is that, in very many of the recently settled parts of North America, every operation that the wool undergoes, from the taking off of the fleece to the cutting and making up the cloth, is performed in the farmer's house and by his own family. A similar state of things caused a similar practice to prevail in England a century ago, and, at present, keeps up many of those manufactures which are properly termed domestic, in many other parts of Europe. In Canada it is not uncommon for the farmer to have, not only the whole processes that wool undergoes til it comes to be worn, carried on by members of his own family, but also to get a great variety of other things made by them, which he could not procure otherwise by sending to an inconvenient distance. . . . the vegetables that supply his table, the animals he slaughters for it, the cider that refreshes his meals, the very sugar that sweetens his tea, and all that variety of fruits, that would attract the most fastidious appetite, are the produce of his own fields, and orchards, and woods. (ibid., 57, 230)

More than any other author whom we have seen, Rae did not oppose self-sufficiency as such. Instead, he kept his eye on the social relations of self-sufficiency, even though he couched his analysis in religious rather than economic terms.

For Rae, frugal independence could be the route to the development of a powerful bourgeoisie. Alternatively, it could represent a stubborn resistance to capitalist social relations. The Scottish Presbyterians used their self-sufficiency to harden their moral fibers; Catholics and other less respectable groups sunk in the face of the challenge of self-sufficiency, as far as Rae was concerned. Consequently, "There is not, in truth, a prouder man than the Canadian farmer. He has no superior; he is not dependent on the assistance, scarcely on the co-operation, of a single individual" (Rae 1828, 230).

Unfortunately, Rae believed that such pride was not characteristic of all independent farmers. Only the Scottish farmers, whose "feelings . . . are totally opposed to the principles and spirit of the Church of England" could claim such independence. Rae alleged that the typical representative of this group "had raised himself and his family from indigence to abundance." Such people formed "a class powerful enough to govern" (ibid.).

Rae saw another class, one "weak enough to be governed" (ibid.). Their fate was somewhat different. In Rae's view:

> There are many individuals from Ireland, Scotland, and England, whose finances are exhausted, ere they reach Canada, and who are burdened with large and young families. It is impossible for these men, immediately to pursue, what has probably been their original plan, and directly push into the wilderness. They absolutely require to have previously provided some small sum for the expense of the journey, some necessary tools and utensils, and provisions for themselves and families, until they can reasonably expect to draw subsistence from the land, they had come to occupy. To obtain these indispensable, their only resource, in general, is to betake themselves to some town or village, or to its neighborhood, and then, from what they may be able to save from their wages, to collect a sum sufficient for their purpose. Years are thus inevitably consumed by the emigrant, and very often, ere he has attained his purpose, old age presses on him, or he yields to the temptations to intemperance, which new habits and foreign manners expose him to, or he sets out prematurely, and sinks under the united pressure of severe toil, want, and disease. (ibid., 249)

Rae's ideas about capital and the social division of labor combined to form a moralistic theory of primitive accumulation. If people could be induced to have a higher effective desire of accumulation, the prevailing rate of return would be lower. With a lower rate of return, the class composition of society would be transformed.

In this way, Rae used his vision of morality to sanction primitive accumulation. He clearly saw that neither primitive accumulation nor a market-based accumulation process would bring material gains for the working class that would be commensurate with the moral progress that it promised. In an essay, which has since been lost, he explained:

> It is in the nature of this progress [of modern civilization] to convert the original simple and rude tools, first, into instruments of greater cost and efficiency, and these again into complex and difficultly con-

structed machines, still more costly and still more efficient. The distaff becomes a spinning wheel; and that changing its form, and wrought by other powers, is made part of a woolen factory. The rough edged blade of the original knife is first cut into a regular saw, and wrought by one hand; it is then put into a frame, which two men operate; and this, in turn, by means of a crank and opinions, is made to go by water, and becomes a saw mill. . . . And so it is with all our implements, they are passing on to great machines. . . . And yet there was a question which might possibly have occurred to the philosophic philanthropists of that day. "Who are to be the owners of these great machines? Will the mechanics and artisans who now wield the tools own the machines, or will they be the property of a distinct class?" . . . So constantly has it occurred that it may be said it has invariably happened, that the former artisans, in giving up their tools, have never become the owners of the machines which have succeeded them. These Machines . . . come to be owned by a distinct class. The operative has no property share in the industrial operation, he owns nothing but his hands and the art of using them fitly. For opportunity to use them, and for pay for their use, he depends on the owner of the machine. He suffers in consequence a degradation in the social scale. Formerly he was a small capitalist, now it is the characteristic of his condition to be a mere operative, destitute of capital. (cited in R. James 1965, 57–58)

To make matters worse, Rae expected that the new technology would reduce the demand for skilled labor: "As art advances from its first rude elements, the hand does less, the instrument more" (1834, 353). In the course of such development, some would prosper and some would fail. Rae came close to recognizing that the probable outcome for any individual would depend upon class origins, but instead he turned to racially based explanations. Nonetheless, Rae managed to produce an extremely valuable analysis of primitive accumulation.

Why did Rae fail to win recognition for his obviously original analysis? His emphasis on personal and racial causes of poverty were not uncongenial to classical political economy. Even today, economists sometimes look to cultural, ethnic, and religious characteristics as a major determinant of growth (see Hall and Jones 1997).

Rae fell from favor because he, like Steuart, advocated state action to further economic development. Consequently, like Steuart, he was slighted. Take the case of Nassau Senior, whose own theory of capital owed much to the unacknowledged influence of Rae. Someone put the question to Senior, how such a fine economist as Rae could oppose free trade if the case against market interference were so self-evident. Senior responded, "Oh, I never looked at that part of the book; what I am referring to is a certain chapter on the accumulation of capital, and other discussions of a like kind." The disappointed questioner gave up on political economy as a result of this encounter:

> He thought that pedants who were so afraid of entangling themselves in the labyrinth of their own science, that they would not follow a man whose genius and power they admitted a single step off the beaten road, lest they should find no end . . . were no guides for me, because it was clear that they could not have any confidence in themselves. (Doyle 1886; cited in R. James 1965, 167–68)

In the end, Senior parlayed his reputation as a political economist into a successful public career. His theory of capital was barely distinguishable from Rae's. Boehm-Bawerk then appropriated much of Senior's capital theory as his own. Later, Boehm-Bawerk "discovered" Rae, whose capital theory seemed to be strangely similar to his own. This brief moment of recognition soon passed. Today, Rae lies largely forgotten. His papers, which were deposited at the University of Hawai'i, have long disappeared.

Conclusion

Reading the modern histories of economic thought, neither Gourlay, Wakefield, nor Rae appear to have much to teach us about the subject. In fact, all three saw much that classical political economy preferred to obscure. They brought the subject of primitive accumulation to the fore. All three were rewarded with silence.

Consequently, in the agrarian question and the agrarian crisis the heart of the matter is not simply the removal of obstacles to the advance of agricultural technique, but what way these obstacles are to be removed, what class is to effect this removal and by what methods.—V. I. Lenin, *The Agrarian Question in Russia at the End of the Nineteenth Century*

Lenin and the Forging of Revolutionary Smithianism

STRANGE BEDFELLOWS: LENIN AND SMITH

The fallacy of Adam Smith's vision of the market has been a recurrent theme of this book. Some support for a Smithian interpretation of history may be found in a most unlikely ally—Lenin.

The convergence of such disparate individuals casts considerable light on the works of both. Although Lenin wrote as an avowed antagonist of Smith, his major anti-Smithian polemic was directed only at Smith's proposed resolution of value into wages and profits. In reality, Smith and Lenin shared a number of concerns. Each found himself in a country in which a relatively rapid rate of capitalist development required the eradication of the residues of earlier social formations. Like Smith, Lenin looked forward to rapid economic change as a means of transforming the psychology of the masses in his land.

An independent British scholar, Mark Jones, upon reading an early draft of this work, commented that Marx had never seen the squalor of a Russian village and Lenin had no firsthand experience of a British factory. As a result, Lenin might have sounded a different tone from Marx and the Marxists, who wrote from a western European environment.

In contrast to marxists such as Rosa Luxemburg, who saw primitive accumulation as an ongoing process occurring on a world scale, the early Lenin, like Smith, believed that the vestiges of previous economies were naturally dissolving as a direct result of market forces (see Luxemburg 1968, chap. 27). In fact, Lenin was much more explicit than Smith about the relationship between capitalist development and the evolution of the social division of labor. For Lenin (1893, 99–100), "the concept 'market' is quite inseparable from the concept of the social division of labour—that 'general basis of all commodity (and consequently, let us add, of capitalist) production' as Marx calls it."

In one sense, Lenin parted ways with Smith. Lenin was careful to maintain the distinctions between capitalist and precapitalist modes of production. Smith generally obscured them. As Lenin (ibid., 93) noted: "In the historical development of capitalism two features are important: 1) the transformation of the natural economy of direct producers into commodity economy, and 2) the transformation of commodity economy into capitalist economy. The first transformation is due to the appearance of the social division of labour—the specialisation of isolated (N.B.: this is an essential condition of commodity economy), separate producers in only one branch of industry." Lenin, of course, is a controversial figure, revered by some, despised by others. He enjoyed the advantage of the historical experience of the nineteenth century, but so did all his contemporaries. Nonetheless, a dispassionate reading of his works will reveal that whatever one may think of his methods and his goals, Lenin, more than anyone else, clearly addressed the subject of the social division of labor. Writing more than a half century before George Stigler's (1951) celebrated article on the division of labor appeared, Lenin observed:

> The growth of small production among the peasantry signifies the appearance of new industries, the conversion of new branches of raw material processing into independent spheres of industry, progress in the social division of labor, while the swallowing-up of small by large establishments implies a further step forward by capitalism, leading to the triumph of its higher forms. . . . it is quite natural that in a more developed part of the country, or in a more developed sphere of industry, capitalism should progress by drawing small handicraftsmen into the mechanized factory, while more remote regions, or in backward branches of industry, the process of capitalist development is only in its initial stage and manifests itself in the appearance of new branches and new industries. (Lenin 1898, 382)

Lenin (1893, 101) cited another Russian author, Vestnik Yevtropy (1893), on the changing social division in the United States:

> Recently, in the United States, the woodworking factories are becoming more and more specialized, "new factories are springing up exclusively for the making of, for instance, axe handles, broom handles, or extendible tables. . . . Machine building is making constant prog-

ress, new machines are being continuously invented to simplify and cheapen some side of production. . . . Every branch of furniture making, for instance, has become a trade requiring machines and special workers. . . . In carriage building, wheel rims are made in special factories (Missouri, Arkansas, Tennessee), wheel spokes are made in Indiana and Ohio, and hubs are made in special factories in Kentucky and Illinois.

Like Smith, Lenin had an eye for the positive developments in the countryside, but without Smith's blind spot for the harsher aspects of rural development. Although Lenin (ibid., 107) did not share the infatuation of Smith's successors for the consumption of baubles, he applauded the changing standard of living that was being adopted: "The rapid development of commodity economy and capitalism in the post-Reform epoch has caused a rise in the level of requirements of the peasantry."

Lenin (ibid.) was especially pleased with the cleanliness that these changes were bringing. Even more importantly, Lenin, like Smith, welcomed the potential of such capitalist development to eliminate dependency, or what he termed "the Asiatic abuse of human dignity that is constantly encountered in the countryside" (Lenin 1894, 235).

In an extended passage based on his study of the *Statistical Returns for the Moscow Gubernia,* Lenin penned one of the finest descriptions of the passage from precapitalist society to capitalism in the countryside. These words are especially striking because many of the same features that Lenin cites are identical to the examples used earlier by Steuart:

> As industrial occupation spreads, intercourse with the outside world . . . becomes more frequent. . . . They buy samovars, table crockery and glass, they wear "neater" clothes. Whereas at first this neatness of clothing takes the shape, among men, of boots in place of bast shoes, among the women, leather shoes and boots are the crowning glory . . . of neater clothing; they prefer bright, motley calicoes and kerchiefs, figured woolen shawls and similar charms. . . . In the peasant family it has been the custom "for ages" for the wife to clothe her husband, herself and the children [Steuart mentions that the same practice was common in his Scotland]. . . . As long as they grew their own flax, less money had to be spent on the purchase of flax, less money had to be spent on the purchase of cloth and other materials required for clothing, and this money was obtained from the sale of poultry, eggs, mushrooms, berries, a spare skein of yarn, or a piece of linen. All the rest was made at home. (Lenin 1894, 121)

The report then illustrated the manner in which commercial production was ousting traditional manufactures:

> Lace was made mainly by young women of more prosperous or larger families, where it was not necessary for all the women to spin flax or weave. But cheap calico gradually began to oust linen, and to this other circumstances were added: either the flax crop had failed, or the wife wanted to make her husband a red calico shirt and herself a smarter dress, and so the custom of weaving various sorts of linen and kerchiefs at home for peasants' clothing gradually died out. . . . That explains why the majority of the population do all they can to make articles for sale, and even put their children to this work. (ibid., 121–22)

Both Lenin and Smith were in complete agreement that capitalist development was "natural." Lenin differed from Smith only in his conviction that the rise of large-scale industry was also natural. Was Lenin wrong, or should I withdraw my claim that Smith's theory of development was a failed ideological venture?

Lenin and the Narodniks

We have already seen that the practical schemes of Wakefield had given lie to Smithian dogma. Why would Lenin, in effect, stand as a throwback to Smith? In part, Lenin's Smithian understanding grew out of his opposition to the Narodniks, whom he held responsible for the fate of his brother, who was executed for participating in a Narodnik plot to assassinate the Tsar (Weiller 1971).

The Narodnik economists, such as Vasily Vorontsov and Nikolai Danielson, took the position that capitalism was foreign to Russian soil. They protested against efforts of the state to implant capitalism artificially in Russia (Lenin 1894, 213; see also Walecki 1969). These attempts, such as the promotion of the Russian railroad system, were indeed both clumsy in execution and oppressive in effect (see von Laue 1963). Since much of the investment was imported, the net impact of this program would have been to restrict the home market, thereby stifling native Russian industry.

The distortions caused by the artificial promotion of capitalism were all the more destructive because of the gargantuan scale of the typical Russian manufacturer. In 1914, only 17.8 percent of Russian industrial workers were employed by firms with fewer than one hundred workers. In the United States, 35 percent of the industrial workers were employed by such establishments. In Russia, 41.4 percent of the industrial workers were in the pay of giant businesses with more than one thousand workers. Around Moscow, such firms employed 57.3 percent of the workers. The comparable figure for the United States was only 17.8 percent (Trotsky 1932, 8).

The Russian economy suffered from the usual symptoms of a dualistic economic growth pattern. The Narodniks preferred to avoid the costs associated with capitalist development in Russia by building socialism on the basis of the traditional village economy.

Lenin denounced their plans. The peasant's life was a constant round of toil. Maxim Gorky (1922, 370), the novelist, conveyed the sense of the Russian village in the following words: "The technically primitive labour of the countryside is incredibly heavy, the peasantry call it strada from the Russian verb 'stradat'—to suffer."

In contrast with the Narodniks, who condemned capitalism as an unnatural intrusion into the wholesome world of traditional Russian village life, Lenin interpreted the spontaneous growth of capitalism in the Russian countryside as part of a larger evolutionary process that would eventually lead to a socialist society.

Lenin (1913, 377) argued that peasants were not being crushed by railroads, but rather by the burdens of manual labor. To tread the Narodnik path, Lenin charged, was to be swept away by romantic illusions. Lenin asserted that the villages were not the bulwark of traditional social relations that the Narodniks thought them to be. Capitalism had already taken firm root in the countryside. He insisted:

> Russia is a capitalist country, that the power of the workers' tie with the land in Russia is so feeble and unreal, and the power of the man of property so firmly established, that one more technical advance will be necessary for the "peasant" (?? who is living by the sale of his labour-power) into a worker pure and simple. . . . [Despite] its general wretchedness, its comparatively tiny establishments and extremely low productivity of labour, its primitive technique and small number of wage-workers, peasant industry is capitalism. (Lenin 1894, 210, 217)

In this respect, Lenin's opinion squares with that of many modern, mainstream agricultural economists, who see peasants as precise maximizers (Schultz 1964, chap. 3; see also the references in Hagen 1980, 129). Lenin (1921a, 218) extrapolated from this observation, "Free exchange and freedom of trade . . . inevitably lead to a division of commodity procedures into owners of capital and owners of labour-power."

The Narodniks, in short, addressed capitalism in terms of the state's success in promoting it. Lenin analyzed capitalism in terms of its spontaneous growth within the villages. In this sense, Lenin may be termed Smithian, while the Narodniks may be credited with picking up the mantle of Steuart.

Lenin could also find support for his position that capitalist development was natural in Engels's *Anti-Dühring* (see, for example, Engels 1894, 195–96); however, Engels was engaged in an attack on Dühring's ridiculous "force theory," according to which Dühring all but denied any influence to economic forces inherent to the law of motion of capital. In this venture, Engels naturally avoided the subject of primitive accumulation.

Lenin's class analysis bore some similarity to Smith's. Smith saw the progressive bourgeoisie as a spontaneous outgrowth of the village economy. The established bourgeoisie were more or less in league with the forces of mercantilism. Accordingly, Smith did not regard them highly. Lenin, too, wrote off the liberal Russian bourgeoisie as incapable of promoting development (see Kingston-Mann 1980, 133).

Just as Smith unfairly criticized his mercantilist rivals, Lenin occasionally got carried away in his polemic with the Narodniks (Weiller 1971). Lenin may be charged with misreading some of his opponents; he may even have underestimated the potential of cottage industries "to gather up fragments of time" (see Georgescu-Roegan 1971, 252); nonetheless, he did provide a consistent revolutionary interpretation of Russian conditions.

Lenin and Smith Again

Lenin obscured the affinity of his analysis with that of Smith by identifying Smith with the Narodniks. However, this identification misrepresented Smith's purpose. Like the Narodniks, Smith did set out to show how market forces came to replace traditional relations of production. In direct opposition to the Narodniks, however, Smith attributed the evolution of the market to natural forces rather than the state.

Lenin and Smith also shared an interest in the social division of labor. Although Smith did not explicitly analyze the social division of labor, his antagonism toward traditional self-provisioning showed that he favored an intensification of the social division of labor evolved.

The social division of labor was Lenin's central concern in one of his first known works, *On the So-Called Market Question.* In Lenin's Smithian-like analysis, "the expansion of markets is made to serve both as condition and effect of capitalist development, obscuring the manner in which capitalist relations take root and the determinants of their specific course" (Tribe 1979, 4; see also Crisenoy 1979, 20). In his most important work on the subject, *The Development of Capitalism in Russia,* Lenin

(1974, 37–39) repeated three times in the first three pages the assertion that the social division of labor was the basis of commodity production.

Furthermore, like Smith, Lenin insisted that no external measures were needed to separate households from their means of production. If the peasantry were to gain access to the land, "it will not abolish capitalism; on the contrary it will create a broader foundation for its development, and will hasten and intensify purely capitalist development" (Lenin 1905, 440).

Smith and Lenin were at one in their reading of the American experience as well. Sounding more Smithian than Smith, Lenin (1974, 85; see also 1908, 140) contended that, "in America, it was not the slave economy of the big landlords that served as the basis of capitalist agriculture, but the free economy of the free farmer working on free land, free from all medieval fetters, free from serfdom and feudalism." He may well have been correct, although quantification is difficult in this sort of matter.

We do know that early American farming was predominately a process of capital accumulation (Bidwell and Falconer 1941, 82–83; for a later period see Primack 1966). The homesteading family often pushed itself as hard as any slave driver could push his crew. Moreover, a relatively small share of its efforts were directed toward providing itself with consumption goods.

Hard work was not enough. Between 1710 and 1775, for example, per capita incomes were estimated to have grown at a modest 0.4 percent per year (Lee and Passell 1979, 20). Improved standards of living in the United States awaited the introduction of the intensive use of slavery to produce the exports that formed the economic base of the country.

True, slavery had its limits. Eventually, the slave system ran up against the dual barriers of soil depletion and the contradiction between the incentive system of slavery and the need for higher productivity, as well as the development of more advanced production techniques that were inappropriate for a slave system. By the time of the Civil War, the eclipse of southern agriculture was well underway. Hinton Rowan Helper (1860, 53) calculated that the combined cotton, tobacco, hay, hemp, and sugar harvest of the fifteen slave states was worth less than the hay crop of the free states. Still, Helper, like Lenin, overlooked the enormous contribution of earlier slave labor in the process of accumulation in the United States.

Lenin's Reinterpretation of Petty Production

To his credit, Lenin displayed a capacity to learn from current events. After the 1905 revolution, in which the peasants were supportive, Lenin significantly modified his stand on the role of the peasantry. This change did not represent a recantation of his economics, but rather a strengthening of his confidence about the degree to which capitalism had already established itself (Lenin 1907, 233).

Based on his reading of the American experience, Lenin posed two alternative paths for the Russian countryside: either the nation could distribute the land to replicate northern American conditions; or, it could give the land to large landholders who could maintain large estates such as were found in Prussia. Lenin wrote: "Both these solutions each in their own way facilitate the adoption of . . . higher technique, both are in line with agronomic progress. The only difference between them is that one bases this progress on the acceleration of the process of squeezing poor peasants out of agriculture and the other bases it on the acceleration of the process of the labor rent system by destroying the feudal latifundia" (Lenin 1908, 136). Consequently, Lenin (ibid.) believed that "the essence of the agrarian question and of the agrarian crisis is not the removal of the obstacles to raise agriculture to a higher level, but how these obstacles are to be removed, which class is to remove them and by what means."

Lenin (1918, 377) also judged the American path to be "the most democratic . . . [and to cause] the masses less suffering." Moreover, the American path was the most congenial to capitalist development (see also Lenin 1907, 238–42; 1908, 40–42). Lenin (1974, 91) contended that the American path "would inevitably withdraw the majority of these owners, whose position is hopeless in capitalist society from agriculture, and no 'right to the land' would be powerful enough to prevent this."

Lenin (1907, 241) confidently summed up his position with the conclusion that "peasant farming . . . evolves in a capitalist way and gives rise to a rural bourgeois and rural proletariat." Here again, Lenin's conclusions were identical to those of Smith.

Although Lenin may have underestimated the importance of slavery to the U.S. economy, his imagery of the U.S. path was consistent with the experience of history. No matter what Wakefield said about the ease of taking up farming in the United States, potential farmers faced numerous obstacles, which became greater with the passage of time. By the nineteenth century, a typical farm cost about $1,000 to establish (Danhof 1941). The extension of farming to new western lands glutted the markets and dropped prices to disastrously low levels (Field 1978). Around Cincinnati, corn prices sank to six cents per bushel in some districts; in others, they fell so low that corn was burned as fuel instead of wood (Gideon 1948, 215; for a theoretical discussion of this sort of phenomenon see Marx 1963–71, pt. 2, 302). Credit was hard to find. The rates farmers had to pay were exorbitant, running as high as 120 percent for short-term loans (Gates 1960, 73). Especially in New England, where land was relatively scarce and infertile, farmers had to have recourse to debt in order to set their children up in farming (see Martineau 1837, 181).

The distribution of wealth in the United States, which had previously remained relatively stable during colonial times, began to become much more unequal after 1774 (Williamson and Lindert 1977). As a result, the U.S. economy began to create a substantial native-born industrial labor force out of the pool of largely self-sufficient producers. At first, these workers were women in the Northeast, left behind by the relatively more substantial exodus of men (Wright 1978, 118–19).

By the time Lenin was composing *The Development of Capitalism* in Russia, farms had become an important source of industrial labor in the United States. Between 1860 and 1900, at least twenty farmers migrated to the city for each worker who took up farming. Ten farmers' sons took up residence in the city for each one who became a farm owner (Shannon 1945, 356–59; see also Goodrich and Davison 1935).

Unlike Smith, who rhapsodized about people moving to new professions by virtue of the pull of better opportunities, Lenin emphasized the push of hopelessness to explain the migration from the countryside. Although the mathematical calculations are formally identical in either case, the social chemistry is not.

The actual mechanism by which a native proletariat emerged in the United States was slightly more complex than what Lenin suggested. When times turned bad, people tended to return from the city to the farm. After the business cycle moved upward once again, the migration to the city could recommence on a larger scale. Andre Gunder Frank, for example, noted that as late as the 1958 recession, the city of Detroit alone lost 50,000 workers and their families to the subsistence farms of the southern and border states (Frank 1975, 30). Similar forces determined the flows of immigration into the United States. For instance, Mexican immigration to the United States is highly correlated with inadequate rainfall in Mexico (Cornelius 1979).

Marx suggested that this pattern of ebb and flow into the countryside dated back as early as the fifteenth century. He remarked that in the course of each cycle, the "peasantry turns up again, although in diminished number, and in a progressively worse situation" (Marx 1977, 912).

In any case, the coincidence of periods of prosperity and rural exodus was consistent with the schema of Smith, who emphasized the association of the migration with opportunities in the city. Lenin, however, more accurately identified the underlying forces that drove the people from the countryside.

In conclusion, the United States offered more substantial support for Lenin's model of development than it did for Smith's.

Lenin on the Process of Differentiation in the Countryside

Both Lenin's Russia and Smith's Britain shared one crucial characteristic: poverty was making the life of the self-sufficient household difficult, if not impossible. This poverty was not a natural result of resource endowments, but the product of centuries of exploitation. Recall Marx's (1963–71, pt. 2, 237) portrait of England:

> Nowhere in the world has capitalist production, since Henry VII, dealt so ruthlessly with the traditional relations of agriculture, adapting and subordinating the conditions to its own requirements. In this respect England is the most revolutionary country in the world. Wherever the conditions handed down by history were at variance with, or did not correspond to the conditions of capitalist production on the land, they were ruthlessly swept away; this applied not only to the position of the village communities but to the village communities themselves, not only to the habitats of the agricultural population but to the agricultural population itself, not only to the original centres of cultivation but to cultivation itself.

We have already made the case that this transition often occurs over long periods of time (chapter 2). What happens when the household finds itself in an environment that is dominated by feudal employers?

Lenin (1908, 140) agreed with the analysis of the classical political economists: under such conditions, the lower the level of paid wages, the more people would produce for themselves. He did not suggest, as Steuart and others had, that such an arrangement would substantially benefit capital. Instead, Lenin was certain that it would only serve to preserve backward forms of production instead of promoting the accumulation of capital. Just as Engels observed in Germany, in Russia, too, the functioning of the household served to restrict capitalist development.

Lenin, however, understood the essence of the classical theory of primitive accumulation. He knew that once the traditional sector becomes sufficiently impoverished, poor peasants will have no choice but to accept wage labor. As a result, poverty, in this setting, did not reflect a disadvantage for capitalist development; rather, it was an important tool for organizing society according to its own interests.

In Russia, poverty in the traditional sector had become so extreme that Lenin saw great promise in the near term. In his mind, "The rapid development of commodity economy and capitalism in the post-Reform epoch has caused a rise in the level of requirements in the 'peasantry,' too: the peasants have begun to live a 'cleaner' life (as regards clothing, housing, and so forth" (Lenin 1893, 107). Yet Lenin (1894, 211) also observed that the desire for cheap calico prints and the like was causing household production to die out. In the process, traditional rural society evolved into a rich mix of economic strata ranging from the landless laborer to the successful peasant, whom the Russians called a Kulak. Unlike Smith, Lenin devoted considerable attention to the specifics of this process of differentiation in the countryside.

We can interpret some of Lenin's analysis in terms of the exchange of labor power. Think back to the earlier example in which the typical household could produce all its own needs in four hours of labor (see chapter 4). Some households will require more time; others less. Thus, if the working day for a wage laborer is eight hours, an inefficient household that needs seven hours to take care of its own needs would be less likely to resist the conditions of wage labor.

In practice, the actual process of differentiation will not be as simple as the following discussion implies (see Deere and de Janvry 1979). Nonetheless, it will conform to the broad outlines that follow. Under the assumption that the household would earn the same standard of living whether it produced for itself or purchased commodities with wages, the inefficient household would have less to lose from wage labor than a more efficient one that required only two or three hours to produce the same goods.

What, then, determines the degree of inefficiency of a household? For Lenin, efficiency was synonymous with modernization. He mocked the pretended efficiency of traditional producers. Yes, traditional producers could sometimes compete with modern industry, but only by lowering their standard of living to an abysmal level (Lenin 1898, 400, 419). The answer will depend, in part, on purely technical phenomena. Better seed, more careful application of work, and superior equipment will all improve the efficiency of a small peasant farm.

Primitive Accumulation or Capital Accumulation?

Lenin, like Marx, stressed the technical and economic forces that condemned traditional producers to extinction. Of course, a family's access to the means of production is not the result of technology alone. Karl Kautsky (1899, 24), whose work on agriculture won the enthusiastic praise of Lenin, demonstrated how political acts, such as cutting off the peasant's freedom to gather firewood or hunt game, increased the number of hours that a family would have to work to produce the same amount of use value.

Families could cope with the difficulties resulting from primitive accumulation by curtailing their standard of living. For example, the consumption of meat seems to have fallen with the pressures put on the traditional peasant economy (ibid., 30). More productive households could try to overcome their difficulties by bringing more produce to market (ibid., 16).

Two factors complicate this latter approach: many households do not possess enough capital to bring a sufficient amount to market; and, if all households were to follow this strategy, a glut of produce would follow, such as we described in the case of the corn burned for fuel. Alternatively, families could attempt to maintain their standard of living by earning wages. In any case, the logic of the market guides the process of differentiation. Some households, whose degree of efficiency was indistinguishable from those of their neighbors in earlier years, demonstrate an aptitude for earning profits. Others, who were not able to compete, lose their property to more successful producers. Thus the surviving operations could increase their production while employing the propertyless workers to labor on their expanded holdings.

Despite his interesting discussions of examples of primitive accumulation, Kautsky glossed over the importance of the initial pressures of this process. For the most part, he accepted that economies of scale and specialization alone cause the process of differentiation. At times, Kautsky's faith in the efficiency of market forces seemed unbounded. He even went so far as to praise the efficiency of the division between mental and manual labor (Kautsky 1899, 101). Lenin, too, put excessive trust in market forces, assuming that those peasants who prospered were technically superior.

Emmanuel LeRoy Ladurie, studying an earlier period, argues that a different sort of mechanism was also at play. He describes the activities of Guillaume Massenx, a successful French proprietor who was born about 1495. Here, we find the acquisition of land based on usury and the reduction of costs by withholding tithes, ostensibly as an act of solidarity with the Reformation (LeRoy Ladurie 1974, 127–28). Massenx's break with traditional behavior may or may not have been socially beneficial. Certainly, it was consistent with the accumulation of capital. Yet we get no indication that Massenx was necessarily more efficient in using the means of production in producing commodities—only that he was better able to profit from market conditions.

"Men of small beginnings," the later counterparts of Massenx, appear to have formed the core of the emergent capitalist class (Hammond and Hammond 1819, 2–3; see also Hilton 1978; Moore 1966, 9–11). Others, such as Massenx's neighbors who forfeited their property in default of their debts, formed the proletariat.

Smith looked on the energy and enterprise of such successful people with favor. Indeed, they contrasted sharply with the decadent nobility whom he despised. His emphasis on the role of "stock" paralleled Lenin's insistence that success was not the result of personal virtue; it was a consequence of the possession of capital (Lenin 1974).

For Lenin, the Russian victims of the indigenous Massenxes of his day would have no other way to turn but to the Communist Party. The faster the process proceeded, the sooner the messy work of revolution would be completed. Implicit in this analysis is the idea that exactions imposed by earlier economic formations furthered capitalist development (see Brenner 1977; Banaji 1977). As Lenin (1974, 199; see also Marx 1977, 875) observed, "Life creates forms that unite in themselves with remarkable gradualness systems of economy whose basic features constitute opposite."

Lenin's Partial Recantation of Smith

Obviously, Lenin would have taken exception to this characterization of his work as Smithian. Even today, at times, Smithian is used as a rather harsh pejorative among people on the Left. For example, Robert Brenner (1977) flings the accusation at such influential theorists as Andre Gunder Frank, Emmanuel Wallerstein, and even Paul Sweezy. Surprisingly, Brenner (1977, 76–77) then himself sounds a Smithian note by asserting that the "original pressure" for the breakdown of feudalism came from the increased demand for English cloth.

This use of the expression, "Smithian," reflects Smith's attempt to advocate capitalist society without acknowledging the existence of the means that were historically necessary to create it. That position was essential, not so much as a practical plan, but to build support for his ideological justification of capital. After all, by the time Smith was writing, British agricultural society had already been formed, for the most part, in conformity with the needs of capital. Thus, England appeared to be well ordered.

In contrast, parts of Scotland still remained inadequately integrated into a more general social division of labor. Even so, for Smith, the standard of living of the Highlanders seemed to be low enough that they, too, could soon be absorbed into the social labor process through the workings of the marketplace. Thus, artificially created poverty did not appear to be necessary.

Smith's nemesis, Steuart, was less concerned with ideology. For him, too much work remained undone. The world still stood in want of statesmen to carry out statesmen-like business, such as the clearing of the estates. The pace of Smithian development was too slow for him. Wakefield intended to develop this approach on a global scale. With Lenin, the outcome of the process would reach a much more advanced stage—world revolution.

Lenin, to his sorrow, soon learned the limits of his Smithian ideology. Although Smithianism may have been useful in his ideological struggle against the Narodniks, capitalism had not proceeded as far as he had thought.

Consequently, Lenin turned to the market to help create the appropriate social conditions to establish socialism. The New Economic Policy was a masterpiece of practical finesse that contained a goodly number of theoretical ironies. Market relations were to be marshaled to build socialist relations. Concessions to individual incentives were to become the road toward constructing a broader basis of cooperation (on this, see Bettelheim 1976).

At this time, Lenin's use of the market was more akin to Steuart than Smith. Smithian theories gave way to the statesman-like actions implicit in Steuart. Lenin came to the Steuart-like recognition that "our task is to organize commodity production" (Lenin 1921b, 95–96; cited in Bettelheim 1976, 484) and to "establish proper relations between" the working class and the peasantry (Lenin 1921a, 404).

Stalin and Mao

As Steuart had observed long ago, people had to glean before they could reap (see chapter 7). Accordingly, the Soviets constructed the New Economic Policy to foster growth within the peasant sector as a basis for future socialist development (Lenin 1921a, 355).

After Joseph Stalin took over the reigns of power, the imagery of Steuart continued to echo in the Party deliberations. Stalin (1928, 169) called for a shift in policy relative to "the bond between town and country, between the working class and the main mass of the peasantry." He emphasized the role of producers' goods delivered to the peasantry rather than the consumer goods, as Steuart had done. Accordingly, he recommended a "bond . . . based not only on textiles, but also metals" (ibid., 170).

Stalin's (ibid.) bond, unlike Steuart's, was intended "not to preserve classes but to abolish them." His program of collectivism, therefore, was ironically justified in terms of cementing the bond between the town and the country (Stalin 1929, 60–72). Ultimately, the Russian countryside was also cleared of many "superfluous mouths" (Steuart 1767, 1:58, 198).

Like the Soviets, Mao Tse-Tung expressed a desire to establish "relations of production and exchange in accordance with socialist principles." Accordingly, he continued, "more and more appropriate forms are being sought" (Mao 1956, 294). China, however, had learned much from the mistakes of the Stalin era, but not enough (see Mao 1955a, 221; 1956, 291).

Unlike Stalin, Mao believed that the proper arrangements could not be created by fiat. Fiat, unfortunately, can become habitual. Yet, Mao's successors, sounding like almost plagiarists of Steuart, proposed an almost entirely economic program to "link the interests of the state, collective, and individual directly so that every person in an enterprise takes it as a matter of his own *material interests* to be concerned about fulfilling the state plan and about what results the enterprise management achieves" (Hu Chiao-mu 1978, pt. 2, 21; emphasis added).

Mao (1955b, 260), in contrast, stressed the importance of "political work as the lifeblood of economic work." Mao, thus, stood for the substitution of the visible bond of politics for the invisible hand of Smith (see Wheelwright and McFarlane 1970, 122).

In this sense, Mao's vision may nonetheless properly be called Smithian. In spite of the best precautions, he recognized that "the spontaneous forces of capitalism have been steadily growing in the countryside" (Mao 1955a, 201). The antidote for these Smithian forces of reaction was a patient "Smithian" program of socialist development. Mao insisted that economic calculations be performed on a long-term basis (1945, 75; 1947, 124). He also shared Smith's idea of a largely rural, agriculturally led development that would eventually produce the highest possible level of industrialization. Like Smith, he favored agriculture (Mao 1956, 286).

The most crucial parallel between Smith and Mao concerns their attitudes toward people. Smith, shorn of his ideology, represented a statement of confidence in the abilities of the emergent capitalist class to bring about a progressive development of society. Mao's theoretical work, too, was a vigorous affirmation of the abilities of the great masses to lift society to heights previously unknown, if only they were allowed an appropriate environment in which their abilities could flourish.

Such sentiments accurately echoed Marx's vision. Indeed, Marx's socialism may be said to be the proper heir to the best of classical political economy in this regard.

The Case of W. Arthur Lewis

The categories of political economy, such as primitive accumulation, shape its vision; they also define its blind spots. To give a fairly recent instance, one of the great failures of modern development economics has been its long neglect of food production.

The tone for much of the current work in development economics was set by W. Arthur Lewis, beginning with his classic 1954 article, "Economic Development with Unlimited Supplies of Labour." Lewis declared himself to be in the tradition of classical political economy. Indeed, although Lewis's article was not entirely faithful to the letter of classical political economy (see Darity and Hurt 1981), it did reflect the spirit of that literature.

Lewis attempted to understand how the seemingly unlimited supply of nonwage labor could be tapped. He even rehabilitated the categories of productive and unproductive labor in arguing for the necessity of squeezing the peasant producers (Lewis 1958, 8).

Lewis was not entirely candid. Like the classical political economists, he noted that

> the wage level in the capitalist sector depends upon earnings in the subsistence sector. . . . This is one of the worst features of imperialism . . . ; it is to their [the imperialists'] advantage to keep wages low, and even in those cases where they do not actually go out of their way to impoverish the subsistence sector, they will at least very seldom do anything to make it more productive. In actual fact, the record of every imperial power in Africa in modern times is one of impoverishing the subsistence economy. (Lewis 1954, 149)

Lewis interpreted primitive accumulation to be an important feature of imperialism, especially in Africa, but it had nothing to do with the market. In fact, Lewis advocated a vision of economic development in which the subsistence sector would disappear as quickly as possible so that market forces could rescue people in the colonial lands.

In describing how owners of plantations forced workers off the lands, Lewis (ibid., 149) even appealed to the authority of Marx. Why, then, should the conflict between capitalists and those who engage in self-provisioning be limited to colonies? Was Lewis pointing to a racial or ethnic bias as the root cause of poverty in the colonies? He was silent in this regard.

Lewis saw no conflict between the goals of the classical political economists and the welfare of people in the subsistence sector. On the contrary, he counseled underdeveloped countries to follow the advice of classical political economy: increase savings and investment so that capitalist employers can hire the excess agricultural labor that leaves the countryside. The interests of capital and labor are apparently supposed to be united.

Classical political economy ostensibly took a similar position. With Smith, all evils are laid at the feet of mercantilist practice: capitalism was the source of salvation. Yet hidden within the works of classical political economy was the uncomfortable truth that capital would profit by attacking the ability of people to provide for themselves.

Thus, Lewis was true to the tradition of classical political economy in lauding laissez-faire theory without openly discussing the interventionist practices that accompanied it. Those who followed Lewis without fully understanding the classical policies fell into a grave error.

The classical economists were always mindful of the importance of food price policy. Lewis's followers, who listened only to his lectures on the beneficial effects of capital, ignored that aspect of classical political economy. The case of Lewis again shows that a proper reading of the classics may have significant practical implications. The effects of Lewis's policies have been disastrous for agriculture in the less developed countries.

Conclusion

The conclusions reached in this book should be obvious by now. First and foremost, this book was intended to show that primitive accumulation was a crucial force in the process of capitalist development—not just during a precapitalist past or even some imagined moment when feudal society suddenly became capitalist. Rather, primitive accumulation played a continuing role as part of capitalist development.

In addition, I attempted to demonstrate that primitive accumulation has been shown to be a theoretical category that is especially valuable in analyzing the accumulation of capital in general. The category of primitive accumulation is central to understanding the evolution of the social division of labor.

This book reveals that the classical political economists' purported adherence to the values of laissez-faire was thin indeed.

In fact, classical political economy and primitive accumulation are inextricably entwined. True, the seeds of capitalism had been planted long before the age of classical political economy, but never before and nowhere else had the process of capital accumulation been so intense. The classical political economists took a keen interest in promoting primitive accumulation as a means of fostering capitalist development, but then concealed that part of their vision in writing about economic theory. By calling attention to the role of primitive accumulation in classical political economy, this book points to the need to revise the traditional reading of classical political economy. Within this context, Adam Smith becomes less original. His significance emanates from his ideological vigor in advocating laissez-faire and his eventual success in obfuscating all information that might cast doubt on his ideology.

Others, such as Wakefield and Rae, took a substantially more realistic view about the nature of accumulation, although later economists cast their analysis aside to create the impression of a humanitarian heritage of political economy. Judging from the literature of the history of economic thought, this revision of history has succeeded mightily. *The Invention of Capitalism* represents a plea to correct this legacy of error and omission.

Rather than discuss these results in more detail here, or even summarize them once again, I would prefer to direct our attention to an unmentioned theme of this book that deserves further study. In calling for the acceleration of primitive accumulation, classical political economy displayed a keen sense of the underlying forces of capital accumulation. Given the social relations of production, the small-scale producer represented an unmistakable barrier to the advance of capital.

In fact, the classical political economists realized that self-provisioning did not have to be restricted on account of its failure, but rather because of its success. Even while the Industrial Revolution was proving its enormous potential, small-scale producers displayed a remarkable tenacity. True, in many cases, they held on only by lowering their standard of living, yet that factor was not always a primary cause of their ability to continue. Small-scale production has its own economies, its own efficiencies. In the long run, they may not be equal to those of modern, capital-intensive production, but where capital is scarce, such technologies are particularly competitive.

The lessons that can be drawn from the classical political economists' analysis of small-scale production may be especially useful for poor, emergent socialist states. Such societies may do well to adopt a transitional program that relies heavily on the potential of technologies similar to those used by the traditional household sector. Obviously, in working out this sort of program, classical political economy did not provide a blueprint, but, then, neither did Marx. Although classical political economy was originally written to aid capital in the exploitation of labor, it may, nonetheless, prove to be a crucial source of inspiration. Perhaps one of the by-products of this book will be to rekindle an interest in this aspect of classical political economy.

References

Abeille, Louis Paul. 1768. *Principles sur le liberte du commerce des grains.* Amsterdam: Desaint.

Achenwall, Gottfried. 1767. *Some observations on North America from oral Information by Dr. Franklin.* In vol. 13 of *The papers of Benjamin Franklin,* edited by Leonard W. Larabee and William B. Wilcox. New Haven, Conn.: Yale University Press, 1959–.

Adams, John. 1780. Letter to John Luzac, 15 September 1780. In vol. 7 of *The works of John Adams,* edited by Charles Frances Adams. Boston: Little, Brown, 1856.

——. 1819. Letter to William B. Richmond, 14 December 1819. In vol. 10 of *The works of John Adams,* edited by Charles Frances Adams. Boston: Little, Brown, 1856.

Adams, Thomas R. 1969. The British pamphlets of the American revolution for 1774: A progress report. *Proceedings of the Massachusetts Historical Society* 81:31–103.

——. 1971. The British look at America during the age of Samuel Johnson. Typescript: John Carter Brown Library, Providence, R.I.

Adler, Moshe. 1985. Stardom and talent. *American Economic Review* 75, no. 1 (March):208–12.

Aglietta, Michael. 1979. *A theory of capitalist exploitation: The U.S. experience.* Translated by David Fernbach. London: New Left Books.

Akhtar, M. A. 1979. An analytical outline of sir James Steuart's macroeconomic model. *Oxford Economic Papers* 31, no. 2 (July):283–302.

An alarm to the people of England. 1757. London: J. Scott. Kress-Goldsmith collection, reel 698, item 9215.

Aldrich, Robert. 1987. Late-comers or early-starter? New views on French economic history. *Journal of European Economic History* 16, no. 1 (September):89–100.

Allen, G. C. 1929. *The industrial development of Birmingham and the Black Country, 1860–1927.* London: George Allen and Unwin.

Althusser, Louis. 1970. From capital to Marx's philosophy. In *Reading capital,* edited by Louis Althusser and Etienne Balibar. London: New Left Books.

Alvord, Clarence Walworth. 1917. *The Mississippi valley in British politics: A study of the trade, land speculation, and experiments in imperialism culminating in the American revolution.* 2 vols. Cleveland, Ohio: Arthur H. Clark.

Ambirajan, S. 1977. *Classical political economy and British policy in India.* Cambridge, U.K.: Cambridge University Press.

American husbandry. 1775. Edited by H. J. Carmen. New York: Columbia University Press, 1939.

Ames, Fisher. 1854. *Works of Fisher Ames.* Edited by Seth Ames. Boston: Little, Brown.

Anderson, Gary M., William F. Shugart II, and Robert Tollison. 1985. Adam Smith in the customshouse. *Journal of Political Economy* 93, no. 4 (August):740–59.

Anderson, James. 1777a. *Observations on national industry.* New York: Augustus M. Kelley, 1968.

——. 1776. *An inquiry into the nature of the corn-laws.* Edinburgh.

Anikin, A. V. 1975. *A science in its youth: Pre-Marxian political economy.* New York: International Publishers.

Appleby, Joyce Oldham. 1976. Ideology and theory: The tension between economic liberalism in seventeenth-century England. *American Historical Review* 81, no. 3 (June):499–515.

——. 1978. *Economic thought and ideology in seventeenth-century England.* Princeton, N.J.: Princeton University Press.

Arbuthnot, John. 1773. *An enquiry into the connection between the present price of provisions and the size of farmers.* London: T. Cadell. In Kress-Goldsmith collection, reel 1024, item 10958.

Arnot, R. Page. 1955. *A history of the Scottish miners from earliest times.* London: George Allen and Unwin.

Arthur, W. Brian. 1989. Competing technologies, increasing returns, and lock-in by historical events. *Economic Journal* 99 (March):116–31.

Ashley, P. 1920. *Modern tariff history: Germany, United States, and France.* London: Murray.

Ashton, Thomas S. 1925. The records of a pin manufactory, 1814–1821. *Economica* 15 (November):281–92.

——. 1948. *The industrial revolution.* London: Oxford University Press.

——. 1972. *An economic history of England: The eighteenth century.* London: University Paperbacks.

Aspromourgos, Tony. 1986. Political economy and the social division of labour: The economics of Sir William Petty. *Scottish Journal of Political Economy* 33, no. 1 (February):28–45.

——. 1988. The life of William Petty in relation to his economics: A tercentenary interpretation. *History of Political Economy* 20, no. 3 (fall):337–56.

Athar, Hussain, and Keith Tribe. 1981. *Marxism and the agrarian question.* Vol. 1 of *German social democracy and the peasantry, 1890–1907.* Atlantic Highlands, N.J.: Humanities Press.

Atkins, P. J. 1977. London's intra-urban milk supply, circa 1790–1914. *Transactions of the Institute of British Geographers* 2, no. 3:383–99.

Auden, W. H., ed. 1956. Introduction to *Selected writings of Sydney Smith.* New York: Farrar, Straus and Cudahy.

Bagehot, Walter. 1880. *Economic studies in the works of Walter Bagehot.* Edited by Forrest Morgan. vol. 5. Hartford, Conn.: Travelers Insurance Company, 1889.

Bailey, Elizabeth E., and Ann F. Friedlander. 1982. Market structure and multiproduct industries. *Journal of Economic Literature* 20, no. 3 (September):1024–48.

Bailyn, Bernard. 1955. *The New England merchants in the seventeenth century.* New York: Harper and Row.

Baldwin, Carliss Y. 1983. Productivity and labor unions: An application of the theory of self-enforcing contracts. *Journal of Business* 56, no. 4 (April):155–85.

Balibar, Etienne. 1988. The notion of class politics in Marx. *Rethinking Marxism* 1, no. 2 (summer):18–51.

Balint, Michael. 1965. On love and hate. In *Primary love and psycho-analytic technique.* New York: Liveright Publishers.

Banaji, Jairus. 1977. Modes of production in a materialist conception of history. *Capital and Class,* no. 3 (autumn):1–44.

Bancroft, George. 1854. *History of the United States, from the discovery of the American continent.* 10 vols. Boston: Little, Brown.

Barber, William J. 1975. *British economic thought and India, 1600–1858: A study in the history of development economics.* Oxford: Clarendon Press.

Bardhan, Pranab K. 1973. Size, productivity, and returns to scale: Analysis of farm-level data in Indian agriculture. *Journal of Political Economy* 81, no. 3 (November–December):45–66.

——. 1979. Wages and unemployment in a poor agrarian economy: A theoretical and empirical analysis. *Journal of Political Economy* 87, no. 3 (June):479–507.

Barrios de Chungra, Domitila. 1979. Let me speak! *Monthly Review* 30, no. 9 (February):42–54.

Barton, John. 1817. Observations on the circumstances which influence the condition of the labouring classes in society. In vol. 2 of *Economic writings*, edited by Georges Sotiroff. Regina, Canada: Lynn.

——. 1833. In defense of the corn laws. In vol. 2 of *Economic writings*, edited by Georges Sotiroff. Regina, Canada: Lynn.

Baumol, William. 1976. Smith versus Marx on business morality and the social interest. *American Economist* 20, no. 2 (fall):1–6.

Beaglehole, John C. 1955–67. *The voyage of the endeavour, 1768–1771.* Vol. 1 of *The journals of Captain James Cook on his voyages of discovery.* Cambridge, U.K.: Cambridge University Press.

Bearington, F. 1975. The development of market gardening in Bedfordshire, 1799–1939. *Agricultural History Review* 23:23–47.

Becker, Gary S. 1965. A theory of the allocation of time. *Economic Journal* 75, no. 299 (September):493–517.

Beechy, Veronica. 1977. Some notes on female wage labour in capitalistic production. *Capital and Class,* no. 3 (fall):45–66.

Bell, John Fred. 1960. Adam Smith: Clubman. *Scottish Journal of Political Economy* 7, no. 2 (June):108–16.

Bellers, John. 1696. *Proposals for raising a college of industry, etc.* In *The life of Robert Owen,* by Robert Owen. London: Effingham Wilson, 1857.

——. 1714. *Essay towards the improvement of physick.* In *John Bellers, 1654–1725: Quaker, economist, and social reformer, his writings reprinted.* London: Cassell, 1935.

Benians, E. A. 1926. Adam Smith's project of an empire. *Cambridge Historical Journal* 1:249–83.

Benson, Lee. 1950. Achille Loria's influence on American economic thought. *Agricultural History* 24:182–99.

Bentham, Jeremy. 1787a. Letter to Dr. Smith. In *The correspondence of Adam Smith,* edited by Ernest Campbell Mossner and Ian Simpson Ross. Oxford: Clarendon Press, 1977.

——. 1787b. Defence of usury. In *Jeremy Bentham's economic writings,* edited by Werner Stark. 3 vols. London: George Allen and Unwin, 1952.

——. 1790. Letter to Dr. Smith. In *The correspondence of Adam Smith,* edited by Ernest Campbell Mossner and Ian Simpson Ross. Oxford: Clarendon Press, 1977.

——. 1797. *Panopticon, or the inspection house.* In vol. 4 of *The works of Jeremy Bentham,* edited by John Bowring. New York: Russell and Russell, 1962.

——. 1822. *Analysis of the influence of natural religion on the temporal happiness of mankind.* Reprint, The psychology of economic man. In *Jeremy Bentham's economic writings,* edited by Werner Stark. 3 vols. London: George Allen and Unwin, 1952.

——. 1830–31. *History of the war between Jeremy Bentham and George the third, by one of the belligerents: Extracted as selections from Bentham's narrative regarding the panopticon penitentiary project and from the correspondence on the subject.* In vol. 11 of *The works of Jeremy Bentham,* edited by John Bowring. New York: Russell and Russell, 1962.

——. 1952. *Jeremy Bentham's economic writings.* Edited by Werner Stark. 3 vols. London: George Allen and Unwin.

374

——. 1954. The psychology of economic man: Extracts arranged by Werner Stark." In vol. 3 of *Jeremy Bentham's economic writings*, edited by Werner Stark. London: George Allen and Unwin, 1952.

——. 1962. *Constitutional code*. Vol. 9 of *The works of Jeremy Bentham*, edited by John Bowring. New York: Russell and Russell, 1962.

——. n.d. *Outline of a work entitled pauper management*. In vol. 8 of *The works of Jeremy Bentham*, edited by John Bowring. New York: Russell and Russell, 1962.

Berg, Maxine. 1980a. *The machinery question and the making of political economy, 1815–1848*. Cambridge, U.K.: Cambridge University Press.

——. 1980b. Proto-industry, political economy, and the division of labour, 1700–1800. Coventry: University of Warwick, Department of Economics.

——. 1986. *The age of manufactures: Industry, innovation, and work in Britain, 1700–1820*. Oxford: Oxford University Press.

Berger, Peter. 1963. *Invitation to sociology: A humanistic perspective*. Garden City, N.Y.: Doubleday.

Bergue, Augustin. 1976. Alternance agricole et urbanisation au Japon. Paper read at the Symposium on Urban Growth in France and Japan. 30 September, Tokyo.

Berkeley, George. 1740. *The querist*. In vol. 4 of *Complete works*, edited by A. C. Fraser. Oxford: Clarendon Press, 1901.

Bettelheim, Charles. 1976. *Class struggles in the U.S.S.R.: First period, 1917–1923*. New York: Monthly Review Press.

Bidwell, Percy Wells. 1916. Rural economy in New England. *Transactions of the Connecticut Academy of Arts and Sciences* 20:251–76.

Bidwell, Percy Wells, and John I. Falconer. 1941. *A history of agriculture in the northern United States, 1620–1860*. New York: Peter Smith.

Billingsly, John. 1798. Uselessness of commons to the poor. *Annals of Agriculture* 31.

Bishton, J. 1794. *General view of the agriculture of Salop with observations for its improvement*. Brentwood: P. Norbury.

Black, R. D. Collison. 1960. *Economic thought and the Irish question, 1817–1870*. Cambridge, U.K.: Cambridge University Press.

Black, R. D. Collison, and Rosamund Koenigkamp. 1972. Biographical introduction to *Biography and personal journal*, by William Stanley Jevons. Vol. 1 of *Papers and correspondence*. London: Macmillan.

Blackstone, William. 1775. *Commentaries on the laws of England*. 6th ed. 4 vols. Dublin: Company of Booksellers.

Bogart, Ernest Ludlow, and Charles Manfred Thompson. 1927. *Readings in the economic history of the United States*. New York: Longmans, Green.

Böhm-Bawerk, Eugen von. 1959. *Capital and interest*. 3 vols. South Holland, Ill.: Libertarian Press.

Bonwick, Colin. 1977. *English radicals and the American revolution*. Chapel Hill: University of North Carolina Press.

Boserup, Ester. 1965. *The conditions of agricultural growth: The economics of agrarian change under population pressure*. Chicago: Aldine.

Boswell, James. 1799. *Boswell's life of Johnson*. Edited by George Birkbeck Hill. 6 vols. Oxford: Oxford University Press, 1971.

Bowring, John, ed. 1962. *The works of Jeremy Bentham*. 11 vols. New York: Russell and Russell.

Bowsher, Norman N. 1980. The demand for currency: Is the underground economy undermining monetary policy? *Monthly Review of the Federal Reserve Bank of Kansas City* 62, no. 1 (January).

Boylan, Thomas A., and Timothy P. Foley. 1992. *Political economy and colonial Ireland: The propagation and ideological function of economic discourse in the nineteenth century.* London: Routledge.

Branson, Roy. 1979. James Madison and the Scottish enlightenment. *Journal of the History of Ideas* 40, no. 2 (April–June):235–50.

Braverman, Harry. 1974. *Labor and monopoly capital: The degradation of work in the twentieth century.* New York: Monthly Review Press.

Bray, Charles. 1841. *The philosophy of necessity.* 2 vols. London: Longman, Orme, and Green.

Brenner, Robert. 1977. Origins of capitalist development: A critique of neo-Smithian marxism. *New Left Review,* no. 104 (July–August):25–92.

Brief, Richard P. 1965. Nineteenth century accounting error. *Journal of Accounting Research* 3, no. 1 (spring):12–31.

Brockway, Lucille. 1979. *Science and colonial expansion: The role of the British royal botanic gardens.* New York: Academic Press.

Broderick, George C. 1881. *English lands and English landlords.* London: Cassell Petter, Galpin and Co.

Buecher, Karl. Hausindustrie aus dem Weihnachtsmarkt. In vol. 2 of *Die Entstehung der Volkswirtschaft.* Tübingen, 1893.

Bukharin, Nikolay, and E. Preobrazhenski. 1922. *The ABC of communism: A popular explanation of the program of the communist party of Russia.* Ann Arbor: University of Michigan Press, 1966.

Burke, Edmund. 1759. Review of *The Theory of Moral Sentiments.* In *Annual Register.* 6th ed. London: J. Dodsley, 1777.

Burns, Scott. 1976. *Household, inc.* New York: Doubleday.

———. 1979. What self-reliance is worth. *Organic Gardening* (May):86–92.

Byington, Margaret. 1910. *Homestead: Households of a milltown.* New York: Arno Press, 1969.

Cairncross, Alexander R. 1958. Economic schizophrenia. *Scottish Journal of Political Economy* 5, no. 1 (February):15–21.

Campbell, Robert. 1953. Sir James Steuart: A study in the development of economic thought. Ph.D. diss., University of California, Berkeley.

Campbell, T. D., and I. S. Ross. 1981. The utilitarianism of Adam Smith's policy advice. *Journal of the History of Ideas* 42, no. 1 (January–March):73–92.

Cannan, Edwin. 1929. *A review of economic theory.* London: P. S. King and Sons.

Cantillon, Richard. 1755. *Essai sur la nature du commerce en general.* Edited by Henry Higgs. New York: Augustus M. Kelley, 1964.

Carey, Lewis J. 1928. *Franklin's economic views.* Garden City, N.Y.: Doubleday, Doran and Co.

Carrier, Lyman. 1918. *American Husbandry,* a much overlooked publication. In *American husbandry,* edited by H. J. Carman. New York: Columbia University Press, 19xx.

Carter, Ian. 1980. The Highlands of Scotland as an underdeveloped region. In *The rural sociology of the advanced societies: Critical perspectives,* edited by Frederick H. Buttel and Howard Newby. Montclair, N.J.: Allanheld and Osmun.

[Chalmers, George.] 1805. Anecdotes of the life of sir James Steuart. In *The works: Political, metaphysical, and chronological,* Sir James Steuart. New York: Augustus M. Kelley, 1967.

Chambers, J. D., and G. E. Mingay. 1966. *The agricultural revolution, 1750–1880.* New York: Schocken Books.

Chamley, Paul. 1965. *Documents Relatifs a sir James Steuart.* Paris: Librairie Dalloz.

Chandler, Alfred C. 1977. *The visible hand: The managerial revolution in American business.* Cambridge, Mass.: Harvard University Press.

Chatfield, Michael. 1977. *A history of accounting thought.* Huntington, N.Y.: Robert E. Krieger.

Chayanov, A. V. 1966. *The theory of peasant economy.* Edited by Daniel Thorner, Basil Kerblay, and R. E. F. Smith. Homewood, Ill.: Richard D. Irwin.

Child, Josiah. 1751. *A new discourse of trade,* 5th ed. Glasgow: Robert and Andrew Foulis.

Chinn, Dennis L. 1979. Rural poverty and the structure of farm household income in developing countries: Evidence from Taiwan. *Economic Development and Cultural Change* 27, no. 2 (January):283–301.

Chitty, J. 1812. *A treatise on the game laws and on fisheries.* 2 vols. London: W. Clarke and Sons.

Clarke, Richard N., and Lawrence H. Summers. 1980. The labour scarcity controversy reconsidered. *Economic Journal* 90, no. 357 (March):129–39.

Coats, A. W. 1958. Changing attitudes toward labour in the mid-eighteenth century. *Economic History Review* 11:35–51.

———. 1962. Adam Smith: The modern appraisal. *Renaissance and Modern Studies* 6:26–48.

———. 1971. The classical economists and the labourer. In *The classical economists and economic policy.* London: Methuen.

Cobbett, William. 1806–20. *The parliamentary history of England.* 36 vols. New York: Johnson Reprint Co., 1966.

———. 1830. *Rural rides.* 2 vols. London: J. M. Dent.

———. 1831. *Cobbett's two-penny trash-politics for the poor.* 2 vols. London.

Cole, Arthur Harrison, ed. 1968. *Industrial and commercial correspondence of Alexander Hamilton, anticipating his report on manufactures.* New York: Augustus M. Kelley.

Coleman, D. C. 1988. Adam Smith, businessmen, and the mercantile system in England. *History of European Ideas* 9, no. 2:161–70.

Colletti, Lucio. 1979. *Marxism and Hegel.* Translated by Lawrence Garner. London: Verso.

Collier, Frances. 1930. An early factory community. *Economic Journal* 2 (supplement):117–24.

Collins, E. J. T. 1969. Harvest technology and labour supply in Britain, 1790–1870. *Economic History Review* 32, no. 3 (December):453–73.

The colonial policy of Great Britain, by a British traveller (Philadelphia). 1816. In *Readings in the economic and social history of the United States,* edited by Felix Flugel and Harold U. Faulkner. New York: Harper and Brothers, 1929.

Colquhoun, Patrick. 1815. *Treatise on the wealth, power, and resources of the British empire.* London: Joseph Nawman; New York: Johnson Reprint, 1965.

Comito, Terry. 1971. Renaissance gardens and the discovery of paradise. *Journal of the History of Ideas* 32, no. 4 (October–December):483–506.

Conner, Paul W. 1965. *Poor Richard's politicks: Benjamin Franklin and his new American order.* New York: Oxford University Press.

Considerations on the game law. 1772. Edinburgh. Kress-Goldsmith collection, reel 1010, item 10847.

Conway, Stephen, ed. 1988. *January 1809 to December 1816.* Vol. 8 of *The correspondence of Jeremy Bentham.* Oxford: Clarendon Press.

Cooke, Jacob E. 1967. The reports of Alexander Hamilton. In *Alexander Hamilton: A profile,* edited by Jacob E. Cooke. New York: Hill and Wang.

Cooper, Thomas. 1830. *Lectures on the elements of political economy.* New York: Augustus M. Kelley, 1971.

———. 1833. *A manual of political economy.* Washington, D.C.: Duff Green.

Cornelius, Wayne A. 1979. Migration to the United States: The view from rural Mexican communities. *Development Digest* 17, no. 4 (October):90–101.

Cowherd, Raymond G. 1977. *Political economists and the English poor laws: A historical study of the influence of classical economics on the formation of social welfare policy.* Athens: Ohio University Press.

Coxe, Tench. 1794. *A view of the United States of America.* New York: Augustus M. Kelley, 1964.

Cranston, Maurice. 1957. *John Locke: A biography.* New York: Macmillan.

Cressey, Peter, and John MacInnes. 1980. Voting for Ford: Industrial democracy and the control of labour. *Capital and Class* 11, no. 2 (summer):5–33.

Crouzet, F., ed. 1972. Introduction to *Capital formation in the industrial revolution.* London: Methuen.

Cunliffe, Marcus. 1979. *Chattel slavery and wage slavery: The Anglo-American context, Mercer University Lamar memorial lectures,* no. 22. Athens: University of Georgia Press.

Currey, Cecil B. 1965. *Road to revolution: Benjamin Franklin in England, 1765–1775.* Garden City, N.Y.: Doubleday.

———. 1972. *Code number 72. Ben Franklin: Patriot or spy?* Englewood Cliffs, N.J.: Prentice-Hall.

Danhof, Clarence. 1941. Farm making costs and the "safety valve." *Journal of Political Economy* 49, no. 3 (June):217–59.

Darity, William A., Jr., and Keith Hurt. 1981. The origins of the doctrine of unlimited supplies of labor. Paper presented at the annual meeting of the History of Economics Society, June 1981, East Lansing, Mich.

Daunton, Martin J. 1995. *Progress and poverty: An economic and social history of Britain, 1700–1850.* Oxford: Oxford University Press.

David, Paul A. 1975. *Technical choice and innovation in economic growth: Essays on American and British experience in the nineteenth century.* Cambridge, U.K.: Cambridge University Press.

Davies, D. 1796. *The case of the labourers in husbandry.* Dublin. In Kress-Goldsmith collection, reel 1855, item 16797.

Davis, David Brian. 1966. *The problem of slavery in western culture.* Ithaca, N.Y.: Cornell University Press.

Davis, John. 1803. *Travels of four and a half years in the United States of America; during 1798, 1799, 1800, 1801, and 1802.* New York: H. Caritat; reprinted privately, 2 vols. Boston: Bibliophile Society, 1910.

Deane, Phyllis. 1957. The industrial revolution and economic growth: The evidence of early British national income estimates. *Economic Development and Cultural Change* 5, no. 1; reprinted in *The causes of the industrial revolution in England,* edited by R. M. Hartwell. London: Methuen, 1967.

Deane, Phyllis, and W. A. Coale. 1967. *British economic growth, 1688–1959.* 2d ed. Cambridge, U.K.: Cambridge University Press.

de Canio, Stephen, and Joel Mokyr. 1977. Inflation and the wage lag during the civil war. *Explorations in Economic History* 14, no. 2 (October):311–36.

de Crèvecoeur, J. Hector St. John. 1782. *Letters from an American farmer.* New York: Dutton, 1972.

de Crisenoy. 1979. Capitalism and agriculture. *Economy and Society* 8, no. 1 (February): 9–25.

Deere, Carmen Diana. 1976. Rural women's subsistence production in the capitalist periphery. *Review of Radical Political Economy* 8, no. 1 (spring):9–17.

Deere, Carmen Diana, and Alain de Janvry. 1979. A conceptual framework for the empirical analysis of peasants. *American Journal of Agricultural Economics* 61, no. 4 (November):601–11.

Defoe, Daniel. 1724–26. *A tour through the whole island of Great Britain.* Baltimore, Md.: Penguin, 1971.

Dempsey, Bernard. 1960. *The frontier wage.* Chicago: Loyola University Press.

Devine, T. M. 1976. The colonial trades and industrial investment in Scotland, c. 1700–1815. *Economic History Review* 29, no. 1 (February):1–14.

De Vivo, Giancarlo. 1985. Robert Torrens and Ricardo's "corn ratio" theory of profits. *Cambridge Journal of Economics* 9, no. 1 (March):89–92.

Diamond, Daniel E., and John D. Guilfoil. 1973. *United States economic history.* Morristown, N.J.: General Learning Press.

Dickey, Laurence. 1987. *Hegel: Religion, economics, and the politics of spirit, 1770–1807.* Cambridge, U.K.: Cambridge University Press.

Diener, R. A. V. 1991. Cultural dissolution: A societal information disaster; The case of the Yir Yoront in Australia. In *Great information disasters: Twelve prime examples of how information mismanagement led to human misery, political misfortune, and business failure,* edited by F. W. Horton and D. Lewis. London: Aslib.

Dillard, Dudley. 1967. *Economic development of the North Atlantic community.* Englewood Cliffs, N.J.: Prentice-Hall.

Dobb, Maurice. 1963. *Studies in the development of capitalism.* New York: International Publishers.

Dockes, P. 1969. *L'espace dan la pensee economique du XVIeme siecle.* Paris: Flammarion.

Domar, Evsey. 1970. The causes of slavery or serfdom. *Journal of Economic History* 30, no. 1 (March):18–32.

Dorfman, Joseph. 1966a. *The economic mind in American civilization, 1606–1865.* 2 vols. New York: Augustus M. Kelley.

———. 1966b. "Piercy Ravenstone" and his radical tory treatise. In *A few doubts as to the correctness of some opinions generally entertained on the subjects of population and political economy,* edited by Joseph Dorfman. New York: Augustus M. Kelley, 1966.

Doyle, Sir Francis Hastings. 1886. *Reminiscences and opinions of Sir Francis Hastings Doyle.* New York.

Draper, Hal. 1978. *The politics of social classes.* Vol. 2 of *Karl Marx's theory of revolution.* New York: Monthly Review Press.

Duckham, Baron F. 1969. Serfdom in eighteenth-century Scotland. *History* 54, no. 181 (June):178–97.

Dudden, Arthur Power. 1971. *Joseph Fels and the single tax movement.* Philadelphia: Temple University Press.

Dyos, Harold J., and Michael Wolff. 1973. The way we live now. In *The Victorian city: Images and reality,* edited by Harold J. Dyos and Michael Wolff. vol. 2. London: Routledge and Kegan Paul.

Earle, Carville, and Ronald Hoffman. 1980. The foundation of the modern economy: Agriculture and the costs of labor in the United States and England, 1800–1860. *American Historical Review* (December):1055–94.

Edmonds, Thomas Rowe. 1833. *Practical, moral, and political economy.* New York: Augustus M. Kelley, 1969.

Edwards, Edward. 1827. On agriculture and rent. *Quarterly Review* 36, no. 51:391–409.

Eiselen, Malcolm R. 1928. *Franklin's political theories.* Garden City, N.Y.: Doubleday, Doran and Co.

Eisner, Robert. 1979. Total income, total investment, and growth. Paper presented at the annual meeting of the American Economic Association, 29 December.

———. 1988. Extended accounts for national income and product. *Journal of Economic Literature* 26, no. 4 (December):1161–84.

Emerson, Ralph Waldo. 1940. Ode inscribed to W. H. Channing. In *The selected works of Ralph Waldo Emerson,* edited by Brooks Atkinson. New York: Modern Library.

Engels, Friedrich. 1845. The condition of the working class in England in 1844. In *Marx and Engels, 1844–1845.* Vol. 4 of *Collected works,* Karl Marx and Frederick Engels. New York: International Publishers, 1975.

———. 1847. "The agrarian programme of the chartists." In *Northern Star* (6 November); reprinted in vol. 6 of *Collected Works,* Karl Marx and Friedrich Engels. New York: International Publishers, 1975.

———. 1881. The peasant question in France and Germany. In vol. 3 of *Selected works in three volumes,* Karl Marx and Frederick Engels. Moscow: Progress Publishers, 1969–1973.

———. 1887. The housing question. In vol. 2 of *Selected works in three volumes,* Karl Marx and Frederick Engels. Moscow: Progress Publishers, 1969–1973.

———. 1891. The origin of the family, private property, and the state. In vol. 3 of *Selected works in three volumes,* Karl Marx and Friedrich Engels. Moscow: Progress Publishers, 1969–1973.

———. 1894. *Anti-Dühring: Herr Eugen Dühring's revolution in science.* Moscow: Progress Publishers, 1969.

———. 1954. *Dialectics of nature.* Moscow: Foreign Languages Publishing House.

Ensor, George. 1818. *Inquiry concerning the population of nations.* New York: Augustus M. Kelley, 1967.

Escher, Hans Caspar. 1814. Letters from England. In *Britain under the regency: The diaries of Escher, Bodmer, May, and Gallois, 1814–1818,* edited by W. O. Henderson. New York: Augustus M. Kelley, 1968.

Everitt, Alan. 1967. Farm labourers. In *1500–1640.* Vol. 4 of *The agrarian history of England and Wales,* edited by Joan Thirsk. Cambridge, U.K.: Cambridge University Press.

Ewen, Stuart. 1976. *Captains of consciousness: Advertising and the social roots of consumer culture.* New York: McGraw-Hill.

Fage, Anita. 1952. La vie et l'oevrre de Richard Cantillon, 1697–1734. In *Richard Cantillon: Essai du commerce en general.* Paris: Institut National d'Etudes Demographiques, 1952.

Fay, C. R. 1932. *The corn laws and social England.* Cambridge, U.K.: Cambridge University Press.

———. 1956. *Adam Smith and the Scotland of his day.* Cambridge, U.K.: Cambridge University Press.

Fetter, Frank Whitson. 1943. The early history of political economy in the United States. *Proceedings of the American Philosophical Society,* 87. Reprinted in *Economic thought: A historical anthology,* edited by James A. Gherity. New York: Random House, 1965.

———. 1953. The authorship of articles in the *Edinburgh Review,* 1807–1847. *Journal of Political Economy* 61, no. 3 (June):232–59.

———. 1957. Introduction to *The economic writings of Francis Horner in the "Edinburgh Review,"* edited by Frank Whitson Fetter. New York: Kelley and Milman.

——. 1980. *The economist in parliament, 1780–1868.* Durham, N.C.: Duke University Press.

Field, Alexander. 1978. Sectoral shift in antebellum Massachusetts. *Explorations in Economic History* 15, no. 2 (April):146–71.

Finch, G., ninth earl of Winchilsea and fourth earl of Nottingham. 1796. *Letter to the president of the board of agriculture on the advantages of cottagers renting land.* In Kress-Goldsmith collection, reel 1581, item 16622.

Fite, Gilbert C., and Jim E. Reese. 1965. *An economic history of the United States.* 2d ed. Boston: Houghton Mifflin.

Fleisig, Heywood. 1976. Slavery, the supply of agricultural labor, and the industrialization of the South. *Journal of Economic History* 36, no. 3 (September):572–97.

Flink, James J. 1975. *The car culture.* Cambridge, Mass.: MIT Press.

Fogel, Robert William, and Stanley Engerman. 1974. *Time on the cross: The economics of American negro slavery.* Boston: Little-Brown.

Folbre, Nancy. 1980. Patriarchy in colonial New England. *Review of Radical Political Economy* 12, no. 2 (summer):4–13.

Foner, Eric. 1970. *Free soil, free labor, free men: The ideology of the republican party before the civil war.* New York: Oxford University Press.

Foner, Philip S. 1975. *From colonial times to the founding of the American federation of labor.* Vol. 1 of *History of the labor movement in the United States.* New York: International Publishers.

Forster, Nathaniel. 1767. *An inquiry into the causes of the present high price of provisions.* London: J. Fletcher. In Kress-Goldsmith collection, reel 887, item 10309.

Foster-Carter, Aidan. 1978. Can we articulate "articulation"? In *The new economic anthropology,* edited by John Clammer. New York: St. Martin's Press.

Foucault, Michel. 1965. *Madness and civilization: A history of insanity in the age of reason.* New York: Harper Torchback.

——. 1979. *Discipline and punish: The birth of the prison.* New York: Vintage.

Fox-Genovese, Elizabeth. 1976. *The origins of physiocracy: Economic revolution and social order in eighteenth-century France.* Ithaca, N.Y.: Cornell University Press.

Fraginals, Manuel Moreno. 1978. *El Ingenio.* 3 vols. Havana: Editorial de Ciencias Sociales.

Frank, Andre Gunder. 1975. *On capitalist underdevelopment.* Bombay: Oxford University Press.

——. 1978. *World accumulation, 1492–1789.* New York: Monthly Review Press.

Franklin, Benjamin. 1782. *Information for those who would remove to America.* In vol. 8 of *The writings of Benjamin Franklin,* edited by Albert Henry Smyth. New York: Macmillan, 1905–1907.

——. 1783. Reflections on the augmentation of wages which will be occasioned in Europe by the American revolution. In vol. 2 of *The works of Benjamin Franklin,* edited by Jared Sparks. Boston: Hilliard Gray.

——. 1905–7. *The writings of Benjamin Franklin.* Edited by Albert Henry Smyth. 10 vols. New York: Macmillan.

——. 1959–. *The papers of Benjamin Franklin.* Edited by Leonard W. Larabee and William B. Wilcox. New Haven, Conn.: Yale University Press.

——. 1964. *The autobiography of Benjamin Franklin.* New Haven, Conn.: Yale University Press.

Freudenberger, H., and G. Cummins. 1976. Health, work, and leisure before the industrial revolution. *Explorations in Economic History* 13, no. 1 (January):1–12.

Friedman, Milton. 1962. *Capitalism and freedom.* Chicago: University of Chicago Press.

Furniss, Edgar. 1965. *The position of the laborer in a system of nationalism.* New York: Augustus M. Kelley.

Garnett, R. G. 1971. Robert Owen and community experiments. In *Robert Owen, prophet of the poor: Essays in honour of the two-hundredth anniversary of his birth,* edited by Sidney Pollard and John Salt. Lewisburg, Pa.: Bucknell University Press.

Gates, Paul. 1960. *The farmers' age: Agriculture, 1815–1860.* New York: Harper and Row.

George, M. Dorothy. 1953. *England in transition.* Baltimore, Md.: Penguin Books.

——. 1964. *London life in the eighteenth century.* New York: Harper and Row.

Georgescu-Roegen, Nicholas. 1971. *The entropy law and economic process.* Cambridge, Mass.: Harvard University Press.

Gerschenkron, Alexander. 1962. Economic backwardness in historical perspective. In *Historical perspective: A book of essays.* Cambridge, Mass.: Harvard University Press.

Gherity, James A. 1993. An early publication by Adam Smith. *History of Political Economy* 25, no. 2 (spring):240–82.

Gideon, Siegfried. 1948. *Mechanization takes command.* New York: Oxford University Press.

Gilbert, Geoffrey. 1980. Economic growth and the poor in Malthus' essay on population. *History of Political Economy* 12, no. 1 (spring 1980):83–96.

Gilder, George. 1981. *Wealth and poverty.* New York: Basic Books.

Goodrich, Carter, and Sol Davison. 1935. The wage earner in the westward movement, part 1. *Political Science Quarterly* 50, no. 2 (June):161–85.

Goodwin, Craufurd D. W. 1961. *Canadian economic thought: The political economy of a developing nation, 1814–1914.* Durham, N.C.: Duke University Press.

Gordon, Barry. 1976. *Political economy in parliament, 1819–1823.* New York: Barnes and Noble.

Gorky, Maxim. 1922. On the Russian peasantry. In *Peasants and peasant societies: Selected writings,* edited by Teodor Shanin. Baltimore, Md.: Penguin Books.

Gorz, Andre. 1968. *Strategy for labor.* Boston: Beacon Press.

Gould, Stephen J. 1988. Pussycats and the owl. *New York Review of Books* 35, no. 3 (3 March): 7–10.

Gourlay, Robert Fleming. 1822. *General introduction to statistical account of upper Canada.* London: Simpkin and Marshall; New York: Johnson Reprint, 1966.

Gourne, Edward G. 1894. Alexander Hamilton and Adam Smith. *Quarterly Journal of Economics* 7, no. 2 (April):328–44.

Graham, H. Grey. 1937. *The social life of Scotland in the eighteenth century.* London: A. C. Black.

Grampp, William. 1960. *The Manchester school of economics.* Stanford, Calif.: Stanford University Press.

——. 1965. *Economic liberalism.* 2 vols. New York: Random House.

——. 1974. Malthus and his contemporaries. *History of Political Economy* 6, no. 3 (fall):278–304.

——. 1979. Adam Smith and the American revolutionists. *History of Political Economy* 11, no. 2 (summer):179–91.

Gray, Malcolm. 1951. The kelp industry in the Highlands and islands. *Economic History Review* 4, no. 2 (May):197–209.

Great Britain. 1840. *Reports from the assistant handloom weavers' commissioners on the West Riding and Ireland.* Vol. 23 of *Parliamentary papers.*

Greer, Edward. 1979. *Big steel: Black politics and corporate power in Gary, Indiana.* New York: Monthly Review Press.

Grigg, D. B. 1974. *The agricultural systems of the world: An evolutionary approach.* Cambridge, U.K.: Cambridge University Press.

Groenewegen, Peter D. 1969. Turgot and Adam Smith. *Scottish Journal of Political Economy* 16, no. 3 (November):271–87.

Guest, R. 1823. *A compendius history of the cotton manufacture.* Manchester, U.K.: Joseph Pratt.

Habakkuk, H. J. 1967. *American and British technology in the nineteenth century: The search for labour-saving inventions.* Cambridge, U.K.: Cambridge University Press.

Hagen, Everett E. 1980. *The economics of development.* 3rd ed. Homewood, Ill.: Richard D. Irwin.

Hale, E. E., and E. E. Hale Jr. 1887–88. *Franklin in France.* 2 vols. Boston: Roberts Bros.

Halevy, Elie. 1956. *Thomas Hodgskin.* London: Benn.

———. 1961. *A history of the English people in the nineteenth century.* Vol. 2 of *The liberal awakening, 1815–1830.* New York: Barnes and Noble.

Hall, Charles. 1805. *The effects of civilization on the people in European states.* New York: Augustus M. Kelley, 1965.

Hall, Robert E., and Charles I. Jones. 1997. Levels of economic activity across countries. *American Economic Review* 87, no. 2 (May):173–77.

Halsband, Robert. 1956. *The life of Lady Mary Wortley Montagu.* Oxford: Clarendon Press.

Hamilton, Alexander. 1961. *The papers of Alexander Hamilton.* Edited by Harold C. Syrett. New York: Columbia University Press.

Hamilton, James C. 1879. *Life of Alexander Hamilton: A history of the republic of the United States of America.* 2 vols. Boston.

Hammond, J. L., and Barbara Hammond. 1919. *The skilled labourer, 1760–1832.* New York: Harper and Row, 1970.

———. 1927. *The village labourer, 1760–1832.* London: Longmans, Green, and Co.

Hansard's Parliamentary History. 1830. 3d ed. Vol. 1. (26 October–30 December).

Hariot, Thomas. 1588. *A briefe and true report of the new found land of Virginia.* In *The Roanoke voyages, 1584–1590,* edited by David Beers Quinn. 2 vols. London: Hakluyt Society.

Harris, Donald. 1988. The circuit of capital and the "labour problem" in capitalist development. *Social and Economic Studies* 37, nos. 1–2 (March–June):15–31.

Harris, Marshall. 1953. *Origin of the land tenure system in the United States.* Ames: Iowa State University Press.

Hartmann, Heidi. 1976. Women's work in the United States. *Current History* 70, no. 416 (May):215–19.

Hartwell, Ronald Max. 1978. Adam Smith and the industrial revolution. In *Adam Smith and the wealth of nations, 1776–1976,* edited by Fred R. Glahe. Boulder: Colorado Associated University Press.

Harvey, David. 1976. Labor, capital, and class struggle around the built environment in advanced capitalist societies. *Politics and Society* 6, no. 3:265–97.

Hayek, Friedrich A. von. 1932. *Prices and production.* New York: Macmillan.

———. 1945. The use of knowledge in society. *American Economic Review* 35, no. 4 (September):519–30.

———. 1948. *Individualism and economic order.* Chicago: University of Chicago Press.

———. 1959. *The counter-revolution of science: Studies in the abuse of reason.* Indianapolis, Ind.: Liberty Press.

Hegel, Georg Wilhelm Friedrich. 1821–22. *Lectures on the philosophy of world history.* Cambridge, U.K.: Cambridge University Press.

Helper, Hinton. 1860. *The impending crisis of the south: How to meet it.* New York: A. B. Burdick.

Henneau-Depooter, Louis. 1959. *Miseres et luttes sociales de Jans le Haunaut, 1860–1890.* Brussels: Universite libre de Bruxelles.

Herrick, Chessman A. 1926. *White servitude in Pennsylvania: Indentured and redemption labor in colony and commonwealth.* Freeport, N.Y.: Books for Libraries Press, 1970.

Higgs, Henry. 1931. The life and work of Richard Cantillon. In *Essai sur la nature du commerce en general,* edited by Henry Higgs. New York: Augustus M. Kelley, 1964.

Hill, Christopher. 1964. *Puritanism and revolution: The English revolution of the seventeenth century.* New York: Schocken Books.

——. 1967. *Society and Puritanism.* New York: Schocken Books.

Hilton, Boyd. 1977. *Corn, cash, commerce: The economic policies of the tory governments, 1815–1830.* New York: Oxford University Press.

Hilton, Rodney. 1978. Reasons for inequality among medieval peasants. *Journal of Peasant Studies* 5, no. 3 (April):271–84.

Himmelfarb, Gertrude. 1985. *The idea of poverty: England in the early industrial age.* New York: Vintage Books.

Hobbes, Thomas. 1651. *Leviathan.* Baltimore, Md.: Penguin, 1968.

Hobsbawm, Eric J. 1974. Custom wages and workload in nineteenth-century industry. In *Workers in the industrial revolution,* edited by Peter N. Stearns and Daniel J. Walkowitz. New Brunswick, N.J.: Transaction Books, 1964.

Hobsbawm, Eric J., and George Rude. 1968. *Captain swing.* New York: Pantheon.

Hollander, Samuel. 1971. The development of Ricardo's position on machinery. *History of Political Economy* 3, no. 1 (spring):105–35.

——. 1979. *The Economics of David Ricardo.* Toronto: University of Toronto Press.

Hollis, Patricia. 1973. *Class and conflict in nineteenth-century England.* London: Routledge and Kegan Paul.

Hopkins, A. G. 1966. The Lagos strike of 1897: An exploration in Nigerian labour history. *Past and Present,* no. 35 (December); reprinted in *Peasants and proletarians: The struggles of third world workers,* edited by Robin Cohen, Peter C. W. Gutkind, and Phyllis Brazier. New York: Monthly Review Press.

Horn, Pamela. 1981. *The rural world, 1750: Social change in the English countryside.* New York: St. Martin's Press.

Horner, Francis. 1843. *Memories and correspondence of Francis Horner, M. P.* Edited by Leonard Horner. 2 vols. London: John Murray.

Hu Chiao-mu. 1978. Observe economic laws, speed up the four modernizations. 3 pts. *Peking Review,* nos. 45–47 (November 10, 17, 24).

Hudson, Michael. 1992. *Trade, development, and foreign debt: A history of theories of polarisation and convergence in the international economy. Volume 1: International Trade.* London: Pluto Press.

Hughes, J. R. T. 1976. *Social control in the colonial economy.* Charlottesville: University Press of Virginia.

Hughes, Robert. 1987. *The fatal shore: The epic of Australia's founding.* New York: Knopf.

Hume, David. 1751. An inquiry concerning the principles of morals. In vol. 4 of *The philosophical works of David Hume,* edited by T. H. Green and T. H. Gross. Aalen: Scientia Verlag, 1964.

——. 1752a. Of the original contract. In *Essays: Moral, political, and literary,* edited by Eugene F. Miller. Indianapolis, Ind.: Liberty Press.

384

——. 1752b. On the populousness of ancient nations. In *Essays: Moral, political, and literary*, edited by Eugene F. Miller. Indianapolis, Ind.: Liberty Press.

——. 1752c. Of taxes. In *Essays: Moral, political, and literary*, edited by Eugene F. Miller. Indianapolis, Ind.: Liberty Press.

——. 1752d. On commerce. In *Essays: Moral, political, and literary*, edited by Eugene F. Miller. Indianapolis, Ind.: Liberty Press.

——. 1752e. Of interest. In *Essays: Moral, political, and literary*, edited by Eugene F. Miller. Indianapolis, Ind.: Liberty Press.

——. 1752f. On the first principles of government. In *Essays: Moral, political, and literary*, edited by Eugene F. Miller. Indianapolis, Ind.: Liberty Press.

——. 1769. Hume to Morellet, 10 July 1769. In *David Hume: Writings on economics*, edited by Eugene Rotwein. Madison: University of Wisconsin Press, 1955.

——. n.d. *History of England.* 5 vols. Philadelphia: Porter and Coates.

Humphries, Jane. 1976. Women: Scapegoats and safety valves in the great depression. *Review of Radical Political Economy* 8, no. 1 (spring):98–121.

——. 1977. The working class family, women's liberation, and class struggle: The case of nineteenth century British history. *Review of Radical Political Economy* 9, no. 3 (fall):25–41.

Hutcheson, Francis. 1749. *A short introduction to moral philosophy.* 5th ed. Philadelphia: Joseph Cruckshank, 1788.

——. 1755. *A system of moral philosophy.* 2 vols. New York: Augustus M. Kelley, 1968.

Hutchison, Terence. 1988. *Before Adam Smith: The emergence of political economy, 1662–1776.* Oxford: Basil Blackwell.

Hayse, Richard. 1971. Richard Cantillon, financier to Amsterdam, July to November 1720. *Economic Journal* 81, no. 324 (December):812–25.

Ignatieff, Michael. 1978. *A just measure of pain: The penitentiary in the industrial revolution, 1750–1850.* New York: Pantheon.

Inglis, Brian. 1971. *Poverty and the industrial revolution.* London: Hodder and Stoughton.

Institut National d'Etudes Demographiques. 1966. *Pierre de Boisguilbert ou la naissance de l'economie politique.* 2 vols. Paris: Institut National d'Etudes Demographiques.

International Bank for Reconstruction and Redevelopment. 1977. *Papua New Guinea: Its economic situation and prospects for development.* Washington, D.C.: World Bank.

James, Patricia. 1979. *Population Malthus: His life and times.* London: Routledge and Kegan Paul.

James, R. Warren. 1965. Introduction to *John Rae, political economist: An account of his life and a compilation of his main writings.* 2 vols. Toronto: University of Toronto Press.

Jefferson, Thomas. 1787. Notes on Virginia. Extracted in *The rise of American economic thought*, edited by Henry William Spiegel. New York: Chilton, 1960.

——. 1788. Letter to Thomas Diggs, 19 June 1788. In vol. 13 of *The papers of Thomas Jefferson*, edited by Julian P. Boyd. Princeton, N.J.: Princeton University Press, 1950.

——. 1817. Forward to *A treatise on political economy*, by Destutt du Tracy. Detroit: Center for Health Education, 1973.

——. 1950–. *25 February to 31 October 1785.* Vol. 8 of *The papers of Thomas Jefferson*, edited by Julian P. Boyd. Princeton, N.J.: Princeton University Press.

Jensen, Joan M. 1980. Cloth, butter, and boarders. *Review of Radical Political Economy* 12, no. 2 (summer):14–24.

Jevons, William Stanley. 1972. *Biography and personal journal.* Vol. 1 of *Papers and correspondence*, edited by R. D. Collison Black and Rosamund Koenigkamp. London: Macmillan.

Johnson, Arthur. 1909. *The disappearance of the small landowner.* London: Oxford University Press, 1963.

Johnson, Samuel. 1774. *A journey to the western islands of Scotland.* Vol. 9 of *The works of Samuel Johnson,* edited by Mary Lascelles. New Haven, Conn.: Yale University Press, 1971.

Jones, Eric L. 1988. *Growth recurring: Economic change in world history.* Oxford: Clarendon Press.

Kalm, Per. 1770–71. *Travels in North America, 1748–1750.* Edited by J. R. Forster Jr. 3 vols. London: Warrington.

Kaplan, Steven L. 1976. *Bread, politics, and political economy in the reign of Louis XV.* 2 vols. The Hague: Martinus Nijhoff.

Kautsky, Karl. 1899. *The agrarian question.* Translated by Pete Burgess. London: Zwan, 1988.

Kawakasu, Heita. 1986. International competition in cotton goods in the late nineteenth century: Britain versus India and East Asia." In vol. 2 of *The emergence of a world economy, 1500–1914,* edited by Wolfram Fischer et al. Wiesbaden: Franz Steiner.

Kelley, Florence Finch. 1906. An undertow to the land: Successful efforts to make possible a flow of the city population countryward. *Craftsman* 11 (December):294–310.

Kemp-Ashraf, P. M. 1966. Introduction to the selected writings of Thomas Spence. In *Life in literature of the working class: Essays in honor of William Gallagher,* edited by P. M. Kemp-Ashraf and Jack Mitchell. Berlin: Humboldt University.

Kent, Nathaniel. 1775. *Hints to gentlemen of landed property.* London: J. Dodsley. In Kress-Goldsmith collection, reel 1072, item 11247.

Ketton-Cremer, R. W. 1965. Johnson and the countryside. In *Boswell, Johnson, and their circle: Essays presented to Lawrence Fitzroy Powell,* edited by Mary Lascelles et al. Oxford: Clarendon Press.

Keynes, John Maynard. 1936. *The general theory of employment, interest, and money.* New York: Macmillan.

———. 1938. Adam Smith as student and professor. *Review of Economic History* 3 (February):33–46.

———. 1963. *Essays in biography.* New York: W. W. Norton.

Kiernan, Victor. 1991. Modern capitalism and its shepherds. *New Left Review,* no. 183 (September/October):75–94.

Kindleberger, Charles. 1976. The historical background: Adam Smith and the industrial revolution. In *The market and the state: Essays in honour of Adam Smith,* edited by Thomas Wilson and Andres S. Skinner. Oxford: Clarendon Press.

———. 1984. Financial institutions in economic development: A comparison of Great Britain and France in the eighteenth and nineteenth centuries. *Explorations in Economic History* 21, no. 2 (April):103–24.

King, John. 1981. Utopian or scientific? A reconsideration of the Ricardian socialists. Typescript, University of Lancaster.

Kingston-Mann, Esther. 1980. A strategy for marxist bourgeois revolution: Lenin and the peasantry, 1907–1916. *Journal of Peasant Studies* 7, no. 2 (January):131–57.

Kippis, Andrew. 1842. *The life of sir James Steuart Denham of Coltness and Westshield.* Edinburgh: Maitland Club.

Knox, William. 1769. *Controversy between Great Britain and her colonies, reviewed.* London: J. Almon.

Koebner, Richard. 1959. Adam Smith and the industrial revolution. *Economic History Review* 11, no. 3:381–91.

Kolko, Gabriel. 1978. Working wives: Their effects on the structure of the working class. *Science and Society* 42, no. 3 (fall):257–77.

Kroos, Herman E., and Charles Gilbert, eds. 1972. *American business history.* Englewood Cliffs, N.J.: Prentice-Hall.

Kropotkin, Peter. 1901. *Fields, factories, and workshops.* New York: Greenwood Press, 1968.

———. 1906. *The conquest of bread.* New York: New York University Press, 1972.

Kuczynski, Jürgen. 1967. *The rise of the working class.* New York: McGraw-Hill World University Library.

Kuznets, Simon. 1965. *Economic growth and structure.* New York: W. W. Norton.

Lancaster, Kelvin John. 1966. A new approach to consumer theory. *Journal of Political Economy* 74, no. 2 (April):132–57.

Landes, David S. 1987. What do bosses really do? *Journal of Economic History* 46, no. 2 (June):585–623.

Lascelles, Mary. 1971. Introduction to *A journey to the western islands of Scotland,* by Samuel Johnson. Vol. 9 of *The works of Samuel Johnson.* New Haven, Conn.: Yale University Press.

Laslett, Peter. 1971. *The world we have lost: England before the industrial age.* New York: Scribners.

Latour, Bruno. 1987. *Science in action: How to follow scientists and engineers through society.* Cambridge, Mass.: Harvard University Press.

Lazonick, William. 1978. The subjugation of labor to capital: The rise of the capitalist system. *Review of Radical Political Economy* 10, no. 1 (spring):1–31.

Lee, Sidney, ed. 1879. *Dictionary of national biography.* Vol. 58. London: Smith Elder and Co.

Lee, Susan Previant, and Peter Passell. 1979. *A new economic view of American history.* New York: W. W. Norton.

Lemon, James T. 1967. Household consumption in eighteenth-century America, and its relationship to production and trade: The situation among farmers in southeastern Pennsylvania. *Agricultural History* 41, no. 1 (January):58–70.

Lenin, Vladimir Ilyich. 1893. *On the so-called market question.* In vol. 1 of *Collected works.* Moscow: Foreign Languages Publishing House, 1960–70.

———. 1894. *What "the friends of the people" are and how they fight the social democrats.* In vol. 1 of *Collected works.* Moscow: Foreign Languages Publishing House, 1960–70.

———. 1898. *The handicraft census of 1894–1895 in Perm Gubernia and general problems of the "handicraft industry."* In vol. 2 of *Collected works.* Moscow: Foreign Languages Publishing House, 1960–70.

———. 1905. *Petty-bourgeois and proletarian socialism.* In vol. 9 of *Collected works.* Moscow: Foreign Languages Publishing House, 1960–70.

———. 1907. *The agrarian program of social democracy in the first Russian revolution, 1905–1907.* In vol. 13 of *Collected works.* Moscow: Foreign Languages Publishing House, 1960–70.

———. 1908. *The agrarian question in Russia at the end of the nineteenth century.* In vol. 15 of *Collected works.* Moscow: Foreign Languages Publishing House, 1960–70.

———. 1913. *The land question and the rural poor.* In vol. 19 of *Collected works.* Moscow: Foreign Languages Publishing House, 1960–70.

———. 1921a. *Report on the substitution of a tax in kind for the surplus grain appropriation, March 15.* In vol. 32 of *Collected works.* Moscow: Foreign Languages Publishing House, 1960–70.

———. 1921b. *Report of the Moscow Gubernia conference of the Russian communist party.* In vol. 33 of *Collected works.* Moscow: Foreign Languages Publishing House, 1960–70.

———. 1921c. *The tax in kind: The significance of the new policy and its conditions.* In vol. 32 of *Collected works.* Moscow: Foreign Languages Publishing House, 1960–70.

———. 1974. *The development of capitalism in Russia.* Moscow: Progress Publishers.

Leontief, Wassily W. 1966. *Input-output economics.* New York: Oxford University Press.

LeRoy Ladurie, Emmanuel. 1974. *The peasants of Languedoc.* Translated by John Day. Urbana: University of Illinois Press.

Leslie, T. Cliffe. 1888. *Essays in political economy.* New York: Augustus M. Kelley, 1969.

Letter to editor. 1757. *London Magazine*, no. 26 (February):87.

Levy, Hermann. 1966. *Large and small holdings.* Translated by Ruth Kenyon. New York: Augustus M. Kelley.

Levy, S. Leon. 1970. *Nassau W. Senior, 1790–1864.* New York: Augustus M. Kelley.

Lewis, William Arthur. 1954. Economic development with unlimited supplies of labour. *Manchester School* 22, no. 2 (May):139–91.

———. 1958. Unlimited labour: Further notes. *Manchester School* 26, no. 1 (January):1–32.

———. 1976. The diffusion of development. In *The market and the state: Essays in honour of Adam Smith,* edited by Thomas Wilson and Andrew S. Skinner. Oxford: Clarendon Press.

List, Friedrich. 1841. *Das Nationale System der politischen Ökonomie.* Jena: Gustav Fischer, 1950.

Locke, John. 1698. *Two treatises on government.* Edited by Peter Laslett. 2d ed. Cambridge, U.K.: Cambridge University Press, 1967.

Longfield, Mountifort. 1834. *Lectures on political economy delivered in Trinity and Michaelmas terms, 1833.* Dublin: Richard Millikan and Sons; reprinted in *The economic writings of Mountifort Longfield,* edited by R. C. D. Black. New York: Augustus M. Kelley, 1971.

Lowe, Joseph. 1823. *The present state of England in regard to agriculture, trade, and finance.* London: Longmans, Hurst, Rees, Orme, and Brown.

Luxemburg, Rosa. 1968. *The accumulation of capital.* New York: Monthly Review Press.

Macpherson, C. B. 1962. *The political theory of possessive individualism: Hobbes to Locke.* London: Oxford University Press.

———. 1987. Property as means or end. In *The rise and fall of economic justice and other essays.* Oxford: Oxford University Press.

Madison, James. 1787. Appointment of representatives in the legislature. In vol. 10 of *The papers of James Madison,* edited by William Hutchinson and William Rachal. Chicago: University of Chicago Press, 1962–.

———. 1962–. *The papers of James Madison.* Edited by William Hutchinson and William Rachal. Chicago: University of Chicago Press.

Magnusson, Lars. 1987. Mercantilism and "reform" mercantilism: The rise of economic discourse in Sweden during the eighteenth century. *History of Political Economy* 19, no. 3 (fall):415–33.

Magubane, Bernard Makhosezwe. 1979. *The political economy of race and class in South Africa.* New York: Monthly Review Press.

Main, Jackson Turner. 1965. *The social structure in revolutionary America.* Princeton, N.J.: Princeton University Press.

Maital, Schlomo, and Patricia Haswell. 1977. Why did Ricardo (not) change his mind? On money and machinery. *Economica* 44, no. 176 (November):359–68.

Maitland, James, eighth earl of Lauderdale. 1804. *An inquiry into the nature and origin of public wealth.* New York: Augustus M. Kelley, 1966.

Malthus, Thomas Robert. 1803. *Essay on the principle of population.* Edited by Donald Winch. Cambridge, U.K.: Cambridge University Press.

———. 1820. *Principles of political economy*. In vol. 2 of *The works and correspondence of David Ricardo*, edited by Piero Sraffa. Cambridge, U.K.: Cambridge University Press, 1951.

———. 1836. *Principles of political economy, considered with a view of their practical application*. New York: Augustus M. Kelley, 1951.

———. 1966. *The travel diaries of T. R. Malthus*. Edited by Patricia Jones. Cambridge, U.K.: Cambridge University Press.

———. 1976. *An essay on the principle of population: Text, sources, and background criticism*. Edited by Philip Appleman. New York: W. W. Norton.

Mandeville, Bernard. 1723. *The fable of the bees*. Edited by F. B. Kaye. Oxford: Clarendon Press, 1954.

Mantoux, Paul. 1961. *The industrial revolution in the eighteenth century: An outline of the beginnings of the modern factory system in England*. New York: Harper and Row.

Mao Tse-tung. 1937. On contradiction. In vol. 3 of *Selected works*. Peking: Foreign Languages Press, 1967.

———. 1945. Policy work for liberated areas. In vol. 4 of *Selected works*. Peking: Foreign Languages Press, 1965–77.

———. 1947. Greet the new high tide of the Chinese revolution. In vol. 4 of *Selected works*. Peking: Foreign Languages Press, 1965–77.

———. 1955a. The debate on the co-operative transformation of agriculture and the current class struggle. In vol. 5 of *Selected works*. Peking: Foreign Languages Press, 1965–77.

———. 1955b. Editor's notes from socialist upsurge in China's countryside. In vol. 5 of *Selected works*. Peking: Foreign Languages Press, 1965–77.

———. 1956. On the ten great relationships. In vol. 5 of *Selected works*. Peking: Foreign Languages Press, 1965–77.

Marcus, Steven. 1974. *Engels, Manchester, and the working class*. New York: Vintage.

Marglin, Stephen. 1974. What do bosses do? The origins and functions of hierarchy in capitalist production. *Review of Radical Political Economy* 6, no. 2 (summer):33–60; reprinted in *The economic nature of the firm: A reader*, edited by Louis Putterman. Cambridge, U.K.: Cambridge University Press, 1986.

Marshall, Alfred. 1927. *Principles of economics: An introductory volume*. 8th ed. London: Macmillan.

Martineau, Harriet. 1837. *Society in America*. In *Readings in the economic and social history of the United States*, edited by Felix Flugel and Harold Faulkner. New York: Harper and Brothers.

Marx, Karl. 1842. Proceedings of the sixth Rhine province assembly, third article: Debates on the law of thefts of wood. In *Marx and Engels, 1835–1843*. Vol. 1 of *Collected works*. New York: International Publishers, 1975.

———. 1845. On Friedrich List's book, *Das Nationale System der politischen Oekonomie*. In *Marx and Engels, 1844–1845*. Vol. 5 of *Collected works*. New York: International Publishers, 1975.

———. 1847. *The poverty of philosophy*. New York: International Publishers, 1963.

———. 1852. The eighteenth brumaire of Louis Bonaparte. In vol. 1 of *Selected works in three volumes, Karl Marx and Friedrich Engels*. Moscow: Progress Publishers, 1969–1973.

———. 1853a. "Elections—Financial clouds—The duchess of Sutherland and slavery. In *Marx and Engels, 1851–1853*. Vol. 11 of *Collected works*. New York: International Publishers, 1975.

———. 1853b. The future results of British rule in India. In vol. 1 of *Selected works in three volumes, Karl Marx and Friedrich Engels*. Moscow: Progress Publishers, 1969–1973.

——. 1858. The Chinese trade figures. In *Karl Marx on colonialism and modernization*, edited by Schlomo Avineri. Garden City, N.Y.: Doubleday, 1968.

——. 1859. *A contribution to the critique of political economy*. New York: International Publishers, 1970.

——. 1865. Wages, price, and profit. In vol. 2 of *Selected works in three volumes*, Karl Marx and Friedrich Engels. Moscow: Progress Publishers, 1969–1973.

——. 1963–71. *Theories of surplus value*. Moscow: Progress Publishers.

——. 1965. *Precapitalistic economic formations*. New York: International Publishers.

——. 1967. *Capital*. Vols. 2 and 3. New York: International Publishers.

——. 1970. *Critique of political economy*. New York: International Publishers.

——. 1974. *Grundrisse*. New York: Vintage.

——. 1977. *Capital*. Vol. 1. New York: Vintage.

——. 1981. *Capital*. Vols. 2 and 3. New York: Vintage.

Marx, Karl, and Friedrich Engels. 1846a. Feuerbach: Opposition of materialist and idealist outlook. In vol. 1 of *Selected works in three volumes*. Moscow: Progress Publishers, 1969–1973.

——. 1846b. The German ideology. In *Marx and Engels, 1845–1847*. Vol. 5 of *Collected works*. New York: International Publishers, 1976.

——. 1942. *Selected correspondence*. New York: International Publishers.

——. 1973. *Marx/Engels werke*. Berlin: Dietz.

——. 1975. *Selected correspondence*. Moscow: Progress Publishers.

——. 1985. *Letters: Marx and Engels, January 1860–September 1864*. Vol. 41 of *Collected works*. New York: International Publishers, 1975.

Marx, Leo. 1964. *The machine in the garden: Technology and the pastoral ideal in America*. New York: Oxford University Press.

Matsukawa, Shichiro. 1965. An essay on the historical uniqueness of Petty's labor theory of value. *Hitotsubashi Journal of Economics* 5, no. 2 (January):1–11.

Matthaei, Julie. 1982. *An economic history of women in America*. New York: Schocken Books.

Mayer, Margit, and Margaret A. Fay. 1977. The formation of the American nation-state. *Kapitalstate*, no. 6 (fall):39–90.

McCoy, Drew R. 1982. *The elusive republic: Political economy in Jeffersonian America*. Chapel Hill: University of North Carolina Press.

McCulloch. John Ramsey. 1824. Political economy. In John McVickar, *Outlines of political economy*. New York: Augustus M. Kelley, 1966.

——. 1825. Evidence given before the select committee on Ireland. *British Parliamentary Papers* 8:811–35.

——. 1841. *Statements, illustrative of the policy and probable consequences of the proposed repeal of the corn laws*. Edinburgh.

——. 1845. *The literature of political economy: A classified catalogue of select publications*. New York: Augustus M. Kelley, 1964.

——. 1848. *A treatise on the succession to property vacant by death: Including inquiries into the influence of primogeniture, entails, compulsory partition, foundations, &c. over the public interests*. London: Longman, Brown, Green, and Longmans.

——. 1854. *A treatise on the circumstances which determine the rate of wages and the condition of the labouring classes*. New York: Augustus M. Kelley, 1967.

McGregor, Pat. 1992. The labor market and the distribution of landholdings in pre-famine Ireland. *Explorations in Economic History* 29, no. 4 (October):477–93.

McKendrick, Neil. 1961. Josiah Adams and factory discipline. *Historical Journal* 4, no. 1:30–55.

McNally, David. 1988. *Political economy and the rise of capitalism.* Berkeley: University of California Press.

———. 1993. *Against the market: Political economy, market socialism, and the Marxian critique.* London: Verso.

Medick, Hans. 1988. Industrialisation before industrialisation? Rural industries in Europe and the genesis of capitalism. *Indian Economic and Social History Review* 25, no. 3:371–84.

Meek, Ronald L. 1963. *The economics of physiocracy.* Cambridge, Mass.: Harvard University Press.

———. 1976. *Social science and the ignoble savage.* Cambridge, U.K.: Cambridge University Press.

———. 1977a. New light on Adam Smith's Glasgow lectures on jurisprudence. In *Smith, Marx, and after: Ten essays in the development of economic thought.* London: Chapman and Hall.

———. 1977b. Smith, Turgot, and the four stages theory. In *Smith, Marx, and after: Ten essays in the development of economic thought.* London: Chapman and Hall.

———. 1977c. Smith and Marx. In *Smith, Marx, and after: Ten essays in the development of economic thought.* London: Chapman and Hall.

———. 1977d. The development of Adam Smith's ideas on the division of labour. In *Smith, Marx, and after: Ten essays in the development of economic thought.* London: Chapman and Hall.

Meillasoux, Claude. 1972. From reproduction to production: A marxist approach to economic anthropology. *Economy and Society* 1, no. 1 (February):93–105.

Melotti, Umberto. 1977. *Marx and the third world.* London: Macmillan.

Mendels, Franklin F. 1972. Proto-industrialization: The first phase of the process of industrialization. *Journal of Economic History* 32, no. 1 (March):241–61.

———. 1975. Agriculture and peasant industry in eighteenth-century Flanders. In *European peasants and their markets,* edited by William N. Parker and Eric L. Jones. Princeton, N.J.: Princeton University Press.

Merivale, Herman. 1841. *Lectures on colonization and colonies, delivered before the University of Oxford, 1839, 1840, and 1841.* London: Longman, Orme, Brown, Green, and Longmans.

Merrington, John. 1976. Town and country in the transition to capitalism. In *The transition from feudalism to capitalism,* edited by Rodney Hilton. London: New Left Books.

Michl, Thomas. 1993. Adam Smith and the new economics of effort. In *Economics as worldly philosophy: Essays in political and historical economics in honour of Robert L. Heilbroner,* edited by Ron Blackwell, Jaspal Chatha, and Edward J. Nell. New York: St. Martin's Press.

Mill, James. 1826. *Elements of political economy.* In *James Mill: Selected economic writings,* edited by Donald Winch. Chicago: University of Chicago Press, 1966.

Mill, John Stuart. 1848. *Principles of political economy with some of their applications to social philosophy.* Vols. 2 and 3 of *Collected works,* edited by J. M. Robson. Toronto: University of Toronto Press, 1965.

Millar, John. 1806. *The origin of the distinction of ranks; or an inquiry into the circumstances which give rise to influence and authority in the different members of society.* 4th ed. Edinburgh: Blackwood.

Mirabeau, Marquis de. 1756. *L'Ami des Hommes.* Paris.

———. 1763. *Philosophie rurale.* vol. 1. In Kress-Goldsmith collection, reel 798, item 9836.

Mirowski, Philip. 1982. Adam Smith, empiricism, and the rate of profit in eighteenth-century England. *History of Political Economy* 14, no. 2 (summer):178–98; reprinted in *Against Mechanism: Protecting Economics from Science.* Totowa, N.J.: Rowman and Littlefield, 1984.

Mitchel, John. 1847. *Irish political economy.* Dublin.

Mitchell, Broadus. 1957–62. *Alexander Hamilton.* 2 vols. New York: Macmillan.

Mokyr, Joel. 1983. *Why Ireland starved: A quantitative and analytical history of the Irish economy, 1800–1850.* London: Allen and Unwin.

———. 1990. *The lever of riches: Technological creativity and economic progress.* New York: Oxford University Press.

Montagu, Lady Mary Wortley. 1966–67. *The complete letters of Lady Mary Wortley Montagu.* 3 vols. Oxford: Clarendon Press.

Montgomery, David. 1979. *Workers' control in America: Studies in the history of work, technology, and labor struggles.* Cambridge, Mass.: Cambridge University Press.

Moore, Barrington, Jr. 1966. *Social origins of dictatorship and democracy: Lord and peasant in the making of the modern world.* Boston: Beacon Press.

Moore, Wilbur. 1951. *Industrialization and labor.* Ithaca, N.Y.: Cornell University Press.

———. 1955. Labor attitudes toward industrialization in underdeveloped countries. *American Economic Review* 45, no. 2 (May):156–65.

Morely, Derek Wragge. 1954. *The evolution of an insect society.* London: George Allen and Unwin.

Morgan, Edmund. 1975. *American slavery, American freedom: The ordeal of colonial Virginia.* New York: W. W. Norton.

———. 1976. *The challenge of the American revolution.* New York: W. W. Norton.

Moser, Arthur. 1966. *Getting agriculture moving: Essentials for development and modernization.* New York: Frederick A. Praeger.

Mossner, Ernest Campbell. 1954. *The life of David Hume.* Austin: University of Texas Press.

Mossner, Ernest Campbell, and Ian Simpson Ross, eds. 1977. *The correspondence of Adam Smith.* Oxford: Clarendon Press.

Mun, Thomas. 1664. *England's treasure by foreign trade.* In *A select collection of early English tracts on commerce,* edited by John R. McCulloch. London: Cambridge University Press, 1970.

Munsche, P. B. 1980. *Gentlemen and poachers: The English game laws, 1671–1831.* Cambridge, U.K.: Cambridge University Press.

Murphy, Antoin E. 1986. *Richard Cantillon: Entrepreneur and economist.* Oxford: Clarendon Press.

Myers, Ramon H. 1980. *The Chinese economy: Past and present.* Belmont, Calif.: Wadsworth.

Nallet, Henri, and Clause Servolin. 1978. *Le paysan et le droit.* Paris: Institut National de la Recherche Agronomique, Economie et Sociologie Rurales.

Needham, Joseph. 1969. *The grand titration: Science and society in east and west.* Toronto: University of Toronto Press.

Nef, John U. 1932. *The rise of the British coal industry.* 2 vols. Freeport, N.Y.: Books for Library Press.

Nelson, Frederick J., and Willard W. Cochrane. 1976. Economic consequences of federal commodity programs. *Agricultural Economics Research* 28, no. 2 (April):52–64.

Newsinger, John. 1996. The great Irish famine: A crime of free market economics. *Monthly Review* 47, no. 11 (April):11–19.

Nietzsche, Friedrich. 1954. *Thus spoke Zarathustra*. In *The portable Nietzsche*, edited by Walter Kaufmann. New York: Viking.

Nordhaus, William, and James Tobin. 1972. Is growth obsolete? In *The measurement of economic and social performance*, edited by Milton Moss. New York: Columbia University Press.

North, Douglass C. 1966. *The economic growth of the United States, 1790–1860*. New York: W. W. Norton.

Nurske, R. 1953. *Problems of capital formation in underdeveloped countries*. Oxford: Basil Blackwell.

Nutter, G. Warren. 1976. *Adam Smith and the American revolution*. Washington, D.C.: American Enterprise Institute.

O'Brien, D. P., and A. C. Darnell. 1978. Torrens, McCulloch, and the "digression on Sismondi": Whose digression? Working paper, Department of Economics, University of Durham.

O'Brien, Patrick K., and Keyder Caglar. 1978. *Economic growth in Britain and France, 1780–1914: Two paths to the twentieth century*. London: George Allen and Unwin.

O'Connor, Feargus. 1845. The land plan . . . In *Class and conflict in nineteenth-century England*, edited by Patricia Hollis. London: Routledge and Kegan Paul, 1973.

———. 1848a. Free trade and the land plan. In *Class and conflict in nineteenth-century England*, edited by Patricia Hollis. London: Routledge and Kegan Paul, 1973.

———. 1848b. A treatise on the small farm system and the banking system. *Labourer* 3:54–100.

O'Connor, Michael J. L. 1944. *Origins of academic economics in the United States*. New York: Garland, 1974.

Ogg, F. A., ed. 1906. *Personal narratives of travel in Virginia, Maryland, Ohio, Indiana, Kentucky, and of a residence in the Illinois territory, 1817–1818*. Cleveland.

Olwig, Karen Fog, and Kenneth Olwig. 1979. Underdevelopment and the development of the "natural" park ideology. *Antipode* 11, no. 2:16–25.

Ommer, Rosemary E. 1986. Primitive accumulation and the Scottish clann in the old-world and new. *Journal of Historical Geography* 12, no. 2 (April):121–41.

On agriculture and rent. 1827. *Quarterly Review* 36, no. 51:391–409.

Owen, Robert. 1813. Second essay on the formation of character. In *A new view of society and other writings*, edited by G. D. H. Cole. London: Dent, 1949.

———. 1857. *The life of Robert Owen*. London: Effingham Wilson.

Panzer, John C., and Robert D. Willig. 1981. The economics of scope. *American Economic Review* 71, no. 2 (May):268–72.

Pascal, Roy. 1938. Property and society. *Modern Quarterly* 1, no. 2 (March):167–79.

Peffer, William. 1891. *The farmer's side: His troubles and their remedy*. New York.

Pennant, Thomas. 1771. *A tour in Scotland*. Chester.

———. 1772. *A tour in Scotland*. 2d ed. London: B. White.

———. 1774. *A tour in Scotland*. 3d ed. 2 vols. Chester.

Perelman, Michael. 1977. *Farming for profit in a hungry world: Capital and the crisis in agriculture*. Montclair, N.J.: Allanheld, Osmun.

———. 1987. *Karl Marx's crisis theory: Labor, scarcity, and fictitious capital*. New York: Praeger.

———. 1988. *Keynes, investment theory, and the economic slowdown: The role of replacement investment and q-ratios*. London: Macmillan.

———. 1991a. *Information, social relations, and the economics of high technology*. London: Macmillan.

———. 1991b. Energy and agricultural production. In *Ethics and agriculture: An anthology on current issues in world context,* edited by Charles V. Blatz. Moscow: University of Idaho Press.

Pesciarelli, Enzo. 1989. Smith, Bentham, and the development of contrasting ideas on entrepreneurship. *History of Political Economy* 21, no. 3 (fall):521–36.

Pessen, Edward. 1973. *Riches, class, and power before the civil war.* Lexington, Mass.: D. C. Heath.

Pettengill, John. 1981. Firearms and the distribution of income: A neo-classical model. *Review of Radical Political Economics* 13, no. 2 (summer):1–10.

Petty, Sir William. 1662. Treatise of taxes and contributions. In vol. 1 of *The writings of sir William Petty,* edited by C. H. Hull. Cambridge, U.K.: Cambridge University Press, 1899; New York: Augustus M. Kelley, 1963.

——. 1683. Another essay on political arithmetick. In vol. 1 of *The writings of sir William Petty,* edited by C. H. Hull. Cambridge, U.K.: Cambridge University Press, 1899; New York: Augustus M. Kelley, 1963.

——. 1687. A treatise of Ireland. In vol. 2 of *The writings of sir William Petty,* edited by C. H. Hull. Cambridge, U.K.: Cambridge University Press, 1899; New York: Augustus M. Kelley, 1963.

——. 1690. Political arithmetick, 1690. In vol. 1 of *The writings of sir William Petty,* edited by C. H. Hull. Cambridge, U.K.: Cambridge University Press, 1899; New York: Augustus M. Kelley, 1963.

——. 1691. *Verbum Sapienti.* In vol. 1 of *The writings of sir William Petty,* edited by C. H. Hull. Cambridge, U.K.: Cambridge University Press, 1899; New York: Augustus M. Kelley, 1963.

——. 1927. *The Petty papers: Some unpublished papers of Sir William Petty,* edited by the Marquis of Lansdowne, 2 vols. London: Constable.

Philipponeau, Michel. 1956. *La vie rurale de la banlieu Parisienne: Etude de geographie humaine.* Paris: Librairie Armand Colin.

Plath, Raymond Arthur. 1939. *British mercantilism and the British colonial land policy in the eighteenth century.* Ph.D. diss., University of Wisconsin.

Platteau, Jean-Philippe. 1978. *Les economistes classiques et le sous-developement.* 2 vols. Namur, Belgium: Presses Universitaires de Namur.

Pocock, J. G. A. 1971. *Politics, language, and time: Essays on political thought and history.* New York: Atheneum.

——. 1985a. The mobility of property and the rise of eighteenth-century sociology. In *Virtue, commerce, and history: Essays on political thought and history, chiefly in the eighteenth century.* Cambridge, U.K.: Cambridge University Press.

——. 1985b. Hume and the American revolution: The dying thoughts of a north Britain. In *Virtue, commerce, and history: Essays on political thought and history, chiefly in the eighteenth century.* Cambridge, U.K.: Cambridge University Press.

Pollard, Sidney. 1965. *The genesis of modern management.* Cambridge, Mass.: Harvard University Press.

——. 1978. *The industrial economies, part 1: Britain, France, Germany, and Scandinavia.* Vol. 7 of *The Cambridge economic history of Europe,* edited by Peter Mathias and M. M. Postan. Cambridge, U.K.: Cambridge University Press.

Pollexfen, Sir Henry. 1700. *Discourse of trade.* London: John Baker.

Ponce, I. 1870. *Traite d'agriculture pratique et d'economie rurale.* Paris: Librairie Agricole de la Maison Rustique.

Postan, M. M. 1966. England. In *The Cambridge economic history of Europe.* Vol. 1 of *The agrarian life of the middle ages,* edited by M. M. Postan. Cambridge, U.K.: Cambridge University Press.

Postlethwayt, Malachy. 1751. *The universal dictionary of trade and commerce, translated from the French of the celebrated monsieur Savary.* 2 vols. London.

Pownall, Governor. 1776. *A letter from governor Pownall to Adam Smith, L.L.D., F.R.S., being an examination of several points of doctrine, laid down in his inquiry into the nature and causes of the wealth of nations.* In *The correspondence of Adam Smith,* edited by Ernest Campbell Mossner and Ian Simpson Ross. Oxford: Clarendon Press, 1977.

Prezzolini, Giuseppe. 1967. *Machiavelli.* New York: Farrar, Straus and Giroux.

Price, Richard. 1783. *Observations on the importance of the American revolution and the means of making it a benefit to the world.* London.

Primack, Martin. 1966. Farm capital formation as a use of farm labor in the United States, 1850–1910. *Journal of Economic History* 26, no. 3 (September):348–62.

Prothero, Iorwerth. 1969. Chartism in London. *Past and Present,* no. 44 (August):76–105.

Puckle, James. 1700. England's path to wealth and honour. In *A collection of scarce and valuable tracts,* edited by John Ramsay McCulloch. London, 1814.

Quesnay, Francois. 1757. Grains. In *The economics of physiocracy: Essays and translations,* edited by Ronald L. Meek. Cambridge, Mass.: Harvard University Press, 1963.

———. 1758. Tableau economique. In *Quesnay's tableau economique,* edited by Marguerite Kuczynski and Ronald Meek. New York: Augustus M. Kelley, 1972.

Rabbeno, Ugo. 1895. *American commercial policy.* New York: Macmillan.

Rae, John. 1895. *The life of Adam Smith.* New York: Augustus M. Kelley, 1965.

Rae, John. 1825. Sketches of the origin and progress of manufactures and of the policy which has regulated their legislative encouragement in Great Britain and in other countries. *Canadian Review and Literary Journal,* no. 3 (March); reprinted in vol. 1 of *John Rae, political economist: An account of his life and a compilation of his main writings,* edited by R. Warren James. Toronto: University of Toronto Press, 1965.

———. 1828. Letter to the honourable Mr. Stanley, on the relative claims of the English and Scotch churches in Canada. *Religious, Literary, and Statistical Intelligencer* (August); reprinted in vol. 1 of *John Rae, political economist: An account of his life and a compilation of his main writings,* edited by R. Warren James. Toronto: University of Toronto Press, 1965.

———. 1834. *Statement of some new principles on the subject of political economy.* Boston; reprinted in vol. 2 of *John Rae, political economist: An account of his life and a compilation of his main writings,* edited by R. Warren James. Toronto: University of Toronto Press, 1965.

———. 1862. Letter to R. C. Wyllie, March 1862. In vol. 1 of *John Rae, political economist: An account of his life and a compilation of his main writings,* edited by R. Warren James. Toronto: University of Toronto Press, 1965.

Ransom, Roger, and Richard Sutch. 1977. *One kind of freedom: The economic consequences of emancipation.* Cambridge, U.K.: Cambridge University Press.

Rashid, Salim. 1992. Charles James Fox and the wealth of nations. *History of Political Economy* 24, no. 2 (summer):493–97.

Rattner, Sidney, James Soltow, and Richard Sylla. 1979. *The evaluation of the American economy.* New York: Basic Books.

Ravenstone, Piercy. 1824. *Thoughts on the funding system and its effects.* London: J. Andrews, 1966.

Ray, Rajat Kanta. 1988. The bazaar: The changing structural characteristics of the indigenous section of the Indian economy before and after the great depression. *Indian Economic and Social History Review* 25, no. 3 (July–September):263–318.

Raymond, Daniel. 1823. *Elements of political economy.* 2d ed. Baltimore, Md.: F. Lucas Jr. and E. J. Coale.

Redford, Arthur. 1926. *Labour migration in England, 1800–1850.* Manchester, U.K.: Manchester University Press.

Reid, Douglas A. 1976. The decline of St. Monday. *Past and Present*, no. 71 (May):76–101.

Rendall, Jane. 1978. *The origins of the Scottish enlightenment.* New York: St. Martin's Press.

Review of Sir James Steuart, *An Inquiry into the principles of political oeconomy.* 1767a. *Critical Review* 23 (May–June):321–29, 411–16; and 24 (July):24–32.

Review of Sir James Steuart, *An inquiry into the principles of political oeconomy.* 1767b. *Scot's Magazine* 29 (April):199–201.

Review of Sir James Steuart, *An Inquiry into the principles of political oeconomy.* 1767c. *Monthly Review* 36 (May–June):365–78, 464–76; and 37 (July):116–25.

Review of American husbandry. 1776. In *American husbandry*, edited by H. J. Carman. New York: Columbia University Press, 1939.

Review of Steuart's Works. 1806a. *Literary Journal* 1, no. 3 (March):225–35.

Review of Steuart's Works. 1806b. *Monthly Review; or Literary Journal, Enlarged* 50 (June): 113–21.

Review of cottage industry by William Cobbett. 1823. *Edinburgh Review* 38, no. 75 (February):105–25.

The reviewers reviewed in a letter to the editor of the political register. 1767. *Political Register and Impartial Review of New Books* 1, no. 2 (June):121–28.

Ricardo, David. 1822. *On protection to agriculture.* In vol. 4 of *The works and correspondence of David Ricardo*, edited by Piero Sraffa. Cambridge, U.K.: Cambridge University Press.

———. 1951–73. *The works and correspondence of David Ricardo.* Edited by Piero Sraffa. 11 vols. Cambridge, U.K.: Cambridge University Press.

Rich, E. E. 1967. Colonial settlement and its labour problems. In vol. 4 of *The Cambridge history of Europe*, edited by E. E. Rich and C. H. Wilson. Cambridge, U.K.: Cambridge University Press.

Robbins, Lionel Charles. 1939. *The economic basis of class conflict and other essays.* London: Macmillan.

———. 1958. *Robert Torrens and the evolution of classical economics.* London: Macmillan.

Robertson, A. J. 1971. Robert Owen, cotton spinner: New Lanark. In *Robert Owen, prophet of the poor: Essays in honour of the two-hundredth anniversary of his birth*, edited by Sidney Pollard and John Salt. Lewisburg, Pa.: Bucknell University Press.

Robertson, William. 1769a. *A view of the progress of society in Europe, from the subversion of the Roman empire, to the beginning of the sixteenth century;* reprinted in The progress of society in Europe: A historical outline from the subversion of the Roman empire to the beginning of the sixteenth century, edited by Felix Gilbert. Chicago: University of Chicago Press, 1972.

———. 1769b. *The history of the reign of the emperor Charles the fifth.* 3 vols. Philadelphia: J. B. Lippincott Co., 1884.

———. 1777. *The History of America.* In *The works of William Robertson, D.D.*, 12 vols. London, 1817.

———. 1781. *The history of Scotland.* 2 vols. London: T. Caddell.

Robinson, Edward A. G. 1932. *The structure of competitive industry.* New York: Harcourt Brace and Co.

Robinson, Harriet H. 1898. *Loom and spindle, or life among the early mill girls.* Kailua, Hawai'i: Pacifica Press, 1976.

Rodbertus-Jagetzow, Johann Karl. 1851. *Sociale Briefe an von Kirchmann, Dritter Brief.* Berlin.

———. 1899. *Das kapital.* Reprinted as vol. 2 of *Aus den literaschen Nachlass von Carl Rodgertus-Jagetzow,* edited by H. Schumacher-Zarchlin, A. Wagner, and T. Kozak. Berlin: Puttkammer und Muhlbrecht.

Rodney, Walter. 1974. *How Europe underdeveloped Africa.* Washington, D.C.: Howard University Press.

Rosenstein-Rodan, Paul. 1943. Problems of industrialization of eastern and south-eastern Europe. *Economic Journal* 53, nos. 210–211 (June–September):202–11.

Ross, Eric. 1973. *The leviathan of wealth: The Sutherland fortune in the industrial revolution.* London: Routledge and Kegan Paul.

Rothschild, Emma. 1992. Adam Smith and conservative economics. *Economic History Review* 45, no. 1 (February):74–96.

Rotwein, Eugene, ed. 1955. *David Hume: Writings on economics.* Madison: University of Wisconsin Press.

Routh, Guy. 1977. *The origin of economic ideas.* New York: Vintage.

Rude, George. 1980. *Ideology and popular protest.* New York: Pantheon Books.

Rudkin, Olive D. 1966. *Thomas Spence and his connections.* New York: Augustus M. Kelley.

Rule, John. 1987. The property of skill in the period of manufacture. In *The historical meaning of work,* edited by Patrick Joyce. Cambridge, U.K.: Cambridge University Press.

Rumford, Count. 1795. Of food: And particularly the feeding of the poor. In vol. 5 of *Collected works of Count Rumford,* edited by Sanborn C. Brown. Cambridge, Mass.: Harvard University Press, 1968–1970.

Ruskin, John. 1866. *Crown of wild olives.* Vol. 1 of *Works of John Ruskin,* edited by E. J. Cook and Alexander Wedderburn. New York: Library Edition, 1903–12.

Sachs, William S. 1953. Agricultural conditions in the northern colonies before the revolution. *Journal of Economic History* 13, no. 3 (summer):274–90.

Salvemini, Gaetano. 1954. *The French revolution, 1788–1792.* London: Jonathan Cape.

Samuel, Raphael. 1973. Comers and goers. In vol. 1 of *The Victorian city,* edited by H. J. Dyos and Michael Wolff. London: Routledge and Kegan Paul.

Samuels, Warren. 1966. *The classical theory of economic policy.* Cleveland, Ohio: World Publishing.

———. 1973. Adam Smith and the economy as a system of power. *Review of Social Economy* 31, no. 2 (October):123–37.

Samuelson, Paul A. 1989. Ricardo was right! *Scandinavian Journal of Economics* 9, no. 1:47–62.

Say, Jean-Baptiste. 1821. *Letters to Malthus on several subjects of political economy and the cause of the stagnation of commerce.* Translated by John Richter. New York: Augustus M. Kelley, 1967.

———. 1843. *Cours Complet d'economie politique.* Brussels: Societe Typographique Belge.

Say, J. B. 1880. *Treatise on political economy.* Translated by C. R. Princep. 4th ed. New York: Augustus M. Kelley, 1964.

Schlesinger, Arthur. 1945. *The age of Jackson.* New York: Book Find Club.

———. 1986. *The cycles of American history.* Boston: Houghton Mifflin.

Schoenhof, Joseph. 1893. *The economy of high wages.* New York: G. P. Putnam.

Schor, Juliet B. 1991. *The overworked American: The unexpected decline of leisure.* New York: Basic Books.

Schultz, Theodore. 1964. *Transforming traditional agriculture*. New Haven, Conn.: Yale University Press.

——. 1968. Institutions and the rising value of man. *American Journal of Agricultural Economics* 50, no. 5 (December):1113–22.

Schumpeter, Joseph A. 1950. *Capitalism, socialism, and democracy*. 3d ed. New York: Harper and Row.

——. 1954. *History of economic analysis*. New York: Oxford University Press.

Schuyler, Robert Livingston, ed. 1931. *Josiah Tucker: A selection from his economic and political writings with an introduction by Robert Livingston Schuyler*. New York: Columbia University Press.

Schwartz, Herman M. 1994. *States versus markets: History, geography, and the development of the international political economy*. New York: St. Martin's Press.

Scitovsky, Tibor. 1976. *The joyless economy: An inquiry into human satisfaction*. New York: Oxford University Press.

Scott, William R. 1934. Adam Smith and the Glasgow merchants. *Economic Journal* 44:506–8.

——. 1965. *Adam Smith as student and professor*. New York: Augustus M. Kelley.

Seligman, E. R. A., ed. 1910. Introduction to *An inquiry into the nature and clauses of the wealth of nations*, by Adam Smith. London: Everyman's Edition.

Selkirk, Thomas Douglas. 1805. *Observations on the present state of the Highlands of Scotland with a view of emigration*. London: Longman, Hurst, Rees, and Orme; New York: Johnson Reprint, 1969.

Semmel, Bernard. 1970. *The rise of free trade imperialism*. Cambridge, U.K.: Cambridge University Press.

Sen, S. R. 1957. *The economics of Sir James Steuart*. Cambridge, Mass.: Harvard University Press.

Senior, Nassau. 1827. Letter to Charles Poulett Thompson, 28 March. In *Letters on the factory act, as it affects the cotton manufactures*; reprinted in *Selected writings on economics: A volume of pamphlets, 1827–1852*. New York: Augustus M. Kelley, 1966.

——. 1831. *Three lectures on the rate of wages with a preface on the causes and remedies of the present crisis*. New York: Augustus M. Kelley, 1959.

——. 1832. *A letter to lord Howick on a legal provision for the Irish poor*. 3rd ed. London: John Murray.

——. 1836. *An outline of the science of political economy*. New York: Augustus M. Kelley, 1951.

——. 1841. Grounds and objects of the budget. *Edinburgh Review* 73 (July):503–59.

——. 1868. *Journals, conversations, and essays relating to Ireland*. 2d ed. 2 vols. London: Longmans, Green, and Co.

——. 1871. *Journals kept in France and Italy*. 2d ed. 2 vols. London: Henry S. King.

——. 1928. *Industrial efficiency and social economy*. Edited by S. Leon Levy. 2 vols. New York: Holt.

Shannon, Fred. 1945. A post mortem on the labor safety-valve theory. *Agricultural History* 19, no. 1 (January):31–37.

Shaw, A. G. 1966. *Convicts and the colonies*. London: Faber and Faber.

Shireff, Patrick. 1835. *A tour through North America*. In *Readings in the economic history of the United States*, edited by Ernest Ludlow Bogart and Charles Manfred Thompson. New York: Longmans and Green, 1927.

Sinclair, Sir John. 1803. Observations on the means of enabling a cottager to keep a cow by the produce of a small portion of arable land. In *Essays in miscellaneous subjects*; reprinted in *The Annual Register* 45 (1805):850–57.

Sismondi, Jean-Charles-Léonard Simonde de. 1827. *Nouveaux principles d'economie politique.* Paris: Calman-Levy, 1971.

Skinner, Andrew S. 1966. Introduction to *An inquiry into the principles of political economy,* by Sir James Steuart. 2 vols. Chicago: University of Chicago Press.

———. 1976. Adam Smith and the American economic community: An essay in applied economics. *Journal of the History of Ideas* 37, no. 1 (January–March):59–78.

———. 1981. Sir James Steuart: Author of a system. *Scottish Journal of Political Economy* 28, no. 1 (February):20–42.

———. 1993. Sir James Steuart: The market and the state. *History of Economic Ideas* 1, no. 1: 1–43.

Sklar, Martin J. 1988. *The corporate reconstruction of American capitalism, 1890–1916.* Cambridge, U.K.: Cambridge University Press.

Slicher van Bath, B. H. 1960. The rise of intensive husbandry in the low countries. In *Britain and the Netherlands: Papers delivered at the Oxford-Netherlands historical conference, 1959,* edited by J. S. Bromley and E. H. Kossman. London: Chatto and Windus.

Smelser, Neil J. 1959. *Social change in the industrial revolution: An application of theory to the British cotton industry.* Chicago: University of Chicago Press.

Smith, Abbot Emerson. 1927. *Colonists in bondage: White servitude and convict labor in America, 1607–1776.* Chapel Hill: University of North Carolina Press.

Smith, Adam. 1755–56. Letters to the editor of the *Edinburgh review.* In *Essays on philosophical subjects,* edited by W. P. D. Wightman and J. C. Bryce. Oxford: Clarendon Press, 1980.

———. 1759. *The theory of moral sentiments.* Edited by D. D. Raphael and A. L. Macfie. Oxford: Clarendon Press, 1976.

———. 1762–63. *Lectures on rhetoric and belles lettres.* Edited by John M. Lothian. London: Thomas Nelson, 1963.

———. 1790a. The principles which lead and direct philosophical enquiries, illustrated by the history of astronomy. In *Essays on philosophical subjects,* edited by W. P. D. Wightman and J. C. Bryce. New York: Clarendon Press, 1980.

———. 1790b. Of the nature of that imitation which takes place in what are called the imitative arts. In *Essays on philosophical subjects,* edited by W. P. D. Wightman and J. C. Bryce. New York: Clarendon Press, 1980.

———. 1937. *An inquiry into the nature and causes of the wealth of nations.* New York: Modern Library.

———. 1976. *An inquiry into the nature and causes of the wealth of nations.* Edited by R. H. Campbell and A. S. Skinner, 2 vols. New York: Oxford University Press.

———. 1977. *The correspondence of Adam Smith.* Edited by Ernest Campbell Mossner and Ian Simpson Ross. Oxford: Clarendon Press.

———. 1978. *Lectures on jurisprudence.* Edited by R. L. Meek, D. D. Raphael, and P. G. Stein. Oxford: Clarendon Press.

Smith, E. Peshine. 1853. *A manual of political economy.* New York: Garland, 1974.

Smith, John. 1616. A description of New England. In vols. 4 and 5 of *The English scholars' library,* edited by Edward Arber. Birmingham, U.K., 1884.

Smith, J. Russell. 1925. *Industrial and commercial geography.* 2d ed. New York: Henry Holt.

Smith, Sydney. 1819. Game laws. *Edinburgh Review* 31, no. 62 (March):295–309.

———. 1821. Spring guns and man traps. *Edinburgh Review* 35, no. 69 (March):213–34.

Smith, Thomas C. 1966. *The agrarian origins of modern Japan.* New York: Atheneum.

Smith, Vernon L. 1992. Economic principles in the emergence of humankind. *Economic Inquiry* 30, no. 1 (January):1–13.

Smollett, Tobias. 1766. *Travels through France and Italy*. Edited by James Morris. New York: Praeger, 1969.

Smout, T. C. 1969. *A history of the Scottish people, 1560–1830*. New York: Charles Scribner's Sons.

Smuts, Robert W. 1959. *Women and work in America*. New York: Columbia University Press.

Sohn-Rethel, Alfred. 1978. *Intellectual and manual labour: A critique of epistemology*. London: Macmillan.

Soltow, J. H. 1959. Scottish traders in Virginia, 1750–1775. *Economic History Review* 12, no. 1 (August):83–98.

Spence, Thomas. 1807. *The restorer of society to its natural state*. 2d ed. London.

Spengler, Joseph J. 1959. Adam Smith's theory of economic growth, part 2. *Southern Economic Journal* 26, no. 1 (July):1–12.

——. 1968. The political economy of Jefferson, Madison, and Adams. In *American studies in honor of William Kenneth Boyd*, edited by David Kelley Jackson. Freeport, N.Y.: Books for Libraries Press.

Spenser, Edmund. 1591. Complaints: Mother Hubbard's tale. In vol. 7 of *The works of Edmund Spenser: A variorum edition*, edited by Edwin Greenlaw et al. Baltimore, Md.: Johns Hopkins University Press, 1932–49.

Spiegel, Henry William. 1960. *The rise of American economic thought*. Philadelphia: Chilton.

Sraffa, Piero. 1951. Introduction to *The works and correspondence of David Ricardo*, edited by Piero Sraffa, 11 vols. Cambridge, U.K.: Cambridge University Press.

Stalin, Josef. 1928. Industrialization and the grain problem: Speech, 9 July 1928. In vol. 11 of *Works*. Moscow: Foreign Languages Publishing House, 1954.

——. 1929. The right deviation in the C.P.S.U. (B): Speech delivered at the central committee and the control commission of the C.P.S.U. (B) in April 1929. In vol. 12 of *Works*. Moscow: Foreign Languages Publishing House, 1954.

Stark, Werner. 1944. *The history of economics in relation to social development*. London: Kegan Paul.

Stearns, Peter N. 1974a. National character and European labor history. In *Workers in the industrial revolution: Recent studies of labor in the United States and Europe*, edited by Peter N. Stearns and Daniel J. Walkowitz. New Brunswick, N.J.: Transaction Books.

——. 1974b. Working-class women in Britain, 1890–1914. In *Workers in the industrial revolution: Recent studies of labor in the United States and Europe*, edited by Peter N. Stearns and Daniel J. Walkowitz. New Brunswick, N.J.: Transaction Books.

Steuart, Sir James. 1767. *An inquiry into the principles of political economy, being an essay on the science of domestic policy in free nations*. Vols. 1–4 of *The works: Political, metaphysical, and chronological*. New York: Augustus M. Kelley, 1967.

——. 1769. *Considerations on the interest of Lanark*. In vol. 5 of *The works: Political, metaphysical, and chronological*. New York: Augustus M. Kelley, 1967.

——. 1772. *The principles of money applied to the present state of Bengal*. In vol. 5 of *The Works: Political, metaphysical, and chronological*. New York: Augustus M. Kelley, 1967.

——. 1966. *An inquiry into the principles of political economy*. Edited by Andrew S. Skinner. 2 vols. Chicago: University of Chicago Press.

Stevens, David. 1975. Adam Smith and the colonial disturbances. In *Essays on Adam Smith*, edited by Thomas Wilson and Andrew S. Skinner. Clarendon: Oxford University Press.

Stewart, Dugald. 1811. Account of the life and writings of Adam Smith, L.L.D. In *The Works of*

Dugald Stewart, 5 vols. (London: T. Caddell and W. Davies); reprinted in *Adam Smith: Essays on philosophical subjects*, edited by W. P. D. Wightman and J. C. Bryce. Oxford: Clarendon Press, 1980.

——. 1855. *Lectures on political economy.* Edited by Sir W. Hamilton. 2 vols. New York: Augustus M. Kelley, 1968.

Stigler, George. 1951. The division of labor is limited by the extent of the market. *Journal of Political Economy* no. 3 (June):185–93.

Strauss, Eric. 1954. *Sir William Petty: Portrait of a genius.* Glencoe, Ill.: Free Press.

Suffield, Edward, III (Baron). 1825. *Considerations on the game laws.* London.

Suggestions on the propriety of reintroducing British convict labour into British North America by a Canadian. 1824.

Sward, Keith. 1972. *The legend of Henry Ford.* New York: Atheneum.

Sweezy, Paul. 1980. Japan in perspective. *Monthly Review* 31, no. 9 (February):1–14.

Swift, Jonathan. 1723–24. The drapier's letters. In *The drapier's letters and other works*, vol. 10 of Collected Works, edited by Herbert Davis. Oxford: Basil Blackwell, 1959.

——. 1726. *Gulliver's travels.* In vol. 2 of *Collected works*, edited by Herbert Davis. Oxford: Basil Blackwell, 1959.

——. 1729. A modest proposal for preventing the children of poor people in Ireland from being a burden to their parents or country; and for making them beneficial to the publick. In vol. 12 of *Collected works*, edited by Herbert Davis. Oxford: Basil Blackwell, 1964.

——. 1731. The answer to the craftsman. In vol. 12 of *Collected works*, edited by Herbert Davis. Oxford: Basil Blackwell, 1964.

Taper, Bernard. 1979. Miniaturizing agriculture. *Science 80* 1, no. 1 (November).

Taplin, William. 1792. *An appeal to the representative on the part of the people respecting the present destructive state of the game and operative spirit of laws erroneously said to be framed for its increase and preservation.* London. In Kress-Goldsmith collection, reel 1500, item 15143.

Tatham. W. 1799. *The political economy of inland navigation.* London: Robert Faulder. In Kress-Goldsmith collection, reel 1648, no. 17736.

Taussig, Michael. 1979. Black religion and resistance in Columbia. *Marxist Perspectives* no. 2 (summer):84–117.

Tawney, Richard H. 1926. *Religion and the rise of capitalism: A historical study.* New York: New American Library, 1947.

Taylor, John. 1818. *Arator: Being a series of agricultural essays, practical and political, in sixty-four numbers.* Edited by M. E. Bradford. Indianapolis, Ind.: Liberty Classics, 1977.

Taylor, Paul S. 1972. *Georgia plan, 1732–1752.* Berkeley: University of California Institute for Business and Economic Research.

Teichgraeber, Richard F., III. 1986. *"Free trade" and moral philosophy: Rethinking the sources of Adam Smith's wealth of nations.* Durham, N.C.: Duke University Press.

Temin, Peter. 1971. Labor scarcity in America. *Journal of Interdisciplinary History* 1, no. 2 (winter):251–64.

Temperly, Howard. 1977. Capitalism, slavery, and ideology. *Past and Present* 75 (May):94–118.

Temple, William. 1758. *A vindication of commerce and the arts.* In Kress-Goldsmith collection, reel 712, item 9321.

——. 1770. *Essay on trade and commerce.* London.

Therborn, Goran. 1976. *Science, class, and society: On the formation of sociology and historical materialism.* London: New Left Books.

Thick, Malcolm. 1985. Market gardening in England and Wales. In *1640–1750: Agrarian change*. Vol. 5 of *The agrarian history of England and Wales*, edited by Joan Thirsk. Cambridge, U.K.: Cambridge University Press.

Thirsk, Joan. 1967a. Enclosing and engrossing. In *1500–1640*. Vol. 4 of *The agrarian history of England and Wales*, edited by Joan Thirsk. Cambridge, U.K.: Cambridge University Press.

——. 1967b. Farming techniques. In *1500–1640*. Vol. 4 of *The agrarian history of England and Wales*, edited by Joan Thirsk. Cambridge, U.K.: Cambridge University Press.

——. 1978. *Economic policy and projects: The development of a consumer society in early modern England*. Oxford: Clarendon Press.

Thomas, Brinley. 1980. Towards an energy interpretation of the industrial revolution. *Atlantic Economic Journal* 8, no. 1 (March):1–15.

——. 1985. Food supply in the United Kingdom during the industrial revolution. In *Economics of the industrial revolution*, edited by Joel Mokyr. Totowa, N.J.: Rowman and Allanheld.

Thomas, Gabriel. 1698. *An historical and geographical account of Pennsylvania and of west New Jersey*. Harrisburg, Pa.: Aurand Press, 1938.

Thomas, Keith. 1964. Work and leisure. *Past and Present*, no. 29 (December):50–66.

Thomas, Sir William Beach. 1936. *Hunting England: A survey of the sport, and of its chief grounds*. London: B. T. Batsford.

Thompson, Edward P. 1963. *The making of the English working class*. New York: Vintage.

——. 1967. Time, work, discipline, and industrial capitalism. *Past and Present* 38:56–97.

——. 1971. The moral economy of the English crowd in the eighteenth century. *Past and Present* 50 (February):76–136.

——. 1975. *Whigs and hunters: The origin of the black act*. New York: Pantheon.

——. 1991. *Customs in common*. New York: New Press.

Thompson, Noel. 1977. Ricardian socialists/Smithian socialists: What's in a name? Research paper, University of Cambridge.

——. 1984. *The people's science: The popular political economy of exploitation and crisis, 1816–1834*. Cambridge, U.K.: Cambridge University Press.

Thompson, T. Perronet. 1808. Letter to miss Baker, June 6. In *General T. Perronet Thompson, 1783–1869*, edited by Leonard G. Johnson. London: George Allen and Unwin, 1957.

Thornton, William Thomas. 1869. *On labour: Its wrongful claims and rightful dues*. London: Macmillan.

Thweatt, William O. 1974. The digression of Sismondi: By Torrens or McCulloch? *History of Political Economy* 6, no. 4 (winter):435–53.

Tigar, Michael E., and Madeleine R. Levy. 1977. *Law and the rise of capitalism*. New York: Monthly Review Press.

Tobias, J. J. 1967. *Crime and industrial society in the nineteenth century*. New York: Schocken Books.

Tocqueville, Alexis de. 1848. *Democracy in America*. New York: Doubleday, 1966.

——. 1858. *The old regime and the French revolution*. Translated by Stuart Gilbert. Garden City, N.Y.: Doubleday, 1955.

Tollison, Robert D. 1984. Adam Smith as regulator. *History of Economics Society Bulletin* 6, no. 1 (summer):38–39.

Tomlinson, Jim. 1986. Democracy inside the black box? Neo-classical theories of the firm and industrial democracy. *Economy and Society* 15, no. 2 (May):220–50.

Torrens, Robert. 1808. *The economists refuted*. London: S. A. and H. Oddy.

——. 1817. A paper on the means of reducing the poor rates and of affording effectual and permanent relief to the labouring classes. Appendix to *Colonization of South Australia*, London, 1935.

——. 1828. *Substance of a speech delivered by colonel Torrens in the house of commons.* London: Longmans, Rees, Orme, Brown, and Green.

——. 1833. *Letters on commercial policy.* London: London School of Economics and Political Science, 1958.

——. 1835. *Colonization of south Australia.* London: Longman, Rees, Orme, Brown, Green, and Longman.

——. 1839. *Three letters to the marquis of Chandos on the effects of the corn laws.* London: Longman and Co.

——. 1842. *A letter to the right hon. Sir R. Peel. in the budget: A series of letters on financial, commercial, and colonial policy.* London: Smith Elder and Co.

Townsend, Joseph. 1786. A dissertation on the poor laws by a well wisher to mankind. In *A select collection of scarce and valuable economic tracts,* edited by John R. McCulloch. New York: Augustus M. Kelley, 1966.

Tribe, Keith. 1978. *Land, labour, and economic discourse.* London: Routledge and Kegan Paul.

——. 1979. Introduction to de Crisenoy. *Economy and Society* 8, no. 1 (February):1–8.

Triffen, Robert. 1940. *Monopolistic competition and general Equilibrium theory.* Cambridge, Mass.: Harvard University Press.

Trollope, Anthony. 1929. *Hunting sketches.* Hartford, Conn.: Edwin Valentine Mitchell.

Trotsky, Leon. 1932. *The Russian revolution: The overthrow of tzarism and the triumph of the soviets.* Edited by F. W. Dupee. New York: Doubleday.

Tsuzuki, Chushichi. 1971. Robert Owen and revolutionary politics. In *Robert Owen, prophet of the poor: Essays in honour of the two-hundredth anniversary of his birth,* edited by Sidney Pollard and John Salt. Lewisburg, Pa.: Bucknell University Press.

Tucker, Josiah. 1758. *Instructions for travellers.* Dublin: William Watson. In Kress-Goldsmith collection, reel 712, item 9323.

——. 1776a. *Four tracts on political and commercial subjects.* 2d ed. Gloucester.

——. 1776b. *A series of answers to certain objections against separation from the rebellious colonies.* Gloucester.

Tully, Alan. 1973. Patterns of slaveholding in colonial Pennsylvania: Chester and Lancaster counties, 1728–1758. *Journal of Social History* 6, no. 3 (spring):284–305.

Turgot, Anne Robert Jacques. 1766. Reflections on the formation and distribution of wealth. In *A select collection of scarce and valuable tracts,* edited by John R. McCulloch. New York: Augustus M. Kelley, 1966.

Tuttle, William N., Jr. 1967. Forerunners of Frederick Jackson Turner: Nineteenth-century British conservatives and the frontier thesis. *Agricultural History* 41, no. 3 (July):219–27.

Tyron, Rolla Milton. 1917. *Household manufacturers in the United States, 1640–1860.* New York: Augustus M. Kelley, 1966.

Urquhart, Robert. 1996. The trade wind, the statesman, and the system of commerce: Sir James Steuart's vision of political economy. *European Journal of the History of Economic Thought* 3, no. 3 (autumn):379–410.

U.S. Department of Agriculture. 1997. *Agricultural statistics, 1979.* Washington, D.C.: Government Printing Office.

Vicker, Ray. 1981. Portable workplaces: Computer terminals allow more people to work at home instead of commuting. *Wall Street Journal,* 4 August, 46.

Viner, Jacob. 1927. Adam Smith and laissez faire. In *The long view and the short.* Glencoe, Ill.: Free Press, 1958.

——. 1965. Guide to John Rae's life of Adam Smith. In *The life of Adam Smith,* by John Rae. New York: Augustus M. Kelley.

——. 1968. Man's economic status. In *Man versus society in eighteenth century Britain: Six points of view*, edited by James L. Clifford. Cambridge, U.K.: Cambridge University Press.

——. 1972. *The role of providence in the social order: An essay in intellectual history*. Philadelphia: American Philosophical Library.

von Laue, Theodore H. 1963. *Serge Witte and the industrialization of Russia*. New York: Atheneum.

Wakefield, Daniel. 1804. *An essay on political economy*. 2d ed. London: F. C. and J. Rivington.

Wakefield, Edward Gibbon. 1829. Letter from Sydney: The principle town of Australasia. In *The collected works of Edward Gibbon Wakefield*, edited by M. F. Lloyd Pritchard. Glasgow: Collins, 1968.

——. 1831a. Letter from P—— to Lord Howick, no. iii. *Spectator* (8 January).

——. 1831b. Facts relating to the punishment of death in the metropolis. In *Collected works of Edward Gibbon Wakefield*, edited by M. F. Lloyd Pritchard. Glasgow: Collins, 1968.

——. 1831c. *Swing unmasked, or the causes of rural incendiarism*. London: Effingham, Wilson. In Kress-Goldsmith collection, reel 2543, no. 2672.

——. 1834. *England and America*. Boston: Harper and Row.

——. 1835. Commentary to *An inquiry into the nature and causes of the wealth of nations*, by Adam Smith. 6 vols. London: Charles Knight.

——. 1836. Response to question 610. In *The report of the select committee on the disposal of public lands in British colonies, British parliamentary papers*.

——. 1841. Letter to the colonization commissioners, June 2, 1835. Appendix to *The report on the select committee on south Australia, parliamentary papers*.

——. 1849. *A view of the art of colonization in letters between a statesman and a colonist*. Oxford: Clarendon Press, 1914.

Walecki, Andrzej. 1969. *The controversy over capitalism*. New York: Oxford University Press.

Walker, Katheryn E., and Margaret E. Woods. 1976. *Time use: A measure of household production of family goods and services*. Washington, D.C.: Center for the Family of the American Home Economics Association.

Wallace, Robert. 1809. *A dissertation on the numbers of mankind in ancient and modern times*. Edinburgh: Archibald Constable.

Wallas, Graham. 1919. *The life of Francis Place*. 3rd ed. New York: A. A. Knopf.

Walpole, Horace. 1937–74. *The Yale edition of Horace Walpole's correspondence*. Edited by W. S. Lewis. 38 vols. New Haven, Conn.: Yale University Press.

Walsh, Vivian, and Harvey Gram. 1980. *Classical and neoclassical theories of general equilibrium: Historical origins and mathematical structure*. New York: Oxford University Press.

Ware, Norman Joseph. 1924. *The industrial worker, 1840–1860*. Boston: Houghton-Mifflin.

——. 1931. The physiocrats: A study in economic rationalization. *American Economic Review* 21, no. 5 (December):607–19.

Waterman, Anthony M. C. 1998. Reappraisal of "Malthus the economist," 1933–1997. *History of Political Economy* 30, no. 2 (summer):293–334.

Weber, Max. 1921. *Economy and society: An outline of interpretive society*. Edited by Guenther Roth and Claus Wittich. New York: Bedminster Press, 1968.

——. 1923. *General economic history*. Translated by Frank Knight. New York: Collier Books, 1961.

Webster, Daniel. 1879. First settlement of New England: A discourse delivered at Plymouth on the 22nd December 1820. In *The great speeches and orations of Daniel Webster, with an essay on Daniel Webster as a master of English style*, edited by Edwin P. Whipple. London: Sampson, Low, Marston, Searle and Rivington.

Weiller, Jean. 1971. Preface to *Nouveaux principles d'economie politique*, by Jean-Charles-Léonard Simonde de Sismondi. Paris: Calman-Levy.

Weld, Isaac, Jr. 1800. *Travels through the states of North America, and the provinces of upper and lower Canada, during the years 1795, 1796, and 1797.* 4th ed. 2 vols. New York: Johnson Reprint Co., 1968.

Wells, Roger A. E. 1979. The development of the English rural proletariat and social protest, 1700–1850. *Journal of Peasant Studies* 6, no. 2 (January):115–39.

Wermel, Michael. 1939. *The evolution of classical wage theory.* New York: Columbia University Press.

Western, J. R. 1965. *The English militia in the eighteenth century: The story of a political issue, 1660–1802.* London: Routledge and Kegan Paul.

Wetzel, W. A. 1895. Benjamin Franklin as an economist. *Johns Hopkins University Studies in Historical and Political Science* (September).

Weulersse, Georges. 1910. *Le Mouvement Physiocratique en France, de 1756 a 1770.* 2 vols. New York: Johnson Reprint Co., 1968.

——. 1959. *La Physiocratie a la fin du regne de Louis XV, 1770–1774.* Paris: Presse Universitaires de France.

Wheelwright, E. L., and Bruce McFarlane. 1970. *The Chinese road to socialism: Economics of the cultural revolution.* New York: Monthly Review Press.

Whitney, Lois. 1924. Primitivistic theories of epic origins. *Modern Philology* 21, no. 4 (May): 337–78.

Wicksteed, Philip H. 1910. The common sense of political economy. In vol. 2 of *The common sense of political economy, and selected papers and reviews on economic theory*, edited by Lionel Robbins. London: Routledge and Kegan Paul, 1933.

Wieser, Friedrich von. 1927. *Social economics.* Translated by A. Ford Hinrichs. New York: Augustus M. Kelley, 1967.

Wight, Andrew. 1778–84. *Present state of husbandry extracted from reports to the commissioners of the annexed estates.* 4 vols. Edinburgh: T. Caddell.

Wilensky, H. 1961. The uneven distribution of leisure: The impact of economic growth on "free time." *Social Problems* 9:35–56.

Wilentz, Sean. 1984. *Chants democratic: New York City and the rise of the American working class.* New York: Oxford University Press.

Wiles, Richard C. 1968. The theory of wages in later English mercantilism. *Economic History Review* 31, no. 2 (April):113–26.

Wilkinson, Olga. 1964. *The agricultural revolution in the East Riding of Yorkshire.* York: East Yorkshire Local History Society.

Williams, Samuel. 1809. *Natural and civil history of Vermont.* 2d ed. 2 vols. Burlington.

Williams, William Appleman. 1966. *The contours of American economic history.* New York: Quadrangle.

Williamson, Jeffrey G., and Peter H. Lindert. 1977. Long-term trends in wealth inequality. Discussion paper, Institute for Research on Poverty, Madison, Wis.

Willis, Karl. 1979. The role in parliament of the economic ideas of Adam Smith, 1776–1800. *History of Political Economy* 11, no. 4 (summer):505–44.

Wilson, Thomas, and Andrew S. Skinner, eds. 1976. *The market and the state: Essays in honour of Adam Smith.* Oxford: Clarendon Press.

Winch, Donald. 1966. *James Mill: Selected economic writings.* Chicago: University of Chicago Press.

——. 1975. *Classical political economy and colonies.* Cambridge, Mass.: Harvard University Press.

——. 1978. *Adam Smith's politics: An essay in historiographical revision.* Cambridge, U.K.: Cambridge University Press.

Wisman, Jon D. 1989. Straightening out the backward-bending supply curve of labour: From overt to covert compulsion and beyond. *Review of Political Economy* 1, no. 1 (March):94–112.

Wittfogel, Karl. 1931. *Die Wirtschaft und Gessellschaft Chinas.* Leipzig.

Wittkowsky, Georgy. 1943. Swift's modest proposal: The biography of an early Georgian pamphlet. *Journal of the History of Ideas* 4 (June–October):75–104.

Wordie, J. R. 1974. Social change on the Levenson-Gower estates, 1714–1832. *Economic History Review* 27, no. 4 (November):593–605.

Wordsworth, William. 1802. Preface to the second edition of lyrical ballads. In vol. 2 of *The poetical works of William Wordsworth*, edited by E. de Selincourt. Oxford: Clarendon Press, 1944.

Wright, Gavin. 1978. *The political economy of the cotton south: Households, markets, and wealth in the nineteenth century.* New York: W. W. Norton.

Wynne-Edwards, V. C. 1962. *Animal dispersion in relation to human behavior.* New York: Hafner.

Young, Arthur. 1774. *Political arithmetic, part 1.* London.

——. 1794. *Travels in France during the years 1787–1788–1789.* Garden City, N.Y.: Anchor Books, 1969.

Zahler, Helene Sarah. 1941. *Eastern working men and national land policy.* New York: Greenwood Publishers, 1969.

Index

Michael Perelman is Professor of Economics at California State
University. He is author of *The Natural Instability of Markets:
Expectations, Increasing Returns, and the Collapse of Markets*
(1999); *Class Warfare in the Information Age* (1998); *The
Pathology of the U.S. Economy* (1996); *The End of Economics*
(1996); *Information, Social Relations, and the Economics of
High Technology* (1991); *Keynes, Investment Theory, and the
Economic Slowdown: The Role of Replacement Investment
and Q-Ratios* (1989); *Marx's Crises Theory: Scarcity, Labor, and
Finance* (1987); *Classical Political Economy: Primitive
Accumulation and the Social Division of Labor* (1984); and
*Farming for Profit in a Hungry World: Capital and the Crisis in
Agriculture* (1977).

Library of Congress Cataloging-in-Publication Data
Perelman, Michael.
The invention of capitalism : classical political economy
and the secret history of primitive accumulation /
Michael Perelman.
Rev. ed. of: Classical political economy. 1984, c1983.
Includes bibliographical references and index.
ISBN 0-8223-2454-7 (cl. : alk. paper)
ISBN 0-8223-2491-1 (pa. : alk. paper)
1. Classical school of economics—History.   2. Economics—
History.   3. Division of labor—History.   4. Capitalism—
History.   I. Title.   II. Perelman, Michael. Classical political
economy.
HB94.P47 2000   330.15'3 21—dc21   99-045625